Two Sides of the Beach

The invasion and defense of Europe in 1944

Edmund Blandford

CASTLE BOOKS

This edition published in 2001 by Castle Books
A division of Book Sales, Inc.
114 Northfield Avenue, Edison, NJ 08837

This edition published by arrangement with and permission of
Airlife Publishing Ltd
101 Longden Road, Shrewsbury, SY3 9EB, England

First published in the UK in 1999
by Airlife Publishing Ltd

British Library Cataloguing-in-Publication Data
  A catalogue record for this book
  is available from the British Library

ISBN: 0-7858-1367-5

The information in this book is true and complete to the best of our knowledge. All recommendations are made without any guarantee on the part of the publisher, who also disclaims liability incurred in connection with the use of this data or specific details.

Typeset by Phoenix Typesetting, Ilkley, West Yorkshire
Printed in England by Biddles Ltd, Guildford and King's Lynn

Introduction

In a broadcast to the French people on 2 October 1940, Prime Minister Winston Churchill vowed that Britain would never weary, never give in, and would rid Europe of the Nazi pestilence and so save the world from another Dark Age.

It took another four years of 'blood, toil, tears and sweat', scheming and much money before Britain and its allies were finally in a position to return to the continent, a date which went down in history as 'D-day' – 6 June 1944.

This work is intended as a contribution to the existing literature on the subject, and deals chiefly with the struggle in Normandy between the Germans and their principal enemy through five years of war, the British.

Edmund L. Blandford

With grateful thanks to all the British and German contributors who made this book possible, but especially those who were at the sharp end.

Contents

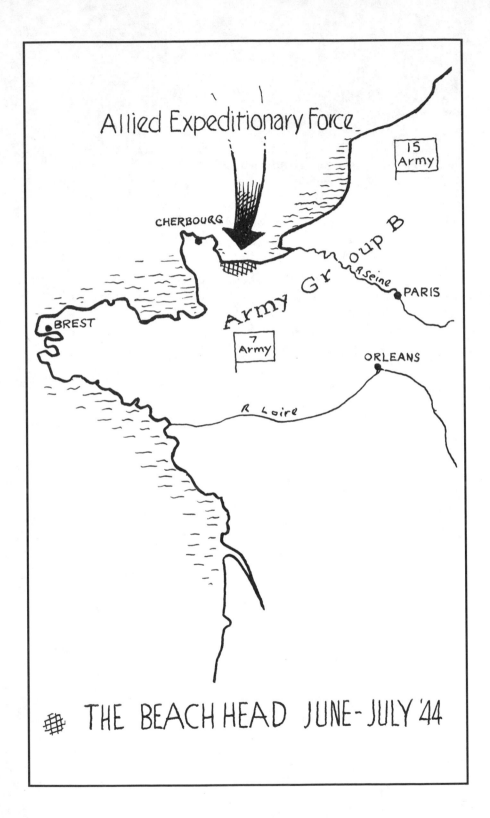

Allied Expeditionary Force

15 Army

CHERBOURG

Army Group B

Seine

PARIS

BREST

7 Army

ORLEANS

R Loire

THE BEACH HEAD JUNE - JULY '44

1 Generals and Soldiers

In the business of war it is the man that counts . . . if you have got men who are mentally alert, who are tough and hard, who are trained to fight and kill, who are enthusiastic and have that infectious optimism and offensive eagerness that comes from physical wellbeing, and then you give these men the proper weapons and equipment – there is nothing you cannot do . . . Every officer and man must be enthusiastic and have the light of battle in his eyes . . . Every officer and man must have only one idea, and that is to peg out claims inland, and to penetrate quickly and deeply into enemy territory. After a long sea voyage and landing, followed by fighting, a reaction sets in and officers and men are often inclined to let up and relax. This is fatal.
– General Bernard Law Montgomery, commander of the ground forces for the Normandy invasion, in *Memoirs*

I had never seen so many decorations as he used to wear. They stretched from armpit to armpit. He should have been a general in the time of the Romans when he could ride around in a chariot. And he had the world's most unfortunate voice, a high-pitched woman's squeak.
– Kay Summersby, of General George Patton, in *My Affair with Eisenhower*

That son of a bitch, he's a thorn in my side!
– General Dwight D. Eisenhower, Supreme Commander, Allied Expeditionary Force, on Montgomery

You must have faith in God, you must have confidence between the commander and his troops.
– Montgomery, in *Memoirs*

In all my years of service I have never known our army to be in such good heart in preparation. Everything possible has been done to make them ready for the coming operation which will not only be the biggest ever undertaken by a British army, but the greatest military undertaking ever, of that I am convinced. Monty is brimming with confidence, as are we all, even though we know a hard fight lies ahead of us.
– diary of Lieutenant-General Miles Dempsey, CO 2nd Army

The whole Corps is in very good fettle and is as ready for the coming battle as they can be. I have inspected all the units and feel very satisfied they will do their utmost. One particular aspect has

been of some concern: as expected the desertion rate has doubled, but is still comparatively low considering the vastness of the undertaking ahead.
– diary of Lieutenant-General George Bucknall, CO 30th Corps

I was knocked into the sea in 1940, and I didn't like it! Now I'm looking for a sea into which I can throw the Germans! I never start a battle until I have won the air fight; this is in progress, the RAF is knocking the Hun for six. When it is won we will invade – not before.
– Montgomery to his troops, spring 1944

As a British general I regard it as an honour to serve under an American command. General Eisenhower is captain at the helm and I am proud to serve under him.
– Montgomery

It was with great indignation I saw your picture in *The Listener* of May 4th of General Montgomery. I should think you took your copy of old Ghandi, or a man of 100 years old. I call it an insult to the General, he looks like a dead man instead of a living one.
– Mrs M. E. Tozer, commenting on Augustus John's portrait as reproduced in the magazine

Esprit de corps is everywhere, the troops are in amazing spirits.
– Lieutenant, King's Own Scottish Borderers

Confidence can be detected everywhere.
– Lieutenant, 11th Armoured Division

Outwardly simple in character, the parade was really the result of most detailed instructions which had come direct to 8th Corps HQ from the General's personal staff. Everything, including the 'spontaneous' surge forward (around him), was laid on by a master of publicity.
– Household Cavalry historian commenting on Montgomery's tours of troop camps before D-day

The only good German is a dead one!
– Eisenhower

Soldiers, Sailors and Airmen of the Allied Expeditionary Force! You are about to embark on the Great Crusade . . . the eyes of the world are upon you . . . your task will not be an easy one . . . Good Luck! And let us all beseech the blessing of Almighty God upon this great and noble undertaking.
– Eisenhower to troops before D-day

Good hunting on the mainland of Europe!
– Montgomery

Bill Bradley was born and lived in London all his life: 'When D-day came I was in hospital having an operation on my big toe, then I went on sick leave and missed the invasion and I wasn't really sorry.'

Rex Williams was called into the army at the age of eighteen:

❝ It was late 1943, and after squarebashing I was sent to the Shropshires [King's Own Shropshire Light Infantry]. They seemed a good bunch of lads and I settled down. There were blokes from the Midlands – Coventry, Rugby, Leicester, places like that. The Sergeant was a bit of a bollocker, but he went off on a course and we weren't sorry. His place was taken by an easier chap to get on with – so long as you didn't mess him about.

We went through all the training and lectures and it wasn't too bad, except when it rained; I hated that, getting wet and hanging about in the fields and woods with all the noise going on, when all I wanted was to get back to camp and have a bath and a hot meal. When it got to May 1944 we packed up and moved south in trucks and we knew it was the real thing. Like all the lads in our lot we'd never been in action and felt scared. We thought we'd lose a lot of men.

The waiting was the worst part. We set up tents in Dorset and had a very boring time with more lectures, briefings and a few local route marches. Then at last it was time and we went off in trucks to Portsmouth where we were amazed by the sight of so many ships of all kinds. It took us a long time to get sorted out and by the time we got aboard it was dark and we were all very tired and fed up. We had some hot supper and curled up in blankets and had biscuits on the deck. We had some transport there so some lucky blokes slept in the trucks. ❞

Bill Molden was an American posted to the Hampshire Regiment:

❝ My folks had emigrated to the States earlier in the nineteenth century and I was always very anxious to visit the old country. In 1939 I managed to work my passage across the Atlantic on a liner and as soon as I landed I told a Customs Officer I wanted to join the British Army. I guess he thought I was mad and he told me to go to a recruiting office in Southampton. I figured I could do myself some good by getting a free meal ticket in the army and seeing something of the country that way.

At the recruiting centre they were not hopeful. The Sergeant-Major told me he'd look into it, so I found myself a room and had a look round the town. It was very different to the USA but I loved it. Next day when I went back to the recruiting office they told me to try the War Office in London. So I caught a train and enjoyed all that wonderful country-side. But when I finally found the War Office an officer told me they could not take foreigners in their army. He said things might change if war came. Of course I was very disappointed and when I called for advice at the American Embassy they sent me to a club – of all things. But I found a lot of Americans there who seemed to be either trying to get home or to join up, mostly with the RAF; they thought I was crazy to want to fight on the ground. It was August and I didn't want to fight, I only wanted that free meal ticket so I could see something of the old country. But one fellow told me I should have joined the Canadian Army as that was easy and they would probably have sent me over anyway. This seemed a very good idea except I didn't have the money to re-cross the Atlantic!

So I found myself somewhere to stay and a few days later I went again to a recruiting office and found it jam-packed with men, all trying to join something. I got talking to some of these lads and they were amazed to learn I was a Yank. One of them was an upper-crust type who suggested I pretend I had been living overseas, but this meant showing my passport and there would be red tape. In the end he told me to say I was a long-lost relative of his and give the same address in the West End. Which is exactly what I did, and I was accepted into the British Army. We were told to go home and wait for call-up, so he took me to a swanky restaurant for a meal. Well, I was called up a month later and met the fellow on the train as we were both going to the camp at Catterick in Yorkshire. In fact, we did a month's training together before he was sent off to become a u/t officer and I never saw him again.

Before I passed out with the training battalion, which was quite a thrill, I met a girl called Mary who was a charming lass. We began dating regularly and I guess I fell in love as after I'd been sent away we wrote to each other, but my letters got less and less frequent and then I stopped, which was sad as she was truly a very nice girl. And by the way, the officer type I'd met told me – too late – that I would most likely have got in the army OK if I'd first joined the TA, the Territorial Army.

I was posted to several different units, first of all the Essex Regiment. But later, in 1941 I think it was, I was sent up to Liverpool with a draft and we expected to go out to join the 8th Army. Instead I found myself guarding a stores depot where there'd been some thieving. Then I was posted south, to the Hampshire Regiment, and settled down to a life in barracks which wasn't bad. We had the usual exercises and plenty of drill and I met a girl in Winchester who took me home to meet her folks who were very kind to me. Then a minor diplomat came to see me – he seemed to have learned about my being in the British Army. He did his best to persuade me to transfer to the US forces as some Yanks were beginning to arrive in the country. I told him I was quite content where I was. And by then I had made Corporal and had stopped writing to my girl back home, but I kept sending letters and cards to my folks in Washington who I guessed must be anxious about me. I found out later that not all of these arrived, due to the Battle of the Atlantic I guess.

Then the Sergeant-Major talked me into taking a third stripe; I wasn't too happy about it but it happened. Quite often I'd be with a bunch of the lads in the pub and because of my accent they'd try to pin down my origin. They could hardly believe it when I told them I was a Yank; they said, 'You must be mad! Why don't you join your own army? Think of all that better pay – and the women!' But I stayed the course as I reckoned I knew the ropes in the British Army by then and had become keen to get over to France into a fight. I'd been all those years in the British Army and wanted to give something back for all they'd given me, that was my way of looking at it. **"**

In July 1944, owing to heavy infantry losses in the British 2nd Army, a comb-out took place in Britain to find replacements, several thousand men being provided by the RAF, mostly from the RAF Regiment – but not all. John Stewart's leisured life was about to reach its end. 'I was in the RAF for three years, a surplus but very fit stores clerk at the large base at Burtonwood in Lancashire where the build-up was fantastic and led to pilfering from both inside and out. The Yanks were coming in; my days were mostly spent doing nothing.' A very rude awakening was to come in July.

Robert Sherwin was from Bridport in Dorset, so it seemed natural that after conscription at the age of eighteen and completion of his basic training he should enter his home county regiment, the Dorsets, though many men never enjoyed such a 'home' posting. 'I used to get home fairly frequently, but when I left home after my last weekend leave my mum had tears in her eyes. I don't think she expected to see me again.'

John Vowles lied about his age to get into the Marine Commandos. 'My dad had been in the Marines in the last lot and I'd always wanted to be a soldier. The Commandos seemed special; I was lucky to get in them. I lived in Portsmouth all my life. I had a young brother who was keen to get into the navy, but he was only sixteen, and I had an older sister in the ATS. I got into 47 Royal Marine Commando in time for the invasion. It was all a great adventure.'

Jim Parkinson, like Rex Williams a soldier in the King's Own Shropshire Light Infantry (or the 'Koslies'), was from Birmingham and admits to having been a 'bit of a wanderer'. 'I had several different jobs before volunteering for the army during the invasion scare in 1940, though at twenty-five I was not due for call-up then as I worked for the GPO telephones as a repairman. I thought the army would be an adventure and with the invasion coming I'd see plenty of action! Instead I spent the whole war doing very little except training and bull, but we had an easy time compared to some, so didn't complain. In any case, by 1943 we were certain we'd be in our own invasion.'

David Ickson was from Ilminster in Somerset and was very interested in tanks as a schoolboy. 'When I was called up in 1942 I volunteered for them and trained on the old Covenanters and Crusaders before seeing my first Churchill, which had a tiddly little two-pounder gun as it was one of the early types and useless. But by D-day we were using the latest types with a six-pounder [57mm], which was much better, but no match for what Jerry could throw at us.'

He, like other tank men who went to Normandy, would have to learn the hard way in the armoured battles to come. The Churchill had been rushed out by the American-owned Vauxhall Motors during the emergency of 1940 after the BEF had lost over 63,000 vehicles including all its tanks in France. Eventually, the Churchill tank group of firms produced 5,640 Churchills of all marks, and although the type did good work in Tunisia and Italy it was never a match for the heavier-gunned German types, and especially the Panther and Tiger. It was the Labour MP Mr Stokes who made a special point of raising British tank deficiencies in Parliament, to be fobbed off (not unusually in public wartime debate) by Winston Churchill, for one, with misleading and untrue statements designed to reassure the troops and the public. But there could be no fooling the men at the front.

John Holt joined the armoured corps as early as 1940, training on a Covenanter. 'The new Churchill was too slow and only had a two-pounder [40mm] gun. It was months before we received any, but the training was quite fun, apart from breakdowns and the feeling we had a long way to go before we could match the enemy. We were more confident by 1944 after pep talks about our overwhelming power. Of course, it all changes when you go into action, as we found out. Yet we had our successes and were lucky to come out of our first action in one piece.'

Jimmy McPartland was a Glaswegian, and wanted to become a Highlander. 'I'd always been mad on Jock soldiers in their kilts, but never had a chance to wear one at all after call-up as it was all square-bashing and bull in battledress. I was dead keen to fight the Germans!'

Captain Roy Leighton was a liaison officer between the various Guard units in Normandy and explains how the Guards Armoured came to be formed:

❝ I was already in the Welsh Guards in 1941 when we were paraded and told that volunteers were needed to form an armoured regiment which would be composed of men like ourselves from the different Guards regiments. I was one of those who stepped forward. At the time I was a subaltern and had no experience whatever of tanks or armoured cars. But those who volunteered were all very keen; I think there were several dozen of us and it was not long before we left our chums and went off to learn something about armour.

We went to Dorset where we met a few hundred other bods from the other Guards and at once went into training, both in lectures and looking over old tanks which were in some cases the old Vickers, so really ancient. But there were Covenanters and Crusaders and a few others such as the Matilda and Valentine. Before long we were sorted into trades and as an officer I had to learn how to command a tank in action, and also to know something about the other lads' jobs, and it was all very interesting.

Over the next few years I think I can say we mastered our trades but were very disappointed when we weren't sent into action. By the time of D-day we were raring to go, but were then further disappointed as we did not get over there until July. We were really very frustrated indeed. **99**

Lieutenant-General Fritz Bayerlein's command, the so-called *Panzer Lehr* division, had been formed, like two other divisions (9th and 10th SS), principally to combat the Allied invasion, originating as a 'lehr' or demonstration unit and formed from the *panzer* training schools at Potsdam and Bergen. From eastern France it was transferred to Budapest in Hungary where it added the 901st Infantry Lehr Regiment, thereafter comprising two panzer grenadier regiments, the 130th *Panzer* Regiment, plus armoured artillery, engineer, signals and anti-tank battalions. In this form it returned to the Orleans area of France in May 1944, moving to Le Mans in June, one of the strongest divisions in the German Army with 109 tanks, forty assault guns and 612 halftracks – double the normal army complement of the last-named. As a 'demonstration' division it could be expected to prove a formidable opponent of expert soldiers, but Bayerlein was a worried man, as he confided to his colleagues:

66 *Panzer* Lehr has a prime duty on the invasion coast, but we are based well inland and unable to maintain the standard of training I demand, this due to a number of factors:

1 – the fuel situation, which becomes ever more critical;
2 – the nature of the local terrain, which prevents realistic manoeuvres;
3 – indecision at higher levels, which has resulted in a series of orders as to our location, all of which have been countermanded.

As a result I believe there is a real danger that when the invasion does come we will be caught in the wrong place. I believe Rommel agrees with this. The Field Marshal is always on the move along the coast and believes that if the enemy invasion forces are not defeated in the first few hours then we will lose, if only because of their air superiority.

What also worries me is that no firm tactical decisions have been made; every time our proposals are put forward no complete agreement is reached. The general consensus of opinion seems to be that we must wait and see. The people at 15th Army and von Rundstedt himself continually state the need to maintain strong forces in the Calais area, believing it is the most suitable place for an invasion. Rommel is scathing in countering this; he says for that very reason the enemy will avoid it! This seems obvious to him and we of Army Group B agree. Rommel insists the Bay of Seine is the most likely spot for a landing. I am sure he will be proved correct.

As to the general state of preparedness in matériel, apart from the fuel situation I am well satisfied. We are well equipped and have the experience to do a good job in defence, though from what I know of the Allied air power we are in for a difficult time. We know what we can expect from Göring and his *Luftwaffe*! We rarely see them! We have made our own intelligence assessment of the Allied strengths and weaknesses on the ground; I fear if they are allowed to build up sufficient strength in matériel and manpower they will overwhelm us. They are capable in time of fielding a huge army on the continent. As to the British, I know them from experience. We are in for a tough fight. Even though I have no great fears over their tank arm I feel that once allowed to establish themselves they will never let go.

As to our *Führer*, I have never looked upon him as other than a Nazi figurehead, though he certainly has some amazing abilities. He is not the kind of man I see as honourable to lead Germany in any sort of conflict. I have heard rumours of a plot against him, but no details, and I never concern myself with such things. I hope Rommel stays clear of anything like that. It would be a very great shock to know he was involved. **"**

Major-General Gunther Blumentritt, Chief of Staff to C-in-C West, shared Bayerlein's concerns:

" In Army Group B Rommel has done everything possible I believe to prepare the defences, but the uncertainties remain and will do until after the enemy lands his main force. We can rely on one thing: the Russians will desert at the first opportunity! As to our intelligence of the enemy's preparations, the *Luftwaffe* have not been of the greatest help, though we are sure of the great concentrations of ships in the southern ports, especially in the area Portsmouth, Plymouth and Weymouth. It will need greater watching. Our listening service is monitoring the channels to the French Resistance and I believe they will provide an excellent pointer to the exact date. In the SS divisions we have excellent quality, yet even there they are to a considerable degree untried men. **"**

As a Colonel, Bayerlein had narrowly escaped capture and death at Alamein, allegedly taking to his heels while the then commander of the *Deutsches Afrika Korps*, General von Thoma, stood his ground to be bagged by the advancing British. Lieutenant-General Edgar Feuchtinger was another desert veteran who escaped capture, though the 21st *Panzer* was virtually destroyed in North Africa:

" We took some hard knocks in the desert, but now we are rebuilt and I have done my utmost to instil a renewed *esprit de corps* in the division. We have been able to get the vehicles we needed, but the men are another matter. So many veterans have been lost in Africa and Russia, but I am sure that by the time the invasion season is upon us we will have solved the problem within the constraints of our situation. Things are not perfect. The fuel situation is a constant problem; we are not allowed to carry out large-scale manoeuvres because of this and the nature of the countryside, which is very claustrophobic and thick with villages and farms to prevent combat in its more realistic terms. As a result too many of our exercises are carried out on map tables, which is all very well in theory. I had hoped to practise a large-scale invasion alert and send the division helter-skelter to the beaches, but this seems unlikely to happen. It is all very frustrating and I know our colleagues in Army Group B are of the same mood. Our conferences with 15th Army are stultifying; it is an effort to try and get some reality into our thinking and planning. We are always told the *Führer* will not allow this or that.

As to the SS divisions, naturally they are of good value, but it is impossible to play with them as they are all under Hitler's control. And I must say von Rundstedt does not show the flexibility he should, even though he has no love for the *Führer*. He has an excellent military brain, but has become stultified through inaction.

The French play only a small part in our calculations. What activities the Resistance indulges in, such as espionage and sabotage, do not affect us, even though we must take it for granted our dispositions are known to the enemy because of French spies.

We have become good colleagues of Rommel and the other commanders in northern France. We are all much of the same mind. Once the Allies are permitted to gain a foothold they will build up overwhelming strength. For that reason the invasion must be defeated on the beaches. 〞

Kurt Meyer earned his laurels in the Balkans and Russia before being appointed second-in-command of the newly formed 12th *SS Hitlerjugend* division later in 1943.

❝ Gentlemen, comrades, I have been appointed deputy under General Fritz Witt, who I know very well by experience. I have every confidence in him. Our new division will now enter serious training here in Belgium, which will last several months. From my long experience in the East I feel competent to take on this honourable task and confident the division will attain its combat status to help protect the invasion front. As you realise, it is difficult to place our units at concentration points since we do not know exactly where the blow will fall. For this reason the *Führer* and others, including Rundstedt, believe it wise to hold the *panzer* divisions back from the coast in readiness so they can be moved swiftly to any one point where the chief landing takes place. In this view I and some others agree; elsewhere there are those who disagree.

The 1st *Leibstandarte SS* are nearer the invasion front, but we are all spread too thin, and I fear time will prove of the essence when the Allies do come. 〞

At the time of this situation conference with his officers, '*Panzer*' Meyer was a *Waffen-SS Gruppenführer*, or Lieutenant-General; he would soon become the youngest full general in the German forces. His fear that the time factor would be crucial in the early stages of the coming battle would prove to be justified, though even Meyer, with his great combat experience, had no idea how time would be bought at his expense by the Allied air forces. Confidence in his division would have been shaken had he appreciated the terrible ordeal soon to face them – not that there was anything Meyer could have done about this. A total lack of preparation to face air attack by the enemy's tactical air power went unnoticed, even though the desert veterans of the German Army could have enlightened him on this danger.

It is interesting to compare 12th SS with 21st *Panzer*, which according to one authoritative source was the only *panzer* division in the West unfit for service on the Eastern Front, being equipped in some units with inferior tanks of foreign manufacture (i.e. Czech and French), some of them lightweight.* It was also weak insofar as it contained only one infantry segment (104th *Panzer Grenadier* Regiment). By comparison 12th SS contained not only the standard engineer, signals, artillery and anti-tank battalions, but two infantry regiments plus a 'projector' battalion of heavy multiple mortars (the 'Moaning Minnies'), totalling some 20,000 men in all. Its training cadres were supplied by the 1st SS, the average age of its soldiers alleged to be only seventeen; the truth was probably eighteen, and photographs seem to bear this out. Neither were they large, physical supermen.

Since 1940 Himmler and his staffs had endeavoured and succeeded in building up the strength of their SS divisions, so that by 1944, while practically every division in the German Army had been cut down through attrition to around 10,000 men, the SS divisions were maintained at around double that number, and were always stronger in armour. This was achieved despite the fact that every one of the 'classic' SS divisions had been decimated during the protracted and bitter battles in the East. For example, of the 17,265 soldiers of the 3rd *SS Totenkopf* division who invaded the USSR on 22 June 1941, 12,625 had become casualties by the following March, with only 5,029 being replaced. Despite an 80% loss rate, the division lived to fight again in the best SS tradition as a 'fire brigade' unit in Russia after being withdrawn to France for rebuilding as a full-fledged panzer division. Diverted by the impending Mediterranean crisis and then ordered back to the Russian front, *Totenkopf*'s extraordinary and often insubordinate commander Eicke managed to gain a month's respite from his superiors (Himmler and Hitler) in order to try and bring his depleted division back to full strength. How he did this would require a whole chapter. Suffice to say that his efforts, while untypical of the SS as a whole, do illustrate the great energy and zeal displayed by the German military in times of crisis.

* *Hitler's Legions* by Samuel W. Mitcham, Leo Cooper, 1984.

Eicke was saddled with thousands of sub-standard recruits, boys fresh from labour service without discipline (on SS lines) and lacking physique. These he worked from dawn to nearly midnight on gruelling physical training and combat exercises, while armed parties of SS veterans toured the French countryside, confiscating every usable vehicle and converting it to their use. By the time his month was up, 120 trains were required to transport *Totenkopf* to Kiev in the Ukraine, the jumping-off point for the battle zones. The soldiers had huddled frozen in box cars for two weeks on that journey.

Eicke was ruthless, as evidenced by his earlier 'exploits', and due for death soon afterwards. Meyer and the other SS commanders, by contrast, had no such problems in the West where conditions, at first, were heavenly in comparison to those in the East. Only in 1944 did they greatly deteriorate when the Allies inaugurated their transport interdiction campaign through the bombing and strafing squadrons which, incidentally, cost the lives of somewhere around 10,000 French civilians.

If some emphasis has been put on the SS, this is because in the Normandy match it was they who provided the backbone and became the greatest obstacle to the Allied advance. Many German Army units would fight stubbornly on the coast, but once this defensive crust was broken the cudgel was mainly in the hands of men like Meyer, Sepp Dietrich, Hausser and Ostendorff (the latter on the American front). How was it that the Germans could take 'kids' who were invariably undernourished by Allied military standards, certainly only average or smaller physically, and somehow transform them into fighting 'fanatics'?

The results of SS-type training (rather than indoctrination in the ideological sense) show in the accounts that follow when the 'Normandy experience' is viewed from the German side.

2 Alarm!

Soon after the Germans occupied Paris in 1940 General Kurt von Briessen, commanding the 19th Infantry Division, is alleged to have ordered his troops to withdraw from the city owing to the sexual depredations of the French female population, or at least to try to prevent his men falling into the fleshpots of those members of the population most inclined to curry favour with the conquerors. This did indeed refer to the notion of the *femme fatale*. The occupiers found that French women were so disgusted with their own menfolk who had fled or given up that they willingly offered themselves to the strapping, lusty specimens of Teutonic manhood who goose-stepped before their commanders that sunny mid-June in Paris.

The French had been assured by propaganda that their enemy *le boche* were short of everything, half starved, petrol starved, unwilling conscripts forced into a Nazi war. The grey columns stamping through the streets of the capital were obviously wanting in nothing – or so it seemed. They would, the citizens soon discovered, be plundering the shops for all manner of goods, the ordinary *landser** purchasing everything in short supply in the homeland, whether high-quality stylish French shoes or perfume, and always in exchange for notes whose value had been set heavily in the conquerors' favour. This sweeping up of French goods by legal means was of course prior to the arrival of the Hitlerian agents (and Göring) who would simply loot items of culture on a grand scale.

The German occupation of France signalled the start of a weakening process among the *Wehrmacht* troops left as occupiers, a kind of tainting by occupation and, above all, inaction. For even though many of the original combat units were withdrawn later, a residue remained who saw no more action whatsoever until struck by the great Allied invasion four years later. Apart from the *Waffen-SS* divisions to come, the army units received (from 1941) a thin stream of second-class soldiers and barely fit men, units rounded out by foreign volunteers usually guaranteed to surrender at the first opportunity. By 6 June 1944, only a kernel of German Army and SS troops in France were veterans of combat, and even then they were often men recovering from wounds. The 'lots of little Germans' had not really materialised among the French population, though some leavening of native blood by the

---

* The German equivalent of Tommy, poilu, doughboy.

friendly enemy was inevitable. For the Germans life in the West in four years of war had proved agreeable, whatever ordeals lay ahead; service life proved no more than routine, seldom irksome. All this changed dramatically on 6 June.

Dieter Hartmann-Schultze was a *panzerjäger* (anti-tank) gunner with the 711th Infantry Division stationed in the beach head area designated as a landing point for the British 2nd Army. The day before he had obtained leave to visit a sick comrade in the German military hospital at Amiens, some 240 kilometres from his base, cadging a lift in one of his unit's supply trucks. Late that evening they set off back to Normandy. As the truck sped with dimmed headlamps through the dark French lanes, Dieter's thoughts alternated between the inevitable contest on the coast when the Allies landed, and more agreeable images of his girlfriend Ulrica back home in Freiburg. The couple planned to marry, though Dieter felt unsure if it was wise to enter into such a partnership in his circumstances – 'I was fearful in fact about surviving the invasion battle.'

Suddenly their truck was stopped by two military policemen who warned them of possible enemy parachutists ahead, this fact possibly signalling the start of the invasion.

❝ We were frightened, but decided we must return to our unit as quickly as possible. We saw searchlights and *flak* and flashes in the sky and once stopped to listen. All we heard was the sound of aircraft, but then it seemed small-arms fire. We consulted our map, trying to decide which route to take. We had no idea where the enemy parachutists could be, if in fact any had landed at all. So we drove on cautiously for another hour until quite suddenly we ran into a German patrol and were made to identify ourselves. The Lieutenant warned us we might run into a paratroop ambush, so we felt even more scared. But we drove on and encountered several more alarms before safely reaching our own unit just before dawn. As soon as we had rested we were told enemy airborne troops were in the area and we must get to our guns. We then heard sporadic small-arms fire to the east and knew the reports were true – unless it was all an enemy trick and our people were firing at each other!

I ran to join my comrades who were already in a small bunker near our anti-tank battery overlooking the beach. Our guns were 75s and very powerful. Then one of our lookouts raised the alarm in great excitement as he saw the first ships on the horizon through his night binoculars. We rushed outside. It was now lighter and we saw the fantastic fleet which amazed us. And soon we saw the first flashes from the battleships' guns and rushed for cover as the huge shells came rushing over. In shelter we stayed for a whole hour as the terrific cannonade continued, until at last our Sergeant told us to get to our guns. We found to our amazement that only one gun had been damaged, even though a huge number of shells and bombs from planes had fallen about us. There was smoke and the smell of explosives everywhere and as we reached our gun the first smaller calibre fire from weapons on the ships and landing craft began reaching us, so we lay flat and waited. **"**

Hans Ulrich Hanter was a member of a mortar team in the 716th Infantry Division stationed in the immediate coastal front north of Caen and west of the river Orne. He had hoped to travel just inland from the military zone long cleared of inhabitants to visit a friendly French farmer to barter German beer and cigarettes for eggs, butter, and whatever else was available. For this purpose he had permission to use a VW jeep.

" The French were not hostile in most cases and we did business with them. Neither had we suffered from spies or acts of sabotage, so we were on reasonably good terms with the population. We had been inspected by Field Marshal Rommel on several occasions. He used to come with his entourage and make a very thorough inspection of the whole sector, even walking on the beach, and he seemed satisfied that we had done all we could to prepare our defences. Although we were helped by French labour in the building of the larger concrete forts, our own bunkers were constructed by ourselves.

When I saw that huge fleet I knew we were lost. The RAF and Yankees were overhead all the time dropping bombs. The naval bombardment had been bad and continued right up to the moment the troops began to land. Even then it did not stop, simply shifting to other targets. Yet, although some positions were destroyed, many remained virtually undamaged, strangely enough. **"**

As indicated, these two divisions, 711th and 716th Infantry, would absorb the brunt of the British–Canadian assault on D-day. Neither was in the van of crack German units, nor were they in any way 'traditional' divisions or veteran in any sense of the word, except perhaps by way of being long used to occupation duties. In fact, both divisions were formed specifically for that purpose in order to free other, more combatworthy units for the great offensive in Russia.

The 711th was formed in April 1941 of older men and sent to northeastern France as a static unit guarding the Channel coast against possible British raids, and naturally to 'oversee' the French population by a German military presence. In December of the same year it was shifted to Rouen, but by the spring of 1944 the 711th was quartered around Deauville, on the coast some distance east of the Orne and under the 15th Army's jurisdiction. Private – or, to give him his proper title, *Kanone* – Schultze would have been based on the extreme western sector of his division's perimeter, where the Allied force assigned to combat them from the sea was the 4th Commando and the 1st Special Service Brigade. However, these elite troops' first task was to relieve the airborne units already dropped hours before in the zone behind this German coastal battery which was well placed to enfilade the eastern segments of the 9th Brigade units (2nd East Yorks and 1st South Lancs).

Always weak, the 711th comprised only two infantry regiments, an artillery battalion, plus engineers and signals. Whereas the standard German Army infantry division in, say, 1940 stood at around 15,000 men, units such as this were by 1944 only mustering about 10,000 to 11,000 troops. However, British rigidity in 'establishments' was not followed in the *Wehrmacht*, which was very flexible. Even though establishments in the British forces were not always adhered to, it can be assumed that for D-day that of nearly 18,500 men for the infantry divisions would have been standard, though it has to be remembered that only single battalions were landed from such divisions in the first wave of shock troops. In any case, regimental battalions were assigned to other divisions in this operation or even made 'LOB' – 'Left Out of Battle' – as a safeguard against the destruction of the first-line troops of the unit already committed to action.

The remarks on the 711th Infantry also apply to the 716th, formed at the same time from older age groups and sent to Normandy in May 1941. It remained in permanent occupation of the Caen sector until 1944 when, like its 'sister' division, it was virtually destroyed fighting the British 2nd Army. Unlike the 711th, this division did not apparently contain a reconnaissance company. Its task was an even more formidable one, for it faced the bulk of the British–Canadian landing force and without rapid reinforcement stood little or no chance of preventing the invaders landing.

However, the term 'older men' as applied in military terms to these front 'static' divisions must be qualified: none of the German witnesses testifying here was over thirty years old, the average age being nearer twenty-five. With the SS it was a different matter.

Christian Hubbne, like his comrades of the 716th Infantry, had been expecting the invasion for some time:

❝ But when it came it was a terrible shock, as the scale of it was over-whelming. We slept in a bunker not far from the shore and went to bed as usual that night. But soon after six o'clock we were roused by our Sergeant-Major who yelled that an enemy fleet was off shore and we must get to our battle stations at once. We rushed about in great confusion and fear, trying to eat something and drink coffee while pulling on our equipment. It took us almost fifteen minutes to reach our position in a fortified bunker which included machine-gun posts overlooking the beach. We were west of the river Orne and north of Caen.

I will never forget our first sight of that invasion fleet. The horizon was filled with ships of all kinds and of course huge battleships all lined up in the grey light of dawn. We were amazed and frightened; we had never seen anything like it and wondered how we could possibly repel such an armada. Of course, there was no sign of our own navy or *Luftwaffe* and we felt betrayed! Our Sergeant tried to steady our nerves, but I could see he was as amazed as we were. Then our Lieutenant came to remind us of all the drills we had done and not to fire until the enemy was in the water and at their most vulnerable. We knew all that, but wondered if we would still be alive to act at all. And sure enough not long after that the terrible bombardment began and it went on and on. We had not expected anything like it and cowered in our holes waiting to be buried alive or blown to bits. The great shells from the battleships made a fantastic noise and the ground shook when they detonated. We guessed that all the seafront houses and our defences were being smashed. The bombardment seemed to go on for a very long time and all the while the air was also filled with the sound of bombers hammering away at us.

Then, at last the noise seemed to lessen and our Sergeant told us to stand to as the enemy were about to land, so we jumped to our weapons, trembling with fear and from the effects of the bombardment. One of the units on our left was composed of Eastern 'volunteers' from Russia, I believe, who looked very Asiatic in appearance; I wondered if they had survived and would surrender at once.

Then we could see the enemy landing craft coming in to the shore and the warships still firing. We forced ourselves to get ready. **99**

Other German soldiers had been alerted hours before, men like Georg Huttler of 711th:

66 We were put on alert at our HQ in the early hours of 6 June and in a short time I, as a Sergeant, was detailed to take out a patrol with four vehicles around the local countryside. We were in a state of some anxiety and complete uncertainty as to the situation. All we knew was of reports of airborne landings at various points.

I had twenty men with me and we set off as soon as we were ready, other patrols went in other directions. After about half an hour we stopped to listen. It was very dark and some of the men said they had seen small lights across some fields. So I sent six men to investigate while we remained on high alert close to our vehicles. After they had gone I heard suspicious noises closer at hand, so I took four men with me to investigate, being very cautious and stopping every few metres to listen. We heard stealthy movements and felt certain we had found the parachutists. We dropped down ready to open fire, but at once a lot of shouting and shooting broke out not far away. I feared our transport was under attack so ran back to find some airborne had stumbled on our position and a sharp fight had taken place. The British had quickly gone to ground and then vanished. So we waited and then took a cautious look round but saw no more sign of them. I rounded up my men and we left the area. But I sent a message back to our HQ, and when we arrived there we found turmoil as the whole division was turning out to repel the invasion in the first light of dawn. "

Another soldier roaming the French countryside in the dark was Lieutenant Peter Lusse of the 716th:

" I went out before dawn after the alert with a small patrol to investigate reports of airborne landings. It was completely dark so we had no idea of the true situation, and until we had exact information it was difficult to make decisions. I had twelve men in two vehicles, an armoured car and VW jeep. We were well armed and fully alert and very surprised to meet a Sergeant with a woman, obviously French and in some state of alarm. He said he had been escorting her home and seen shapes coming down from planes passing overhead and knew at once they were parachutists. They were in some panic as they were not supposed to be out and she was obviously breaking the curfew. He seemed very relieved to see us, so I told him to send the woman off and get into the VW, which he did.

We then made a slow search of the local roads, but it was so dark it was hard to see anything. I then stopped and ordered the men to get out of the vehicles and listen. We heard stealthy movements coming towards us. Everyone jumped into cover and soon we saw two figures coming along the edge of the road. When they saw our vehicles they dropped down and began crawling towards them, and as soon as they passed us we leapt out and captured them. They were British parachutists, one a Corporal. We disarmed them and rushed them back to HQ, with difficulty as we had little room in our two vehicles. They seemed both relieved yet disappointed to be taken prisoner. We asked them all sorts of questions but they simply shrugged their shoulders and said, 'It's the invasion, you will soon be beaten', and things like that. I then had to go out as it was getting light and I never saw them again. "

Fritz Buchte of the 711th was another who had never fired a shot in anger from his machine-gun, and like his friends was relieved to have been left out of action 'in view of the state of things on the war fronts'. Life in France had been quite good with just about enough to eat and leaves to return to Germany. When last at home his wife had asked him if he thought the invasion would come; he replied: 'Of course, but I'll try to get back to you in one piece!'

" We saw the huge armada and then the bombardment started. Later the Sergeant rushed up and told us enemy airborne troops were already behind us and this was very alarming. Not that there was anything we could do about that, and we soon learned that they would be attacked by our panzers. We had to shelter from the bombardment which went on for a long time and was the worst experience of my life. Then at long last the Sergeant called us back to our posts as the enemy were coming in landing craft of all sizes and we guessed there would be tanks too. We had six anti-tank guns well sited to cover the beach but some of these had been knocked out by the bombardment. Yet we were very surprised to find many of our bunkers were still complete and undamaged. So we set up our guns and made ready to fire as the first Allied troops landed. **"**

Franz Grabmann had survived two years in the desert war as a Lieutenant in the 21st *Panzer* Division:

" I was lucky to escape as I was wounded and flown out to Sicily, then Italy and home. After I had recovered I was posted to France and the new 21st *Panzers* where I met two old comrades, which was excellent. I looked forward to a quieter time in France and indeed that's what happened, with enough to eat. But by 1944 and the threatened invasion we had begun to wonder about our future. I had attended many conferences which were inconclusive, but we did our best. Our other concern was over the training of the men, most of whom had no experience at all in combat – this was a constant difficulty. We tried, but all the best veterans and leaders had gone. Our equipment was fair to good, and although we did not have things on the same lavish scale as the SS we were fortunate in most things, though some of our tanks were Czech or French. All the bulk of the best armour went to the SS and Eastern Front. For example, we had not a single Tiger tank, only the SS in France had some of these.

I well remember one exercise which was 'fought' on the theory that the Allies had landed strong airborne forces at the same time as seaborne units landed in our region, which is where we believed the invasion would come. But we failed because of the conflicting ideas and uncertainties. Personally, I felt we should have been nearer the coastline, but it was more open there and this would have meant more danger from air attack. In fact, we always had to remain widely dispersed for that reason. **"**

Like other units, the 21st *Panzers* were alerted by the reports coming in of widespread airborne landings. The fact that considerable numbers of paras had fallen in the wrong place was of course unknown to the Germans, and indeed this scattering of airborne soldiers proved advantageous to the Allies. Because of the uncertainty of the situation Lieutenant Grabmann and his comrades received no orders. 'We had not the fuel to go chasing about the countryside looking for odd groups of parachutists, so it was daylight before we received real news which was of the invasion armada off shore. We then knew we were in for a great battle and prepared accordingly. Even then it was some time before one of our columns went off on reconnaissance, to be ambushed successfully by British airborne troops.'

Heinrich Siebel was an anti-tank gunner with the 711th and already on watch duty when the invasion fleet came over the horizon. 'I reported the sight to my Sergeant who ran out and shouted, "*Jesu! Mein Gott!*" and ran off to the telephone. I sat gazing at the sight for some time until my comrades arrived, then we manhandled our gun into position, removed the covers and set up the ready ammunition. Then we continued staring at the armada until the bombardment began, when we ran to shelter.' Shelter comprised a large bunker well protected by sandbags, with mines and wire to the front and flanks and a little exit path to the rear. The gunners had in fact been taking some coffee until the British shells began to arrive. 'All went into chaos, with smoke and destruction. We never thought we could survive and in fact quite a lot of damage was caused. Yet our gun remained intact with enough clearance to fire. Our Sergeant was wounded and went away; a Corporal took charge.'

For hundreds of Germans the very first moments of coming under fire were both terrifying and frustrating. To be head down in an earthen hole under tremendous bombardment from the many warships and unable to hit back was unnerving, to put it mildly. Hans Ludwig Weiner was woken up by a kick delivered by his close friend Georg, who shouted, 'The Tommies are here!' 'I jumped from my cot in a state of great alarm and started to pull my clothes on. Everyone was rushing about and I heard orders being shouted. It was dawn and when we rushed to our bunkers a great noise arrived overhead and the first great naval shells began exploding. The concussions were terrific, but there were no signs of troops landing.'

About an hour later these men of the 716th Infantry were called out of shelter by their NCOs to man their weapon posts. 'I was a machine-gunner. My good friend Georg helped me to set up the weapon. We were in a great state of fear as we had never been in action before. The shells continued to come over, but although great damage was done, we were not hit. When I first looked out to sea I could hardly believe my eyes – the horizon was covered in ships of all kinds. We could see the flashes from the warships' guns and then saw the landing craft which came nearer and nearer, some larger ones we believed containing tanks, so I hoped our anti-tank guns had survived.'

3 Assault

Except for the 47th Royal Marine Commando, the 1st Battalions of the Hampshire and Dorset regiments were the first wave of assault troops put down on the right flank of Gold beach in the British invasion sector, the American troops of 1st US Army to their right, a gap of some miles between the two armies. John McLaughlin of the 1st Battalion, Hampshire Regiment, recalled:

❝ We jumped from our LSI* in a great funk with a hell of a lot of noise going on, somewhere around 7.30 a.m., rushing up the shingle as fast as our loads would allow. I was a Corporal and realised I was in the lead with plenty of chaps behind me. I heard shouts and grunts but didn't look back. Only after we hit the deck further up the beach did I find that three men I knew were dead. The bullets were whining about us and hitting the beach stones with all kinds of muck flying about as a result. We lay behind some wreckage from the bombardment and I tried to locate our Sergeant but couldn't see him, which irritated and disappointed me as he was a big chap. I saw several men lying about and guessed they'd been hit. The rest of the platoon were still struggling up the beach and two more went down before they could reach comparative safety.

I knew I had to make a move, so I shouted, 'Come on lads, any more for the Skylark?' and felt a bit silly as no one took any notice. They didn't want to stick their heads up, but I thought we could reach a broken wall without too much trouble. So I shouted 'Come on!' and started moving towards it; the others followed reluctantly. One or two stuck themselves up too far and got hit, but not seriously. We had some very good medics and the wounded were soon under care. ❞

Ted Viger of the 1st Dorsets was also scrambling up the beach at that time:

❝ We jumped out under heavy fire and in great fear and tension. One of our lads fell face down into the water, but nobody stopped. I rushed up the sand and shingle with bullets whizzing past me and actually reached the top of the beach in amazement as I heard yells and screams behind me on each side which sounded bad. Our medics soon attended to the wounded. I lay head down in a state of funk with the remaining lads falling down around me in the same state, but we grinned in great

* Landing Ship Infantry

relief to be alive. The noise was pretty terrific and we heard some Jerry machine-guns going not far away. A Lieutenant and Sergeant came up and urged us on, so we crawled off that beach a little way and lost two more men. There was green grass and muck and debris and the smell of explosives and ruined houses. There was a lot of mist and smoke. When I glanced back I was amazed at the sight of the invasion fleet. It made me feel we couldn't lose. **99**

The Hants and Dorsets comprised 231 Brigade which included assault engineer units of the 79th Armoured Division, known as 'the Funnies' because of the unusual nature of their equipment. The 79th was commanded by the pioneer of specialist armour, Major-General Hobart, whose unorthodox ideas on the subject had so offended the War Office that he was got rid of – posted to Egypt. After his return he resigned rather than face further humiliating frustration from his superiors, the Blimps at the 'War House' who seemed determined not only to prevent the development of a modern tank arm, but much else that would bring the British Army up to date.

Astonishingly, the man whose ideas were to save many lives in Normandy and elsewhere was, by the summer of 1940, serving as a Corporal in the Home Guard. Rescued by Winston Churchill, he was reinstated and encouraged to get on with designing tanks that could fulfil special tasks in battle areas. It was even then an uphill struggle; suitable vehicles were just not available, but by 1943 an amazing array of armoured bulldozers, bridge layers, mine clearers and heavy mortar tanks had joined the engineer units. By D-day these vehicles were organised into assault regiments and assigned roles in the coming invasion. It was thanks to these that the British and Canadian casualties on 6 June were far lighter than expected and why, by contrast, the American losses on Omaha beach were so heavy. For despite being offered the 'Funnies' by Britain, the Americans declined such help – and suffered accordingly. The 'DD' (Duplex Drive) tanks – Shermans – were shared by both armies, though some sank after launching.

It was a source of wonder and disappointment to both Britons and Americans that so many of the German defence bunkers survived the tremendous and prolonged bombardment. Sufficient enemy soldiers remained with the nerve to resist the attackers, causing thousands of casualties. By and large, the many thousands of man-hours expended by Rommel's men on the beach obstacles proved a waste of time. Some were rendered harmless by the extraordinary bravery of special teams who went in before the main invasion fleet arrived; the remaining 'Rommel asparagus' was much nullified in effect by the invaders' arrival at high tide. Few of the landing craft and amphibious tanks struck the obstacles.

Some idea of the actual numbers of men involved in the assault wave on the British beach can be obtained. As indicated earlier, the well-concealed defenders were not faced with the mass human wave tactics used by the Soviets on the Eastern Front. In theory at least, the German MG42 machine-guns with their fantastic rate of fire (1,200 rounds per minute) should have been easily able to annihilate the comparatively small numbers of British soldiers leaping from their landing boats. It was always an incredible wonder to the surviving attackers that they gained the scant cover available at the top of the beach.

In combat, no matter what great numbers may be involved overall, it all comes down to action on the platoon scale. It was a soldier's own platoon mates who faced death that morning, and in fact this narrows down to a section: one section comprised an NCO, Bren gunner and eight riflemen; three sections made a platoon and three platoons made a company, with four companies to a battalion and three battalions making an infantry brigade. While establishments might lay down unit strengths, these were in practice hard to maintain at an exact level, for through sickness and above all casualties units would fall below strength. It would be rare during a campaign to find a company at its full strength of 120 men, or therefore a battalion at 480 soldiers. Down at section level a sergeant armed with a Sten or Thompson sub-machine-gun could well find himself followed not by nine men but half a dozen or less. Over a few months or even far less time infantry battalions often suffered 100% casualties, so that even if such a unit was still in existence later the faces would be largely new.

The greatest turnover would have been in company commanders, the captains and lieutenants who fought and messed with the men in the field. A great number of these never survived the Normandy battle. Whoever rushed forward at the head of his troops stood the highest chance of being killed or maimed, so once an officer had vanished from the action his place would by necessity be taken by the next ranker in line, the higher NCOs who are generally considered to have been the backbone of the army – any army. If the sergeant-majors or sergeants 'copped it' then the corporals found themselves in charge, but in the confusion and uncertainty of a field action would all too often find themselves out of sight of most of their company, or even what remained of their platoon. One of the eye-witness accounts in this work will demonstrate how one brave NCO would even find himself totally alone in an attack.

On the immediate left flank of the Dorsets was the 6th Battalion of the Green Howards (Princess of Wales' Own Yorkshire Regiment), among whom was Ron Wilson:

❝ When I rushed up the beach I had a bad feeling we would not reach the top as the fire against us was very heavy and flanking. I said a prayer – God Almighty, save us! – and ran like hell. But we were carrying heavy loads and it seemed ages before I crashed down further up the beach and I realised with enormous relief I was still in one piece. A lot of the other chaps reached me, but when I looked back I saw at least six bodies lying about, some just in the water, and they were I reckoned dead.

Our NCOs shouted at us to watch out for the tanks and some were the funnies and two were hit and brewed up which was very disappointing. Then a Sherman went past us with its guns firing and I saw a funny disappearing through a sea wall, so the Sergeant told us to get after it. Which we did. **"**

Flanking the Green Howards on the immediate left was the 5th Battalion of the East Yorks. Jim Tolson recalled:

" I was wounded in the knee as I rushed up the beach and I thought, 'Oh God – not me!' I fell down in a heap, thankful I didn't have to run any further with all my gear. The pain was bad and I moaned a bit. My mates ran past and one was killed. Then a medic reached me; he'd been hit in the arm but did his best and I must say they were a great bunch and very brave. I just lay there on my back looking at the sky and wondering how long it would be before I got home. I almost forgot about the noise and my mates.

The medic called one of his mates who came and tore my trousers and said it was only a scratch. And when I could look I was amazed to see he was right. It was a bad cut, a bullet graze, and, as they insisted, I tried to get up and found it wasn't so bad after all. I had a weird feeling of relief but disappointment that perhaps I wouldn't get home after all. The medic bandaged me up and they ran off, so I crawled up the beach to my mates who seemed surprised to see me. But when they went on the Lieutenant told me to hang on at the rear, which is what I did. **"**

John Venables was a Sergeant in the 48th Royal Marine Commando. The commandos were a new force in the British Army, their name derived from the Boer fighters of the South African War, originally conceived by Prime Minister Winston Churchill as an élite corps of volunteers capable of raiding and harrying the Germans in the occupied territories. As was often the case with Churchill, his inspirations were sometimes carried into fantasy; in this case he envisaged strong columns including armour landing on the French shore and striking inland to create alarm and despondency among the enemy. It took several memos from 'Winnie' to get any action from the hidebound War Office staff, who hated the thought of any kind of élite troops who could well escape their control. But once kicked into action the right men for that kind of dangerous work were soon forthcoming: intrepid, bold, brave adventurers who set about selecting the volunteers for hazardous duty.

The original commandos proved no more than a nuisance value to the enemy, but their pinpricks could sometimes be painful, enough to sting the *Führer* into ordering such men executed when captured.

From among these first commandos emerged men willing to try even greater hazards – that of parachuting, the first British airborne troops. By 1942 the Royal Marines had formed their own commando units, designed of course for amphibious operations, and by D-day it was the navy commandos who formed most of these élite troops. A 'Commando' establishment was not based on the army concept, being in effect a weak battalion comprising 'troops', the strength of these varying in both number of men and equipment. On 6 June the 48th RM Commandos landed on the right flank of the 30th British Corps front, on Sword beach, with the Canadians on their right. They were part of the 4th Special Service Brigade, their sister unit to the left 41 RM Commando.

John Venables:

❝ As our craft touched the shingle the bullets were zipping all round us and into the ship. We jumped out and waddled up the beach just as a Sherman DD tank came by. I called out to our lads to get behind it and run forward. As I did so I sort of overbalanced as we were all carrying heavy loads. I fell over next to the front left track of the tank and in that split second I thought I'd go right under it and be squashed flat. The next second I was grabbed from behind and thrown aside by very strong arms. I was amazed as the Sherman missed me by inches and as it went past I got a face full of exhaust fumes. I saw one of our other NCOs rushing up the beach, a chap I never really knew, and he had saved my life. By the afternoon he was dead. ❞

The 1st Battalion South Lancs with the 1st East Yorks were the assault troops of the 8th Brigade on the left flank of Sword beach, part of the 3rd British Infantry Division which had been Montgomery's old unit in France in 1940. Their parent formation was the 1st British Corps. As such, the invading infantrymen landed slightly north-east of Caen and close to the mouth of the river Orne on their immediate left, by Ouistreham. Scattered just inland were paras and glider troops of the 6th Airborne, these soldiers tasked to keep the beach-head clear of enemy reinforcements.

Dennis Cartwright of the 1st South Lancs jumped into a foot of sea water 'with a great splash', his best mates alongside: 'We tried to get off that damned beach which was covered by Jerry fire and I thought, if only I could run faster, but it was impossible with all that stuff on me. There were lots of bits of debris in the sea swell and smoke and noise and it seemed an age before we reached the shelter of a knocked-out DD tank with no sign of the crew. Our Lieutenant and NCOs ran up to urge us on behind them, but we were very reluctant to do this because of all the fire going on.' Charlie Hansen of the 2nd East Yorks recalled:

❝ We went in with none of the yelling you see in films. It was every man for himself as we tried to get up the beach in one piece. No one wanted to stop for a wounded mate, though I did see it happen. One bloke who stopped and tried to pick up his pal was himself killed. That shook me as I'd never seen anything like it. I was really too soft to be in battle; the noise upset me a good deal and I preferred to keep my head down. But with so much going on I was too curious and our Lieutenant had said, 'Well boys, this is history, you'll be able to tell your children and grandchildren all about it.' Course, he was trying to imply we'd be alive to do so! We weren't very optimistic, with all that shooting and the chaps falling. I could see quite a way up the beach and knew some units were having a far worse time. Yet when I looked back and saw our own lads struggling up that beach I was amazed that so many made it. And I felt terrifically relieved and began to feel better. **"**

On the eastern flank of the British was the 1st Special Service Brigade, comprising army commandos led by Lord Lovat which included allied elements – even Germans who had fled Hitler's Reich. Gerald Farquarson and Tom Baker were pals; both had 'great confidence we could win once we got the chance to get ashore. Well, we did that all right and most of our losses occurred inland in the battles that followed. There was a good deal of fire against us, both small and larger calibre stuff, but we managed to follow a DD tank up the beach, to the top where everything came to a halt while we sorted ourselves out and the tank took on targets. There were a few men lying about, but I think our casualties were quite light really.'

Rex Williams of the Shropshires, like many other soldiers, was disturbed in mid-Channel by the advent of bad weather which caused the landing craft to rock and brought sickness to the troops, the pills they had been given ineffective. By then they had been told the invasion was on, there would be no cancellation. Added to the constant drone of planes overhead were the sudden great cannonades from warships big and small as they rained fire on the German beach defences. It was almost impossible to gain any view of the shoreline from the landing ships, whether LCIs or LSTs – hardly touring craft, with no ports; more like oblong open-topped boxes with engines and manned by small Royal Navy crews who knew their job and were vulnerable in the stern to German fire. The short voyage to shore seemed an age of terrible stomach-turning suspense and racket, in fact about half an hour until officers told their men to get ready, to buckle on their equipment. Men who felt bad, queasy with retching in some cases, forced themselves to face a worse ordeal. And as the craft lost speed near the shoreline the rocking motion eased and to the disappointment of all they realised the Germans had not been annihilated by the tremendous bombardment from the sea. Shells and bullets were now hurtling down the beach at them.

" We could hear shells exploding on the sea and beach, machine-guns rattling and all sorts of other noise. My tummy was rolling as we stepped off onto the ramps either side of the landing craft and I tried to keep calm. My mates went down in front with more blokes I knew behind me. We were so overloaded with gear I almost overbalanced into the water. But I made it. My legs felt like jelly through nerves. I tried to run up the beach but it was no use, I just couldn't. So I said out loud, 'Fuck it!' and simply walked until I was with a bunch of the lads lying down near a Sherman tank that seemed to be out of action. It was quite chaotic, with thousands of men trying to unload with vehicles and get up the beach. We kept our heads down as there was stuff flying about. Then a Lieutenant I didn't know told us to get off the beach and into the grass and sand dunes. **99**

Tim Holdsworth landed with 41 Royal Marine Commando: 'We had quite a few casualties from well-sited German machine-guns and when I finally got into cover we had got a few hundred yards inland among the first houses, where I lay down in a sweat.'

Meanwhile, parachutists of 6th Airborne had been inside enemy territory for hours, many in some confusion owing to their being delivered outside the designated drop zone, as Peter Firmin related:

66 I dropped into Normandy with a clear idea of what to do, but it all looked different on the ground in darkness, in the wrong place and alone. But after a while I found some other chaps and we set off along the edge of a field, stopping every so often to try to locate more men. Eventually we numbered about twenty including a Sergeant who took charge. We went on till we found a lane where we set ourselves up in case the Jerries came along. We reckoned we could find out where we were when daylight came. I was with two chaps with a Bren. There was a lot of noise all night with the planes going over and as it began to get light the offshore bombardment began and we gave a bit of a cheer.

The Sergeant sent out some small patrols in two directions, and one of these soon came back to report Jerries coming our way. So we got ready for them, well hidden behind the hedges with our Stens, grenades and everything.

Then we saw them come into sight, about twelve vehicles with an officer in a truck at the front, an armoured car, the German troops in open trucks, and we let 'em have it. The officer fell dead and the truck caught fire. The noise was terrific, the Jerries were yelling and trying to shoot back but getting knocked down and I saw the last truck in the rear go up in flames as our chaps threw grenades. It was a perfect ambush and after about five minutes only a few Jerries had managed to scuttle back along the lane to safety. **99**

The paras found twenty to thirty Germans left on the road, most of them dead. Documents were taken, at which point more paras under an officer arrived and the group set off to deploy, ready for the expected heavier enemy counter-attack. Other memories of this same action tell of a German column a mile long and some enemy soldiers marching on foot, the rearmost enemy vehicle being knocked out so that the rest were unable to reverse in retreat back along the lane; of one British para at the front intent on taking the German officer's Luger pistol – which he did.

Those vital few minutes before 7.30 that morning made the success of the first phase of the British landing inevitable. Field Marshal Rommel's insistence that the invaders must be stopped on the beaches could not be realised; only on the American Omaha beach did the Germans succeed in inflicting a crisis on the Allies. Despite all the German fire and against the odds, a majority of British infantrymen reached comparative cover to form assault groups led by determined junior officers and NCOs to begin the task of outflanking and taking the defenders in the rear and so rolling up the German coast defences. Then the great build-up could begin unmolested by land, sea or air action. The German Navy's attempts to intervene by U-boat and E-boat caused little bother to the Allied fleet, while the few sorties flown by the *Luftwaffe* seemed more like a pitiful token showing than any serious attempt to cause damage.

However, it was the kind of renewed testing time General Montgomery had warned of. Those first British shock troops surviving the actual landing did indeed lie up on the beach in great relief and thankfulness, most unwilling to leap up and face acute danger again at once. The relieving lethargy that followed miraculous survival was strong and inevitable, the kind of anti-climax that follows moments of deadly, nerve-straining fear. This brief period had come for most after years of waiting, boredom and comparative inaction until, at long last, they had been released into what for very many would prove either their last moments, or weeks, on earth.

The inertia following these early morning terrors was broken by the men with pips and stripes on the khaki battledress, those like Corporal John McLaughlin of the Hampshires:

❝ I had enough men with me to move on, but the trouble was trying to locate the enemy bunkers. I know we all felt very relieved to have got off the beach, but disappointed there were still some Jerry positions intact and apparently untouched by the bombardment. I crept forward and realised the fire was no longer coming our way, so I felt more confident. When I looked back I saw our Sergeant grinning at me and in a minute we were trying to spot the Jerry bunkers which were very well concealed. We went through a broken wall and saw some muzzle flashes, so the Sarge directed some blokes to get round them and off they went at the double. But we then came under flanking fire and had to hit the deck again. However, it was possible to crawl and this we did until we fell into a crater and could decide what to do next. We then rushed on a way until we reckoned we were close to the Jerry positions which we located in a house that had been well knocked about. We managed to get close to the grey walls of the place and threw grenades into the windows and they went off with a hell of a row. Then we rushed in, just as some of the other squads attacked the front of the house. We found several dead Germans and took six prisoners. We next consolidated and counted our losses, which were about twenty in all, killed and wounded. 〝

Ted Viger of the 1st Dorsets recalled: 'We ran along a little gully behind the houses and even though we were under fire it seemed to miss us. We attacked a house with grenades and heard a lot of racket inside and suddenly several Jerries came running out with their hands up. They had thrown off their helmets and looked terrified. We felt really terrific and sent them running off down the beach. Then some of our tanks that were still intact came up and we started to move inland.'

For the German soldiers the terrifying, hour-long bombardment was followed by more fear almost as acute as that suffered by the attackers. Slight relief came from action, as Christian Hubbne of the 716th Infantry recalled:

〝 On the command we opened fire. Then we saw lots of funny-looking tanks coming off the landing craft and I thought, My God, if they get to us we're finished. Some of the tanks sank in the sea, but others rolled up the beach and we could not stop them. But we heard our anti-tank guns firing and three of the tanks were destroyed. The others were shooting at us and all sorts of debris was flying about. I felt something hit my forehead and blood, so I wrapped a handkerchief around my head. Then there was a horrible crash and our bunker filled with smoke. I fell down and saw bodies and thought it was the end. Then the Sergeant came and helped me up and together we started firing again. We used an undamaged machine-gun, but after a short time we heard a lot of noise behind us and realised the enemy tanks and infantry were in our rear.

Suddenly there was a lot more noise and the whole bunker collapsed. A tank had come up and fired a heavy charge that really destroyed everything. It was very dark and filled with choking smoke and I staggered to get out. I could not see my Sergeant and found later he had been killed. There was a lot of debris but I managed to struggle over it and saw faces; some British Tommies helped me out. I had no idea what time it was, I seemed to have been in that hole trying to escape for hours. Next morning I reached England as a PoW and thankful to be alive. 〝

Lothar Vogt had always been more than keen on motorcycles and by 1944 was happily employed in Belgium and France as a despatch rider, his parent unit the 84th Corps under General Marcks.

〝 I often took despatches to 21st *Panzer* and other units near the coast from headquarters. Between eight and eight-thirty a.m. on 6 June I was handed an urgent message for the commander of 21st *Panzer*, General Feuchtinger, and set off as usual. I was warned to be alert as we were not sure how many enemy airborne troops had landed, or where. I rode north-eastwards on my usual route at a good pace, keeping my eyes open but seeing nothing at all unusual.

Then, about halfway to my destination which was a château west of Falaise, I heard shouts and shooting above the noise of my machine and suddenly saw enemy soldiers running in a little wood to my left. I went faster in fear as I thought they must be American parachutists. I kept my head down and raced on at about sixty miles an hour, heard shots and realised I had had a narrow escape. But then it seemed peaceful again and I saw many French civilians moving south. I decided to stop and ask if they had seen the enemy. I saw two men and a woman pulling a horse and cart and asked them in bad French if they had seen British or American soldiers, and they nodded. So I took out my map to try to find a little side road and safer route. I found one and went along it, but after a mile began to see wreckage and realised I was in the battle zone, though I had no idea if the wrecked vehicles were the work of jabos or ground troops. So I slowed down and then took another look at my map. I was on the right road and, I thought, far from the battle which was on the coast.

So I rode on and then saw a great number of aircraft flying in various directions. Next I saw a column of fast-moving vehicles in the distance and decided they were Germans moving to the front. My own route then turned parallel to this other route, but only after I had covered another mile did I realise the column nearby was an enemy one. This surprised me greatly, as they seemed to be travelling due north. So I stopped again to consult my map and saw I was in fact moving eastwards; the road had twisted, and since I was on an unfamiliar route I had become disorientated. I thought the short enemy column must be on reconnaissance so I waited until they had vanished. Then I found my own little road joined with another, which ran towards the enemy. I went on cautiously and then realised it ran directly north – or so I believed. In fact, I was beginning to lose all sense of direction. I had not brought a compass as I had been quite familiar with the usual route for so long I had become over-confident. But I drove on cautiously, wondering what would happen if I was captured and the despatch fell into enemy hands.

Then I distinctly heard the noise of battle and knew I had ridden nearer the beach-head. I had no option but to stop and turn round hurriedly. I had travelled only a few hundred metres when hell came in the form of tracer bullets from across a nearby field. So I forced my head down over the handlebars and drove like mad. A kilometre further on I ran into one of our patrols and screeched to a halt in a cloud of dust, almost falling off my machine.

I discovered they were from 21st *Panzers* and they directed me to the right road. An hour later I had delivered my message and was drinking coffee in the château. I returned to 84th Corps HQ by a more southerly route. **99**

Lieutenant Ulrich Radermann was a paratroop officer who had fought in Crete and been ready to drop on Malta in Operation 'Neptune', but this action never came. Following a well-deserved leave in Germany he was sent with his unit to the Russian Front where he spent 'two long, bad years'. To his and the survivors' relief they were next sent west, to France, 'heaven by comparison', on anti-invasion standby and quartered around Rennes.

66 On the morning of 6 June I was ordered to report to General Meindl, our CO of 5th Parachute Division, and go to 84th Corps and find out what the situation was as we were completely in the dark. We knew only that enemy airborne troops had landed. We had received no orders and it was all very unsatisfactory. Communications were proving difficult owing to air attack and a certain amount of Resistance sabotage. So I selected a Sergeant I knew as very reliable. We had a motorcycle combination and knew the best route to travel.

When we reached 84th Corps HQ we found panic and a complete lack of decision-making. I did not know what to make of it, and when I tried to telephone my own HQ at Rennes and speak to General Meindl it proved impossible to get through. I decided all I could do was try to investigate the situation for myself. It was still quite early, about nine o'clock, when we set off north.

We travelled fairly fast and soon ran into our army patrols who warned us of American parachutists in the area. The soldiers were trying to find them, but it was difficult owing to the woody nature of the countryside. So we rode on cautiously in a northerly direction until reaching a crossroads and a military policeman, who passed on the same warning of enemy paratroops. He was in a rather exposed position and looked very nervous. So on we went, still going north and feeling we now had a better idea of the situation. I decided to travel a few more miles to see if the troops in the beach-head were holding. We almost reached a village a few miles from the sea when we heard shouts and bursts of automatic fire. Our motorcycle went out of control into the side of the road and we were flung off. I was dazed, but my Sergeant was hurt. We found ourselves prisoners of some Americans who had blackened faces and looked very fierce.

They removed our weapons and belts and took us to a little copse where we found an officer with another man who spoke some German. He said, 'You are paratroops like us?' I shrugged my shoulders and the officer asked us questions – where were we going, etc. I refused to answer, so they tied us up with some cords and we were given some whiskey from a small flask. My Sergeant was badly bruised so I asked for medical attention, but the American officer said they had no doctor.

Then most of the Americans left on patrol, leaving two men to guard us who were chewing and smoking, so I whispered to my Sergeant that we could try to escape, but then saw he was in no position to do anything of the sort. So he said, 'Lieutenant, it is your duty to get away if you can. Don't worry – I'll survive!'

He was right, so I pretended to fall asleep. And at the right moment, as the two Americans strolled away, I leapt up and ran off as fast as I could with my hands still tied. The guards ran after me, shouting and shooting, but I had the advantage. I ran like mad through the trees, leapt over several ditches and went under hedges until I reached a little road where I collapsed to rest and see if I had been followed. But no one came, so I got up and ran along the road, hoping it was the right direction. To my great joy I soon met one of our army patrols who untied me. I told them the location of the American paratroopers and they went off to look for them and try to rescue my Sergeant. One of their vehicles drove me back to their field headquarters which was of the 21st *Panzer* Division. From there I was able to get a message to my own HQ at Rennes, and by nightfall I reported to General Meindl.

My Sergeant was not recovered, but remained a PoW. I met him again after the war. **99**

Ron Wilson of the Green Howards, having got off the most exposed part of the beach, was trying with his mates to follow a tank that trundled on behind a house where it was immediately hit by German anti-tank fire.

66 We hit the deck and were ourselves pinned down by fire for some time until another Sherman came along. So we rushed to get behind this one but it was hit and the crew baled out and ran off. We cursed them as windy! We tried to move on but fire was coming at us from many directions, until suddenly it slackened and we were able to move on over broken ground and found several dead Germans with a machine-gun. They looked awful and were the first dead I'd seen. Then our Lieutenant told us to get after a 'funny' that appeared, so we ran off towards it, but the Jerries got that one too. Then the officer pointed out a burning house that still had Jerries inside it, so some of us rushed it, expecting to be hit at any moment. But nothing happened. We rushed in through the back door, fired a few rounds and found only dead Germans. **99**

Dennis Cartwright of the South Lancs was also trying to make ground:

66 Urged on by NCOs, we forced ourselves out of cover and next found some British wounded lying in a ditch waiting for attention.

We moved on at the crouch but were forced to fall flat as enemy fire came at us. We saw two tanks brew up, then managed to get behind a Sherman that came up the beach firing and trying to get behind the ruined houses that still had Jerries in them. Our tank was firing like mad at all of them, but in the smoke and mist we couldn't see which of them to go for first. Then the Lieutenant said, 'Come on lads – follow me!' So we did, and ran slap-bang into heavy fire from a Jerry machine-gun we hadn't seen. I went down in sheer terror and heard chaps bawling like kids who'd been hit. There were bangs and shooting and when I dared to glance up I saw our lads rushing on past a Jerry strong point, so feeling a bit of a twerp I followed.

That was really the end of our first battle in Normandy. We stopped for a few minutes for some hot tea and to count our losses, which were about twenty I think in that first hour, but of those a few rejoined us later. **99**

Charlie Hansen of the East Yorks, 'too soft to be in a battle', had recovered his courage a little on finding himself a survivor of the first wave of troops.

66 After about ten minutes our NCO got us to move, so we followed a Sherman which then got stuck in a ditch beyond the beach and was knocked out with a hell of a bang. There was fire coming at us from a house, so we waited until we saw a DD tank go in and blast the place and the fire stopped coming our way. We moved on with a hell of a lot of noise going on and no idea what was happening until a Captain appeared and directed us to a group of houses, and there we had a hell of a fight as the Jerries had machine-guns and at first it proved impossible to outflank them. We were completely pinned down while the ships offshore and some tanks tried to blast them out, and this took time to arrange. In that time we were under fire from the machine-guns and mortars and had casualties and the medics couldn't get to us, so some men died who could have been saved.

After at least an hour of this the Jerries were beaten. A dozen of them, now dead, had held up a whole battalion with three machine-guns. **99**

Fritz Buchte lay behind his MG42 machine-gun, he and his comrades overawed by the vast armada spreading across the Channel before them. Trying to quell their fear and once the hour-long bombardment on them ended, they made ready to tackle the first landing troops.

66 We opened a heavy fire on them and saw men falling and our bullets hitting the craft, but then tanks appeared. Some went into the sea and we realised they were amphibious. Some never reached the shore, others were hit and caught fire, but others were shooting very accurately. Our bunker was struck several times and we began to get casualties. It was horrible to hear the men yelling in pain in all that other noise. Then we ran out of ammunition so one of my helpers at the gun ran off for more but never returned. We were obliged to use rifles and grenades, but this was very hard as the British tanks and infantry were shooting at us and some got behind us. Suddenly our Sergeant appeared and said, 'It's no use, we're surrounded! We must surrender!'

In view of the murderous fire all round us we had no choice. We tied a white rag to a rifle and stuck it out of a shooting embrasure and that was that. We heard British voices and went out the back, which was very difficult because of all the debris. They made us go down onto the beach where we laid down because of all the shooting still going on. But after a while it got quieter, though not until afternoon were we put aboard a landing craft and taken to England, which was quite an experience as after that I learned much I liked about the English and felt better than I had done for years. **"**

The *panzerjäger* Heinrich Siebel opened fire with his comrades, their first 75mm shell going straight through one of the British landing craft, the second hitting the stern.

" From then on we shot and shot, especially at the strange tanks that came up the beach. It became hard for us to see much because of the smoke, but I believe we destroyed two tanks before our gun received a direct hit. There was a flash and a great bang and I was blown backwards over the concrete floor and knew nothing else for a time. When I woke up I found two of our men dead and more wounded. Our gun was destroyed and all I could think of was escape. I tried to get out through the rear exit, pulling one of my wounded friends with me, but debris made this difficult. There was a lot of shooting, then some British soldiers came and with their help I was able to escape. My comrade was treated, but he died. **"**

On the British left flank the Green Berets pressed on behind their leader, Lord Lovat, among them Gerry Farquarson and Tom Baker:

" We saw a great deal of damage from the bombardment; the whole area was thick with smoke and mist and the noise constant. We had to try to link up with the 6th Airborne lads who'd been on the ground for hours. Once off the beach we got among the houses and that's where we had our first real skirmishes and casualties as the Jerries were well sited and sniping. Some of our lads went down. We pushed on past windows, trying to find cover, which was not easy. Speed was of the essence as we didn't know how hard the airborne were being pressed. Some of our boys bought it among those houses, but Lovat was an amazing leader and rallied us. I saw two Jerries rush out of a house and before you could say Jack Robinson they were dead. Only then did we realise they only wanted to surrender. We were very tense and touchy with all those windows overlooking us and mistakes were made.

Two Jerries had a machine-gun on the roof of a house and we gave them full bursts which knocked the slates off, and one of them waved a hanky from a window and got himself shot. The other one jumped from a window and broke his leg. Soon after that we came across the first airborne lads and were surprised to see them so cocky and in good condition. After that we found little opposition. **"**

Off the beach itself Rex Williams and some other soldiers were directed to a German machine-gun nest which their Lieutenant wanted eliminated.

❝ I didn't want to stick my head up too far. The noise was considerable and glancing along the beach I could see thousands of men, all sorts of vehicles and smoke, and in the distance landing craft burning. And I wondered how the Yanks were getting on. I saw a few bodies here and there, but they were not near us. One of the lads set up a Bren and started shooting at the Jerry position, and the Lieutenant told us to follow him so we could try to outflank the enemy. I kept right down, absolutely terrified as we huddled along the grass and sand until we fell into a shallow ditch full of bodies, both theirs and ours. I was fascinated by this sight, but the officer urged us on, so we actually got to our feet and ran like hell over some dead ground behind a ruined house which gave good cover. There were at least six of us with rifles and Stens; one bloke had a sack of bombs and we all carried grenades.

The Lieutenant said, 'Now then, where's that bloody Spandau?' and started searching the ground with his glasses. There was still a lot of stuff coming over, but somehow we seemed to escape it. Then the Lieutenant spotted our target and pointed out a small hill surrounded by debris, assuring us we could now deal with it. So off went our Corporal Bill something or other, I forget his name, with us crawling along behind him. We left some of our gear behind with two of the lads. The Lieutenant went off to the left with a Sten and some grenades while we went straight on until we could clearly hear the Jerry machine-gun firing – but we still could not see it.

'OK, let's chuck grenades,' the Corporal said. So we each took out a Mills and threw them at the little hill. The noise was pretty terrific and then we heard the Lieutenant shouting for us. But when we raced over to where he was we found him dead, near the Jerry machine-gun post which was a mess, with bodies all round. We crouched down and stared at them. Two had grubby faces and were wearing camouflaged helmets, one had lost an arm and they looked pretty awful.

'Christ,' said the Corporal, 'fancy getting it like that.'

He was staring at our Lieutenant, and took out his ground sheet to cover the body. The Corporal looked round for another officer while one of the lads took the Lieutenant's paybook and Sten. We had no idea what to do next and couldn't see our own Sergeant. But then a Sergeant-Major ran up, sized up the situation and told us to follow him. The rest of our lads came up and we recovered our gear and we trudged on to a wall where we waited for orders and some support as there was a lot of fire coming in our direction. I glanced at my watch, amazed to find two hours had gone by. We had landed in France and I was still alive. I took out some chocolate and sat down in great relief. ❞

Tim Holdsworth of 41 Royal Marine Commando lay flat among the trees and walls about the first houses they had reached inland, surprised to find himself apparently alone as his mates were either lying wounded (or dead) or, like himself, gone to ground.

66 I was a bit surprised to be in one piece. The shock of going into action had hit me quite hard and I'd seen chaps I knew falling all over the place. The trouble was we couldn't see the enemy who had run back and set up new positions, and being Jerries they knew what they were doing and you never had it easy with them. The bullets were smashing about everywhere and I could see that none of us still alive felt like moving. Two DD tanks came along and the bullets were pinging off their armour. When they came closer some of the lads jumped up and got behind them, so I waited my chance and did the same. This way we managed to get along a little lane and seemed to be missing most of the fire until we reached a curve in the road when our tank got hit by an 88 and brewed up. So we all had to hit the deck again. I hid behind a wall with other lads as the Sherman started exploding, like rockets going off. I felt very sorry for the poor beggars inside the tank, but there was nothing we could do for them. The thing was blazing and bullets were still hitting it and the road and trees around us.

After a few minutes an officer appeared and showed us how to get behind the wall and into some undergrowth, so we followed him in fear, but he seemed to know what he was doing and the enemy fire was now missing us completely. We went on through a copse and saw houses across a field and a few Jerries stupidly showing themselves. They seemed to be arguing as to what to do next and had no idea we were near. We let them have it and I think bagged the lot. The officer then led us over to them in a rush and we found all but one dead. He was in a bad way so we left him and ran down a little street until more Jerry fire forced us into one of the houses where we were pinned down. Every time we tried to leave we were fired at. Then at last another Sherman waddled up and started shelling all the houses including ours, so we dived out the back into a little garden and our officer was able to signal the tank crew. By then the Jerries had had it or run off, so we were able to get over the gardens at the back of the house and the whole village was ours. 99

That evening, while 'having some grub' with his remaining mates and waiting for a German counter-attack, they came under shellfire, spraying them with splinters, and Tim was struck in the right foot and put out of the battle. Two days later he was back in England.

The American Bill Molden remarked only on 'some skirmishes' he experienced with the Hampshires, and casualties: 'I got used to the sight of bodies, often in pieces, and they weren't pretty at all. But it's amazing how quickly we got used to the awful sights on the battlefield. You get so you take no notice of them at all. Either they're alive or dead, it's as simple as that.'

Hans Ulrich Hanter and his mortar team received their first fire orders from their Sergeant. From their dugout they could see nothing once in position, and began lobbing their three-inch bombs onto the water's edge.

❝ We had practised this so many times; it was a simple operation and we just went through the same motions. I had sited the weapon, one comrade loaded and another helped. It was very smooth work except we were trembling as it was our first time in battle. Our Sergeant was a veteran of Cassino and the Eastern Front and knew all about war. He did not last long, as very soon we heard a shout that enemy tanks had landed and were shooting at us – we heard no more from him. Then a Corporal appeared and told us he would give the orders. But in a very short time the enemy's own mortars and other fire began to search us out. The noise was fantastic; great smoke columns were shooting up as the tanks that were hit burned.

Then we were forced to take shelter as the battle came too close. We fell into our reserve bunker with rifles at the ready as everything seemed to come in on us. We heard a tank very close by but could see nothing. Then the earth fell in on us and we fought to escape being buried alive. Outside we went and straight into the hands of the waiting Tommies. ❞

Hans Ludwig Weiner of the 716th Infantry, with his comrades, was urged to hold fire until the enemy was in the water:

❝ The first Tommies jumped into the sea, which was quite shallow. The bullets hit them and their craft to good effect and I was a little surprised to see them falling – I don't know why. Never having seen a real battle it did shake me to be hurting those men, even though they were enemies. Even then, in my stupidity I thought I was only hurting them, not killing them!

But we were getting all kinds of fire; bits and pieces were flying all around our embrasures as the Tommies who survived tried to rush behind us. But they seemed to move so slowly as they carried a lot of equipment, and some more fell. There was so much fire going at them I was surprised to see so many survive, and once these reached the upper part of the beach they found some cover and were no longer in our sights.

Then things became very difficult as mortar bombs and machine-guns hit us from the flanks and some of our men shouted that the Tommies were surrounding us. Tanks began shooting at us with cannon and machine-guns and we were forced to get down. Part of our block-house collapsed and we thought we would be buried alive. By some miracle we were not and our Corporal reached us to say all the other men were dead or wounded – but we would not give up. Then some of the Tommies came very close as they fired and we knew it was hope-less. The enemy were shouting and firing and then we ran out of ammunition, so it seemed the sensible thing to surrender, if we could do so without being shot.

I threw my helmet out of the hole at the back and my friends did the same as we had nothing white to wave. They called us out and we managed to escape and found about ten Tommies all pointing their guns at us. After being searched we were told to go and lie on the beach, which was still under fire from our own people. It seemed a very dangerous place to be, but we lay flat and escaped injury. It seemed hours before we were finally taken down to a landing craft for England. **99**

Peter Wolf Agnussen of the 711th Infantry helped provide some of the stiffest and most prolonged opposition to the British invaders on D-day, a battle that went on for hours, the defenders only being finally subdued later on 6 June. 'I was in the front line from the start of the landings on 6 June.' Despite the fact that accounts show the sector occupied by Peter Agnussen as within the boundary of 352nd Infantry, a fact commented on by the late Chester Wilmot in his pre-eminent account *The Struggle for Europe* (Collins, 1954) with a remark on the resistance offered by 'a battalion of 352nd Infantry Division', this witness asserted that he served his term with the 711th only, and was with a detachment of this division in the battle at the sanatorium.

The Hampshires had landed just east of Le Hamel, and escaped the worst of the direct fire across the beaches when men were so terribly slowed by the absurd weight of equipment the War Office had decreed they hump into combat. If these brave troops had been combat loaded with the minimum amount of items necessary for immediate battle, and above all if some little imagination had been used, then fewer men would have died struggling up the shingle. In the short time it took the Hampshires to gain some kind of cover three Crabs (anti-mine flail tanks) crawled up the beach to try to outflank and if possible take the enemy-occupied houses in the rear. Three were knocked out in the attempt, or else bogged down in the marshy ground beyond the beach. Then a third tank charged the largest strongpoint that was now emitting the fire that drove the Hampshires to ground. It was a fortified sanatorium and the occupants were forced by the tank's fire to keep their heads down long enough to allow two companies of Hampshires to bypass it and the little locality of Le Hamel and move into the village of Asnelles, which was just beyond the seafront road. Then the tank was knocked out and that front became impassable because of renewed German fire.

'By some miracle we were spared serious damage,' Agnussen commented with regard to the bombardment. He saw the first infantry unloading and the 'unusual' tanks, some of which had chains that beat the ground, others amphibious.

66 The noise was tremendous and the enemy opened fire. I saw two of the strange tanks knocked out. We were firing through what had been large windows which we had boarded and sandbagged, sticking our weapons through small holes. We had an excellent and wide field of fire and made a very strong impression on the British who were forced to go to ground and made no headway against us at all. Our anti-tank guns were successful in stopping all the British tanks. Our Sergeant and Corporal were manning machine-guns and beside me stood my old friend Hans who had been with me all of my time in France. We had not had a bad life, quite a good one compared with others, but at last the war had reached us and we began to feel we would not survive as the bombardment continued. More tanks appeared and we began to suffer serious damage to our strongpoint, and several men were killed or injured. It was terrible to hear them moaning and there was no chance of evacuating them. Our Captain was a very strong-willed man and came round continually, exhorting us to hold the enemy until help could reach us. He said the 21st *Panzer* would soon relieve us.

The battle seemed to go on and on and soon half our men were casualties and we were running out of ammunition and had nothing to eat at all. Then I received a splinter in my left arm and had to lie down while Hans bandaged it up with a paper roll. Then I returned to my position in time to see two British tanks with heavy mortars opposite our position. The noise was indescribable as they fired great bombs at us. All hell broke loose as the building began to collapse around us. We were forced to retreat to new positions. By then it was late in the afternoon, and I remember looking at my watch and being amazed how much time had passed. Then I saw the Captain consulting with a Sergeant, and I guessed they were wanting to surrender as we had no more ammunition and so many killed and wounded.

Our ordeal ended when the Captain waved a small piece of white cloth and the Tommies came forward, so we threw out our weapons which were now useless and helped remove the wounded. The bodies of our comrades had to wait. **99**

It had taken the Hampshires all morning to subdue the beach dune defences; it was around four o'clock when the Germans in the sanatorium surrendered. The Churchill Petard (heavy mortar) tanks had swayed the balance in that fight, while destroyers and small support craft had battered the Germans further along the beaches, so enabling the Hampshires to push on to Arromanches, which they reached about nine p.m. It was a prime objective, more important than the junction towns of Bayeux and Caen, at least on D-day, for Arromanches had been selected as the site for the British Mulberry artificial harbour, the other to be sunk into position for American use at St Laurent. These amazing constructions, basically hollow concrete shells, had taken much ingenuity and work to construct and were essential for supplying the Allied armies until a port could be captured. Some 37,000 workers had been employed in their making, the two absorbing 144,000 tons of concrete, 850,000 tons of ballast, and 105,000 tons of steel. Even these great and weighty structures, caissons and breakwaters, were susceptible to storm damage. The inclement weather on D-day sank one great caisson being towed across the Channel by an American tug. One of the towlines snapped and seawater seeped into the well of the concrete box which sank with loss of British lives. Later, when the great and unforecast storm hit the Channel on 19 June, the American Mulberry was destroyed while the British harbour was only damaged, allegedly because it had been assembled and installed in position more thoroughly. The supplies unloaded dropped dramatically from over 24,000 tons daily to only 4,000 through the British harbour, parts of the American port being used to repair the other.

This disaster had an immediate effect on Allied operations; already short of ammunition, the gunners were forced to begin using their 'bad weather' reserve. The Americans were already one third behind schedule in requirements. Furthermore, General Montgomery's planned offensive using the fresh 8th British Corps under Lieutenant-General Sir Richard O'Connor was postponed. When the storm struck only one of his three divisions had been landed; the remaining thousands of soldiers were obliged to ride out the weather in rough seas and suffered accordingly.

All this trouble lay ahead on 6 June, and over the following days the battle raged along the coastal strip as the comparatively weak Allied forces strove to maintain and enlarge their foothold. Yet, by midnight on D-day the British had disembarked almost 25,000 men on Gold beach where they suffered under 1,000 casualties; on Sword beach almost 29,000 soldiers were landed with similar losses. Around 26,000 Allied airborne troops had dropped during the previous night, and despite the near catastrophe on Omaha beach, by the end of the first day the Allies had put ashore a grand total of 155,000 men, an amazing achievement.

Hans-Georg Futtler was in a regiment of the 346th Infantry attached to the 711th Division. Most of the unit fought on the immediate beach area, but Futtler's detachment was in reserve until the afternoon when their Sergeant told them the British were trying to advance inland, so they would be hit in the eastern flank.

❝ Off we went on foot at a fast pace, laden with weapons, ammunition and something to eat and drink. I was almost thirty and had never been in action; in fact I had been working in an aircraft factory through the war. But late in 1943 there was a big comb-out and I found myself sent off into the army which did not prove too bad – OK, in fact, as I went to France and it was quite a good life, though we knew things would soon change once the invasion came. I was put into the 346th Infantry but then transferred into the sector of the 711th Division.

When we neared the battle zone the noise was great, with much gunfire and planes in the sky, and I felt terrified. Our Sergeant ordered us into an ambush position near some small houses, so I laid down in a shallow ditch near a little road. We were told there were enemy airborne troops behind us and on one flank, but not to worry about them as the 21st *Panzer* and SS were coming along to deal with them.

Then we heard some bagpipes and this seemed very funny, but in a moment hell broke loose, there was a great deal of shooting, and when I dared glance up I saw a lot of brown figures some way off who were running and dodging and coming nearer. There were also tanks and our guns were shooting at them. I was very frightened as many bullets were coming our way. I shouted to my friend, 'Franz, what shall we do?' because we seemed to be alone, the rest of the squad had spread out. He shouted, 'Wait!' He was an expert soldier and I trusted him and he now came closer to me with his rifle and Schmeisser. So I levelled my own rifle and tried to keep calm as the shooting got worse, and at last Franz said, 'Here they come, now you can get rid of some bullets!'

So I tried to force my head up to see targets and sure enough there were the same khaki figures rushing at us, but every so often they dodged this way and that and fell or got down into whatever cover was available. We started shooting and it felt very satisfactory to be doing something at last. Then, just as I thought we were holding them the Sergeant appeared as if from nowhere and shouted that we must fall back as the British were getting behind us. This made me frightened again, and when we jumped up and ran back the bullets were flying and I expected to be hit at any moment.

We found some of our men behind a house and I was very relieved. Even though some of the British tanks had been destroyed there were more shooting at us, and the house started to burn. But our Sergeant would not let us go, so we kept on firing and firing until at last I could feel the heat in my face and things became very difficult. Only then were we allowed to retreat again. But as we ran off there was a big explosion and the Sergeant and many others were killed or wounded.

I ran after Franz and two others and at last fell behind a hedge, exhausted. We then found we had no more ammunition. We did not know what to do, so Franz said he would try to get help from some-where. He ran off and that was the last I saw of him that day. We lay there trying to keep our heads down and quite suddenly realised we were surrounded. There were British all round us; some rushed forward and shouted, 'Hands up, Fritz!'

I later met Franz on the beach as a PoW. We were taken to England, very glad to be out of that war. **99**

The only German armoured division available to deliver a counter-stroke was 21st *Panzer*. Hans-Georg Petersen was a driver for a Mk IV tank armed with the then standard (for the type) 75mm gun.

❝ We were alerted early on 6 June and manned our vehicles. I had fought in Russia and after receiving a wound in the thigh was sent to the 21st *Panzer* in France which was being rebuilt. I was quite happy there, though by 1944 things had deteriorated for various reasons: the imminent threat of invasion, our lack of proper training and the air raids.

For some time on that day we received no orders. Then, at long last, late in the morning we were ordered into column on the road where our tanks were camouflaged to some degree and we moved off with orders to break through to the sea and wipe out any Allied troops we encountered. That was all.

We went some way with no problems. In my position I could see little and hear nothing but the engine and my commander's orders. He was a veteran Sergeant who had fought in Africa, and like the rest of our crew a good friend. At last I learned the enemy were near and I should be ready to deploy across the fields if necessary. I saw smoke ahead and the Sergeant told us our own infantry were in action. We halted several times and I had no idea what was happening until I suddenly heard bangs and our Sergeant dropped down into the tank and began using his periscope, warning us to get off the road at a second's notice. Because of the obstructing hedges and ditches this would not be easy.

Then I heard greater explosions and saw one of our tanks firing ahead of us. It stopped, but I could not see any targets at all. The road was now blocked, but I saw one of our tanks go through the hedge and I was ordered to follow it. I drove on and went through the hedge with difficulty, and at once saw the tank ahead blow up in flames. The Sergeant shouted orders and the gun crew went into action. I had my visor closed as there were now bullets pinging over the tank and I could hardly see through my periscope because of the smoke. Our seventy-five was banging away, even though I myself had only the vaguest idea where the enemy was. Then the Sergeant shouted, 'Go left! Go left!' So I tried to, and then saw the road we had left and enemy soldiers lying flat, and beyond it the sea which amazed me. Then there was a great deal of noise and I saw British soldiers running away from us as we neared the road again. Then came a hell of a bang and the tank stopped. A lot of smoke came in and we knew we'd been hit. The Sergeant ordered everyone out and I thought, My God, this is the end! We'll be shot – we must try to escape.

The others managed to get out, but I was in such a state of panic it took me much longer, and when I finally did I jumped down and rolled across the grass and saw one of our tracks had been blown off. And I saw my comrades crawling away and some of our own infantry shooting over our heads, and we escaped.

Not long afterwards we were pushed back and ran as hard as we could to the rear of our column, just as a great fleet of planes arrived and we saw parachutes and gliders coming down. We withdrew and that was the end of my first battle in Normandy. ❞

As related earlier, Lieutenant Franz Grabmann was a desert war veteran and had escaped, though wounded, to fight again with the renewed 21st *Panzer* in Normandy, finally receiving orders to take 'serious action' late on the morning of 6 June.

❝ We were to make a strong thrust directly to the coast and west of the Orne, wipe out the enemy and take over the beaches to prevent further landings. By then we were in a state of some excitement, but the enemy planes were overhead and we knew we had been spotted. We had heard the great bombardment on the shore and as we went along the road we heard the sounds of battle. All went reasonably well as we met little resistance and drove on until we could actually see the sea, and then we met stiffening opposition. I was in an armoured car and tried to get off the road several times because of jabo attack. We met a number of our casualties going back and heard our own tanks firing ahead. The situation was confused and not helped by great naval shells that came hurtling over at us, some placed very accurately. We had to disperse our vehicles so much along the route they became ineffective as a fighting column.

However, a motorcyclist told us some of our troops and tanks had actually reached the beach, which was heartening news. Then, like a thunderbolt from the sky came a great aerial column of planes and gliders which despite all our *flak* proceeded to land before us about the area. We were so disheartened we felt we could not continue. ❞

This admission must surely rank as extraordinary, coming from a desert veteran. Yet the situation was confused; whether more resolute action would have sufficed to inflict a real defeat on the British in that zone is open to question. Unstated in the above testimonies is the fact the other units of 21st *Panzer* had already been in action east of the Orne, but this attack was little more than a reconnaissance probe against the drop zone of 6th Airborne, denied help from 12th SS which was barely started on its way to the battle zone when it was broken off. West of the Orne, Lieutenant Grabmann and driver Petersen were part of only one column trying to stem the British advance inland, principally that of the Shropshire Light Infantry, supported by tanks. The most westerly German column thrust out of the Caen suburbs towards the Canadians, who had advanced just beyond Anisy; Grabmann's unit was heading for Periers and the beach. The right-hand group passed the wood at Lebisey where it encountered the 2nd Battalion Shropshires who had set off south after one o'clock. Despite having to divert a company to take a troublesome enemy gun battery in the rear to the west of them, Lieutenant-Colonel Maurice drove his battalion on, only to have them barred by German fire from the wooded area around Lebisey. They were then attacked by twenty-four tanks of 21st *Panzer* which appeared from the west, five of these being knocked out, the rest withdrew.

Events elsewhere and lack of strength now foiled the Shropshires' advance. The lead company commander was killed and the British troops ended their first day consolidating around Bieville. This advance should have been supported by the Royal Norfolks, but that unit's efforts had been delayed by the failure of the Suffolk battalion to capture the strongpoint code-named Hillman north-east of Periers. It was in this action that the lack of real drive began to show among some British commanders, in this case the Suffolks' CO, who having seen his companies rebuffed spent some hours organising a large-scale assault when urgent, driving action was needed to sustain the overall advance.

As to the British airborne column which so unnerved 21st *Panzer*, it was composed of 500 tugs and gliders, plus escorting fighters, and transported the 6th Air-Landing Brigade, artillery, reconnaissance and light tank units to reinforce the 6th Airborne east of the Orne. Grabmann's unit, comprising some fifty vehicles plus an infantry battalion, despite losses, reached the sea. German infantry stood on the beach, amazed and triumphant to find their own defences still apparently intact for some two miles westward from Luc-sur-Mer. Then came the aerial armada. Of the 256 gliders which took off from English bases, one crashed, six force-landed in England, and only one was shot down by German *flak*. Despite enemy shelling of the landing zone, great relief reached the men of 6th Airborne already fighting off probing assaults by elements of 21st *Panzer*. Grabmann's centre column, the strongest, had set off before lunchtime, but it took them hours to move anywhere near the beach zone, by which time their force had been so whittled down by engagements and air and naval bombardment that it stood no chance of holding the strip of beach achieved. Most of the panzer column was in any case still well short of the sea when the British reinforcements arrived by air, the German commanders believing the airborne troops were about to fall about and before them. Shocked and intimidated, the *panzers* and infantry withdrew.

Help was on the way, but it would arrive much too late to bolster this thrust by 21st *Panzers*. Perhaps to Lieutenant Grabmann's surprise, the battle that developed was not with the British airborne who descended east of the river Orne, but with the British units who had advanced from the beach, which 'were well supported by artillery and anti-tank guns. In a short time our armoured attacks were destroyed and we lost control of the battle. A lot of men came streaming back saying the battle was lost, so I went forward myself to investigate and was almost taken prisoner in a surprise attack. We just managed to escape and drive back to our lines. Then came an order to abandon the attack, so we retreated to a point west of Caen to try to set up a blocking position and combat the advancing enemy.'

Hitler, as indeed his commanders and probably most of the troops of the army already engaged or about to be, pinned their hopes on the SS divisions, of which the 12th *Hitlerjugend* was, on D-day, stationed at Lisieux, roughly forty-five kilometres to the east. 'I led my reconnaissance battalion towards the battle zone,' recorded the deputy divisional commander, *Gruppenführer* Kurt Meyer. 'It was evening on 6 June and long before we reached Caen we were attacked from the air and lost quite heavily in vehicles, though most of the boys escaped injury. It was a bad start and I realised we were entering a different kind of war to that I had known in Russia. The lads of 12th SS were mostly teenagers, some in their early twenties; the officers too were young, though we had some veterans of combat like myself. But in Russia the Soviet Air Force was no great problem.'

According to legend, Meyer did not reach Major-General Feuchtinger's headquarters in Caen until around midnight, having encountered obstacles caused by British *jabo* attack – a blazing French bus containing dead civilians – inevitable since the Allied fighter-bombers attacked anything that moved in or near the battle zone. Despite the bad setback suffered *en route*, Meyer still radiated confidence, perhaps arrogance, in the SS manner, for such troops never gave up easily. Their *esprit de corps* was second to none, and most likely the more conservative army commanders were somewhat bemused, if not surprised, by the young SS General's attitude. Yet if anyone could restore confidence it was Meyer. His troops, he told them, were the pick of the Hitler Youth and would soon drive the 'little fish' back into the sea.

❝ As soon as I met the army COs I tried to formulate a plan. Having done this I went off to reconnoitre, using a church tower and other vantage points to see the invasion fleet and troops approaching our zone. I soon became directly involved as naval gunfire sent huge shells landing nearby, which again was a new experience. I was forced to take shelter in one of their enormous craters for some time. Then, after reaching a fresh vantage point, I observed Allied forces I later found to be Canadians advancing towards Caen and hurried off to organise some defence. The bulk of our division was still en route, so next day we did the best we could with what was available, disposing anti-tank and a few SP guns and *panzers*. In fact, we set up a very good ambush.

An enemy column consisting of infantry and tanks was taken completely by surprise, several of the enemy vehicles being destroyed and heavy casualties caused among the infantry. But we ourselves then came under heavy artillery fire, including ship's salvoes. We were forced to withdraw or face destruction. ❞

The Canadian advance had threatened the German airfield at Carpiquet, an important target for the 2nd Army since Montgomery's air marshals had insisted that adequate airfields be captured quickly after the landings so the 2nd Tactical Air Force could perform more effectively. Until then, emergency airstrips would be constructed by men of the RAF's Airfield Construction Wings, but not until the beach head had been enlarged.

The 12th SS *Panzer Division Hitlerjugend* had been formed mainly from the youths of that organisation in the toughening-up camps. Activated on 24 June 1943, it spent most of the next year in Belgium, its training centre outside Brussels also used by other SS divisions. Its cadres were supplied by 1st *SS Leibstandarte* Adolf Hitler (LAH), and comprised veterans of the war in the East. Its deputy '*Panzer*' Meyer earned his Knight's Cross in the brief campaign conducted by LAH in the Balkans before being transferred to take part in the invasion of Russia on 22 June 1941, his work on that front earning him the Swords and Oakleaves. By 1944 he commanded the 25th *SS Panzer Grenadier* Regiment of the new 12th SS and was the senior regimental commander in that division. Historians have written him up as a great admirer of Hitler, both during and after the war.

In April 1944 the division moved to Lisieux in France, and it was from there that eighteen-year-old Matthias Jubell wrote to his parents on 6 June. They were living with relatives, having moved out of the flattened city of Hamburg. Before Matthias could mail his letter his unit, the 2nd *SS Panzer Grenadiers*, was ordered to move out to the invasion front. The youth barely had time to add a hurried 'P.S. – I am moving today!'

❝ We travelled all day in our vehicles, having been warned by our officer to prepare ourselves mentally for our first action, in other words to get ready to receive the shock of battle, one we thought would be a hard but short fight. We were very confident we would win, driving the small Allied landing force into the sea – how little we knew!

I well remember admiring the beautiful countryside and wishing I was on holiday. The next moment someone shouted '*Feindliche flugzeuge! Jabos!*' and we drove our vehicles into the side of the road and dived for cover. This was our first experience of Allied air power and it was terrible. There were a number of *jabos*; I kept my head down and had no idea what type. They roared over us once to make sure of their targets and then began strafing us with cannon and machine-guns, and some of our vehicles went up in flames. I heard shouts and commands and we left cover to try to save any vehicle still intact. Smoke was rising from those destroyed with the equipment, and some lads had been killed or wounded. We had to use one truck as an ambulance and load up the casualties before we could proceed. In this crisis our commander Meyer was extremely effective in trying to restore order and rebuild our shattered confidence. We had been taken by surprise and our *flak* silenced. ❞

Unknown to the SS troops in the stricken column, all this had been witnessed by British eyes.

Now known nationwide, during World War Two the Special Air

Service was almost a secret organisation, very few in number and the elite among parachute forces. Developed from volunteers willing to act in almost suicidal manner, these men had already gained a reputation in the Middle East, Italy and the Balkans. The Battle of Normandy afforded them yet another front, bold adventurers who loved the additional excitement and danger of dropping behind the enemy lines. Lieutenant Reg Hall dropped by parachute into France before daylight on D-day:

" Unfortunately, in the poor light we mistook our location east of the Orne and soon ran into a bunch of Germans. In the fight that followed our Corporal was killed and had to be left behind. We ran off and reached a little copse where we hoped the Jerries wouldn't find us. I believe they mistook us for paratroops – which we were not. Our job was to do a reconnaissance behind the enemy lines, and to do this we planned to pinch some sort of transport as we'd been unable to bring our own. We had a radio, but this had been damaged in landing, so we felt obliged to find out all we could and then get back to the nearest Allied positions.

We had a rest and ate some chocolate with no sign of any Jerries and then set off in open order across the countryside in the direction of Lisieux. As full daylight came we heard the bombardment at sea and smoke going up into the sky and soon the local roads began to get busy with Jerries bobbing about all over the place. But we saw no organised columns of the enemy so pushed on until afternoon when we first saw signs of the enemy in strength. Then we were able to get close to a road to study their insignia, and by their outfits we knew they were of the best – SS. Right then – some of them were still passing us – we were well hidden in a small gully. The first British fighter-bombers appeared and circled overhead for a couple of minutes before strafing the column. We were about 100 yards away and too close really. We saw everything and it was pretty devastating stuff as the planes shot up the front and rear vehicles and then started on the rest. The Jerry *flak* was small calibre stuff and that soon went silent.

The Germans had abandoned their vehicles as soon as the attack started and we could see them desperately trying to get under cover as their stuff was strafed over and over again, with fires breaking out all over the place. Some of the drivers tried to get over the fields but were caught. About ten minutes went by before the planes flew off. We watched the SS trying to get reorganised. After about half an hour the survivors went on while the killed and wounded were taken back to Lisieux in one of the surviving trucks.

After a while we went on and got quite close to Lisieux, where at dusk we were able to find a place to sleep while some of us stayed on watch. **"**

Johann Schmidt joined the 12th SS following the usual labour corps service, finding it all a great adventure in Belgium, with –

❝ splendid officers and NCOs, good food and country walks and runs. There was hard training and lectures during which we were told the Allies would certainly invade the continent soon; we must be ready to drive them back into the sea. He told us frankly that the enemy had great sea power and air forces, but that we were superior soldiers and that was all that mattered. We would beat them on the battlefield, so we felt confident that whatever happened the SS would win. I believed in my country and our rights and being young knew only the Nazi philosophy and outlook. But above all I loved my comrades. We were all good friends. I'm sorry to say that most were killed in the coming battle.

After that first terrible air attack I thought, so that's what the officer meant by Allied air power! We had no idea it would be so bad, and we had not trained for such things. I wondered if we had the strength left to commit ourselves to the battle and throw the Allies back into the sea.

We drove on in much more sombre mood until we could hear gunfire, which grew steadily louder. We had yet to see the sea, but heard lots of planes in the sky and some really heavy explosions which became continuous. Our officers told us to ignore the noise, which was nothing. Some of them went forward to reconnoitre and there was a long delay. In fact, we saw no action at all that day and were deployed about the countryside near Caen. ❞

In fact, not only Meyer's reconnaissance column, which had set off from Lisieux soon after three p.m., but the rest of the 12th SS division, including Johann Schmidt's supply convoy, were repeatedly attacked from the air, and also under restrictions because of the fuel shortage. By the time the surviving vehicles finally reached their assigned assembly area at Evrecy, south-west of Caen, their fuel tanks were almost dry. More bad news came: their fuel dumps had been bombed and burnt by Allied air attack.

Matthias Schmidt describes the successful ambush set up by Meyer:

❝ Then we had our first real battle. A great deal of shelling took place and we were told British and Canadian troops were advancing and we could catch them, give them a beating and drive them into the sea. We all went forward into cover in bushes and trees and set up our weapons. The shelling stopped and we heard tanks and other move-ment. Then, just as we saw the first Shermans and khaki figures, the shelling restarted and our officers ordered us to fire. Everyone sent off a terrific rain of bullets, while our anti-tank guns let fly at the tanks. The enemy fell everywhere and several of the Shermans went up in flames. It was terrific – our confidence returned. Several of the enemy were captured and we discovered they were Canadians and they looked very sorry for themselves.

But then the shells fell thick and fast among us, including huge naval shells which were terrifying, so we were forced to fall back to new positions in some disorder. By then I was in a state of shock and nerves and very hungry. When the rations finally came they were cold. **99**

In this action Edgar Furchte fought as an anti-tank gunner, his detachment having lost two of its weapons before reaching the front, to air attack.

66 We knocked out six Shermans before we were forced to retire by the shellfire. We did our best to camouflage everything as the enemy spotter planes were overhead directing the naval gunfire. So we had a very uneasy night in Normandy and wondered what the next day would bring. We had some coffee and bread and I ate some sausage I had saved from the previous day as we waited for orders, which soon came. The Canadians were trying to thrust around our flank, so we went forward in our half-track, pulling our gun, in short dashes, trying to conceal ourselves. Then our Sergeant-Major showed us into a suitable position and our three guns were set up again and camouflaged. Soon we saw Sherman turrets moving slowly forward along a little road. When the first tank came fully into view through a gap in the hedge we opened fire so quickly it went up in flames at once and blocked the road. Pandemonium followed as the enemy infantry tried to seek us out with heavy fire, destroying our half-track, though the gun remained intact. When the Canadian infantry tried to advance our machine-guns cut them down. Some of the wounded were screaming and this was awful to hear and a new experience for us. I tried to shut out the noise by covering my ears. Fortunately it stopped as the man died. It was very brutal and shocking for us youngsters, as we were.

The burning Sherman was finally pushed aside by the enemy and we prepared to fire again. In the next moment we were deluged with artillery fire and some *jabos* came looking for us. We were forced to pull our gun away into a little wood, eight of us with the shells and bullets flying about us. It was quite terrifying. In fact we were then prevented from firing again by the advancing Canucks and forced to flee for our lives. **99**

Edward Schusske was a Sergeant in the 5th SS Artillery of the 12th Hitler Youth, and related that three of their howitzers were lost to air attack on the route from Lisieux:

66 It was a terrible blow, but we resolved to do our best with the other twelve guns. There was a scramble to find suitable gun sites before we opened our first barrage on 7 June. Our recon unit reported good results, but we were soon spotted by enemy aircraft. Our camouflage was good, but not good enough to escape the bomb carpets which the medium bombers dropped over the landscape, and we lost three more guns. So we were forced to find new positions and this was very difficult as all movement was restricted in daylight. At dusk we started off, but this too proved hard as we no longer had enough tractors. It took us two hours to move one mile, and as soon as we were in position the enemy artillery began ranging on us, which came as a great surprise as we had not even opened fire. It is generally only possible to fix an enemy battery's position by various methods after it has opened fire. So we suspected the French Resistance were reporting our position and sent out patrols to scour the area, but found no one. So we set up our camouflage again and hoped for the best.

Then, when daylight came the first enemy attacks developed so we opened fire again, but after an hour ran out of ammunition and had to wait two hours for more shells to arrive. In that time a very serious situation developed as the enemy infantry advanced and we were forced to take up weapons to defend ourselves. The little brown figures were coming at us across the fields and we were trying to shoot them down. We were not very good with rifles and hit no one that I can recall. But there was an infantry unit on our left with machine-guns and they were far more expert and carried out a spirited counter-attack which drove the enemy away.

As soon as our supply of shells arrived we went into action again and went on firing continuously. Then Meyer arrived on a motorcycle combination and told us we were doing so well he expected us to be on the beaches again soon! He was always a great optimist and did his utmost to sustain morale. I doubt if anyone believed his outbursts, but he always kept us in good heart. **"**

Hans Dischke was an SS infantry Captain of two years' experience in Russia when he was seconded to help train recruits of the 12th SS. He and the other officers met Kurt Meyer:

" It was very interesting as he had a big reputation and I felt he would do all he could to prepare the new division for action on the invasion front. On parade I met Fritz Witt, our divisional commander, who seemed very boyish, and as I knew also had a big reputation as a man of dash and experience. For myself, I was a little older and perhaps a more cautious type. I had joined the armed SS when it was a much smaller force and had only just gained its new title. Some ex-army friends who had transferred to the SS told me it was a much better place to be in all ways, even though there was a certain amount of Nazi nonsense on the political level at the officers school. I must emphasise that we were not in the least bit interested in Nazi philosophy or political theory. We had only one interest, and that was the military side of things, and above all this new idea of an army based on rather different lines. I realise that the Allied side formed certain opinions due to the terrible excesses practised by the Himmler gang of cut-throats, who I again emphasise were never part of our kind of tenets or thinking.

So when I went into the 12th SS I had no thoughts whatsoever of trying to indoctrinate the lads with *Führer*-type philosophy, no matter what they had learned earlier in the Hitler Youth and Labour Corps.

Of course, most had known nothing else, there was nothing we could do about that. We did, however, have a very strong belief in our own country, and since we were engaged in a war we saw it as our duty to win if possible. Certainly, we would die rather than let the Bolsheviks take over Germany.

Then there was the question of military training, which was all that mattered to us officers: how to teach these boys to survive in battle, and this was only possible to a degree. It was, shall we say, in the lap of the gods. All we could do was try to inculcate some of our own experiences and hope they would absorb enough of it to assist them in combat. Our special kind of '*SS esprit de corps*' was a fact, and as far as we were concerned instilled by mutual confidence and real comradeship which produced absolute trust between officers and men to a degree unknown in the German Army. When we reached the battle we never found any reason to believe our methods had not paid off. I saw many youngsters of eighteen to nineteen, or less, who fought to the death with a tenacity that amazed their officers and, I believe, our enemies. Of course, it is impossible to say to what degree they were fighting for '*Führer* and fatherland' and the Nazi way, but I do believe that in the main they had been instilled and inspired by our teachings of comradeship and absolute trust. **99**

Back on the beach, Dieter Hartmann-Schultze was rousted out of his bunker with his terrified comrades by their Sergeant to man their anti-tank gun, astonished by the sight of so many landing craft:

66 And how large some of them were! We fired off some rounds and saw some craft hit and catch fire. But our aim was then spoilt by all the enemy fire coming at us; there were a lot of splinters flying about and two men were wounded. As a loader I became very hot serving the gun. Then we fired at a strange Sherman trying to enfilade us – it blew up and burned. We cheered heartily, but not for long; a machine-gun found us and we were forced to lie flat in great terror. At this point our gun was put out of action so we ran to the bunker for our machine-gun and rifles and began firing at the enemy troops trying to get off the beach. I saw men hit and falling and crying out, others simply folded up quietly, which looked very strange and dreamlike. Then we came under such heavy fire we were forced to run to our reserve position where it was hell as the enemy fire was so heavy we were unable to give battle at all.

The end came swiftly. We were surrounded, with grenades coming at us. There were screams and yells and I found myself almost buried by bodies and debris. Somehow, I fought my way out and was grabbed by a Tommy with a Sten gun and told to lie flat. It was the end of my war, but I had survived in one piece. **99**

4 'The Greatest Ever Armada'

By 1944, paper rationing restricted Britain's larger format news dailies to a mere four pages, while the tabloids (*Daily Mirror, Daily Sketch,* the *Evening Standard* and various smaller provincials) were able to field eight pages. In such parlous times news editors were under stress as to what items must be kept off their meagre pages; stories that would merit considerable column space in peacetime, and certainly in a later era, had to be discarded. So much was happening around the world's war fronts that events and stories worthy of headlines were too often crowded into corner paragraphs or laid aside until no longer news.

The day before General Eisenhower's momentous announcement that the long-trumpeted invasion of France had begun, the newspapers were able to announce the fall of Rome to the US 5th Army under General Mark Clark, the city having been evacuated by the Germans the day before. By this date, 5 June, the invasion fleet was already at sea, having set sail from the south coast ports west of Brighton, to tarry uncertainly in a decidedly unfriendly Channel while Eisenhower and his staffs agonised. Not a word was breathed to the waiting press in Britain. Security was tight. Yet one scare had already alerted the British, who sent agents hurrying to interview an innocent crossword compiler; one of his puzzles printed in a leading newspaper had given the invasion code-word – Overlord. This was no more than a fluke. More serious was the premature and fantastic 'accident' that disclosed the Allied assault almost two days earlier: FLASH: EISENHOWER'S HEADQUARTERS ANNOUNCED ALLIED LANDINGS IN FRANCE.

The report had emanated from Associated Press agency in London and within a minute of reaching America was rushed out by hundreds of radio stations. One columnist writing in Britain's *News Chronicle* on the 5 June remarked on the 'dynamite in the present perfection of channels of public information in America'; half a century on this obsession for news has resulted in agency helicopters buzzing around the sky over major US cities in the mad quest for instant news. That brief announcement across America at about 4.40 in the afternoon brought pandemonium. Thousands turned out into the streets, thousands more stood in one minute's prayerful silence at baseball and polo games, church bells tolled and phone lines became jammed as great numbers of callers sought more information. In Brooklyn, police patrol cars were obliged to control the crowds and try to tell them the news was false.

In France, the German intercept services were forever on watch for clues as to the Allied assault, monitoring BBC broadcasts to the Resistance and all news bulletins. The great clue came loud and clear over the American news wires, only to be scotched five minutes later. What had happened?

At the AP offices in London the news *was* known and a suitable one-line message was prepared to be flashed by teletype across the Atlantic. For the invasion fleet had tentatively started its final countdown, despite the threatening weather and Eisenhower's last-minute, painful decision making. One Joan Ellis, a teletype operator, had run her fingers over the keys in a simple, few seconds' practice run. By accident the machine was 'on' for the Atlantic link-up, and the magic words sped across the ocean, escaping the censor's net.

No word of this seems to have leaked to Britain, though rumours were rife in those tense days as hundreds of thousands of soldiers with all their vast array of equipment crowded the lanes, roads and fields outside the quays and docks of Portsmouth, Southampton, Weymouth and the Isle of Wight, places where some pub landlords refused soldiers a drink, pleading they were out of beer ration. The waiting troops naturally wanted a last drink in England, many anticipating the worst across the Channel. Locals and landlords welcomed their going.

A fresh offensive in Italy, and of course the capture of Rome, had boosted Prime Minister Winston Churchill's approval rating to 88%, according to the latest Gallup poll. That such public soundings could be taken and the results published even in wartime was a tribute to democracy. In the Third Reich, of course, such genuine enquiries by a commercial agency were forbidden, but the *Gestapo* and SD maintained a close ear to the ground on German public opinion, their reports (sometimes surprisingly frank) circulated to appropriate ministers, including Dr Göbbels.

However, on the eve of D-day Churchill and his American allies, so newspapers noted, had aroused sour comment in some quarters by alleged guarded praise for the Spanish dictator General Franco, a leader indebted earlier to Hitler for German military help in the Spanish Civil War (1936–39). Since Franco's opponents had been socialists and Reds they had found a mentor in Stalin, so naturally the Soviets took exception and made appropriate comment in print. In Britain, Sir Richard Acland proclaimed that Anglo-American policy was pointing the way towards a Third World War.

But Churchill and his government were now beyond danger. The national mood had swung too far in his favour since the bad days of 1941–42 when everything seemed to be going wrong. The disasters overtaking Nazi Germany seemed set to continue; the loss of whole armies at Stalingrad, in North Africa, the Allied capture of Sicily and the invasion of Italy had set the pattern of Hitler's decline. By 1944 there was increasing reference in Britain to post-war aims and problems. Such trends had culminated in the famous Beveridge Report setting out a new 'social chapter' for Britain. Politicians, notably Labour, were pronouncing on what must come once it was all over (the war, that is).

However, Nazi propagandists looking for snippets with which to taunt their opponents might have found fresh meat in some tales published in Britain on 5 June: 'The state of affairs in Grantham and other towns is deplorable.' This was the crux of a statement made by the Hon. MP Mr Kendall on behalf of the council for that town in Lincolnshire, the newspaper heading reading 'Critics of US Soldiers'. A petition signed by outraged councillors was forwarded to the Home Secretary, Herbert Morrison, with a request that an inquiry be held. Countering this, the Chief Constable said he had no complaints concerning the behaviour of American soldiers, though in the House of Commons Mr Kendall told how it was 'unfit for a woman to walk unmolested through the town at night or in daytime'. In Kettering a reverend gentleman made similar complaints, stating that the accosting of girls was not only carried out by Americans, and that some women themselves were guilty. Everyone knew the by-then old adage that the Yanks were 'over here, overpaid, and oversexed', that parks in all areas occupied by our allies bore the signs of night-time activity next morning. True, walks through the parks and other open spaces after dark were not really advisable, and not merely because of the strictly enforced blackout; comedians made jokes about tripping over unexpected obstacles. 'Dear John' letters (as the Americans called them) became known to British PoWs in Germany and Poland, the 'other men' not always Americans, though with all they had to offer females inevitably found them tempting.

The US authorities in Britain dealt harshly with offenders of the serious kind, and when a coloured soldier was found guilty of an 'offence' (which could only have been rape), he was sentenced to death, whereupon it was reported in the press that 10,000 people in the West Country area petitioned that his case be reheard. The option of a death penalty was of course very much open in those days in Britain, both for service personnel, civilians and enemy spies. News of executions usually rated a tiny paragraph in the press, as on 5 June when Gunner James Harman Kemp (21) was hung for murdering a Waaf.

Having missed the deadline, British daily newspapers were forced to wait twenty-four hours before publishing the great news story of the invasion. This was, however, used on the afternoon of 6 June by the evenings who provided the brief statement read over the wireless by announcer John Snagge early that morning: 'Under the command of General Eisenhower, Allied naval forces, supported by strong air forces, began landing Allied armies this morning on the northern coast of France.'

This terse announcement was Communiqué No. 1 from SHAEF – the Supreme Headquarters Allied Expeditionary Force.

General Eisenhower himself broadcast a message to the people of western Europe that morning, newspapers reporting that the King would broadcast to the nation that night. The time difference allowed American newspapers to use screaming headlines that took up the whole front page: 'INVASION – SMASHING AHEAD! Nazis say we're 10 miles inland – Sky troops far beyond lines.' By the evening, the British public had the facts via those papers scooping the news in print: '4,000 SHIPS, THOUSANDS OF SMALLER VESSELS, 11,000 AIRPLANES – Invasion going well; tanks ashore – the greatest ever armada.'

However, something of a news blackout was maintained in those first hours, so that news editors rather incautiously used agency reports picked up from enemy sources – Hitler had personally taken charge of the battle and set up his HQ in northern France. This of course was nonsense. The *Führer*'s last visit to Rommel in France had been rudely cut short when a V1 flying bomb on test had run amok and landed nearby. But, oddly, German reports exaggerated Allied success and the range of the landings, telling of these extending from Cherbourg to Calais and of fierce fighting 'in Caen'. British deception measures had succeeded in convincing Hitler and his chiefs that a further or even the main landing would take place in the Calais area, this view encouraged by Mr Churchill's statement in Parliament that the enemy was due for even more surprises, that the Normandy invasion was only the first of a series to come on the continent of Europe. The creation of a spurious 'army' under General Patton amassing in south-east England and the existence of a British mountain division (to threaten Norway) all helped to tighten the Führer's nerves even more.

Both the Allied public and their enemies were in the first hours groping in the dark for real news, the Germans even going so far as to report landings on the Channel Islands, 'vicious fighting' around Rouen, and massed airborne landings near Boulogne. However, except for the enemy bridgehead at Caen, all the landed troops had been thrown back into the sea. As always, German radio was quick to bring news of prisoners, the first of them Private James Griffiths of Newcastle, who is reported to have commented, 'It was tough.' The next named was Sergeant Roger Murray (25) of Bristol, taken from a strayed landing craft at Le Havre.

The two principal leaders of the great and dangerous enterprise were also written up. General Eisenhower, leader of the Allied team, was a fifty-four-year-old Texan whose forebears had fled Germany through religious persecution; his grandfather had trekked the old Oregon wagon trail. He had married in 1916 'after a vigorous courtship'. After the war rumours of an alleged 'affair' with his British-Irish chauffeur, Kay Summersby of the Transport Corps, would erupt, even though her first book on the relationship published in 1948 made no mention of such dallyings. Only later, when dying of cancer in the 1970s, would Miss Summersby write more fully in denying any impropriety between them. She, along with millions of others in Britain, had been won over by Ike's charm and by the famous broad grin, these attributes concealing a chain-smoking soldier who like most American generals used language unfavoured by his land forces commander, General Bernard Law Montgomery. Ike's amiable, energetic personality also masked a short fuse, his red-faced temper usually held at bay until the right moment to explode – as he did following his attendance at a formal luncheon date in London at which Monty at once made known his immediate priority – No Smoking! Eisenhower was furious, unable to light up until leaving. He had of course met Monty in Tunisia during the campaign to clear the Axis forces from North Africa. Monty had found a derisive opposite in General Patton, though in some ways the pair would prove strangely alike. He now got up Ike's nose in no un-certain manner, his aesthetic ways unappealing. Monty saw the Americans as amateurs in soldiering and generalship, and through a series of gaffes, as he has admitted since, drove a wedge between himself and his American comrades.

*   *   *   *

The first locality of size captured by the British was the little town of Bayeux, made famous through the tapestry, one side of which depicted the Norman invasion of Britain. Here the French inhabitants gave their liberators a warm if cautious welcome; after all, they were near the beaches and the enemy could counter-attack, and reoccupy the town. In fact, citizens pointed out some streets where German snipers were still believed to be hiding, and told them that Rommel had only recently visited the area, inspecting the defences and assuring his troops they were impregnable. But, according to these French people, the German soldiers had seemed pessimistic – 'The British and Americans are too strong for us now. But we will fight to the last.'

It was twelve hours before Hitler issued his first order – through his Chief of Staff, General Jodl – for no one had dared wake him following his usual 'after hours' harangues and one-sided monologues. Even then, the (from his view) valid reasons for waiting delayed any decision making. When at last the staff of Army Group B received instructions they were dismayed that Jodl (relaying the *Führer*'s wishes) demanded the Allied lodgement be cleared up by that evening – 6 June. To do this the crack division *Panzer* Lehr must move at once from its quarters at Châteaudon. Rommel's generals knew the order an im-possible one to fulfil. The division's tanks would have to travel 130 miles on their tracks and could not reasonably be expected to reach the battle zone until 8 June.

At the close of D-day and for a while afterwards Field Marshal

Rommel, correct in his forecast of the Allied landing site, was never-theless in agreement with Hitler and Rundstedt that these assaults were very likely diversions, which in turn implied he agreed with their dis-positions of the forces available; 15th Army must remain intact east of the Seine. The only concessions made were the shifting of the 346th Infantry west of Le Havre to enter combat against the British, plus the release of SS Heavy Tank Battalion 501, and a *flak* brigade. The SS unit was equipped with Tigers and these would prove a bane to the British, inducing 'Tiger phobia' so that the type was reported everywhere, despite the fact that of several hundred German tanks on the British–Canadian front, only thirty-six were Tigers. Lesser types destroyed and shown in the Allied press became 'Tigers'. The fifty-seven-ton monsters were largely responsible for a drop in morale which bred rumours and the phobia mentioned, which soon reached the top. Not that edicts by Montgomery designed to counter this malaise helped: the tankers at the sharp end would continue to press on in the sure knowledge that at least three of their own tanks would be needed to knock out a single Tiger – and then only providing they could manoeuvre themselves into a favourable position for a flank shot. In the narrow, hedge-confined lanes of Normandy this often proved im-possible; whole columns of British or Canadian armour would find themselves at a standstill because of just one Tiger straddling their axis of advance.

Not that the German Tiger was invulnerable. It was not, but it was a perfect defensive weapon, and the enemy knew just how to use them. Their vulnerability lay, as with all tanks, in being exposed to infantry anti-tank weapons. The soldiers with nerve able to stalk a Tiger could disable it with the relatively low-velocity Piat bomb, or perhaps simply place Gammon bombs or a bundle of grenades atop the unarmoured engine grille plates behind the great turret. To do this meant freedom from interference by German infantry; like all tank crews they needed to work in conjunction with foot soldiers, but this did not always work out. A tank isolated from such protection was lost.

The British had developed the superb seventeen-pounder anti-tank gun which could fling an 87mm armour-piercing hollow charge shell at great velocity, and this was enough to deal with any German panzer. There were sufficient of these weapons, but not in the tank arm: only three Shermans per squadron were fitted with the gun, and were quaintly called 'Fireflies'. Unfortunately, the American-built tank, though available in great numbers, had a high silhouette and was known as the 'Ronson' by its crews on account of its predilection to brew up easily. It is remarkable that so many tank crews survived the very many 'brew-ups' in Normandy, when life usually depended on a very few seconds in which to escape a blazing coffin. Following the great British–Canadian offensives when hundreds of tanks were knocked out or disabled, grimy and blackened tank crewmen could be seen streaming back to safety; most would recover to fight another day. And many tanks were also made fit again for another battle.

However, the British were better armed to combat the Tiger, as indicated; the Americans had only their M10 tank destroyers carrying an inferior gun plus the British-designed six-pounder (57mm) anti-tank gun. One eminent writer has more recently spoken of the 'great tank scandal', and as an ex-serving officer with the OBE he should know. He comments that while General Montgomery tried to suppress such feelings, he did nothing to alleviate the situation. In truth, of course, it was much too late by 1944. In Britain it was reckoned that four years were needed to design and develop a new tank weapon.

An example of just how much could be achieved by an audacious, fearless opponent with a single Tiger can best be given by quoting the oft-repeated episode at Villers-Bocage.

By 13 June General Dempsey, commanding 2nd Army, had pushed his western corps comprising 7th Armoured and 50th Infantry divisions southwards to attack Tilly-sur-Seulles where they entered battle with *Panzer* Lehr. At this juncture Dempsey ordered the corps to disengage and drive westwards. This they did, entering a gap beside the boundary line with US 1st Army, racing south and meeting no opposition. Dempsey's intention was, if all went well, to have the column swing east, thus threatening not only Evrecy a few miles on, but developing a dangerous pincer south of Caen. The British unit leading this drive was the 4th County of London Yeomanry, not of course dolled out in fancy outfits and riding chargers; only the traditional names remained, and few would survive the increasingly savage defence cuts of a later era.

At around 8.30 a.m. the three Cromwell tanks, armoured cars and scout cars reached the little town of Villers-Bocage, surprising two Germans who fled in their Volkswagen. A few French civilians appeared to greet the men in khaki. The whole column halted, fresh orders were given, and A Squadron, with the Headquarters Squadron, then moved on some way, just out of the town, leaving their infantry echelon to dismount from their half-tracks to stretch their legs and have a smoke. The leading squadrons then stopped themselves while a couple of cars went forward to reconnoitre the Caen highway leading to Evrecy, but more importantly their next objective, some higher ground known on their maps as Point 113. The personnel of the armoured column themselves took a break, and it is possible that if they had kept moving the disaster which quickly followed would never have happened – at least not on the same scale.

Perhaps for the first time, it is described by a British eye-witness, the then Lieutenant Edward Hartly of A Squadron:

❝ We were in column on one side of the little road, taking it easy while one or two cars went on ahead. Suddenly, we heard a crash and looked round to see this great Tiger lurching across the road. We were stunned for a second or two. I was at the end of A Squadron column and sitting on the bonnet of my armoured car when I heard this noise of a tank engine revving and saw the Tiger. We leapt off our vehicles; some jumped into them. Almost at once there was an almighty bang as the 88 fired and scored its first hit which made a hell of a splash of flame. I yelled to my driver to reverse, but this took a few seconds. When we did move backwards I watched in amazement as the Tiger came rolling along the road, firing rapidly and scoring a hit every time. Then we reached a point where the road widened slightly and were able to turn round and scuttle away from there as fast as we could. There were bods running in all directions, explosions and yells and smoke going up. **99**

Lieutenant Hartly reached the infantry in town, yelling a warning that a German Tiger was on the loose and coming in their direction. The men needed no second warning, leaping into their carriers and retreating from the town. After a quarter of an hour it became evident the battle in the lane outside the town was over: 'We went back to investigate and found all the carnage. There were burning vehicles and bodies and men in a state of shock, others trying to help the wounded. It was a terrible scene. There was no sign of the Tiger. Then some medics arrived and began their work and we began getting reorganised. It was quite a setback for us.'

A 'setback' is really putting it mildly. The commander, Lord Cranley, was among those killed; he had served in the desert war, as had many of his men. Even accounts published in these times mention this soldier being 'killed or captured', as well as varying the number of vehicles lost. In fact, just five Germans in that Tiger had carried out this execution, without aid from escorting infantry, so there was no question of British prisoners being taken. A total of thirty-seven armoured vehicles were destroyed, including the three Cromwell tanks whose unfortunate crews saw their shells bouncing harmlessly off the 110mm-thick frontal armour plate of the Tiger. The two squadrons were virtually destroyed, the remnants amalgamated into their original parent unit, the 3rd County of London Yeomanry, with the 5th Inniskilling Dragoon Guards taking their place in that corps.

The British armoured brigade commander, Brigadier Bill Hinde, sometimes known as 'Loony' on account of his fearlessness, consolidated his troops around Villers-Bocage, while some British tanks that reached Point 213 were surrounded and destroyed by Tiger *Abteilung* 501. However, when Lieutenant-General Bayerlein ordered Panzer Lehr and the Tigers to recapture Villers they went in minus infantry, who failed to arrive until later that day – and paid the price. In the attack the German *panzers* lost heavily, six Tigers and several Mk IVs being lost, and the assault failed. But this advantage was not exploited by British corps commander General Bucknall, who continued to use his infantry against Tilly; 7th Armoured continued to be too weak in

Above: General Bernard Montgomery, commanding Allied land forces in Normandy, with (left) Lt-Gen. Richard O'Connor CO XIIIth Corps, and Lt-Gen. Miles 'Bimbo' Dempsey, CO British 2nd Army, who was knighted in July 1944.

Left: Lt-General Dempsey with corps commanders: Lt-Generals Crocker (left) and Bucknell.

Below: Major-General 'Pip' Roberts, CO 11th Armoured Division.

Top Left: Field Marshal Gerd von Rundstedt.

Top Right: Field Marshal Rommel and SS General Sepp Dietrich.

Above: SS General Paul Hausser, paratroop General Meindl left.

Above Right: SS Colonel (later General) Kurt *Panzer* Meyer CO 12th SS from 16 June 1944.

Right: General Erich Marcks, commander of 84th Corps.

Above: Commandos disembark into the sea under fire.

Left: Royal Navy crews manned the landing craft.

Below Left: 'Funnies' of the 69th Brigade Group negotiate 'Rommel's asparagus' obstacles under fire.

Below Right: British infantrymen were over-loaded for such an assault landing.

Above and Centre:
Some confusion results as commandos try to disembark into the sea: the bicycles were soon discarded.

Below: Sword Beach: heads down as the bullets fly. The man at bottom left has been hit in the face.

Above: Commandos prepare to move off the beach.

Left: Commandos follow a DD Sherman tank to attack the German battery at Oiustreham.

Below: The momentum of this first advance was not maintained.

Top Left: A well camouflaged German *Sturmgeschutz* IV en route to the front.

Above: A German supply column after attack by British *jabo* near Mailly-le-Camp.

Left: Lt-Col Max Wunsche, CO 12th Hitler Youth *panzers.*

Below: A halftrack of 12th SS moves to confront the British

Above Left: Among 716th Division troops were Russians only interested in fighting Stalin.

Above Right: Luftwaffe field divison troops proved of little value.

Left: Well camouflaged German motorised infantry move cautiously towards the action, and (*Bottom Right*) 40-ton Panthers with crews taking final orders. The Panther proved the best all-round tank of the war.

Above: Sergeant Willi Fey and crew with Tiger of Heavy Tank Battalion 102, IInd SS *Panzer* Corps.

Right: SS troops drive into Villers Bocage; knocked out Cromwell ahead and disabled *Panzer* IV on left.

Below: Waffen-SS infantry move up in the Orne sector.

infantry to plunge forward. In defence, Bucknall had lost both his escort tanks 'to a Tiger' when visiting the 7th, and now feared that division was too strung out and vulnerable, especially as a fresh German division, the 2nd 'Vienna' *Panzers*, had arrived undetected from Amiens.

Originally from its home base of Würzburg, the 2nd *Panzers* had gone into Austria in 1938, and by the outbreak of war most of its troops were from that country, and suffered heavy losses in Poland, later fighting in France (1940), then Russia before being rebuilt and stationed in France.

Thomas 'Tommy' Hindler became a Corporal in the 2nd *Panzers* and related that while the unit was known as the 'Vienna' division, the title was never used officially. 'We had a lot of very good tanks, Mk IVs, Panthers, plenty of armoured cars and self-propelled artillery, but in the opening battle against the British few infantry took part. I manned a machine-gun in an armoured car and we did create some panic among the enemy columns, which were taken by surprise. However, within half an hour we came under air attack and were forced to disperse or withdraw. We then became involved in positional warfare for a time.' It is probable that the 2nd *Panzers* lost some infantry as prisoners, since the record shows the new German arrivals were soon identified.

Karl Fischer was another armoured car gunner in that unit:

66 We were very proud of our unit, even though we had suffered an almost 100% turnover in personnel since 1939. I was from Vienna, like many of my friends, though some had been lost in Poland, France and in the East. When we moved from Amiens in June 1944 we were well equipped and anxious to give a good account of ourselves. We made quite good progress and saw no enemy aircraft at all, and took the British by surprise.

We began to reconnoitre near Tilly late on 8 June, but it became too dark to do much. Next morning we observed the enemy attacking the town; they did not appear to have seen us so our CO ordered us to attack the British in the flank. We moved very fast along a little road, lost sight of the enemy, then ran into them and opened fire with cannon and machine-guns and caused a fair amount of panic. The enemy tanks then opened fire on us. Our own tanks deployed and a fierce battle took place in which the British attack on Tilly was stopped. But they held their ground and some, I believe, went on south of the town. 99

It was that engagement which complicated the British plans and led to the onset of a less fluid situation.

Peter Linke had been an instructor with the *Panzer* Lehr regiment at Potsdam and had never been in real action until June 1944:

66 This situation was rectified when we went into action against the British in June when we were sent south of Tilly to try to stop the enemy encircling the town. We were involved in fierce fighting and took our first casualties including the loss of six tanks. We then moved west to

attack the British around Villers-Bocage and there we lost several more tanks. In that attack we were accompanied by some Tigers of the SS and felt very confident. But the British had taken up well-sited defensive positions with many anti-tank guns and we stood no chance, partly because we had no infantry. However, though we had to withdraw we did prevent the enemy from advancing further. We then ran out of supplies having had no chance to get properly organised, due to the air attacks and because the division was spread too thin. **"**

Wilhelm Oskawicz was conscripted in 1937 and after recruit training volunteered for the *Panzerwaffe*, and by late 1940 had taken part in the campaign in France in a Mk III tank, going on to fight in Russia the following year, remaining in the East until 1943 when he was transferred to *Panzer* Lehr. Now a Sergeant, he commanded a forty-five-ton Panther armed with a 75mm gun.

" We reached the battle zone in France late on 8 June and went into action at sunset against the British east of Tilly. We took up a hull-down position and managed to stop them. The night proved quiet with little activity, but next morning we came under heavy artillery fire and were forced to move back to new positions. Then we heard the British were outflanking us, so we moved again, and became engaged with the enemy around the town.

That day we ran short of ammunition and our *staffel* was forced to move back for replenishment. In this period we suffered a number of air attacks, but lost only one Panther that went up in flames after a very near miss. Owing to the air attacks our supply convoy could not reach us, so our food became meagre. The division was spread far and wide and it was some time before our baggage convoy could reach us.

Then we learned of a wide gap in our defences near Villers and a battle there, with losses, so some of our unit moved in that direction and we became involved in heavy fighting. I was still with my crew in our Panther south of Tilly, however, when we were hit by several Sherman tanks and caught fire. We managed to scramble clear. We had just reached a new position and done some servicing on our tank. My uniform was singed and when we reached our command car we were treated to some schnapps and whiskey and then hoped for a rest. Instead we were given a Mk IV tank and ordered back into combat. **"**

Corporal Herman Giske was a friend of Wilhelm and was put out of action – though not by the enemy: 'They gave us no time to recon-noitre the ground [near Tilly] because of the urgency of the situation. We had a hard time from *jabos*, medium bombers and artillery and were forced to withdraw, and in that time I broke my leg. I had jumped down off my tank but failed to see a truck coming and in dodging aside I caught my foot in one of our tank tracks. It twisted, I heard a snap, and as my leg broke I fainted. When I came to I was being carried away. I remained out of combat for three months.'

The course of the Normandy battle had in fact been decided in the first couple of days, for despite the bravery of the British foot soldiers and tankers the drive for Caen was lost. Not that their opponents had displayed superior dash and vigour; the 21st *Panzers*, despite its leavening of combat veterans, seemed ill-led and decidedly lacking in the 'Rommel spirit' which had caused the British such problems in the desert war. In fact, in hindsight, one of the most remarkable facts about this new campaign was the apparent total lack of Rommel influence on events. Obviously, this was a very, very different kind of war, and by then the Desert Fox's star was well into descent; Rommel had no chance whatever of displaying his genius for rapid manoeuvre, for it was quite impossible to run rings around his enemy in the Normandy bocage. Apart from which, whatever his success in Africa, he had made enemies; he was the focus of sarcastic comments and outright chagrin from Berlin and in his own army in the desert, the latter from some officers who felt he squandered men in some of his wilder gambles that failed to come off, and who despised his disappearing tricks across the desert wastes when he remained completely out of touch with his rear HQ. There had been those of rank in Africa (and at home) who looked on Rommel as a maverick, a general in temporary favour with Hitler through his successes in the desert war. The British seemed to have regarded him as highly as most of his own men however. The Rommel 'legend' started in the early spring of 1941, was stymied by Montgomery in the autumn of 1942, and extinguished two years later in Normandy.

The truth is, of course, that the much decorated and promoted Rommel had by then become a figurehead, an inspector-general of the coastal defence crust, of little or no account once the invasion happened. And there is another aspect, that of his adherence to the *Führer* and therefore the Nazi cause. It is perfectly obvious that from that angle the near affection afforded him by the British in some quarters (such as in post-war writings) is misplaced. He has been turned into a figure to be sympathised with, virtually a victim of Hitler and Nazism, simply because his mentor fell out with him and easily persuaded him to commit suicide. Is it not untoward to suggest that if the great Rommel had succeeded in throwing the Allies back into the Channel, then his star would have risen fantastically again? He would have been fêted by Hitler, received new honours, perhaps even a cash handout from a *Führer* who by all accounts was not short of a few *Reichsmarks* (after all, he did present one of his other generals with a cash bonus). The fact is, so long as things were going well in the war – and for him as a battle-field general – Rommel was perfectly prepared to stay the Nazi course, remaining in curious ignorance with regard to the terrible deeds going on under his mentor's pitiless gaze. Once his fall began (i.e. after defeats in Africa) he fell into 'bad company' and decided Hitler and his war should come to an end.

Of course, even a Manstein could not have reversed the tide of events in Normandy; even that military genius had come adrift in the morass of the Russian Front. It is fair to say that by the Battle of Normandy General Montgomery's star had reached its high point, whereas that of his old adversary had almost vanished behind a very dark cloud indeed. Montgomery may have gazed at portraits of Rommel (and Rundstedt) on the wall of his battle caravan, though trying to read their intentions by that method was probably press bunkum; the General had by then a pretty fair idea of his opponent's military capabilities, and of course he was well served by Ultra. Whatever reverses he suffered in the campaign, these, plus a couple of errors (the failure to take Antwerp and Arnhem), did not alter the sum total of his victory in Normandy, a battle won through his strategy and control. Whatever his critics cared to say then or later, Monty did dictate the campaign in both its overall concept and, largely, in its day-to-day conduct. The enemy's counter-strokes either never took place because of his interventions, or were frustrated in the act; whatever successes the Germans achieved in the battle, they were always short-lived and achieved at prohibitive cost. But the nature of the battle – Briton versus German – ensured that both sides would suffer heavily. This was out of Montgomery's hands.

It would be churlish not to feel some sympathy for Rommel, whose ill luck was hastened and added to when Spitfires of 602 Squadron caught him on the open road in France, injuring him seriously, though not enough to prevent his being given the opportunity to end it all dishonourably.

Yet the German command gained some hope, for once the British were stymied around Tilly and Villers, and the 51st Highland Division's attack was blunted in the north, it began to look as if the bridgehead might be contained, if not destroyed. And, as soon as things began grinding to a halt, the first weak-kneed doubters rose up, critics of Montgomery's way of doing things, those at SHAEF and at home who had no idea, it seemed, of his strategy. That such ideas should gain ground over the next weeks among the armchair civilian strategists is perfectly understandable, that the same queries should arise among the officers at Eisenhower's HQ less so. It has been said more than once that Monty changed the records after the war to suit his memoirs and assuage his ego; whatever the truth, some facts remain. The General *did* explain his strategy for the coming campaign to high-ranking Allied officers in England on 7 April, and not for the first time. As to the so-called 'Phase Lines', these Monty knew perfectly well could only serve as a rough guide to those executives of his plan; they were never intended as definitive indications of exactly where his forces should stand on any particular date.

It did not really matter in military terms whether the British–Canadian army captured Caen. All that did matter was that the enemy was sucked into a battle of attrition he could not possibly win, destroyed and no longer able to influence events at all. In other words, once the German divisions had been reduced to a helpless collection of leaderless troops without support or hope the Allied armies could simply drive through them, out of the accursed bocage countryside and into the far more open terrain so suitable for fast-moving armoured columns – perhaps the very kind of landscape Rommel could have seen as more his own.

It is the mark of the amateur to imagine that any battle can and must adhere to the plan laid. It rarely happens, and in Normandy a certain amount of adjustment and flexibility were needed as the situation developed. The better generals are not fazed, to use the American term, by what appear to be reverses; so long as a general maintains his nerve and above all a good measure of control then the initiative returns. And, as everyone the least bit familiar with General Montgomery knows, he did above all insist on maintaining his 'battle stance', or ensuring the enemy never allowed him to become unbalanced, which is only another way of saying loss of control.

Monty should have known, along with everyone else at the time (and perhaps even now), that for the British and Canadians to have taken Caen in the first hours would have been a bonus. An important rail and road junction, it was seen as the gateway to better things – the tank country beyond. In denying us Caen, the Germans did seal their own fate, for this was not another Cassino, a cursed mountain that straddled the Allied path, though the simile may seem apparent. It did become the 'crucible' (as one writer put it), the magnet that apparently implied British failure, and was harped upon in various quarters – especially at SHAEF where Monty's most dangerous foes were to be found, notably among his own compatriots. It has been recorded by at least one notable historian that having seen his own COSSAC plan scrapped, Lieutenant-General Morgan used sniping tactics thereafter to undermine Montgomery's, whose amendments were approved by the C-in-C, General Eisenhower. It is said that Morgan lost no opportunity to cast aspersions on this plan, to Monty's great disadvantage since the latter was not at SHAEF once the battle in France began. In this he would be joined by Air Marshal Tedder, the senior Briton on the spot with Eisenhower. Over the coming weeks Monty's tenure as commander of the land armies was to become increasingly shaky, unjustly so, as the sniping criticism gained weight, the General's position hardly helped by his style of command, which was to delegate Freddie de Guingand to do his errand running. Monty did to some extent become isolated in his caravan, perhaps ignorant of what was happening at SHAEF and failing to put in appearances there, if only to re-explain his strategy to his boss and perhaps batten down his critics.

If Ike had really understood (he often said he did to Monty), then he would have shown greater confidence in his commander, who after all had the battlefield experience to know what he was about. Eisenhower, perhaps ever the diplomat in the role given him, did show patience, especially when faced with seeming insubordinate talk from one designated his junior, though not unnaturally Monty far from regarded himself as that in military terms – just the opposite in fact. But Montgomery was a soldier, not a diplomat, and apparently had no idea at all he had committed 'offences' with his new boss from the earliest days. All that mattered to Monty was winning the battle. Let the old fogeys back at SHAEF gossip, results on the battlefield would come. In these difficult days the British hero of the public back home began to realise more fully that his allies the Americans were not fighting one battle but two. At least, that was the way it seemed. For some, at the very least, were fighting with one eye cast backwards, over their shoulder to the politicians and people back home. 'The American people won't stand for that!' Ike might say to Monty, who would retort that battles or wars were not won by public opinion. 'Give 'em the victories and that will be sufficient!' was Monty's attitude.

Nevertheless, Monty allowed himself to be influenced by the democratic, 'All-American' way of running the war, with publicity as one of their personal weapons – and fell into the trap of trying it their way. The General who would not allow visitors to interrupt his cogitations played host to the press, and came a cropper. It was not long before the press statements fell on the Allied public (and SHAEF). From the lips of the great man came bulletins proclaiming great offensives which to the layman (i.e. the press and public) seemed naturally to signal imminent 'breakthroughs', almost on the lines of World War One, with the German 'lines' busted and the victorious British driving across France towards Berlin. In such matters Monty was an innocent; he apparently had no idea of the effect cast not only in the direction given, but above all at SHAEF where Ike was thrown into a mêlée of optimism and expected the best of his ally. After the lack of any such apparent victory, the C-in-C's confidence in Monty began to wane, falling further as each new offensive seemed to fail in its objective. Monty was too busy running the battle to keep travelling to SHAEF to hold hands and reassure the faint-hearted that all would be well.

Things reached a dangerous stage when even Monty's long-time mentor General Sir Alan Brooke at the War Office was obliged to pull out all the stops to save his protégé from being sacked. For, judging by available records, even Winston Churchill had failed, like Eisenhower, to grasp the essential Monty strategy. It was not the PM's way to have to sit back and watch such a protracted slogging match, which is what it seemed to be coming to. It was certainly not the American way. In World War One the Yanks had come in late and gone rushing in without regard for military dictums, and it was the same kind of thinking in Normandy, as confirmed by the writings of Ike's aide Captain Harry Butcher. Eisenhower expected his team to be running with the ball all of the time, just as in an American football game; the whole line had to be on the move, despite the fact that he seems to have appreciated that the destruction of the enemy army was the principal aim.

None of these frictions became known to the public at home, certainly not to the soldiers fighting and dying at the front. Only much later would historians try to dig into the nooks and crevices of the relationships between these leading war protagonists.

*   *   *   *

The eighteen-year-old John Vowles of 47th Royal Marine Commando was amazed on landing in France just before mid-June:

66 All that stuff all over the beaches, you could hardly get off the beach for it. We went to a quiet sector where our chaps were resting. But not for long. We joined up with a troop of veterans who told us we'd be OK as all the real fighting had been done by them. When we asked them what it had been like they said, 'A piece of cake', just like the RAF blokes. But we knew they'd had losses, that's why we were there.

We saw a long line of German PoWs and they were of great interest as they didn't look much good at all. Then we marched to a little village and had some tea where a Captain told us we would cross the fields to reinforce some airborne chaps. This we did, right in the middle of a Jerry barrage which took the wind out of our sails right away. We had to dig in like mad as we were in open fields. I'd only been at it a moment or two when something hit me on the left arm and I dropped my spade. I felt a terrific pain shoot up to my shoulder and called out in pain. Then I felt the blood running down my arm and the Sergeant called the medic who rushed me back to some houses where I took off my jacket and we found a horrible gash in my arm and I fainted. When I came to I was lying on a stretcher and then taken off in a truck. I was back in the UK in less than twenty-four hours and I never went back to the war. 99

The deferred service GPO repairman Jim Parkinson, one of the 'old men' of his platoon in the Shropshires, described how on forming up for their next attack their Lieutenant told them:

66 I won't beat about the bush, it won't be easy, but we can do it. You're well trained and can give a good account of yourselves. We've got plenty of support from the tanks and guns and the good old RAF.'

And he looked round, listening to the sound of our guns, which as always were terrific.

Well, we'd eaten breakfast, hot tea, bread and jam and a few biscuits, and thinking it could be our last meal on earth. I know I was. By then I'd had some of my bravado knocked out of me as I'd seen a few bodies and the noise was nerve-racking. We looked at each other and tried to grin, but I knew we all had the same grinding feeling in the stomach.

Our objective was a road beyond a ditch, and beyond that a little wood. The countryside in Normandy was very attractive and much like England. There were little woods and farms everywhere – and of course the Jerry SS who were our opponents, and they'd fortified everything defendable. Their tanks were dug down and it was very hard to see them at all. We just knew they were there and waiting for us. We'd been told as soon as we arrived; a chap called Brown soon let us know the score. He laughed a lot and tried to put the wind up us, though the Corporal used to say, 'Shut it, you twerp!' As soon as we arrived Brown said, 'Oh-oh! Look who's here, the bleedin' boy scouts! Well, you know who's waiting for us, don't you? Hitler's fucking SS!'

So we were pretty scared as we all thought the SS a lot of bastards. Later we found they were just as scared as we were and ordinary soldiers, but very, very good at it. But we were greenhorns and had a bad time just wondering what we were in for.

I crouched down with my mates with my pig sticker bayonet fixed. I had some grenades in my pouches and wondered if we should be praying. I was never religious, but when you think you're about to get killed you wonder if a prayer might be in order.

Anyway, up we got into full view, trotting up the grassy slope, trying to keep our heads down, ducking every time a shell buzzed over – they were all ours but you never knew when one might fall short. Then we heard our tanks on the left and wished we were behind them. There was a lot more noise from the little wood which we were trying to outflank and some terrific cracks as some of our Shermans were hit and brewed up. There were yells and screams and I realised the Jerry infantry were firing at us. I could hear weird noises and zips as the bullets started flying past us and we ducked down with our faces in the grass until the NCOs ordered us on. Then we forced ourselves up, running doubled over until we reached the little ditch which we found contained bodies – both British and SS. The Sergeant told us to wait while he reccied. There was a lot more noise with the Jerries using airbursts over us, which was awful. I lay cringing in that ditch with the stuff coming down on us until the Sergeant urged us out of it and we ran to some tree stumps, and then I realised there were only about six of us left. I tried to tell myself the others must be under cover elsewhere.

I heard the Sergeant yelling something and thought he meant we were under direct attack. As I lay there I was trembling so much I could hardly hold my rifle straight against the tree. The noise got worse and I heard tanks and thought, I hope to God they're ours! Then I realised the Jerry infantry were rushing at us in short spurts and our blokes were shooting at them. So I forced myself to look round the tree stump and when I saw them I let fly a few rounds, but they kept coming, about one hundred yards from us. Just flashing figures in brown jackets and shooting all the time. Then I saw one of their SP guns firing its machine-gun at us. The earth was flying up all round us in dust and stones so I kept my head down. I expected the SS to get me at any moment and I really was terrified.

Then I saw the Sergeant wave and start running back the way we'd come, so I did the same without looking round and expecting to be hit in the back at any minute. We got back to the ditch and there were just three of us left, including the Sergeant. **99**

John Trenchard went to Sandhurst and passed out a subaltern:

66 No great achievement, as in 1943 they were churning out officers like sausages from a machine. I went over on D-day with the South Lancs. We had some fighting before things settled down a bit and then we went into a small reserve before going into action again, and that was when I had my little adventure.

We were trying to advance towards Caen and not making much headway when we ran into several German machine-guns and a Tiger tank. We tried to deploy to use a Piat on the tank but the machine-gun knocked out the operators and no one else could get near as they had us pinned down. So I ran over and managed by some miracle to get hold of the Piat without getting hit. But I still couldn't get near enough to that Tiger, which was holding up the whole battalion.

At last the Colonel became impatient so he came up to see the situation for himself and was hit in the arm at once. He went back for treatment and then the Tiger changed its position slightly, and while it was doing this I did the same and managed to get quite close to it and get off a shot. But the bomb didn't hit the thing square in the flank, it glanced off the front track, but was near enough to force the driver to withdraw. So we all rushed forward and I took another shot at the damned great thing. This time I hit it on the rear sprocket, which flew off, and in no way could the driver get the thing moving again. Then some of our chaps tried to rush it and drop grenades on the engine cover, but were stopped by machine-gun fire. So I crept forward very slowly until I was able to lob a grenade on the rear of the Tiger, and it went up very satisfactorily. The crew baled out and we took them prisoner. **99**

Bill Dobbs was in the same regiment and was taken prisoner soon after the above incident.

66 We advanced through an orchard, past a little house, when I got separated from the others as we were moving under fire in open order. I lay down among a load of debris near the house and suddenly saw a Jerry pointing his gun at me from the ruins and beckoning me to give up. I had no choice, so I let go my rifle and went over to the house and found about six Jerries, all heavily camouflaged. They searched me and took my paybook and cigarettes and made me get down in the rubble while they chattered away, trying to decide what to do next. They had an NCO with them and I think he wanted me taken off to the rest of their blokes, but the men detailed seemed very hesitant as there was a lot of firing going on.

I had seen my mates disappearing out of sight into a small wood, and I felt very disappointed and wondered if I'd ever get out of it alive. I thought our lot would catch on and start plastering the house – which was exactly what happened. There was a hell of a bang and the Jerries got down flat as I did, and then the stuff came over thick and fast. When the first lull came I heard our chaps calling to each other. The Jerries ran off and left me behind. **99**

Len Wynton was a 'Somersetter', as he called them:

66 I saw my first battle a week or more after D-day. We went up to relieve some 6th Airborne lads who'd been in the thick of it. Just a platoon of them, though their division stayed on through it all. We went up in trucks and passed the airborne coming out and, of course, they made rude remarks and signs. They looked grubby but were in good spirits and I wondered how long we'd last in the line. I had no illusions about the fighting and guessed we'd lost a lot of men, though not in the landings.

I was from Wincanton and worked on a farm till I went in the army at eighteen, but like all the lads I had never been in action so felt pretty scared. We found our positions were the foxholes the airborne had just left. I reckon the Jerries must have been watching the changeover, and to welcome us they lobbed a few shells over and that was nasty. We jumped into the holes and huddled up and our Lieutenant came with an airborne officer to point out where the Jerries were. It was all very new to us, and of course we couldn't see any enemy at all, only the general location and smoke going up from our own bombardment and planes attacking. The noise was always there; it wasn't often you had a few moments' peace in Normandy.

Then, that evening after supper, the Jerries started sending out patrols to try to infiltrate and we all stood to, straining our eyes and ears for some sign of them. It was very jittery and we saw nothing much until someone sent a flare up to our right and the shooting began. There were tracers flying about but nothing in front of us. By daylight I was tired out and starving. Breakfast came late and was cold. But we scoffed it down and then the Lieutenant came and ordered everyone out. He told us we were going to punch out an enemy salient they'd set up in the night. We would outflank them to the right and force them out – or kill the beggars, as he put it.

So we formed up and set off in open order, ready for anything. It was mostly open terrain, with a few trees and bushes. We saw a couple of Shermans to our right and some banging started. Then someone shouted, 'Hit the deck!' So I did, and a load of Jerry mortars came over, plastering us with dirt and mud. The Lieutenant ordered us to keep moving, so we ran like hell over the grass till we reached a small rise, and when we lay down we found we could see a fair way over the fields which were very much like the English countryside. Then we saw our Shermans going in against the Jerries and a big fight going on, and the Lieutenant said we could take them in the flank as planned. We were reluctant to leave that position, but the Lieutenant got up and trotted down the hill and started shooting into some long grass and a hedge. I had just fired off a clip and was about to reload when something hit my rifle, which spun away out of my hands, and I fell down in surprise and fright. The Jerries were behind the hedge and shooting through it and some of our lads were cut down before our Bren marksman set up and raked it from end to end, and that was the end of them. One of the Shermans then came along and ran over the hedge, and I believe there were no survivors – we did not see any of the Jerries get away. When I picked up my rifle it was undamaged, but for a gash in the stock, and it was still workable. **99**

Jack Smith flew Spitfires and was shot down by *flak* not long after D-day:

66 I was with 54 Squadron at Hornchurch. We used to fly to Lympne to top up our tanks and then cross the Channel on patrol, and were often called on to do some strafing over the battlefield. One afternoon we were busy on such a job, trying to knock out a Jerry column some way behind the front, when at low level I felt a thump and the stick went dead in my hands. I knew I'd been hit but the plane didn't go in so I thought the engine was OK and I could make it back to our lines. I did – but only just. I crash-landed in a field a few hundred yards from our artillery positions and the chaps rescued me. Then I found I was in the thick of a battle as the Jerries were attacking and the gunners ran back and turned me over to some other bods and in no time we were diving for cover as all hell let loose. Someone said, 'Can you shoot?' So I said, 'I suppose so!' They gave me a rifle and advised me to keep my head down. The noise was pretty terrific and I just had to see what was going on. All the chaps were firing like mad, and when I looked through a hedge I saw a lot of Jerries in groups rushing from place to place and firing every so often. I could hear the bullets whistling about. I got quite excited and started shooting myself.

Then a Sherman tank came up and started firing and that made a hell of a din. After a bit a Lieutenant said I could clear off with a runner leaving in a jeep. So I handed back the rifle, climbed in the jeep and a couple of hours later I was tucked up in a tent miles away. I got back to England next day. **99**

Montgomery's aim to tie up all the German armour was intended to thwart Rommel's desire to gradually withdraw his *panzers* and replace them with infantry, this advised to OKW (*Oberkommando der Wehrmacht*). The day before the German commander signalled this Montgomery had himself told his chief General Sir Alan Brooke (Chief of the General Staff at the War Office) of his general policy 'to pull the enemy onto Second Army so as to make it easier for First [US] Army to expand the quicker'. So successfully did the British carry out this hard task that no *panzers* were able to disengage in order to either concentrate for a counter-punch or divert to the American front where the doughboys were having a hard enough time trying to break through the German infantry divisions. On 15 June the German forces on the British–Canadian front were estimated to have 520 tanks in combat, against their opponents' 1,350 with only seventy on the American front.

It was this constant pressure by the British and Canadian forces which so eased the American General Collins' path to the port of Cherbourg, which finally fell on 26 June. Not that the American soldiers would have seen any of those days quite in that light; they had to fight every inch of their way through the same difficult country that so favoured the defence. It was in this period that a US Sergeant designed the Sherman 'hedge cutter', which at least helped to lay aside some of the obstructions and expose their enemy.

Before mid-June the two Allied armies had locked their boundary line, the Germans' chance of splitting the two had passed, the grand counter-stroke had not materialised, and it seemed that not only had Rommel 'missed the bus' in his hope of smashing the invaders on the beaches, he had also failed to interrupt their massive build-up, his Army Group powerless to eliminate the bridgehead.

Hans Gilbert was an infantry Sergeant of great experience in Russia. Following leave in Bremen he was seconded to the new 12th SS and took up training duties at Bruges in Belgium.

❝ They proved excellent material. Though not all strapping lads by any means, they were very fit and we were well satisfied with their progress. Of course, they were new to soldiering and had everything to learn. I had some good, experienced comrades and we did our best to prepare the lads for the big battles we knew lay ahead. So when we finally advanced across France we felt the boys were as ready as they could be. Unfortunately, we had not been able to train them for the terrible air attacks that sapped their morale considerably. I know I was very disappointed that they had not had the chance to absorb the first shock of combat in the usual manner. However, they amazed us by their good spirits and willingness to come to terms with the reality of our situation, and I never had the slightest reason to complain of their behaviour and battlefield discipline. ❞

Such comments may strike a raw nerve in some quarters, not only among surviving veterans on the British–Canadian side but among those who have been repeatedly told in the press at intervals ever since those days of SS atrocities in that battle – specifically the shooting of Canadian prisoners. This ugly topic was touched on in *Hitler's Second Army – the Waffen-SS* (Airlife, 1993) by the author, and since this present work includes the experience of prisoners on both sides it seems inappropriate to ignore the sore points. But in mentioning this particular incident both sides of the question will be aired, not merely the Allied view, as is customary, even though any kind of in-depth inquiry is out of place here. Neither is it the intention to air other grievances in this field. Nevertheless, it must surely be pertinent to include a couple of references to apparent previous incidents, though only one may be directly relevant.

In his book *The Longest Day* (Gollancz, 1960), the late Cornelius Ryan quotes one witness, an Able Seaman, who nipped ashore from a landing craft, believing it was 'his chance to get a German helmet for a souvenir'. He saw Canadian soldiers march six German prisoners behind a sand dune, but when the seaman ran up the beach to obtain his souvenir he found the Canadians gone and the prisoners all crumpled up with their throats cut. The sailor turned away sick. He did not get his souvenir.

That incident occurred on the first day of the invasion – 6 June. Some may be familiar with the Hollywood blockbuster film made of the book; naturally, such episodes were left out.

In his excellent book *Caen – Anvil of Victory* (Souvenir Press, 1964), Alexander McKee writes of wild French-Canadians who carried knives going berserk in Normandy to the extent that their officers were forced to draw pistols to restore order. These tough soldiers lived a hard, rough life back home. Saturday nights were spent drinking and brawling.

The story of the shot Canadian PoWs was publicised through a book published in the 1950s by two survivors of the incident, and obviously aroused feelings of disgust for Hitler's SS troops. As mentioned, this episode has been repeated in the British press ever since, and of course in many other publications, yet none has seen fit to print the kind of story given concerning Canadian or indeed Allied misdemeanours, despite the fact that such tales have appeared in various memoirs over the years. Naturally, as the losers our former enemy the Germans were forced to take the 'stick' in all such matters.

The late Kurt Meyer, commander of 12th SS for most of its tenure in Normandy, stated in earlier testimony that the ugly incident concerning shot Canadians was made known to him in the middle of a battle, and that it was not possible to institute an inquiry during the intense fighting in progress. But he did discover that the SS soldier principally involved had found some of his closest friends bound and dead, apparently having been taken prisoner by Canadian troops who were themselves driven back. It appeared to the SS troops that their comrades had been executed, and it was this that triggered off the action later. Such things happen in war, in the heat of battle and sometimes in its immediate aftermath; there are similar cases from our own side of feelings running amok through the loss of friends. One ex-soldier has said to this author, 'We can behave as badly as anyone on the battlefield,' this in regard to a much earlier episode in France 1940.

Meyer, held responsible as officer in command of the division concerned, was later charged with a war crime, even though he was nowhere near the spot where it occurred. As to those who were, they were all killed or vanished in the fighting when from the perhaps 18,000 men of 12th SS, only about 500 survived.

All this lay in the future. Hans Gilbert's arrival in the battle zone saw him leading one of the first attacks and, as he related, it failed to drive the enemy into the sea, 'though we did shake them up a bit and bring them to a temporary halt'.

❝ After the preliminary skirmishes we made an attack on their flank. I rushed forward, followed by several squads of men with weapons trained on the enemy. We were covered by flanking fire from our machine-guns and mortars and managed to take the Canucks by surprise. They broke and ran in all directions and we cut them down with our fire. But they soon recovered and their own machine-guns gave us casualties. I heard some of my boys calling in pain, but in the heat of the action I could do nothing for them. I was lying down shooting at the Canadians who I could see quite plainly. The enemy in their excitement had neglected to take proper cover and lost a lot of men as a result. The noise of course was tremendous, with so much firing going on, but I was used to that kind of thing. I then threw some grenades, changing position frequently, before withdrawing with some of my lads. We did this by simply sliding backwards through the grass so as not to expose ourselves too much. We were largely successful and regained our old positions. These were foxholes [*schutzengraben*], and when the enemy soldiers tried to charge at us in open formation our machine-guns cut them down even further in numbers.

The enemy tactics in such a situation were to hammer us with artillery and air power, which was very bad, and we lost several more men that way. Then as it grew dark we were ordered to change our positions. No sooner had we done this than the enemy let loose a fearful barrage on our old positions, which were of course empty. When dawn came we received a little food and moved off to a new location, this time in a small wood from where we had perfect observation and a better field of fire. But this did not go unnoticed, and presently we were shelled and bombed from the air and had a bad time so that we were compelled to find yet more positions in the more open countryside. From there we were, however, able to observe the enemy very closely, and when he next tried to advance with Sherman tanks our 88s and 50mm anti-tank guns caught them in the open and many were destroyed. The battle went on for hours and once again it was the enemy's artillery and air attacks that gave us most trouble so that we were forced to withdraw. In all this time the boys never complained, despite their lack of sleep and supplies. 🙶

Modern armies carry two kinds of doctor on their medical staffs: the first tend the sick and wounded, the other kind assesses the minds of the soldiers. Richard Stretmann was of the latter kind:

🙶 I was on the divisional staff of 12th SS. It was part of my job to assess the psychological state of the troops, rather than their physical condition, even though I was fully trained in that too. I had been a doctor before the war in Wiesbaden, but when war came my partner was called into the army and I had difficulty working alone. Then one of my sons went into the army also and was killed in Russia. We were very upset, and in 1943 my wife went off to do nursing work and the other son went into the *Luftwaffe*, working with the ground staff. So I saw no point in struggling on in private practice. I was nearly forty, and though I could have stayed where I was I decided to volunteer my services. I had an uncle who had been in Russia with the SS medical services; I had heard some terrible stories from him and felt I did not want to become involved there. Then I heard of a new SS division forming and since it involved youngsters I felt it would be an opportunity for me to serve in some capacity and perhaps stay clear of that awful war in the East. In fact I knew this was possible as my uncle told me the new unit was being raised in the West to help stop the invasion. By then I had taken a staff job and heard all sorts of news and gossip.

With my uncle's help I made a successful application and was assessed by the SS medical department in Berlin. In one of the interviews a medical officer suggested I might be interested in a psychological post, and I told him yes, it sounded interesting. So I went off to Brussels for another interview before meeting General Witt, the 12th SS commander, and some of his staff in a hotel. We then went off to inspect some recruits who looked very young, but fit and keen. Only in that week did I receive a uniform outfit. I was in truth a civilian in uniform, so I had certain privileges and this was a boon to me. For example, at first I stayed in a Brussels hotel, with all expenses paid; then I moved into officers' quarters which were quite comfortable in another hotel, though less luxurious.

I ate with the officers and they took me into their confidence as a staff doctor and I also met other medical staff who proved very friendly. I felt at home, even though I had no military training at all. But I had to appear on some parades which of course were very formal affairs, but no difficulty arose. Then, later that year the men went into a lot of field training and I was called in to help with a few minor wounds, and we had one fatality, which is perhaps quite understandable when live ammunition is used in the field. I saw the body. It was one of the infantry sergeants, a man of experience who should not have been killed. But it was an accident and very regrettable, and no one was to blame.

After some weeks the senior medical officer asked me to start a serious study of the recruits' morale, so I began work. I did this after consideration as to the best way to proceed in the task. I asked one man from each company to come in for an interview, which were conducted on a very informal basis; I asked about their families, etc., and what they thought about the war and the situation in general. In this way I was able to gain a fairly accurate picture of the division's morale and state of battle readiness. I made out my report which went to all the senior officers, including General Witt.

Then, when Christmas came we had some big celebrations and drank to our success in battle. General Witt made a little speech in which he said something like this: 'Gentlemen, comrades, some of us have been through hard times and tough battles, and good days when all seemed right. Ahead lies our greatest test of all. It will be our duty to lead youngsters into combat, lads who have yet to see a shot fired in anger. It will therefore be a great testing time for all of us. I am confident you will acquit yourselves well, in you I place my complete trust.' We then toasted each other and as an observer I could see that a great bond of comradeship held these *frontsoldaten* together.

When we reached France I felt my own testing time had come. Yet it was to prove extremely difficult in a way I had not foreseen, for once battle was joined it proved almost impossible to extract men from the fighting zone to give them tests on the psychological level. It would have been absurd. It therefore fell to my lot to act as a doctor pure and simple, and as a result most of my days were spent tending the wounded, of whom we had a distressingly large number, many of whom failed to survive who should have done but for the pitifully small supplies of the right drugs and treatments. In all this time I felt myself ageing considerably as I had never been trained in the treatment of battlefield casualties, and some of the sights were so bad I almost collapsed in despair and shock.

When the great disaster came of our defeat in August we had been severely reduced. So few of these brave boys survived and I was hard put to justify in my own eyes my own safety behind the front. I was one of the last to escape before the ring closed at Falaise. 〞

That time was as yet far off, for in mid-June the campaign had barely begun. Captain Herbert Wise of the 2nd Green Howards:

〝 The following incident took place after we had established ourselves in France but were engaged in almost continuous combat.

We'd captured some German prisoners and had them under guard in our lines ready to be taken back to the beaches. I'd noticed that one of them looked very young, so I asked him in German how old he was. This is what he said:

'I left school two months ago. I was in the Hitler Youth of course and went straight into a *flak* unit at fifteen. After a while I ran off to an army recruiting office and told them I was seventeen and they accepted me as I had my Hitler Youth papers. I trained as an infantryman and enjoyed it a lot. But after coming here I've been so frightened and sickened I never want to go to war again.' **99**

This kind of comment was, of course, just the kind of material Allied propagandists were looking for; Hitler seemed to be scraping the bottom of the barrel in attempts to prop up his tottering empire.

When Ron Hardy of the Tyneside Scottish landed, he too was surprised by the enormous amount of matériel everywhere:

66 You could hardly move for stores and vehicles. We marched on and saw some Jerry PoWs, and as we drank some tea I felt rather sorry for them as they looked in such a poor state. So I went over to them and offered one a cigarette, which he took gratefully saying things like, '*Krieg kaput – Hitler nix gut!*' and all that kind of thing. Then they asked me what I thought of their army, in broken English. So I told them it didn't look too hot now, did it? One of them laughed and said, 'Well, it has taken you British and Yankees all this time to start winning, hasn't it? Eh?' So I shrugged my shoulders and went back to my mates and told them what they'd said, and one of my mates said, 'Cheeky bleeders! But he's right, you know.'

I wondered how we'd get on when we went into action. Well, a few weeks later I was the only one left unwounded and still on my feet. **99**

Geoff Ryder, of the 2nd Battalion, King's Royal Rifle Corps (the Rifle Brigade), was one more affected by the constant noise of battle:

66 We were near an artillery unit banging away with twenty-five-pounders for hours on end and it gave me such a headache that I asked our Sergeant if I could go off somewhere for a break. He looked at me as if I was mad and said, 'What the hell's the matter with you, laddie?' So I told him I felt ill with a headache. He laughed, as did the other chaps, saying, 'I'll give you a fucking headache, get your fucking head down and I'll send for the nurse!'

Well, that was all very well, but I did have a serious problem, and when we next went forward I told the Lieutenant I felt ill, and had been for some time with acute headaches. So he told me to fall out and go back to the Casualty Clearing Station and ask to see the MO in charge. I did so, but he was too busy and told me to go to the hospital in the rear, and he got on with looking after the wounded as they had a lot of cases. So I wandered outside, not really knowing what to do. I didn't really want to leave the lads and be thought a skiver. Then I saw another doctor who had just finished a spell in the theatre and asked him if I could go to the base hospital for my bad headache, and he said, 'Sorry, you can go to hell for all I care with your bloody headaches, don't waste my time!'

I was shocked and marched off in disgust, intending to go back to the line. But he called after me and made me follow him to a tent where he gave me some little pink pills and said, 'Take one of these every few hours. I'm sure it's just the noise that's affecting your nerves. I'm sorry if I was a bit abrupt, but it's been one of those days.'

I felt so sorry for him, he looked all in. So I thanked him, saluted and left. When I got back to my unit the Sergeant said, 'Where the hell have you been?' So I told him and he didn't know whether to laugh or bawl at me. I took one of the pills and thought about it, had a good laugh, the headaches went away and never returned. **99**

Jim Castle was a tank driver with the Staffordshire Yeomanry:

66 We had a mixture of Churchills and Shermans. There wasn't much to choose between them because of advantages and disadvantages with each. I'd driven both types, but overall I think I preferred the American Sherman because there was more room, but it was a lot higher and more vulnerable.

We were cracking along a road with the Shropshires when we came under awful fire and took a hit in the side of our Churchill, which we called *Daisy*. We didn't catch fire and were able to go on, but slower. I didn't know what the trouble was, but thought it could have been a small calibre hit as we weren't disabled. Then we saw some puffs of smoke ahead and rifle bullets began to ping off our hull. The infantrymen rushed off each side of us and I saw some of them fall as they were hit. I couldn't see much from my position, then our Sergeant warned the gunner of targets ahead and we started banging away.

A few minutes later as we were still advancing we all smelt burning and wondered if we'd been hit again. The tank was still running, but obviously something was wrong, though we didn't want to stop in that position under fire. But a moment later an infantry Corporal appeared in front of us waving at me through my periscope, though of course I couldn't hear a word. So I stopped the thing and he came closer, yelling, 'Your bloody tank's on fire mate!' So we all baled out really smartish, amazed to see flames coming out from beneath *Daisy*, and a moment later she went up with a hell of a roar. **99**

Horst Gisentus was also a tank crewman, but a Sergeant-Major in command of a Tiger of *Abteilung* 501:

66 We took up a blocking position just north of Caen in a little gully off the road. From this position we had an excellent view of the approaches to the area. We were well supported by army infantrymen and mortars and felt secure.

Presently, we saw a lot of enemy vehicles and infantry approaching one mile away. We had them in our sights but waited until the leading vehicle, which was a Sherman, had reached a point one hundred metres from us before opening fire. The Sherman's turret was blown off and the tank caught fire, effectively blocking the road. But some of the other

Shermans turned off into the fields to try to outflank us. So we opened fire at one of them which was stopped, though it did not catch fire. Other Shermans were taken on by our anti-tank guns while we concentrated on those still on the road. After four more shots three of them were burning, the rest withdrew.

At this point a heavy artillery barrage began making things very uncomfortable for us, so I ordered my driver Karl to reverse and try to get into a hedge for concealment. This was not entirely successful, so we jumped out to try to get some foliage to use as camouflage. But the enemy fire reached us again, so we leapt back into the Tiger where we felt a lot safer. This situation continued for some time, with no sign of the enemy column advancing. But when I glanced out of my turret I saw a lot of *jabos*, so got down again and closed the hatch. In no time the whole area came under air attack. The noise was terrific as they fired off rockets at all known or suspected positions. There were concussions all round us, but by some miracle we escaped being hit. When the planes left the artillery started again and the enemy column tried to advance over the fields and along the road, so we started shooting again, and before long the green grass was littered with vehicles of all kinds. Apart from the Shermans there were armoured cars, scout cars and behind them trucks of infantry and supplies. But when I dared look out again I saw two other Tigers burning and our infantry running off under fire. I decided it was prudent to withdraw as we seemed alone, and once the enemy infantry got close they could destroy us with grenades.

This was not easy, for as we reversed we lost our cover and attracted a lot of fire. Most of the shells bounced off our thick hide, but one or two damaged our flanks and tracks, which would not work properly. There were all sorts of unpleasant noises but I ordered the driver to go on and suddenly we ran backwards down a slope, which was amusing, and at last we were clear of the leading enemy troops and also had an excellent field of fire. However, we were then in the open and extremely vulnerable to artillery and air attack, so I had to urge our driver to get on into cover. This we just managed to do before one of our tracks snapped and we were immobilised. I informed our CO by radio and he told me to shoot it out from where we were, he would try to send help. Whether he meant infantry or a tractor I had no idea; there was no chance to repair a broken track under fire. After about thirty minutes' shooting we were out of ammunition and there was no sign of help. The anti-tank fire became intense and at last we were hit and caught fire. We barely escaped with our lives, under fire from the Tommies who closed in. 〝

Felix Wendel was another specialist offered an interesting job after conscription, for he had learnt English and French at school; he could become a translator of documents, or an interrogator with front-line units.

❝ I chose the latter course and volunteered for service with the *Waffen-SS*. This was in September 1940, and before long I arrived at a *Leibstandarte* school to be assessed on my ability to interpret military jargon, which was not brilliant but not really essential at that time. However, I was then sent to an SS language school in Berlin, which proved most interesting. We had not only excellent tutors but listened to enemy radio broadcasts and recordings which we had to translate into German, these always being taken from the BBC.

After two months I was judged satisfactory and posted to an SS training school where I learned something about the fighting units of the SS. Soon after that the war in the East began and all the *Waffen-SS* units became involved, but as I knew no Russian I was left behind in the West and assigned to an SD unit in Holland where I learned some Dutch, but rarely had an opportunity to practise my English. But I soon became involved in other work as the SD set up their own radio intelligence monitoring service.

We had a house in The Hague manned full-time by radio operators, and here I learned how to listen in to the BBC and various other wavelengths for code messages broadcast to secret agents, which of course was all very secret work and extremely interesting. To actually be involved in that sort of thing was exciting and especially taxing in some ways as I felt I was in a sense helping to find spies and saboteurs, but also sentencing them to death. For we were quite successful in finding such people, though the messages themselves were often very hard to decipher, but that was not my job. All I did was note down code letters or even at times messages, such as, 'Dick will not be coming. Perhaps later.' 'Will you make it all ready for us as arranged?'

This seemed extraordinary, to be sending messages in clear language. However, all this was but the start of my real career, as once the invasion started I was sent with other interpreters to the battle zone to interrogate PoWs, and this proved extraordinarily interesting. Interrogators like myself were not assigned to any particular unit, but sent here, there and everywhere, all over Normandy until the big retreat in August. After that I worked around the German border.

I did my first job with the LAH; they had a number of prisoners, British and Canadian. The very first fellow was brought into a little room behind the lines. We had a nice villa also used by some of the officers for operations with radio links to the fighting units. I offered the man a cigarette, which he took gratefully. He was British, a Corporal in a Scots unit, and spoke very broad Scots and I had to listen very carefully in order to understand at times. Of course, I did not use a pen and paper, but had to write up notes later for one of the division staff. Our conversation went like this:

'Have you been well treated?'

'Yes, I s'pose so.'

'Have you any message to send home?'

'Ah – not really. Ah – just say I'm well and not wounded.'
'Have you been over here long?'
'Not long, just a couple of weeks.'
'And how are you finding it, hard is it?'
'Yes, hard enough – in fact, bloody awful.'
'Oh? Do you wish you'd stayed at home?'
'Too true, chum.'
'Do you think the German soldier superior to your own people?'
'I must say, they're damned good though, I'll say that.'
'Do you think the war will last much longer?'
'Oh no, I doubt it. Still, who can say?'
'Would you like to write a letter home?'
'Yes, that would be nice. Can I do that?'
'Would you also like to write a note to your pals?'
'How d'ye mean like, to mah pals?'
'Oh, you can say you are safe and well and hope to see them soon.'
'Ye mean that? How can they get it?'
'Oh, that's easy, we just send it over in a little shell or something, or simply leave it where it will be found.' 99

Felix Wendel states that the prisoner complied and wrote home and to his pals.

66 The first letter we threw away, the other was indeed dropped over to his mates, though I cannot say if any saw it. Possibly not.

I remember a Captain we captured who was wounded, a university graduate. He told me quite casually he had met the King while at Cambridge, so I encouraged him to speak and he did very fully, of his old life and how he wished he had been able to stay on at university, with all the fun and girls they had! But I must say he clammed up completely when I turned to military matters. On the other hand we once had a military policeman who had been badly shaken in battle. They'd been taken by surprise it seemed and had no chance to drive off. When I spoke to him he was still trembling and in quite a state. I tried to calm him with some tea and a cigarette, but I had the impression he was in fear of the SS. I said this to him:

'You've nothing to worry about, I assure you. You're in good hands.'
'I'm sure you're right,' he said, 'but I've heard some rotten stories about the SS.'
'Oh? Such as?'

And he said he'd heard we shot PoWs, that sort of thing. So I told him that was nonsense. After all, we had plenty of PoWs in the rear and he would soon find out the truth of it. Then a Captain came in and asked me to try to find out certain things from the man who was a Corporal. So I pretended the interruption concerned some routine matter and turned the conversation to his home and family. He said he was from Berkshire and not married, but had a girlfriend. So I suggested he write her a short note and one for his pals, just to let them know he was safe. And, do you know, he complied to both requests and even addressed them. So we learned the address of his unit. After that he became much more talkative and spoke of the various people he knew, including 'bastard officers' and things like that, so all in all he did provide a good deal of information.

I often had to hide during air attacks, especially when travelling from one unit to another. Quite often I would be stuck in a jeep in the middle of nowhere with jabos flying overhead, and once after I had left my vehicle it was destroyed and I had to ask for a lift from a passing *Wehrmacht* truck.

One Sergeant we captured was a very belligerent Canadian who demanded to be sent to a PoW camp. I tried to calm him, but he wouldn't listen, so eventually I said, 'Unless you calm down I shall be forced to have you locked up without food or water or anything. All I want is some small co-operation. Your name, rank and anything of non-military value.' Well, he saw sense and before long was telling me a good deal about his life back home in Canada outside Ottawa, and then he began grumbling about the war and casualties in his unit, so out of that I was able to gain a lot.

Then there was a most unusual case, a man who told us he was a fireman. I could not understand what he meant. He wore the usual battledress and no flashes.

'What do you mean, a fireman?'

'I mean I was a fireman before I joined the army, that's all.'

He had a London accent and seemed very friendly and cheerful so I thought it would prove very interesting. He had a smoke and some tea and we chatted about the war and his life as a London fireman. He said he'd been in the *Blitz* and how awful it was.

'Your bloody *Luftwaffe* gave us a bad time you know. That's why we're giving you some back!' And he laughed and seemed very pleased with himself.

So I asked him why he had joined the army and he replied: 'Well, I was fucking-well called up, wasn't I? After all, with the air raids over now we've got too many bleedin' firemen – so here I am!'

I laughed and asked if he wished he'd stayed at home, and he said: 'Nah, not really, I was getting fed up with me old woman and that and thought I needed a change anyway. But I didn't reckon on this lark, did I?'

We laughed, and he would not say another word. **99**

5 The Great Slogging Match

Kurt Meyer had, as he lamented later, been prevented from driving the enemy back into the sea through lack of proper direction from above, but congratulated his troops for at least stabilising the situation. This was achieved after the rest of 12th SS arrived to take up position. 'The great slogging match began and we became bogged down in positional warfare where the enemy in time gained a great advantage in weight of matériel, and above all their continuous air *blitzes* which made all movement difficult by day. This was a new experience for us and proved fatal.'

Two of Meyer's men who finally arrived at the front were the brothers Jakobsen – Hans and Johannes, both Sergeants. They lost their transport to air attack and were obliged to go forward on foot. Soon they were leading small battle groups into action, for their regiment had been hard hit, so Meyer decided to split the remaining personnel into units – *kampfgruppen* – an arrangement that seemed to work well at first. The brothers were newly promoted, with Russian Front experience, but hampered, as were all such veterans, by the lack of visibility in Normandy where at times this could be as little as a 'few metres'.

❝ The Allied planes would appear overhead at first light and the artillery began. About an hour after we had eaten a little, we saw tanks forming up through our glasses and warned our men to prepare. They were very young and anxious to prove themselves, most with no experience whatever, just seventeen or eighteen, but very well camouflaged. We had lost some of our anti-tank guns and were not well protected against tank attack. At this time our tanks were not near us.

Then the British concentrated their fire on us and we saw their tanks advancing and soon we were in hot action against the infantry who swarmed forward in rushes but were cut down by our fire until the attack melted away. We saw tanks trying to outflank us, but these were stopped by our anti-tank fire and some of our own tanks which we realised had been well hidden on our flanks. ❞

Then the battle lessened, so Hans ran to see if his brother was all right, surprised to find him badly wounded in the leg. 'I helped the medics place him in a truck and he went off, never to return to that battle.' When Hans returned to his own position the battle had resumed:

❝ The enemy artillery and machine-guns began firing again and we received an order to fall back – just in time, as a large formation of twin-engined bombers attacked our old positions and devastated them. But we remained intact and returned to our old positions, and when the enemy attacked again that afternoon we drove them off with heavy losses. But that evening we were forced to retire as the enemy artillery fire was causing us so many casualties, and the fire seemed to follow us back to our new positions. Next morning we were ordered to join up with some tanks and attack the British. I gathered about twenty men to me and met the tanks, which were Panthers. Then we hid behind hedges until we were ready. Our multiple mortars put over a great barrage and we rushed across a big field until we could see the flashes from the enemy weapons. Then we began dropping to the ground and firing, then rushing on in great style. But I heard screams as some men were hit and our tanks were all destroyed. The noise was stupendous and then I realised I was all alone, except for one or two comrades who were calling for help. Somehow I managed to roll and slide back through the grass, dragging one of the wounded with me until we regained our starting point again. It had all been a waste. ❞

Uwe Friedemann was a private soldier with the 21st *Panzers* and trying to reach the front in a well-camouflaged convoy of fifty vehicles including tanks. As usual, lookouts to warn of enemy planes were placed on all the vehicles which were spaced along the road. After a while warning came of enemy *jabos*:

❝ We pulled off the road, but there were few trees and hedges, only a few drainage ditches, and everyone scuttled into these. Soon after the enemy planes came screaming down at us, about twelve I believe. I huddled in the ditch with my comrades as the machine-gunning began. No bombs were dropped, but in all that din I could hear some of our vehicles being hit, blowing up and catching fire. Then the last of the planes left. We got out of our hideout and found that only about twelve of our vehicles were still usable. Several men had been killed and wounded, including the CO; these were taken back the way we'd come. I went on with my comrades on foot. But the enemy had not finished with us.

Not long after some Typhoons appeared, so we jumped into a ditch again. They attacked and it was much worse because of the rockets, which made a terrific noise coming down and exploded with very loud detonations. This was hellish, and the planes also fired their cannon, and this time not one of our vehicles remained intact and more men were killed and wounded. Some of us stayed with these who in some cases were crying out, but there was little we could do to help them.

Then a Lieutenant commandeered a passing army truck which was trying to get by the wreckage over a nearby field, and the wounded were loaded up and removed.

We found we had only twenty men still fit for action. It seemed stupid to continue, so we waited about an hour but saw no more planes. Then an armoured car arrived from HQ and we gave them the news and soon we were withdrawn. Many of my comrades were killed in that air attack. **99**

James Dietrich Hanneman was conscripted in 1942 and after recruit training volunteered for the tank arm:

66 I would not be put off by ugly stories I heard of their vulnerability. I felt much safer inside a 'steel coffin'. I went to Münsterlager where we trained on old tanks for some time before going onto a Mk IV which had seen better days. When I finally reached 21st *Panzers* in 1943 I was a gunner in a Mk IV, but soon after we received some Panthers which were very impressive, and I was one of those chosen to train in them. It was not easy to do that in France, where the countryside was so restrictive, but we used a plain east of Caen where we carried our manoeuvring and shooting to some extent until our commanders were satisfied we had reached a set standard of proficiency.

I loved shooting the long seventy-five at targets which were usually made of wood or even straw, though on some occasions we actually used old tanks, usually Czech or French, which was much more satisfactory. **99**

James was quite excited at the thought of going into action when the invasion came, and disappointed when other detachments of his division were chosen to make counter-attacks, one achieving the 'near victory' before being defeated. Then at last his turn came:

66 We took up hull-down positions, well camouflaged in the countryside, and waited for the first enemy tanks to appear. When they did show up along a road my commander closed the turret hatch and ordered us to wait until we were sure of targets. We had six Panthers covering that road, and hoped we would not be spotted by enemy aircraft. Then the first Sherman came into my sights at only about 200 metres; I fired and the shell struck his turret, which blew off in a great bang. The tank was smoking, and when I fired again it blew up in flames and I saw no one get out. Our other Panthers stopped the other enemy tanks, though we could not see them all and waited in case their infantry appeared. None came, and we next saw some of the Shermans breaking out of the road over the fields to try to outflank us.

I followed these targets and chose one before it vanished below a hedge, which were everywhere in that country. It was very much like a game of cat and mouse. I fired but the Sherman went behind some bushes. So I fired once more, and the shell crashed through into the tank which went up in flames at once. We cheered like mad and saw another and another enemy tank knocked out by our comrades. The rest of the enemy then withdrew. So while one of us remained on watch the rest of us had a smoke and drank some tea.

Then we were alerted by radio from our infantry HQ that another enemy column was outflanking us, so we had to hurriedly withdraw a kilometre and take up fresh positions. Then the enemy aircraft found us and things became very difficult. Two of our tanks were knocked out by rockets. We jumped out to throw a lot of foliage over our tank, which was close to a hedge with the gun poking through it ready for action. This soon came when enemy vehicles appeared along the nearest road and we started another battle. There were armoured cars, tanks and infantry who tried to rush across the fields to get within bazooka range. The noise was terrific as we fired like mad; a lot of enemy shells were coming close to us and there was smoke everywhere. I saw several enemy tanks go up in flames, but then we had to withdraw again as we were out of ammunition and the enemy was outflanking us.

We withdrew some way to replenish our supplies and during that time the British advanced and all our ground was lost. Our next battle was closer to Caen, and there we lost our tank.

We were set up ready for defence and well camouflaged – or so we thought. But the enemy spotter planes found our location and before long we suffered a sustained artillery barrage and several of our tanks were destroyed. One of our tracks was blown off by a near miss so we had no choice but to escape on foot. One of our trucks drove us away, then we walked to our depot for a replacement tank. But none was available, and to our amazement the officer there told us to go and fight with the infantry. Not that we could do much, we were not trained for it, so soon we moved back to a new position where to our disgust we were given an old Mk IV tank to start fighting again. **"**

One German weapon which could have had a serious, if not devastating, effect on the battle was misused. The V1 'doodlebug' flying bomb was designed primarily, as its designation (V1 – *Vergeltungswaffe Nr 1* – Revenge Weapon No. 1) suggests, to strike back at London in retaliation for Allied air raids on German cities. The unit concerned with delivering the bombs was *Flak* Regiment 155, commanded by one Colonel Eberhardt whose difficulties were complex. He was under constant pressure from Hitler to start the offensive, but air attacks had so cut up the rail links from the Reich that delivery of the weapons was slow. The planned mass attack for the night 12/13 June saw only nine bombs being launched; of these only one reached London. If the sixty-four launch sites had been built facing north-west the assault could have had a great effect on the invasion harbours, or even on the landing beaches themselves. Once the sites came into use they were more detectable by radar. Allied air attacks were stepped up, and about half of RAF Bomber Command's aircraft engaged in bombing Germany were diverted to the task. By the end of June at least twenty-four of the flying bomb launch sites had been destroyed.

The effects of those bombs reaching London were, however, considerable, for the weapon was indiscriminate and terrifying to those in its path who waited with frayed nerves for the pulse-jet motor to cut. When this happened the bomb dived to earth where its comparatively small explosive load caused widespread damage since the weapon detonated on contact, all of the blast effect being above ground. Deception measures to convince the Germans the bombs were overshooting the capital helped, and a good proportion began falling short or inland from the south coast, in areas like rural Battle and other spots not used to a *blitz*. An increasing proportion were destroyed by the AA gun belt which was rushed south from London, and many more by fighters, including a few of the new Meteor jets, but chiefly by Tempests, Spitfires and Mustangs.

Yet another way of striking at the Allied invasion was missed when new German sea mines were launched too late and in too small numbers. At first unready, the new pressure mines were sown by *Luftwaffe* crews by night off the Normandy beaches, the airmen warned by Grand Admiral Dönitz not to 'lose' any as he was fearful his new secret weapon would be captured intact by the British and copied – which was exactly what happened. Several floated ashore on a French beach where they were soon examined, and tests were begun by minesweeper crews of the Royal Navy who took 'unacceptable risks' in solving the deadly conundrum, for the German mines exploded through reduced water pressure when ships passed overhead. But the British discovered they did not work if vessels proceeded at a slow rate of knots. The British admirals were baffled why Dönitz had failed to drop such mines in the invasion harbours.

As late as 19 June, Rommel was still favouring a second Allied landing, reinforcing Hitler and his OKW's own belief. By that time the balance of power in Normandy had swung against the Germans, for Montgomery had landed twenty divisions; the German Army Group B fielded only elements of eighteen, and these at low strength, so their actual number was around ten. For the second time in his career, Rommel found himself in a trap, a dilemma that in his then current circumstances he could not solve, his forces suffering heavy losses, receiving only a trickle of replacements, unable to divert *panzers* to combat the Americans due to Montgomery's constant pressure. The 2nd SS was slowly progressing north from southern France, and the *Führer* had conceded the release of 1st SS which was en route from Belgium, forced to divert through Paris because all the Seine bridges had been knocked out by Allied air strikes.

Sepp Dietrich, the division's old commander, now commanding 1st

SS *Panzer* Corps (which comprised 12th SS and 21st *Panzer*), was becoming desperate as his forces were ground down in constant battle. On 16 June he signalled to Rommel that British tanks had broken through at Longraye, west of Tilly, that his units had been forced to throw in cooks, drivers and other non-combatants to try to halt the enemy. Next day he protested, 'I am being bled white and getting nowhere!' If he did not receive another eight to ten divisions fast, 'we are finished!'

This crisis was not evident to the British at the front, at Tilly, or the Canadians around Caen. At the first location *Panzer* Lehr fought stubbornly, but although denying the enemy progress were in fact complying with Montgomery's aims. By 25 June the Lehr division would lose 160 officers and 5,400 men; soon after that it became almost non-operational. Around Caen, 12th SS and 21st *Panzer* held a fifteen-mile ring of defence that included 228 tanks and assault guns.

As related, it was the weather that intervened, the storm in the Channel during the night of 18/19 June destroying the American Mulberry anchorage, thus throwing all unloading of supplies onto the British harbour at Arromanches. Not that any real diminution of pressure was felt by the Germans, who not only continued to suffer from artillery and air, but received a great blow that precipitated an even worse crisis for General Dietrich.

On 20 June Hitler produced his own plan to smash the Allies in Normandy: the 1st SS, 2nd SS, 9th and 10th SS, plus the 2nd *Panzers* (*Wien*), the 3rd Parachute Division and *Panzer* Lehr would carry out a mass assault to cut through the Allied front, starting on the left at Caumont and smashing a wedge through the US–British armies to the coast, where they would swing left to destroy the American bridgehead before turning to deliver similar treatment to the British and Canadians. As usual, Hitler failed to allow sufficient time for preparation, Rommel objecting on this point, which sent Hitler into a rage concerning generals not prepared to take risks.

By 23 June SS General Paul Hausser had set up 2nd SS *Panzer* Corps HQ to manage the offensive. Hausser, known as 'Papa' because of his leading role in organising the armed SS through the 1930s, was another ex-German Army officer who, disillusioned with the old ways of the still largely conservative Prussian military hierarchy, had been tempted by others of like background into the more go-ahead *Verfuegungs-SS**, where prospects seemed infinitely brighter. His career had taken off when his fellows elected him inspector-general in charge of training; it was Hausser who set up the V-SS officer training colleges, thought by some to have produced the best field officers in the world. Twice wounded, Hausser had arrived in Normandy with a great amount of

* The 'stand-by' SS; armed political readiness troops.

East Front experience, ready and willing to take on the great responsibility of commanding the first real coordinated German counter-stroke since D-day.

On 23 June, Hausser let it be known that the 40,000 men of 9th and 10th SS would begin arriving from Poland in two days. The ill-fated military nobleman Geyr von Schweppenburg had been assigned control of the assault from *Panzer* Group West, yet another curious anomaly of the German command set-up, soon changed by the RAF.

On 25 June, Rommel, still with a role to play in this plethora of generals, ordered every available piece of transport to bring up three more divisions to reinforce the crumbling front; these were the army's 276th and 277th Infantry, plus the 16th *Luftwaffe* Field Division, all three still some 150 miles away. The background of these units is not without interest, and indicates how Rommel's continued attempt to release *panzer* units and replace them with infantry resulted in his having to scrape the bottom of the barrel, so to speak.

The original 276th Infantry was formed of older men in June 1940 but was dissolved two months later, following the conclusion of operations in France. It was re-formed in December 1943 and sent to south-west France to complete its training, containing ordinary infantrymen now bearing more colourful appellations as a result of Hitler's earlier decree whereby some foot soldiers became 'grenadiers' or 'fusiliers', an echo of an earlier era (hence '*panzergrenadiers*', infantrymen transported into battle in armoured half-tracks, etc). The 276th, of course, contained no armour.

The 277th started its life in similar fashion, formed and disbanded in the summer of 1940, re-formed December 1943 from remnants, but mostly of Austrians. In January 1944 it was sent to Croatia, doubtless as a security unit, before being transferred to southern France.

The 16th *Luftwaffe* Field Division was put together in 1942–43 and served as an occupation unit in north Holland, and originally comprised only two regiments. In June 1944, doubtless to try and boost its coming (futile) role in Normandy, its three-battalion regiments were reduced to only two each in order to form (on paper) a third regiment. Unusually, its commander (Lieutenant-General Karl Schlievers) was an army officer.

Geyr von Schweppenburg had issued a secret order that the grand attack must begin before dusk, and continue through the night. It was all a waste of time. Even before the 9th and 10th SS personnel were fully assembled, Montgomery's army struck first.

The progress of the promised SS divisions from the East had been monitored by British Intelligence, with the aid of Ultra intercepts, and Resistance fighters in France and Lorraine, so that on the morning of 24 June Monty's Ultra liaison officer was able to hand him a paper containing the unwelcome news of these formidable fresh forces entering his battle. Far from being the cautious, ponderous general – on this occasion at least – Monty took swift action to spoil the enemy's plans. First, he cancelled his own proposed and imminent assault on Caen which was to have involved the dropping of 1st British Airborne Division south of the city, which would have virtually surrounded it. He then ordered Lieutenant-General Richard O'Connor to speed into an all-out attack south-east of Caen, the main thrust towards Cheux. This General had made his mark in the early desert war; now he had arrived in Normandy with his 8th Corps, including the 11th Armoured Division and 15th Scottish Infantry Division, which included many famous regiments. The previous assaults by 30th Corps were known as Operation 'Perch'; now Monty settled for the first of several major efforts utilising code-names based on race tracks, a practice that by the light of interpretation put on them by some critics would prove unfortunate. Operation 'Epsom' was, however, a spoiling attack designed yet again to hold off the *panzer* divisions from the Americans, and naturally to forestall completely the planned German counter-offensive. In both aims he succeeded completely.

As a prelude to the British attack a preliminary assault was carried out by 49th (West Riding) Division to clear a ridge at Rauray on what would be O'Connor's right flank. This attack was not large enough to alert the enemy to an even greater effort, and seemed part of continuing British operations east of Tilly. In telling General Eisenhower of the coming attack, Monty said, 'Once it starts I will continue battling on the eastern flank until one of us cracks, and it will not be us.' In other words, attacks were to continue east and north of Caen by the other British–Canadian forces.

One can well imagine the British commander's state of mind at this time, for despite all his outward optimism and control, Montgomery naturally had his anxieties: the throwing away of men's lives on a daily basis, the constant need to be on the alert with many other details to attend to – all the normal lot of a general involved in a great battle. He was therefore irked when an enquiry arrived from the War Minister in London concerning depressing reports of inferior British equipment, especially failures in the new Cromwell tank.

The notion of sloped armour on tanks was hardly new to the British; they had produced the splendidly designed Crusader featuring a turret almost the ultimate in that essential – though carrying a peashooter gun in its early versions. They had, like their enemy the Germans, been tremendously impressed by the Soviet T34. Yet, in 1944, after years of trial and error and hard-learnt lessons, the 2nd Army in Normandy was saddled with yet another inferior tank – inferior, that is, for the job in hand. Developed from other designs that never became operational (Cavalier and Centaur), the Cromwell Mk I carried only a 57mm gun, though its immediate, offshoot predecessor, the Centaur Mk IV, was armed as an assault tank to destroy fortifications with a 95mm mortar. The Cromwell marks (IV, V and VII) carried a 75mm cannon with the new muzzle brake, mounted in a large turret of vertical armour plates almost crudely bolted together, which made a perfect target for German anti-tank weapons.

One might have thought that since the British had (allegedly) been planning a return to the continent since summer 1940, some thought would have been given to the kind of terrain the invading army, and especially its armour, would have to fight in. Unhappily, British pioneering with tanks in 1916 had not been followed up at the War Office and staff colleges by scientific thinking on the best way to use armour; at least, those few who had the right ideas were ignored or side-tracked into less dangerous branches of service. British experience of armoured warfare became based on the desert war and, of course, on the kind of men who, initially at any rate, rode in tanks – the horse soldiers. Men whose mentality was based on the good old cavalry charge were men swiftly removed from this world by the realities of World War Two. But such men died hard and continued to, so that when the Desert Rats and others not strictly of that close-knit fraternity travelled to Normandy with their shiny tanks they had in mind tactics not too dissimilar to those practised in both North Africa and the wide open fenlands of East Anglia, where many of them had trained. Naturally, and perhaps oddly, it is curious that in both Britain and in Normandy the opposing sides were constricted by the nature of the countryside during training, but that is the truth of it. The 'crowded island' of Britain, it seems, even during a life and death struggle, would never permit its pretty landscape to be despoiled by armoured monsters charging over the green fields or ruining the tarmac in country lanes. Anyone who has seen the damage that results from even modest tonnages of armour (or even farm tractors) will know what this can mean in terms of damage claims by angry farmers and irate local councillors.

Yet, knowing as we do that Britain was once joined to and part of the continent of Europe, we see that the similarities mentioned by the soldiers themselves to their own land back home across the Channel had a greater relevance than mere coincidence. For not only had it once been part and parcel of the same landscape, during World War Two it presented conundrums to both invader and defender. But, whereas the German veterans from the wide open spaces of Russia may have felt claustrophobic in the *bocage*, they at once saw its superb defensive potential and used the right tactics when battle came. The British and their allies found their armoured columns jammed nose to tail (at times) in lanes passable by only one vehicle at a time, hemmed in by high banks and twelve-foot-high hedges several feet thick; more defendable terrain could hardly be imagined. Yet, the British military authorities had appealed to the public at home for holiday snapshots of the French coast; they had set up great organisations and gone to extreme lengths of ingenuity in all manner of ways to ensure the success of the Normandy invasion. But, once into the *bocage* the troops seemed dismayed and baffled by their surroundings. It is true to state that the Normandy landscape dictated the battle to a considerable degree, almost as much as Montgomery. It is impossible to hear or read accounts by the men involved without being impressed by this fact.

Obviously, there was really nothing at all the attackers could do about the landscape, no matter how many millions of shells and bombs were expended; the little lanes and byways remained essentially the same, traps for the unwary and quite unsuited to 'cruiser' tanks like the Cromwell. The type's 600hp engine gave it a good turn of speed, but this was of no use at all, and its over-high turret seemed an open invitation to the enemy's high-velocity 75 and 88mm shells ejected from long barrels poking through the hedgerows or cunningly sited at the best available gap.

The other, perhaps more serious, snag with Britain's army in the battle was its lack of expertise in infantry-tank co-operation, stressed by other writers, the unfortunate tankers having to learn again the hard way the folly of charging in minus infantry protection. For many the lesson came too late. The armoured corps motto of 'Through mud and blood to the green fields beyond' loses its relevance when trapped in a blazing hulk.

General Montgomery's response to the War Minister's enquiry ran: 'We cannot have anything of that sort at this time . . . tomorrow we leap upon the enemy. Anything that undermines confidence and morale must be stamped on ruthlessly.' And of course he was right. It was no time for the soldiers to have their morale sapped, even though many knew and had known all along they were battling against the experts who in many cases used better equipment, not merely in armour but in infantry weapons.

Hausser's HQ was a useless entity without divisions to control, but this waiting period for him was about to end, and he would once more take command of an army in combat. Seventy-eight trains had carried the 9th *SS Hohenstaufen* across Poland and the Reich, while a further sixty-two transported the 10th *SS Frundsberg*. Somehow, 2nd *Panzer* (*Wien*) was assembling near Caumont, the 1st SS was arriving in Normandy, while the lesser elements (276th, 277th and 16th LW) were also coming along. The SS men of 9th and 10th had triumphed in the East. Georg Essler was a Panther tank driver in the first named unit: 'The news of our transfer to the West was good. We boarded trains in Poland and our tanks were loaded on flat cars. We were quite excited; people greeted us at the stations in Germany, giving us food and drink. It took us about four days to do that journey, and when we reached Lorraine we had to leave the train as the tracks had been damaged by air attack. We had to unload and check over our vehicles and then begin the slow journey to the front.' In fact, it was a further eight days before the 9th SS began arriving in Normandy.

A similar experience came to Siegfried Lasson, an armoured car driver in the reconnaissance battalion of 10th SS, and when his unit finally arrived they found not a great assembling for the Hausser offensive, but a piecemeal throwing-in to try to stem Montgomery's own pre-emptive strike.

In the battle around Cheux, elements of Meyer's 12th SS were drawn, since they were already spread thin all across the southern perimeter of the Caen front, called in by constant appeals for help from Sepp Dietrich. In the preliminary battle, the British 49th Division had failed to capture the ridge at Rauray, but had forced Meyer to commit his *panzer* regiment in its defence; this unit had, in striking back westwards, broken into *Panzer* Lehr's boundary. It was now the *panzergrenadiers* and engineers of 12th SS who tried to stem Monty's great new assault from the north, its objective to cross the river Odon and seize the high ground beyond. Once the 15th Scottish and the armour had reached the objective beyond the Odon the 43rd (Wessex) Division would move in to take over the ground won.

As so often, the simple directives issued from army HQ resulted in a confused mass of death and destruction, with, in this case, the weather throwing its weight into the struggle. There are two ways to describe a battle – here is one of them.

Two hours after dawn on 26 June, the 15th Scottish Division and 31st Armoured Brigade moved into their first battle under a leaden and threatening sky. Ahead of them the barrage rolled across sodden cornfields and dripping hedges. A minefield checked the tanks but the infantry tramped stolidly on across the Caen–Tilly road and fought their way into the string of hamlets around Cheux, from where an armoured column was to make its rush to the Odon bridges. Mines, mortars and debris in the villages held up the armour. During this pause the Germans recovered from the bombardment and swept the whole area with fire from their positions on Rauray, and the hamlets and woods north of the river. Of this battle, Chester Wilmot wrote later: 'The troops of 12th SS fought with a tenacity and ferocity seldom equalled and never excelled during the whole campaign.'

The British armour stopped; the Scottish reserves were sent in during a torrential downpour. Routes cut through the minefield became rivers of squelchy mud which reduced supporting arms to a crawl. Though stopped by the SS soldiers at Rauray, on the left flank the British reached the railway at Colleville, four miles south of their start line. And there the attack halted.

This brief summary conceals a day that began with disappointment in the mist and drizzle, a morning that swiftly degenerated into confusion, desperation and death. Hamish McDougall was a Private in the 4th Seaforths:

❝ We had a meagre breakfast of tinned beans, dry bread and tea and saw the horrible mist and it was drizzling. So we felt bad about the whole operation. We'd never been in action, and looking at that fog we began to see Jerries everywhere! We went off after the barrage which was fantastic, and of course we'd never experienced anything like it in training. All I could see was two or three mates each side of me as we walked into that cornfield and heard our tanks moving. Before long we heard small-arms fire, but with the fog could see nothing and had no idea where it was coming from, or in fact if we were still going in the right direction. I heard the Lieutenant blow his whistle a few times to give us a clue, but that stopped and we heard bangs as the tanks ran onto mines. Next we heard shouts and hadn't a clue what was going on, but then suddenly, shells were landing among us. 99

The British infantry advancing cautiously through the corn had deviated from their route, owing to the thick mist, and had run slap-bang into their own barrage, still being put down by 500 guns.

66 There was a hell of a bang, and another, and another. We hit the deck and my pal Andy said, 'Christ-all-fucking-mighty – they're ours, I reckon!' It went on for a few minutes as we lay there with our faces down in the dirt and corn with the stuff falling all round us, and the noise was terrific. They were the worst moments of my whole life. Then, thank God, the barrage moved on, so we got up, trembling and pretty useless, and didn't know where the hell we were. There was a lot of shouting and someone was trying to give orders. So we tramped on and suddenly saw Jerries running off through the mist. At last we had something to do and we started firing at them – or, at least, in their general direction. The start of Epsom was a complete balls-up! 99

The troops had hoped the attack would be postponed, at least until the mist cleared, but Montgomery could not delay owing to Hausser's imminent offensive. The weather put paid to any air support; the kind of air blitz the Germans had been suffering was entirely absent that morning. Jim Fiske of the 1st Gordons remarked:

66 We went off in high hopes into the mist, which wasn't too bad where we were, with all our guns banging away, and we thought the Jerries were getting such a pasting it must be a push over. But I remember our Lieutenant, who was English and from public school. He said, 'Don't forget chaps, the Jerries are bloody good at defence, so watch out for surprises, OK?'

Well, they certainly gave us a few. Half an hour later the guns stopped for a few minutes. We were in among some trees, or what was left of them, and suddenly there was fire coming at us from all directions, including our rear. There were yells and curses and we all dropped to the dirt and mud and started shooting, though we couldn't see a thing, partly because of the mist, but also because the Jerries were so well hidden. 99

Indeed, in the mist and through the excellent fieldcraft of the young SS men, the Scots infantrymen had overlooked some German foxholes, the enemy waiting till they had passed before springing to life.

❝ Then our Lieutenant got hit not far from us; he shouted at us to keep moving. So we did. But a lot of blokes never got up from that place, and the officer was one of them. Then we saw some ruined houses – it must have been almost an hour later. I know I looked at my mate's watch and was surprised so much time had passed. We reached those houses with fire coming at us from all directions and blokes falling down and calling for medics. There was a high grey wall and I huddled up against it with my mate Tommy and waited. We had no orders and didn't know which way to move. The battle got worse and we heard tanks and saw a Churchill moving along the street, but it was hit and caught fire. All our mates seemed to have disappeared and we felt alone. In fact, the survivors were still about, but somewhere under cover. With all the stuff flying about it was very confusing. ❞

Angus Jones of the Glasgow Highlanders recalled getting lost in the fog, but pushing on to some trees and houses:

❝ And it rained like hell and we all got fed up with it. We'd never been in action before, it was all very different to what we'd expected. The only consolation, so we thought, was the Jerries who were suffering too, with all that barrage on them. As soon as we reached the ruins we set up for defence and waited for orders, but none came until a Sergeant-Major we didn't know ran up and said, 'Don't hang about lads – get on!' So we did, moving from house to house, under fire from Jerries we couldn't see. There were shells and mortars and small-arms fire zipping and banging around us and a lot of blokes never made it. ❞

James Hayter was a Lieutenant with the Seaforths:

❝ When we finally reached Cheux we were few and minus our tanks. There was nothing to see but mud, water, ruins, smoke and mist, and the air was alive with missiles. I tried to see how many chaps had made it, but this was difficult because of the conditions, but I knew that some were under cover. I lay among some redbrick ruins that were still quite hot to touch. I carried a Sten gun and grenades; I had a Corporal close by and two men not far away with a Bren. All the rest were dead, wounded, or out of sight. Then we heard tanks but had no idea if they were theirs or ours. The noise was fantastic and I couldn't understand how a battle could be fought in such conditions of mist.

But then the mist began to clear and I saw Jerries not far off. They wore brown jackets and were, I thought, trying to collect some of their wounded, so we didn't fire. Then some of our tanks appeared and as they went by we gave them a wave. Two of these Churchills were brewed up, so we were again unsupported. Then the rain came down in torrents so we tried to hide under our capes, but had to stay vigilant. I decided to try and push on, as our orders were to reach the river, but I'd lost my little compass and sense of direction. Then a Captain appeared in a scout car and told us the way before going off. But as soon as we started to move the Jerries let us have it with multiple mortars and all hell broke loose. We were forced to get down in the rubble again and took a beating. Then came a pause in the enemy barrage and we were able to rush off out of Cheux in the direction indicated and joined up with others of a different unit. The mist had thinned and we were getting fire from all directions, including mortars. I felt something nick my right leg, but I kept going. We reached the railway line, I believe, at Colleville, but didn't get any further that day, which had been a bad one. **"**

The Captain who had driven into the mud and fire in Cheux village was Geoffrey Chater, from Chelsea in London. He had been serving on the Seaforths staff, but preferring a field job had managed to get himself employed as a kind of inter-battalion liaison officer. In this battle he had sped from unit to unit, under fire, trying to keep the men on course and moving. 'With so much stuff flying about Cheux was a death trap, thick with mud and great pools of rainwater which grew worse in the sudden downpour. I was able to give directions to a number of groups hiding in the rubble, but then those big mortars came down and my car was blown up off the road. I fell in a heap with my driver who was a Corporal, and we lay there concussed for a while.' Geoffrey Chater was forced to lay up that night, and although the enemy fire quietened, there was sniping.

When the sun burned away some of the mist it was found that the key village of Fontenay le Pesnel had not been attacked at all. The confusion caused by the mist, some infantry losing their way and being clobbered by their own shellfire, the unexpected loss of tank support when the Churchills ran onto the minefield, and the loss of junior officers in the mêlée that followed, all helped to bog down the offensive. The failure of 49th Division to clear the Rauray heights the day before contributed to the hold-up. It has been recorded that not until afternoon did tanks arrive to support the infantry of the Royal Scots at Fontenay, which was immediately south of the ridge at Rauray, cornerstone of the defence provided by the 3/12th *SS Panzergrenadiers* whose positions butted the flank of *Panzer* Lehr. The SS troops hung on to Fontenay, still in occupation at the day's end, by which time four hundred men lay among the ruins of that hamlet alone, the dead and wounded of each side.

The ferocity of this battle, fought over mist-laden fields, through hedgerows and shattered tree stumps, soaked corn and into the hot rubble of tiny villages, so stunned and traumatised many men involved that decades later the reawakened memories of those awful hours still evoke upset. Not only that, the shock to young minds new to such death and terror bred a confusion of impressions, so that recollections have become muddled in later years. Those hours in the rain under constant fire, with little or no idea of locality or even at times direction, have resulted in only a painful montage of nightmarish impressions, two days in fact of hell that have telescoped into one. To be so trapped in the middle of a ferocious enemy, suffering the additional, more natural discomforts of rain and mud, with only an occasional exhortation to 'Get on!' to the cursed river from strangers who appeared and disappeared, knowing most of the lads who had started the day were now dead or maimed – that was enough to test the stoutest hearts.

When those terrible hours under fire drew to a close, the surviving Scots lads splashed on to reach the railway at Colleville. It was the remaining reserves of the Royal Scots Fusiliers and sister unit the Royal Scots who finally gained that objective, as Ron Beckinson, an Englishman in the Royal Scots, recalled:

66 It was late in the afternoon when we saw the ruins of Colleville, including what remained of the station. By then I reckon we had lost over half our men. We lay there, still under fire and wondering what to do next. I felt hungry, thirsty, hot and terrified. The sun had come out and that made it worse as the Jerries could see us clearly. But then came sunset and it got misty and quite chilly again. Our Sergeant was still with us by some miracle and said we had no chance of reaching the Odon bridge that day. So we tried to dig in, but this was difficult lying down. We didn't dare stand up to use our picks and spades. 99

Ron's mate Edward Devlin had also survived the wild dash under fire, with men falling around him:

66 When we got down we were quite out of breath, done for, and in a bad state of nerves. Our officers had vanished long before among some ruins and only our Sergeant kept us going. We expected a counterattack and had no guns or tanks in support that we knew of. We were close to the remains of a big hedge; I can hear even now the bullets coming through it, and we were forced to keep our heads down. Just to our left we could see some ruins – walls and what we thought must be the station – but we couldn't see the railway itself, though our Sergeant told us it was right in front, just a few yards. I believe a Corporal not far away tried to reach it when we first got there, but he was knocked down and killed. 99

Ron Beckinson:

66 We lay there as it started to get dark and quite chilly. Then someone, I don't know who, produced a bag of biscuits and passed some along the line. It then got quiet, and we were warned by our Sarge to be doubly alert. But frankly, we were so tired out and demoralised I think some of

us no longer cared what happened. We'd had such a bad day. As soon as it was properly dark the Sarge sent a chap back with a message, told half of us to try and get some kip while he and one other bloke tried to reconnoitre to the railway. So we lay on our backs after removing our small packs and fell asleep. Apart from an occasional thump from a gun somewhere it was amazingly quiet. **99**

Edward Devlin added: 'We munched the biscuits and fell asleep, and in that time I believe a lot of reorganising went on behind us, as we woke up in pitch darkness and could hear a lot of movement back where we'd come from.'

These men were now at the point of the British spearhead. They had without realising it brought panic and alarm to Sepp Dietrich and his command. That thin line of Scottish infantrymen just yards from the railtracks were now less than one and a half miles from the nearest bridge over the river Odon. That evening, as the spent Britishers lay near the tracks, the SS General reported to the commander of 7th Army, General Dollman: 'If further reinforcements are not brought up tonight a breakthrough on both sides of Cheux cannot be prevented.'

Two battalions of 1st SS had been promised, but these were stuck miles away, out of fuel. The day before, as 49th Division was battering Rauray, Dietrich had called for help from Hausser's new 2nd SS *Panzer* Corps, but Rommel had refused, insisting that the assembling units under Hausser be kept clear of the battle, ordering him to remain no closer than Aunay. But now, with the advent of a fresh British onslaught that threatened to outflank and even encircle Caen, the Field Marshal relented to some extent, and in so doing complied with Montgomery's will to cause the complete frustration of any major German counter-stroke. At nine o'clock that evening, 26 June, Rommel ordered that 'everything which can be assembled by General Hausser must be thrown into the fight', with the proviso that the SS General's own troops (9th and 10th SS) must still not be committed to battle. The 2nd and 21st *Panzers* must each furnish armour while the 2nd SS (then arriving at St Lo) would provide a battle group. It can be seen therefore that both of Montgomery's aims were being realised: not only had he set the south-west corner of the Caen front aflame, his drive was drawing forces from the American sector; not only was 2nd *SS Das Reich* being forced to divert troops and armour, two brigades of mortars were also diverted from the US Army front to try to stem the British drive.

All night long the Germans waited anxiously for news of the British assault, but nothing happened. They had shot their bolt the day before – or so it seemed. This overnight pause deluded the enemy command into the belief that they had scored a 'good defensive victory', and General Dietrich, somehow having scraped together eighty tanks, reported to 7th Army that he now proposed making a counter-attack in the direction of Cheux, which the British had battled into. The apparent inaction gave Rommel the impression Hausser's offensive was still on; 9th and 10th SS would indeed smash through the British on the axis Caumont–Bayeux to the sea.

The Dietrich counter-attack with armour went in on 28 June. Even as the enemy assembled a deluge of British artillery fire began to fall among them. The *panzers* and infantry advanced towards Cheux:

❝ We were lying down behind our gun as a lot of Jerry fire including mortars started coming over, while at the same time a great deal of our own stuff was going in their direction. We were just inside a little wood, the area was full of them, and ahead of us was a lot of open ground. We were well warned and in a few minutes our Sergeant shouted to us to take post at our six-pounder gun, which was well camouflaged with the barrel poking through a little hedge. We had three more not far off and some seventeen-pounders of the RA elsewhere.* I looked over the gunshield and saw a lot of Jerry tanks coming through the smoke of our artillery barrage. The noise got a lot worse and then we saw bunches of Jerry infantry rushing along behind the tanks, which I think were mainly Panthers. They were about half a mile off and soon we opened fire. We couldn't really miss, and pretty soon there were several Jerry tanks stopped and burning or blown to bits, especially by the seventeen-pounders which had a terrific punch. We cheered like mad and saw the Jerry infantry trying to come on, but without the tanks they were simply mown down by machine-guns and few survived. ❞

That was Frank Winton's impression of the German counter-attack from the Royal Scots battalion anti-tank gun positions. The seventeen-pounder guns were much bigger and did indeed pack a hefty punch. Alan Wicks recalled:

❝ Our Sergeant was watching the Jerry tanks through his glasses and made us wait and wait until they were less than half a mile off, which was close range for us. Then we let fly and the results were spectacular. With our first shot we blew a Panther's turret right off and it went up with a whooshing sound and nobody baled out. Our other guns were firing at top rate and I saw two more of the Panthers blow up, one of them like a great firework display. Our second shot blew one sideways and one of its tracks flew off. There was still a lot of our artillery fire going into them but they were then too close and the twenty-five-pounder boys left it to us. I think at least three more Jerry tanks were knocked out right in front of us at close range and many more elsewhere, and they did us no damage, so we were very bucked about that and had

---

* The six-pounder anti-tank guns were issued to battalions; the seventeen-pounders remained Royal Artillery weapons.

some tea as we watched them burn. The Jerry infantry, or what remained of them, just withered away and vanished. **99**

As another account put it: 'Their armoured counter-attack, disorganised by heavy shelling, broke on the anti-tank screen which flanked the Scottish salient; it did not even prevent the 49th from capturing Rauray, nor did it distract O'Connor from his assault across the Odon. A bridge was captured intact, and by the morning of the 28th the main strength of 11th Armoured Division was over the river and its tanks were probing southwards.' Again, simple statements giving only a bald outline of more fierce fighting with all the heartache and death and destruction that entailed.

Panzer Meyer had been rushing from one threatened sector to another, trying desperately to prevent the breakthrough around Cheux, his forces stretched ever thinner, unsupported by other SS and certainly no army units. He recorded these hours later in his memoir *Grenadiere* (1955): 'The mass of British tanks was enough to frighten anyone to death. There was no time to think any more. Only one thing mattered – to keep fighting!'

The 43rd Wessex moved down to take over St Manvieu; the Highland Light Infantry moved out of Haut du Bosq, which was taken over by the 5th Duke of Cornwall's Light Infantry, as Denis Coulsen remembered:

66 We formed up. It was not a bad morning but we were still wet from the soaking we got during the night. We'd had some breakfast but hardly felt like eating. Our battalion was crouched down and ready to go; we had some Churchills of the 7th tanks. Then the whistles blew and off we went down a grassy slope and in no time we began to get fire from two sides and we were pinned down. Our officer was hit at once and we heard no more from him. Our Sergeant tried to get us moving but as soon as he rose up he was hit in the arm and fell down moaning. We lay there quite unable to move; the bullets and shells were whizzing overhead and into the ground about us and some more men were hit. Then there were shells falling among us and some panic came so that first a few and then the lot of us were forced to run back the way we came. I had my head down and I could only see one of my mates and not all that many others of the 500 or so men who started out, but amazingly most of them got back sooner or later. As we crashed down again among the bushes and broken trees I saw our Colonel standing with his glasses by his scout car, and his face was a picture, a mixture of anguish and fury! **99**

Denis's mate John Tilsen also remembered this experience:

66 I ran back in a hell of a sweat just behind Denis with all that stuff flying about us and was very surprised that we were still in one piece. Yes, I saw our Colonel watching, and even before we'd got our breath back the reserve company was sent rushing off down that hill, past the knocked-out Churchills, and they got it just as bad as we did. The medics were fantastic; they went rushing down the slope waving white sheets and Red Cross armbands to get to the wounded, and some were hit. It was awful to see and I just buried my face in my arm. I'd seen enough and I cried. We'd had a bad introduction to combat and no mistake. **"**

The Scotsmen had run straight into fire from elements of the 12th *SS Panzergrenadiers* beside the road south and the Salbey stream, while other SS of the 8th/12th *SS panzers* hit them on their left front. The first drive towards Grainville was stopped; it had been intended to swing left there once the railway was reached, and race across to Odon. Meantime, drama had broken out in their rear for, responding to Rommel's orders, the 2nd *Panzer Division (Wien)* drove north-east to take the British in the flank at Cheux itself, some of their Panthers branching right to hit the DCLI in Haut du Bosq. The main German spearhead caught the battalion HQ and aid post of the HLI. Confusion reigned as the surprised British were forced to grab weapons; anti-tank guns were hurriedly turned about and an attempt was made to repel the enemy. In Cheux two light Honey reconnaissance tanks were destroyed, one of them containing a sleeping Sergeant. Other British tank crews of the 23rd Hussars manning Shermans were lined up waiting south of the ruined village when the commotion broke out behind them. But it was tanks of the Fife & Forfar Yeomanry the shattered HLI saw when they were pulled back to reorganise. The Scotsmen cursed the tankers for not being there on the slope to help them, but the armoured crews (so accounts tell) were 'battened down and deaf to all appeals'. But one tank Lieutenant stated that Shermans were not suited to 'such close fighting'.

Nevertheless, these tanks were ordered to advance, over the crest and into the German fire. The leaders were knocked out at once; the rest of the attack, minus infantry, went astray. One Lieutenant's Sherman had an electrical failure, but escaped back to get repairs, while in Cheux infantrymen and six-pounders battled the invading Panthers. It was the same in Haut du Bosq, where the Duke of Cornwall men had found their first battle of the war. Here, five Panthers were knocked out and four German crewmen captured at a cost of twenty killed and wounded, including the 5th Battalion's CO, Colonel Atherton. The German tanks had again proved just as vulnerable as the British when shorn of infantry protection. That protection had not been provided because of the panicky nature of the German counter-measures that were sent in piecemeal.

Otto Weidinger had come up the much-delayed route from southern France with 2nd *SS Das Reich*, and because of the emergency he had been ordered to take a battle group to assist 2nd *Panzers*, coming under their command. A veteran of the first campaigns and especially the Russian Front, Weidinger had reached the rank of Colonel and would survive the war to write a history of his division that appeared in several volumes. 'We had only just arrived in the American sector near St Lo and gone into action when the British offensive threatened to break through our front.' Weidinger's original orders were to assist in the defence of the front south of Cheux, but on reporting to 2nd *Panzers* after midnight this command from Sepp Dietrich was countermanded by *Panzer* Lehr, who ordered Battlegroup Weidinger to plug a gap between their surviving troops and the Hitler Youth.

❝ We arrived some 1,500 men strong with tanks and other vehicles and were shown our positions and the location of the enemy. We had hardly disposed ourselves in battle formation when the enemy greeted us with heavy artillery and air attacks which disrupted my plans for some hours. Vehicles were lost, but after regrouping we went into the assault on a local level and made some progress until at last the overwhelming enemy artillery and air attacks brought us to a halt. I went forward to see the situation and what could be done and received a small wound in the leg, which was not serious, and I continued to direct operations which became entirely defensive. In fact, not long after that we were forced to break off our part in that sector because of American pressure on our left flank, and from that time on the steady drain of casualties reduced our group to only a few hundred men at most. We lost all our tanks and much other transport with little or no replacements. ❞

When the disaster came weeks later, in mid-August, Weidinger's battlegroup would consist of a few dozen men. His parent division was soon identified in the battle, as were the 9th and 10th SS, whose units were thrown in piecemeal following the British break-in around Cheux on 26 June. Siegfried Lasson, driver of an armoured car with 10th SS reconnaissance, recalled:

❝ I was sent forward in a small column to try to stem the British advance on the right flank of our division. There was a little artillery fire, but we were well concealed in a sunken road. Our car was in the lead and, as I knew, in the most dangerous position. We had once been ambushed in such a position in Russia and I knew things could happen very fast, with little chance to escape. The road was so narrow I could see we would have difficulty turning round if we ran into the enemy, which we surely would sooner or later.

It was fairly early in the morning and I felt tired and hungry as we had not had a good meal for a couple of days. I thought of my family back in Hamburg. They were living in a shack, which was all they had on the outskirts after the terrible air raids on the city. Then we reached a straight part of the road and had still not seen any sign of the enemy, yet we knew they were about and probably watching us. Our men were alert, with weapons at the ready. My CO, a Sergeant-Major of great experience, told me to drive slowly as there was a tree at the end of the road and we could see no further than that. Then he told me to halt while he went forward on foot.

I saw him go forward, bending with his Schmeisser. Then I heard a burst of fire and he vanished. We had no idea what had happened, so I reversed the car while one of our men went forward to investigate. He returned a few moments later to say the NCO was dead. So I reversed further and we met an officer who ordered us to go ahead and find out what we were up against. It seemed foolish and suicidal, but we obeyed. I drove forward again in low gear, and nothing happened. So I speeded up a little, believing the rest of the column was following us. Then quite suddenly shooting broke out and I heard shouts and found we were surrounded by Tommies. There was a great deal of noise, and the enemy vanished. One of the men told me the rest of our column was with us, so we had to go on. I tried to argue, but the senior Private ordered me on, so I engaged another gear and we drove on for a kilometre or so in amazement, with no sign of the enemy. Willi radioed this news to an officer in the command car behind us and he told us to halt and wait. So I stopped the car and the rest of the column came up behind.

Then the officer sent us forward to reconnoitre on foot as there were trees and undergrowth each side of the road. This they did. But no sooner had they started off than a deluge of mortar shells began to fall all around us. We rushed back to our vehicles and the officer ordered us to reverse course. This was easier said than done. We had to drive backwards, but there was a lot of shooting behind us and we guessed we'd been trapped. At that moment I looked out of my port and saw a group of Tommies manhandling an anti-tank gun into the road ahead of us. I shouted a warning to Willi, who said, 'Get a move on!' He opened fire with our machine-gun, but missed the Tommies.

In a moment we were hit by the first shell which knocked off our left front wheel. We were helpless and I thought the next shell would finish us. Very reluctantly, Willi ordered everyone to get out, which we did, just as the gun sent another round into our car, which was wrecked but did not burn. At the same time the enemy began firing machine-guns at us so we raced back and leapt into one of our half-tracks and escaped injury. But we had lost three men and the Tommies advanced so rapidly we were unable to recover the body of our Sergeant-Major.' **

After the slow journey across France which did tank tracks no good at all, Georg Essler of the 9th SS arrived in Normandy.

** We deployed across fields and set up our little camps to await orders, which soon came: we would take part in a big counter-offensive against the British and Americans and drive them back into the sea. With us would be our companion division, the 10th SS, so we felt very confident. But a day or so later the British themselves launched a new offensive from the north so we boarded our vehicles and followed a guide to a fresh attack point. A great battle was in progress and we saw a lot of smoke, and overhead the Allied planes were making constant attacks on our forces. Some of our comrades were already engaged elsewhere, and we received an order to go in and crush a British salient.

We went across the fields with our infantry and at once came under very heavy artillery fire which disrupted everything. There was so much smoke I could hardly see, and I thought it very dangerous if we lost touch with our infantry. Then my commander, who was a Sergeant and a great friend, told us there were enemy tanks ahead, so we opened fire at once. Then the bangs were continuous and I could barely see a thing. Then I was ordered to stop while our gunner shot up some enemy tanks and other vehicles. And then we received a hit on the front of our tank which shook us a bit, but did no real damage. We changed our position and I found I could see the enemy tanks ahead quite clearly in another field, and they were shooting at us. We then found a little dip in the ground and some cover from where we could shoot at the many targets. Then came a series of loud explosions round the tank and we realised we were under artillery fire. So I withdrew, but then we were in open ground and still under heavy fire so I reversed again and saw one of our Panthers burst into flames and two men jumping out. It was all very terrifying.

Our gunner found he could no longer turn the turret, so I turned the tank so that the gun could still fire, and we hit several more of the enemy vehicles, including tanks.

Then something hit us very hard in the flank and we smelt burning. The Sergeant ordered us out quick, so I tried to unfasten my front hatch, but it was jammed. By the time I scrambled up into the turret the whole tank was on fire and my clothing was smoking. I just managed to jump onto the grass when it went up and the ammunition started to explode, blowing me across the ground. I struggled to run away, but my legs collapsed under me. Then I felt strong hands grab me and I was dragged off across the grass into some bushes where we collapsed. It was the Sergeant, and I think he saved my life. When the battle quietened down we were able to rejoin our own lines. 99

Troops of the 43rd Wessex went in to occupy the ground won, one company of the Monmouths entering Mouen, unaware that Battlegroup Weidinger and 2nd *Panzers* (*Wien*) were about to fall on them from the west. Stan Kendall was a Lieutenant:

66 We marched into Mouen in good order with little or no sign of the enemy, who had been cleared by Highlanders of 15th Scottish. We then started to consolidate according to orders and I gave a few directions before sitting down near a ruined house for some tea and consulting my map. A moment or so later some of our chaps at the end of the village ran up to say Jerries were coming. We barely had time to get to our feet before they were upon us, tanks and half-tracks and other stuff, all firing

like mad. There was a wild scramble for cover with stuff flying everywhere, and the ruins were being torn to pieces by shellbursts. In a matter of seconds almost the Jerries were in among us and it was hell, pandemonium and terrific, deafening noise. I tried to get behind a wall but something hit me in the leg and side and I cried out in pain and fell down. I lay there in some agony with all the racket and heard both our chaps and the Germans yelling, and then I passed out.

When I came to it was much quieter and I felt no pain, but ill. I tried to move but couldn't, but then I did manage to turn my head and saw a few Jerries on foot going among the ruins with their weapons at the ready. So I decided to stay put and pretend I was dead. Then vehicles went by and it got very quiet for a short time until quite suddenly a terrific barrage came down and that was hell too. It went on for some minutes, and when it stopped I looked around and saw nothing but smoke and no sign of the Jerries. I managed to drag myself to a wall and passed out again. When I came to I found some Jocks coming in and I was soon being taken away on a stretcher, and three days or so later I was back in England. I lost a leg. **99**

The company of Monmouths had been wiped out, with only some three men including Lieutenant Kendall surviving. British artillery had persuaded the enemy to vacate the locality, but when the 10th Highland Light Infantry tramped through a cornfield towards Mouen they ran unsuspecting into the enemy at point-blank range. Rex Dalglish was a Corporal:

66 Our orders were to occupy and hold Mouen, though few of us had heard of the name; most just thought of yet another ruined village. The area was full of them, and very pretty it was until the war came. We went across a field and reached some corn and I thought we were going to have an easy time. We'd never been in action ourselves though some of our blokes had been in the thick of it and had a bad time. Well, we were in open order and it was not too noisy where we were. Then suddenly I heard a sort of muffled shout and all at once machine-guns opened up right in front of us and we hit the dirt. But it was too late for a lot of our blokes. We started firing like mad but we couldn't see anything and our officer vanished in the corn. I was terrified as the bullets were just cutting through the corn from side to side. I forced myself backwards and thought about trying to dig in, but that was impossible. The firing went on and grenades were going off.

After a few minutes I heard the horrible yells of someone wounded and I saw my mate lying not far away. He was grinning at me and saying something I couldn't catch. Then a whistle blew and I heard our Lieutenant and Sergeant yelling that we should fall back. Well, we had to do that by slithering on our bellies in the mud and corn until at last we were back near a little road and the field where we were able to get up in some cover. There was a ditch and bushes. I reckon half of the blokes were lost in that bloody cornfield. We lay there for some time until a Captain came and ordered us to get off in another direction, which I later found was Colleville. **99**

The measure of anxiety on the German side is shown by the fate of General Dollman, in command of 7th Army. With Rommel and Rundstedt summoned to confer with Hitler at Berchtesgaden, the responsibilities and stress multiplied. The Americans took Cherbourg, the port finally surrendered by its commander General von Schlieben, who was pictured in the Allied press, dressed in muddy overcoat, at the moment of his capture. Hitler, enraged that his order to hold the port seemed to have been ignored, ordered an inquiry; General Dollman, as commander, perhaps saw a court-martial looming. The situation around Cheux seemed to have taken a turn for the worse as the British, far from being cowed into retreat by the fierce resistance, continued to enlarge their corridor, obviously intending to establish a substantial bridgehead beyond the river Odon and take Hill 112 (112 feet above sea level), the dominating feature in the area. General Hausser's plan had been to fight a holding action until his new 2nd *SS Panzer* Corps and the other assembling forces were ready for a concerted blow. But, with more depressing reports flooding in, General Dollman ordered Hausser: '2nd *SS Panzer* Corps must move immediately to clean up the enemy penetrations south of Cheux.'

That morning (28 June) General Dollman died. The belief has persisted and is stated in some histories that he took poison, his dying words that Hausser must attack at once.

In the event, everything went off at half-cock. Attacks on the Scottish corridor by 1st and 12th SS, and probing assaults by 9th and 10th SS were not co-ordinated, and even though, like those on Mouen and Grainville, achieving local success, were soon nullified by British artillery and air strikes. Nevertheless, Hausser still planned to hit the British on the morning of the 29th with the main weight of 9th and 10th SS. But the day dawned fine, the RAF intervened early and Hausser signalled 7th Army his attack would have to be postponed until afternoon. But at 13.40 hrs he stated that artillery and air raids were causing heavy losses; the operation finally went in at 14.30. Obviously, by that time Hitler's original plan had vanished; reality had never made it feasible anyway, and there was no chance of driving any wedge between the Allied armies. In any case, that day the British crossed the Odon.

Angus Jones, Glasgow Highlanders:

66 The same Sergeant-Major told us to support the tanks that were going on to the river to try to rush the bridge. It was agonising progress as the Jerries were plastering us all the way and some more of our blokes vanished. There was not much cover and we felt they were watching us all the time, despite the mist which had come down again. We were getting fire from our right flank and felt we were registered. Then the mist began to clear and we felt exposed. Then, at last, I don't know how long it was, we saw the banks of the river and a lot of bodies all over the place. We rushed forward, and when we saw the water we actually cheered. Then we were deluged with fire, and there was hardly any of us left. I heard some of our tanks go rattling over the bridge, but I didn't dare lift my head to watch. Then I was hit in the arm and passed out. "

Steve Cox, of the same unit:

" We were told by our Lieutenant to pile into some Bren carriers. We'd been in reserve and doubled into Cheux, or what remained of it. We had about six bods in each carrier and raced off across the fields. There wasn't much cover in those things, but we kept our heads down. Then we reached the bridge and saw all those bodies. God knows how many there were – dozens, I reckon. We had no time to wonder about all that. We raced on and when I looked back I saw a couple of our carriers lying on their sides, with bodies sprawled about, dead and wounded or trying to find cover. There was a lot of noise going on as we crossed the bridge and saw tanks manoeuvring and some on fire. Then our own carrier lost a track and ran amok, so we piled out and ran like hell towards some trees which were being cut to pieces by fire. It was a very unhealthy place to be, but we had no choice but to lie flat and hope the Jerry fire would be put down by our artillery. "

That is what happened. Jimmy Archer was there with the Glaswegians: 'After a few minutes our artillery were plastering the Jerry positions and we were able to go on a bit, but not far. There were dead Jerries all over the place and the ground was really chewed up with craters. We fell into a small ditch or something and felt safer. There were just three of us. We heard the Lieutenant shouting the Jerries would be counter-attacking, so we set up our weapons. Then he blew his whistle, so we got up to advance, but the Jerry fire was so accurate we were forced back into our little hole. My helmet was knocked off by a bullet. I felt lucky to have survived.'

Sergeant Rex Winter of the Gordons related how his men got mixed up with other units, 'in that scramble out of Cheux. When by some miracle I reached the bridge over the river I could see all the different insignia on the bodies. We got all mixed up; the battle was so fierce, it was every man for himself. On the bridge I had only three blokes with me, but later we were about twenty, from different units, and we hung on there for hours before being relieved. We left on the backs of tanks and in carriers to get some grub and sleep.'

Captain Geoff Chater was surprised to find the surviving tanks and infantry had captured the bridge at Gavrus: 'We seemed to have got stuck in those cursed ruins of Cheux. I managed to get a lift in a carrier and raced down the slope with other vehicles to find bodies everywhere. The tanks had crossed the little bridge and were fighting with a few pockets of infantry on the other side. The river itself was little more than an oversized stream, with bodies floating in it too.'

Private Bill Bridger was with the Shropshires and bypassed Cheux to his left:

❝ We were with some Churchills and made good progress, with not too much fire coming over us, and then we saw this big stream which our Sergeant said was the Odon river. But I didn't believe him as it looked quite small really. And then we saw a wooden bridge which surprised us, and we never thought the tanks could cross it and they didn't. They had to go on towards Grainville while we went over at – I think it was near Tourmanville. We never really knew the names of all these little places unless we were properly briefed. Quite often our Sarge or Lieutenant would say, 'You see that wood (or those houses, or whatever it was), we've got to get there, let's go!' Or something like that. So on this occasion we had no idea where we were, except that we had reached a very important objective. But just after that we ran into a hell of a lot of fire from Jerries we couldn't see and had to go to ground. After that it was one long ding-dong battle up to Hill 112. ❞

Jimmy Doonan was with the Herefords of 30th Corps:

❝ We were not far behind the Shropshires and crossed the same bridge over the Odon and felt it might not be too bad. I hadn't been with the chaps long as I'd had the flu or something that held me back in England. I'd gone over with some replacements, but when I found the old company and platoon there'd been some losses and changes and I felt almost like a stranger. But when we went on over that river we had to keep hitting the dirt because of the Jerry fire that was almost constant and included those terrible Moaning Minnie rockets that made a terrific screeching sound and went off with a hell of a bang. ❞

Ray Cooke, Sergeant in the Rifle Brigade, with his old friend Jimmy Reynolds, was heavily involved cleaning up German pockets north and west of Cheux:

❝ We saw a lot of dead Germans in brown jackets and also some of our own lads, and they were all very ugly and it gave us quite a fright as we were new to it. We'd been in reserve most of the time and only done one patrol and that was uneventful. Then, after the Epsom business started, we were ordered forward to protect the right flank of the Corps front, and right after seeing those bodies we took a lot of fire from the Jerries and they came at us with tanks and infantry. So we had quite a fight and at one point the Jerries got so close we could see their faces clearly, by which I mean for once we were looking at individuals, young mostly, but grubby and I think as frightened as we were. ❞

Jimmy concurred: 'We captured a couple of them and they looked like overgrown schoolkids beside us and made us feel quite old, even though we were only about twenty! One of these kids asked us in English if he would be able to see London, so I said, 'I suppose so, why?' And he said, 'We believe it is all destroyed!' So we laughed and told him that was rubbish. Actually, we used a different word but he didn't understand that!'

The 9th Cameronians were also among the many different Scots infantry who survived the terrible dash through German fire to the bridge at Gavrus. Reg Tolken was a Lance-Corporal:

❝ We ran down the field like mad after the tanks of the Fife and Forfars and it was hell. We kept passing bodies and wounded lads we couldn't stop for. The noise was terrific from the German shells and all kinds of stuff including rockets. Some of the tanks were hit and went up; one blew up right near me with a great flame that sent hot air rushing past me and almost knocked me down. I didn't stop to look round, although I knew some of the blokes were being hit and were falling. Then I saw the water, but there were bodies everywhere and I felt terrible, quite sick. The bullets kept flying everywhere and it was a while before we rushed over the bridge, and I remember I couldn't recognise any of the chaps there with me. We fell down and then went on across the grass and kept off the little road which we thought must be mined. There were craters and bodies, theirs and ours, and burning tanks and I thought we'd never survive. At last I saw a little gully or ditch and fell into it with only one other bloke with me. Others were lying about wounded and moaning or silent. Not long after that some carriers rushed over with reinforcements and we were relieved. ❞

Some Britons had close encounters with their enemy. Jimmy Dougall of the Royal Scots had had a grand view of the German counter-attack with *panzers* stopped cold by six- and seventeen-pounder anti-tank guns. He had watched one of the latter gun crews nearby –

❝ firing away like mad, and Jerry tanks getting knocked out all over the place. Their infantry kept rushing along in groups and trying to attack us, but we had them all sighted and they were stopped. But they didn't give up and gave us a hell of a pasting with their big mortars and that kept our heads down.

Then the seventeen-pounder was damaged and put out of action, so our Lieutenant told us to withdraw a little, but we kept getting splinters from the trees so we were forced into our foxholes again – just in time, as the Jerries were trying to outflank us in short rushes and were only in sight for a few seconds. They really knew their stuff; you had to be very quick off the mark to catch them. Eventually, some of these beggars were only twenty yards away and that's when things got really nasty. So the Lieutenant suggested – he didn't order us – that we go over with the bayonet. Nobody moved, so he told us to use grenades. It had gone quiet, but we knew some of the Jerries were there as we heard them calling to each other, which was stupid as they gave their positions away. So we started chucking grenades and that finished them completely. Then we left our holes and went over with the bayonet, but all the Jerry kids were dead, except for one and we took him prisoner. His leg had been torn open, so I put a dressing on it and sent him hobbling off to the rear. **99**

6 The Hill of Calvary

After the war, Field Marshal the Viscount Montgomery was one of the first generals to get into print with his account of the Battle of Normandy, which was published in February 1947.* Later, in his *Memoirs*, he expanded this literary field of operations by telling his life story, of boyhood days when, as a not too brilliant and at times troublesome schoolboy, he had startled his parents by opting for a military career. The nature of the second of his books meant that a mere dozen or so pages (of the 575 or so) was devoted to the Normandy campaign.

In this field, inevitably, many other ex-soldiers also felt the need to purge themselves of their experiences in war, from the highest ranks to the lowest, though for various fairly obvious reasons few 'common soldiers' did this. Among the best known works that touched at least on this battle were those of Eisenhower and Bradley; General Patton was killed in a car crash in Germany, so perhaps what might have been the most colourful of the war memoirs never emerged. These leaders of men were of course encouraged, for one thing, by publishers who had most likely been waiting for the end of hostilities and the right moment to corral the biggest names into committing their sins (or glory) to print. In Eisenhower's case he was, soon after the war if not before, being marked down as a possible future president of the USA, and by all accounts was persuaded, if not dragged, into the job. Whatever endearing comments of mutual esteem and loyalty had passed between this American and Montgomery did not prevent sourness and aggravation driving them apart, and it has to be said that it was Monty's own early bash at the literary wicket which perhaps provoked this antipathy.

A similar situation arose *vis-à-vis* Omar Bradley, who, during the actual battle in Normandy, had gone on record agreeing that his then boss Monty had shown him every consideration in overseeing operations, and above all in concurring that in no way could they, as a team, reveal the true nature of Monty's overall strategy. Indeed, Bradley has specifically stated that the 'containment mission' allotted to the British–Canadian forces around Caen was hardly calculated to 'burnish British pride in the accomplishments of their troops'. Bradley commented that in the minds of most people success in battle was measured in terms of mileage gained; the public (and others, even among the higher military, perhaps including Ike) would find it difficult

---

* *Normandy to the Baltic,* Hutchinson & Co, 1947.

to understand that the greater the hornets' nest was stirred up by Monty, the less he would advance. The American General also pointed out that by the end of June, Rommel had concentrated seven *panzer* divisions against the British – 'one was all he could spare for the US front'.

The opprobrium afforded General Montgomery in certain quarters, especially by his sniping enemies at SHAEF HQ, was quite inappropriate from men engaged in the campaign. General Eisenhower would, according to some sources, including Monty, complain petulantly to the British Prime Minister on his field commander's need to 'keep the whole front aflame', as if the hundreds of British and Canadian dead lying about the battlefield signified some kind of truce or inactivity. It was as well the man at the top's comments and ideas remained unknown to the Tommies sacrificing themselves across the Odon.

It is customary and obvious that an attacking army must expect the greater proportion of casualties, while the defenders, in modern war, as often in olden days, fighting from cover, suffer less. In Normandy, the loss rate in proportion to our enemy, at least during the early days, had been running at about 2:1, which was acceptable. The landings had not, as Montgomery had assured many, resulted in a blood bath – at least, not apart from the beach at Omaha. But, as also expected, once the Germans had begun to commit their main *panzer* forces to battle the loss rate had climbed. This, it must be admitted, was in good part due to the tenacity of a military organisation later to be labelled 'criminal', i.e. the SS. It was this collection of mostly young 'criminals' who so decimated the British regiments in Normandy. It is this same force of soldiers who are written up in the press over half a century later with odious comment, as responsible for the ghastly crimes, including atrocities on the battlefield, that resulted in the absurd declaration in 1945 of the SS *as a whole* as being a 'criminal organisation', to be treated accordingly.

It was largely the young soldiers bearing the double lightning flash of the SS who brought about the crippling losses in the Odon valley, before the river Orne, and above all on Hill 112, christened by the Germans *Kalvarienberg* – the Hill of Calvary. One SS trooper quoted Dante: 'Abandon hope all ye who enter here'; historians have written of 'Death Valley'. The enemy claimed the British had suffered 2,000 casualties in the first forty-eight hours of Epsom. Such figures hardly make a 'Somme', even less a 'Verdun'; the first-named battle has been quoted often in recent times as costing the British 60,000 casualties in the first two days of that particular insanity. It cannot be claimed that the flower of British manhood was lost (or wasted) around Hill 112, but it was this struggle south-west of Caen that initiated the start of the break-up of units, the regroupings and, eventually, in July, the incoming flow of some thousands of replacements from the RAF and Royal Navy.

After the war, one ex-SS General said:

❝ That particular battle became known throughout the German forces for its seesaw nature and ferocity. There were very heavy losses on both sides, with whole companies and battalions being wiped out. In some cases, on the German side at least, every single officer was killed and the men fought on, almost without hope of relief, yet never giving in. It must be said the enemy's huge superiority in air power and artillery once again became the deciding factor. A very great deal depended on the outcome of that battle around Caen, for once that city was taken the way became open to the enemy's armoured advance into country far more suitable for such *panzer* operations. It was much more open terrain which lent advantage to the attackers. Once the British enveloped Caen most German commanders realised the Normandy campaign was lost. **❞**

According to Montgomery's own figures, the day before Epsom began (25 June) the Germans were fielding 530 tanks, supported by forty-nine infantry battalions. Five days later, these figures had increased to 725 *panzers* and sixty-four infantry battalions, the tank units approximating the strength of seven and a half *panzer* divisions. Such figures cannot be verified as to exactness; intelligence was at times guesswork and barely approximate. Yet no doubt ever existed then or now that Rommel committed most of his armour to stem Monty around Caen. And the British, in late June 1944, were hammering at what SS General Hausser called the 'back door' to that city. Again, quoting Monty's own figures, 2nd Army casualties by 22 June stood at 10,782, of which 2,006 were dead. A fortnight later they had roughly doubled.

As a great contrast, and bearing in mind the kind of opposition being met by the British around the river Odon, the American operations to capture the port of Cherbourg resulted in 39,000 prisoners, with not one SS soldier among them. This was the German Army's response to Hitler's 'stand and fight' order; as supreme *feldherr*, he was without doubt as disappointed as Churchill had been when 80,000 Allied (mostly British) troops were surrendered at Singapore. The latter event has rightly been called the worst and most humiliating defeat in British military history and propelled morale in Britain to a new low. At Cherbourg the Americans had successfully bombarded their enemy with propaganda via a psychological warfare unit; doubtless the thought of excellent Yankee rations in PoW camp safety led many Germans to give up. Generally speaking, once the Americans got better organised, these PoWs did indeed receive meals on the American pattern, especially of course the many transferred to the US where they lived like kings. Not so those who were captured later on in this battle, at least in one camp where, following the gruesome discovery of death camps such as Belsen, one US commandant introduced a starvation policy for his inmates by way of reprisal.

In launching Epsom, Montgomery knew that whatever the outcome regarding the actual capture of Caen, his main object was virtually certain to be achieved; 'in either event our thrusts would probably provoke increasing enemy resistance, which would fit in well with my plan of campaign'. Bad weather had delayed the Epsom jump-off by at least five days; the 8th Corps was not finally assembled until 25 June. As always with accounts written from the wider, 'big picture' viewpoint, a rather different aspect emerges. The litter of bodies in the Odon valley and on the banks of the river (as well as in it) are covered by passages such as: 'Progress was made during the day in spite of heavy fighting, particularly around Cheux. By the end of the day leading troops were well south of the village with patrols in Grainville and a battalion established in Colleville; elements of 11th Armoured were in Mouen.'

The forces described as 'battalions' and a 'division' were, by accounts given, of lower strength, initially mere tiny pockets, remnants who had by the usual miracles that somehow occur in hot combat survived to fall into comparative and temporary safety. Monty decreed Epsom to be over on 30 June, by which time it is recorded 8th Corps had lost 4,020 men (2,331 from 15th Scottish, 1,256 from 11th Armoured and 43rd Division). To officers and men new to battle the losses had been frightening, and in his excellent book *Overlord – D-Day and the Battle for Normandy 1944* (Michael Joseph), Max Hastings quotes a battalion commander of the 6th King's Own Scottish Borderers who laments, 'We were one big family, I knew every man.' His unit suffered 150 casualties in Epsom, and the Major recalled a briefing given by a psychiatrist before leaving Britain, in which the doctor exhorted officers to allow battle survivors to talk freely of their experiences afterwards. Some would – some that survived the campaign that is – though ex-soldiers do not generally speak extensively to their own immediate families back home. It is not easy to describe harrowing events to civilians; incongruously, therefore, it is the officers who have most told their tales since. Traumas remained, as a result, still present over fifty years on.

Hastings, in his researches, discovered, perhaps to his surprise, that despite all their horrible experiences, the soldiers both at lower and higher level never lost their confidence in Montgomery. Not even when things went horribly wrong, as some allege they did at this time. Hastings alleges that Montgomery wrote 'nonsense' in his post-war accounts of Epsom and other succeeding offensives, that he did himself a disservice by causing controversy and showing a determination to reap personal credit, of distorting history to conform with his own advance planning, and that in doing so he also reaped a whirlwind for what went wrong in Normandy. No sane commander, so Hastings accuses, would have mounted assaults of the kind Monty did in Normandy – which implies that the commanding general of that time was insane. Yet this too is nonsense, for it was not Monty actually running the battle as executive officer on the field of battle. The responsible men in charge were the corps and divisional commanders, and judging by available records from all levels Britain was not especially well served in that direction. The broad concepts of Montgomery were sound, and he was neither by inclination or possibility able to conduct affairs in the field like Rommel. Whatever criticisms are hurled at Monty, and some are justified, they are really directed at what amounts to no more than his personal quirks. He may have been stupid in misjudging personal situations, such as, apparently, ignoring the enormous contribution made by 2nd Tactical Air Force in all his operations, his great lack of 'feel' for these personal relations with fellow officers, something he never lacked when assessing the enemy. One cannot dismiss such failings if they affect the conduct of a war, yet whatever transpired in that direction it made no difference to the outcome in the end.

However, the soldier on the ground, certainly in the earlier Great War, had come to question the sanity of the men at the top, and with every reason. Monty had his own stark experience of war on the ground, and was acutely aware of the bloodbath nature of the fighting in the days of trench warfare, when much seemed to hang on the reputations and vanity of the generals in command. In World War Two, whatever strictures can be levelled at the War Office in London, staff were well aware of the pressing need for greater tank–infantry cooperation, while on the executive combat level General Sir Alan Brooke had, quite early in the war, expressed his opinion of commanders at corps and divisional level in most pungent terms. The only reason he could not boot them out was because there was none fit to replace them. One is left with the impression, after extensive study of the wealth of memoir material, that the average British field officer was a gentleman amateur, playing at war, that the real professionals were on the other side. Was it not Göring who, as a junior officer of the German Army, when describing his spell of exchange duty before World War One with a British regiment, lamented caustically on his hosts' strictures on 'talking shop' in the mess, on their lack of interest in field training (as opposed to the traditional drill and bull), of their only real enthusiasm – for the weekend to arrive when they could change into their blazers and meet their 'popsies'. Such regimental chaps could be very brave on the battlefield, but bravery alone does not win battles. Tactics and management in modern war count for much.

Did the Germans' academy at Potsdam produce the best field officers? Or the various colleges of the *Waffen-SS* in the Reich? Or were such Germans merely the equivalent of their British counterparts, but fighting on the wrong side? Did they take more naturally to war and all its aspects? Certainly, tough Germans turned adventurers had fought in many an army across Europe as mercenaries, including sizeable bands in the armies of both Rome and Britain. Was Sandhurst incapable of producing the right men for the job in Normandy? Similar criticisms had followed the disastrous combats in North Africa; in France 1944 more followed, to be amplified in later memoirs.

In part, the old, tried and trusted system of 'the regiment' lay at fault. This ingrained, 'family' atmosphere made it harder for such battalions to fully integrate into (for them) new forms of warfare where they needed to become really part of a different kind of unit – the tank–infantry striking force spoken of by Montgomery in the latter part of this work. Somehow, despite the years available to them, the War Office never managed (or perhaps tried and failed) to develop such a force. But was this at the heart of the alleged 'failures' in Normandy? For Hastings and others these successive offensives of Monty were expensive flops. One historian points to the immense snarl-up in Cheux as the crux of it all. This small village road at the main axis of advance became a quagmire after heavy rain, so reducing (it is alleged) the British armoured advance to a trickle, something that should never have been allowed to happen.

Then, at general staff level, General Dempsey, dismayed by the performance of two corps commanders, has himself been flayed for his mistaken and premature withdrawal of 11th Armoured from Hill 112, which resulted in its early loss to SS troops after the British infantry had been left unsupported. Was this an example of the 'nervousness' also attributed to the Canadian divisional commander, soon also to come under the hammer? Then, tank troop commanders also lacked dash, assessing risks too great to advance until ordered to by seniors.

The intensity of the fighting in Normandy, mostly due to the terrain, resulted in a troop density very many times higher than on the Russian Front. This produced a constant strain that wore men down, and owing to casualties the normal practice of relieving troops every three or four days did not always apply. One 'casualty' in five was due to battle fatigue. Men broke down, their nervous systems shot, unable to continue. Every man has his limit. Once a man's own stock of courage was used up he became useless and had to be allowed to rest to re-cuperate. Shell-shock cases were different, if genuine, and bad to see, and those who were visibly affected with the gross, uncontrollable, jerking movements were given considerate treatment, as indeed they had been in the earlier war. Those who simply declared they had had enough and were not certifiable by a doctor as useless for combat could be charged, though the severe, unthinking and callous treatment handed out in World War One was not repeated; men were not shot for either cowardice or breaking down in battle.

Men who, in full possession of their faculties, engineered their own removal from the battlefield could be said to have deserted their mates and thereby weakened the section and unit. These were comparatively few. No doubt their chums saw their departure with mixed feelings: good luck to him if he can get away with it, or perhaps 'Running out on us?' For nobody would have stayed if given the choice, British or

German. But duty was duty, allegiance to one's comrades the main thing. A 'Blighty wound' gave one the perfect excuse for leaving; only the very keenest, press-on types would feel regret at being deprived of further combat. Leaving one's best mates was different. Leaving close friends to ensure one's own safety, leaving them in the lurch, was hardly popular. There were weak links among troops, it was inevitable. Officers knew that a certain proportion among ordinary line units would crack and probably run off in terror in the first shock of battle, but most would return later. Problems came with lesser formations, conscripts, unwilling soldiers far removed from the crack airborne, commando and Guard units, and certainly among those units less well trained and disciplined for combat.

On 11 July 1944, No. 3 Casualty Clearing Station received an order that all possible SIW (Self-Inflicted Wound) cases were to be sent to No. 84 BGH (Base General Hospital). Of twenty-one cases investigated by Special Investigation Branch Sergeants at 3 CCS, twelve resulted in men being court-martialled on 13 July, and four men on the 17th. The usual SIW occurred to the hand or foot, but some offenders worked in pairs, shooting each other at a suitable distance to avoid the obvious close-range effect of powder marks. When General Eisenhower visited the US Army hospital at Verviers he found hundreds of men with self-inflicted wounds, and when winter came these actually included frostbite cases and trenchfoot. The incurring of venereal disease became a chargeable offence unless proof of a previous visit to a prophylactic clinic could be proved. One odd case occurred when an officer was found unable to speak – he had swallowed his dentures.

Men deprived of food and drink, unable to sleep, under constant fire and in the grip of fear and uncertainty for days on end will likely break down. At least, the average soldier becomes so debilitated his combat performance suffers. His helplessness to alleviate his conditions increases the frustration so that aggression may be switched to his superiors – if they are still around. Often enough they were not.

It was the job of some intelligence officers on both sides to assess morale and combat readiness of men on both sides. The resulting reports were circulated among the higher ranks who had every interest in following such matters. Naturally, such reports were secret, and no adverse comments were allowed to get near the press and other reporting media. In any case, front reporters, including the BBC radio journalists who regularly sent home recordings, would by their own discretion have omitted anything detrimental to morale, and their reports would have faced censorship in London anyway.

The same battalion Major quoted by Max Hastings related how he could hardly believe his eyes on witnessing a battalion of Tyneside Scottish running away during a German attack on 1 July. His own unit, the King's Own Scottish Borderers, were on the flank. Some divisions were known to be unreliable, not up to some tasks, made up of unseasoned troops, perhaps with weak leadership. Even given a battering, the best soldiers stood firm. One Lieutenant-Colonel arrived with a battalion of the Duke of Wellington's Regiment at the start of Epsom, though the unit was not actually in that offensive but in combat elsewhere. Three days later the officer submitted a damning report on the state of the battalion which he assessed as unfit for battle.

After fourteen days in the line the battalion had lost twenty-three officers and 350 other ranks. The commanding officer and every rank above Corporal at HQ had gone, as had the company commanders. One company had lost all its officers, another had one left (out of three). In the three days of his tenure, the new CO had lost two second-in-commands and one company commander. The battalion had lost most of its transport, all its records and other documents and a lot of equipment. There had been at least five cases of self-inflicted wounds, while every incident involving loss of life brought hysteria or shell-shock cases. Three-quarters of the men had the jumps, with nerves badly affected by shell and mortar fire. Young replacements caved in simply through the noise of their own nearby artillery in action; this kind of behaviour tended to infect others. A 'large number' of men kept leaving their positions for one pretext or another, until sent back by the MO or battalion commander. Yet the men as a whole seemed cheerful enough – until combat began. Unhelpful was the fact that half the battalion were replacements who had not had time to get to know their NCOs and officers, partly because these leaders had been forced to remove all rank insignia through the enemy habit of picking them off as preferred targets. It worked both ways: officers did not know these men and time was needed to rebuild confidence and trust, but daily casualties prevented this. Discipline in the unit was bad; what *esprit de corps* had existed earlier had vanished.

There is no doubt this battalion had suffered, but it was a similar story with every front unit in Normandy, including the Americans, who suffered even greater casualties. One can imagine the state of mind of the new CO as he saw his unit cracking up into a collection of demoralised individuals. Even officers of the rank of Major had fled for safety when mortars fell, to be ordered back by their commander – only to be killed. In one incident the Lieutenant-Colonel had been forced to draw his pistol to drive back troops running away. This commander stated candidly in his report that he realised that as a regular soldier he was jeopardising his career by reporting his findings, and requested that the unit be pulled out of combat. Certainly it did his prospects no good at all. Commanders were expected to be ruthless in pulling units together that were falling apart. When Montgomery read the report he is alleged to have reacted furiously, passing comment to the Secretary of State for War, James Grigg in London, that the Lieutenant-Colonel was not a 'proper chap', that the battalion must be disbanded at once – which it was.

The very idea that British soldiers could flee before a German attack would have surprised and shocked people at home, but then, as in the earlier war, no such reports could ever reach them. Not that the above story was typical of British line units. Soldiers became used to the steady turnover in faces, though it was seldom that units cut down in size through casualties ever got back to full establishment strength. The question of actual numbers will be looked at, since rarely do historians give a full picture of this aspect.

Naturally, the doubling and even trebling of Allied casualties over the Germans' does not preclude reports in all quarters of the enemy's own heavy losses, for no matter how good they were at concealment, the air strikes and artillery sought them out. One British prisoner among his enemies suffered one air raid from his own side and was moved to wonder how the British troops would have reacted to such treatment. The SS soldiers in particular, despite having such an enormous weight of metal and more thrown at them, seemed able to absorb such constant punishment, the survivors carrying on to inflict the heaviest casualties on the attackers. Even the completely green young troops of the *Waffen-SS* seemed capable of astonishing performances which, judging by accounts, can only be attributed to that special brand of *esprit de corps* inculcated by their leaders in training that always seemed to give them a distinct edge over their army counterparts. There is no doubt they were superior to the average Tommy or GI in field combat, but in some respects they were inferior to the very best British soldiers – the airborne and commando troops whose toughening-up courses were the hardest to surmount. But in one all-important respect the comparison comes out equal, for such troops believed above all in themselves and their élite status. They had been told this, it was driven into them, and they behaved accordingly to preserve their reputation, to uphold their unit's honour. In such top formations the bond of comradeship was great.

It is not stretching the truth, perhaps, to look on British failures in this and other battles as reflective of the national character, while on the other hand the absurd propaganda concerning the 'Huns' or 'Boche', the goose-stepping 'Nazi' automatons who rushed *en masse* into battle like unfeeling, unthinking clods or peasants rebounded. For in the main the enemy proved to have much the same human feelings and characteristics as the Tommy. It was Churchill who wrote early on of the 'dull mass of German infantry', thickheads without imagination and above all without initiative. The reverse was generally the truth, as many Allied soldiers discovered. One cannot entirely overlook the kind of regime imposed on the German people by Hitler and his Nazis, a system designed to achieve total control over a population, this exercised through some 80,000 policemen and very many more in paramilitary units and, of course, the hidden army of informers working through the *Gestapo* and SD. Yet a nation that had produced such a bevy of great composers, scientists, philosophers and more was not to be crushed in spirit by the likes of a passing dictator; the Germans retained their human dignity and qualities that had made them a major force in Europe. Not that our wartime Prime Minister would give voice to such sentiments in those days, though moments came when his customary eloquence gave vent to what he knew to be the truth in such matters. Churchill's greater love seemed, however, at times to be for words rather than truth, despite all his great qualities.

It was, and still is, amazingly after all these decades, the 'Nazi' soldiers the British were fighting during the war. Every single man in uniform on the other side was a 'Nazi', which was fine propaganda, though never the truth. But then truth, using the well-known adage, is the first casualty in war. So why, one might ask, do we still hear through our media of 'Nazi soldiers' inflicting this or that crime somewhere around Europe? Generally speaking, a soldier was a soldier on the battlefield, whatever his nationality. Witness this letter from a German soldier called Heinrich in Normandy early in July 1944:

❝ Dear Helga,

I am well and keeping myself as safe as I can in the circumstances. Things may not be exactly as I would wish them, but like my comrades I try to make the best of it. We have had some marvellous weather lately, though the sun has been a little too hot for me, and as you know I have a sensitive skin. A few days ago when we went away for a short rest I found a pool and had such a marvellous bathe; it refreshed me wonderfully, and to sit on the grass later and let the sun dry me felt wonderful. I only wish I could do this more often.

I hope you and the children are well. I want Marie to do well at school. She is a darling and I so long to see them both. How is Berti getting along with his maths? I know he was a little weak in that subject at school.

I am shortly going to send you a little present, something unusual from the front. I hope it will serve to remind you all of your Heinrich. Until I see you again my dearest wife, I love you – ever.

Your ever loving Heinrich. **❞**

Then there is this letter and appeal from a Lieutenant to his parents at home in battered Berlin:

❝ My Dearly Beloved Parents,

Here in France all goes well with me. I am at this moment away from all the noise and enjoying a quiet rest in a little hospital as I have hurt my foot in a small accident quite unconnected with the fighting. I will not talk about it as it is so trivial, but it required proper treatment and that meant going to hospital.

Well, how are you? I hope not doing too badly, what with the air raids etc. My heart goes out to you at this time and I do so wish I could be there to do something to help. I know you have Aunt Matthilda to be of use but she is no longer young and I am sure in need of help herself.

The doctor has just seen me and says I am progressing very well and will be allowed to leave soon. In which case I will soon be back with my good comrades, and glad of that.

If you can send me any books, especially detective stories, I will be in heaven. There is a great deal of trouble involved in getting reading matter here and I have read my meagre stock over and over.

Until I see you soon (I hope), I send you my dearest love and best wishes always.

Your loving son, Peter. **"**

Apart from one or two aspects, the letters could easily have been written by British soldiers to their loved ones at home. However, there is no doubt that even in close relations the traditional British reserve played its part; it may have come as a surprise to most Britons to learn, then if not later, that their enemy the Germans carried a strong streak of sentiment in them and in the right circumstances were quite capable of expressing it.

As to the Germans' own intelligence assessment of the British, one report which fell into our hands spoke of the Tommy's best quality as his physical endurance; the enemy did not think highly of his attacking quality or his initiative, the lack of this noticeable in the NCOs who too often did not seem to be in the 'wider picture' like their officers. When setbacks came the British soldier was incapable of acting on his own; all in all he was inferior material to his opposite number, the German *landser*. Unlike Churchill's assessment, the German soldier was taught to be self-sufficient, especially in crises, when officers and NCOs were lacking; at least, that is the indication. He was taught to act with speed, whether in attack or in reacting in defence to a changing situation. The latter is evident from German moves in various episodes, such as at Arnhem, or before when the Allied armies drove back the remnants of the German Army and *Waffen SS* to their own homeland. The ability to take swift measures in crisis astounded the Allies.

An ex-SS general has made the following comments on the British forces:

" Although I never personally fought against them, I learned much of their military capabilities from my own military upbringing and contact with other officers and men. This convinced me they were a very tough adversary who, unlike the Russians, never used manpower wastefully, or squandered troops in so-called 'human wave' tactics. Undoubtedly, there were shortcomings due to various factors which were, I must say, also present in the German Army. For example, the use of horses was widespread in our army, even in 1944, whereas the level of motorisation in the British Army was remarkable. I also saw to my own cost the hugely successful use of air and artillery power such as we never achieved on any battlefield. As to the personal qualities of the soldiers themselves I never doubted their bravery at all, only their lack of the right training. 99

These are fair comments, but those earlier on British Army NCOs are not; such men were and still are regarded as the backbone of the army, and in most forces. Among the most audacious and remarkable (and largely unsung) escape stories of World War Two are those of British Army sergeants.

The Battle of Normandy became the army's great testing ground. As to the actual physical condition and stature of British soldiers at the time, in terms of fitness they were better off than ever before, thanks in part to the equalising factors of wartime rationing before call-up. Overall, the men in Britain were reasonably fed, and became fit for battle through the many bouts of PT and other exercising carried out over the pre-invasion weeks, months or years. The question of stature is far more complex, and to delve into it thoroughly is beyond the scope of this work. One tank soldier whose comments went into print later remarked with some awe on the superb physical specimens he saw among German bodies on the battlefield, comparing them unfavourably with the comparatively motley collection of Tommies passing by. One may argue that 'big 'uns' last a lot longer in tough conditions than 'little 'uns', but fighting ability and spirit do not depend on size.

Hitler's Nazified Germany, by its very nature and aims, set out to produce a nation of super-fit soldiers. By and large they succeeded; the Nazis loved to show off their Apollos and Amazons, bronzed and naked but for the scantiest of coverings – females included. They were the products of a regime heading for war on a grand scale, and looked it. By contrast, the state organisations which ensured such physical well-being were entirely absent in Britain where passing fads such as hiking and cycling received a good amount of publicity during the inter-war years. Joining the Boy Scouts or Territorial Army did little to improve the national health and stature. However, there had been great improvements in this direction since the Victorian era when terrible housing and malnutrition – near starvation in some cases – were rife. It is a fact that Hitler, in forcing Europe into war, actually improved the lot of the working classes (as they were known) in Britain; the British *hausfraus*, for instance, were able to ensure their fair share of rations, more balanced meals at reasonable cost. A great levelling out of eating habits made for a greater standard of health among the eligible fighting men. The army took care of them once in uniform; even though some camp cookhouses proved deficient, there were always canteens to top up in.

The British Army landed in France in 1944 was the largest, best equipped, and fittest ever. It has been the practice since, and particularly in 'D-day anniversary' publications as well as many memoirs and searching records by historians, to quote large figures denoting the great number of Allied troops landed after 6 June 1944 but seldom does the reader obtain the scantiest picture of what these grand figures meant in terms of actual fighting men at the front.

A British division was one of the largest, if not the largest, among the warring nations – some 18,500 men for the infantry formations in 1944 establishment. But just how many of these 18,500 comprised combat soldiers? One section was ten men; a platoon comprised three sections, and a company four platoons (120 men); there were four companies in a battalion (480 men), three battalions in a brigade (1,440 men) and three brigades in a division (4,320 men). Add, say, three machine-gun battalions totalling 900 men, and you are left with 5,220 fighting men. That leaves 13,280 soldiers out of the fighting formations, which on the face of it seems an absurd proportion. In fact, this number needs further clarification. For added to the combat units were other 'front personnel' such as headquarters troops and drivers manning Bren carriers and other essential transport, those responsible for the dangerous job of delivering ammunition to the men in the foxholes etc. and not to be confused with drivers (DMT = Driver, Motor Transport) who manned the supply routes in the rear.

As a rough guide, therefore, the number of fighting men in a British infantry division in Normandy in 1944 should have been around 8,000 – which still leaves 10,500 men in a non-combat role. This body is known as the 'tail' of a formation, its essential support services comprising cooks, medics, dentists, bath houses, clerks, everyone considered part of the modern division at war. Naturally, this 'other' great organisation had grown in size and importance since the early Victorian era when only the most primitive (by later standards) troop care was practised. The scale and standard of medical services in the Crimean War, for example, was scandalous; enormous improvements had taken place since those dark days. But, as society itself in Britain progressed in material welfare, the men in the forces expected more.

The strength figures for an infantry division given here are, however, something of a 'golden mien', and seldom in reality achieved, and for various fairly obvious reasons. For a start, men went sick; more importantly, when battle was joined the casualties began to flow back to the CCS (Casualty Clearing Stations), and the daily wastage could reach prodigious proportions. Old hands have described how in fact their 'sections' would all too often be down to less than half a dozen men. This was inevitable, and it was the same for the enemy. Sepp Dietrich reported by 20 June that company strengths in *Panzer* Lehr, 21st *Panzer* and 12th SS were only twenty-five to thirty-five men, and by the end of that month the numbers had been further reduced to nineteen in Lehr, even though that division had received 1,800 reinforcements since D-day. By the end of the British assault in Epsom, *Panzer* Lehr had virtually ceased to exist as an effective combat division.

It can be seen, then, that when official and other historical records tell of a regiment achieving this or that in combat, it was (for a start, for the British at least) most likely the remains of a battalion, because of the new practice of splitting up regiments between corps to try to avoid the horrendous regimental losses which had occurred in World War One. In that war whole streets and districts in British cities, towns and villages mourned the loss of great numbers of young men who had been lured into volunteering *en masse*, all too often ending up in the same regiment. These calamities were aided by the 'pals' system, whereby young men were encouraged to persuade their chums to go with them to the local recruiting office where jovial Sergeant-Majors ushered them through the formalities, and in no time the cannon fodder found themselves enrolled in what were to go down in military history as the 'pals battalions'. They have been well recorded in recent years in several volumes. The annihilation of such units in France during the Great War robbed communities of their menfolk. No such calamity would befall Britain again – or so the War Office decreed. So, county regiments were split by battalions between the British corps in Normandy, and though the losses incurred in the hard slog through that summer were considerable, they did not match the horrific and senseless bloodbath of the earlier war, and in the context of the new system casualties were spread fairly evenly throughout Britain.

When comparing the British infantry division with its German counterpart, as regards numbers, it is fairly useless to use those of the German Army itself as a yardstick, for by 1944, as indicated earlier, these divisions had been considerably reduced in troop strength. The only point worth bearing in mind is the scale of support services, which was certainly far smaller in the German units. We are left therefore with the divisions most in action against the 2nd Army, those who created the most formidable obstacle: the *Waffen-SS* units. This seems especially applicable in view of the fact that these divisions were always maintained up to a great level of combat readiness – until they entered battle, of course. So it is appropriate to assume an almost exact equivalent in establishment strength between the British and SS infantry divisions, the German unit breaking down as follows.

The actual 'tail' of administration, inclusively, would be only about 5,000 men, which leaves 13,500 fighting troops, as against the British 8,000. This figure would have been very chastening to the British in Normandy, had they known it. However, bad as the comparison seems, there were, even with the SS, attenuating factors. Again, drivers and other personnel are included in the *kampfbereitschaften* – the combat units – and not only those men. There were others such as company runners, medics and various troops, such as signals and clerks. The difference lies in the level of training, for not one of these 'extra bods' was in the least untrained; he was a complete, all-round combat soldier every bit as capable of taking his place in the fighting line as the regular 'full-time' infantryman. Which means that, generally speaking, the

Above: Wounded shelter by a disabled Petard tank and (*Left*) death and debris before a German blockhouse.

Below: The first German prisoners.

Right: Loading the deadly 88mm dual-purpose gun.

Below: A 'Moaning Minnie' multiple rocket mortar with crew.

Bottom: A 5.5-inch gun of the Royal Artillery. Note photographer at bottom right.

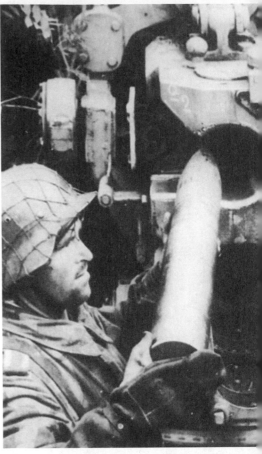

Above: 'Order group' for 2nd Co. 101 Heavy Tank Battalion.

Left: Young SS troops watch passing Allied air power.

Below: Major Prinz (9th SS) maps an attack near Caen.

Above: Shermans on the start line for Operation Goodwood.

Right: Lightly armoured recce cars were often at the point of an advance.

Below: A Sherman Firefly of 3rd Royal Tanks crossing the Caen-Vimont railway.

Above: A welcome break between battles, Sherman tankers write home while comrades sleep.

Left: The 27-ton Cromwell mounted a 75mm cannon: speed and manoeuvrability gave it some advantage.

Below: Sherman crews of 13/18th Hussars do their chores before the next attack.

Above: Near the
Odon on 28 June
1944 – a Tommy in
cover near dead
German and
knocked out Tiger.

Right: A 6-pounder
anti-tank gun of 3rd
Division.

Below: A wounded
Canadian is tended
while others keep
watch.

Above: An ammo truck explodes after being struck by German fire.

Left: A Spitfire IX downed beside the road of advance.

Below: Spectacular results follow air attack on German ammunition supply.

Above: Rest and watch, men of the Wessex Regiment.

Top Right: Troops of the Duke of Cornwall's Light Infantry digging in.

Centre Right: A patrol of the 5/7th Gordon Highlanders move warily through the Bois de B'Avent.

Right: Scottish soldiers watch a Sherman Firefly with 76.2mm (17-pounder) gun.

greater number given of SS combat personnel is correct, and the difference lies in practice, for obviously a number would not normally be in the line at all, only taking up arms in an emergency. Even so, and this assumption has been confirmed by an SS combat veteran, the proportion still weighed heavily in the Germans' favour.

But, as an enormous counterweight which swung the balance against the enemy was the Royal Artillery and RAF, sometimes aided by the USAAF. It would not be profitable to speculate on the 'if' factor – i.e. what might have been the outcome if the Germans had been aided by an artillery arm of like calibre and a *Luftwaffe* still capable of effective riposte. By D-day the British artillery regiments were so well attuned to the tasks in hand that their part in battle became greater than ever before. In World War One massed artillery were used to batter the German lines not just for an hour or two, but for days on end. Once the great 'shell shortage' scandal was overcome by Lloyd George, the artillery in France were able to, and did, expend vast quantities of ammunition, much of which acted as a giant, constant rotavator of French soil on and about the German trench systems, which were expertly constructed but seldom able to withstand such sustained, heavyweight bombardment indefinitely. That was the main role of the British artillery in that war.

In World War Two things were different. By 1942 the field regiments of the RA had begun to master the art of intervention in battle to such a degree that when D-day came they played a far greater and often quite decisive role in every heavy engagement. Every single German counterattack of any size was either at the very least considerably hampered by shellfire, or broken up completely before it could get underway. Even those attacks that were launched received such treatment by the artillery that their effect was so nullified that the infantry in their foxholes were that much more easily able to repel the enemy. The term 'Queen of the Battlefield', if such a phrase is appropriate in such a destructive context, most certainly applies to the Royal Artillery in Normandy.

And, as shown, the comparatively new art of anti-tank gunnery reached its zenith in 1944, at least so far as pure gunfire is concerned, though already being supplemented by bazooka weapons which ultimately meant that longer-range, wire- or radio-guided and hand-held rocket weapons superseded even the devastating hollow-charge shells coming into use in 1944. But, as things stood, the somewhat inferior Piat (Projectile Infantry Anti-Tank) was the standard close-range British infantry weapon for use against German armour, the battalion six-pounder AT guns of 57mm of limited use. The seventeen-pounder (87mm) AT tank was the best, and some figures regarding its capabilities are worth looking at. The penetrating powers of its shells were: 149mm of armour at 100 yards; 140mm of armour at 500 yards; 130mm of armour at 1,000 yards; in other words, up to five and three-quarter inches of solid metal.

The power of the seventeen-pounder (that was its shell weight) was greatly increased by the introduction of the new 'discarding Sabot' ammunition in August 1944. But the problem with such weapons was that they were towed and difficult to get into action in some terrain, especially the narrow lanes of Normandy. Against well 'announced' German armoured counter-attacks the weapon was supreme, its missiles capable of piercing even the 110mm frontal armour plate of the Tiger.

Whether the long, proud traditions of the British county regiments were eroded by their being divided up is arguable; what is significant is their lack of integration with armoured forces.

*   *   *   *

We last saw the unlucky troops of the Highland Light Infantry ambushed by deadly German machine-gun fire that swathed through the corn and their own ranks as they moved towards Mouen. The Scotsmen had been tormented and cut down by an enemy they never saw, ever since entering the battle. Now, at last, a fresh company rushed in to make a ferocious attack, catching the SS men in their hideholes at last. Ron Arkwright of B Company, HLI, recalled:

❝ We had heard all about the terrible ambush to our blokes and felt sick. At first we wanted to get away from the whole area, which seemed to have been so bad for us. Then a Captain came with a Lieutenant – we were sitting about on the grass just outside Cheux. They told us we could now get at the buggers and take care of them – the SS. They were the exact words used. So we perked up a bit and got ready, and soon after that two Sergeants led us off carrying Stens and grenades and soon we went into the fields. There was some corn and a few bushes and then we heard shouts and bangs and we dashed forward firing like mad and yelling our heads off. It was fantastic but terrible, as we saw all these bodies of our own chaps and then Jerries in brown jackets, some dead, some wounded, some firing or trying to get away. We showed no mercy at all; we fired in all directions and just wiped out the lot. We were so worked up into a rage and that was that.

When we got through their positions there was nothing to see and we soon came under a bit of fire from elsewhere, so we dug ourselves in for a while. I felt completely worn out and all in a sweat, and I kept seeing all those poor Jocks lying there dead and I felt sick and cried. ❞

Alan Crichman was a Cameronian Corporal and experienced the battle for the Odon:

❝ We rushed down the field after some Shermans. Some were hit and went up with a bang, but we rushed on and I heard the boots thudding and men falling and sometimes tripping up in the mad rush to reach some sort of cover. There wasn't any really, apart from bits of bushes and bodies, and there were plenty of those.

I was amazed when I suddenly saw the little bridge. I think the place was called Gavrus. The river was so small and the banks high and there were bodies everywhere. I stared at all this for some seconds, oblivious of all the fire coming down on us and the racket going on as the Shermans went on, those that could. And when I fell down the grassy bank I found I was lying among the dead and some of them were just as if still alive but for their staring eyes. I'd never seen anything like all that before and it made me feel very bad yet strange and fascinated. It was odd, but there wasn't much blood on those chaps. It was as if they'd suddenly been frozen in the middle of doing something unusual. They were really like dummies.

I came to as another bloke fell on me to get some cover, and he laughed when he saw the look on my face. Then a Sergeant yelled at us over the bridge, 'What the fuckin' 'ell d'ye think you're playin' at? This ain't no picnic! Get up off your arses and get up here ye buggers!' He spoke broad Scots, much more than I did. So very reluctantly we pulled ourselves up and with heads down ran over the bridge after the tanks. The Sergeant said we had to reach the next river which was the Orne and some way off. But we never got there. The Jerry stuff was coming down on us and we fell into one of the many craters and just lay there panting and not caring. The Sergeant had vanished and we never saw him again. It was some time before a few more blokes reached us from some other mob, and a long while before an officer came and told us to get back and dig in by the Odon, which we did. And later on still, I can't really remember, the Jerries counter-attacked and we fell back over the river. **99**

Tom Reynolds was an eighteen-year-old infantry Private with the Argyll and Sutherland Highlanders:

66 After we'd left Cheux, which was a hell of a mess and packed with transport and guns, I saw a lot of bodies and tanks all over the slope down to the Odon. There were a lot more blokes going down to the river and the whole area was under fire, so this made it hard for the medics to get down there and try to help the wounded. I must say their bravery was quite fantastic as none of them carried weapons, but they never hesitated to go in and do everything they could.

We had carriers, but they filled up, so I trotted down the hill with other bods and found we were getting in fire from the Jerries, but I don't think it was so bad as before. I know while we were waiting in Cheux it was coming down thick and fast, including those terrible mortars. When we looked down towards the river we could see all these khaki heaps and knew we were going into the worst place and wondered if we'd see the day out. We were reinforcements and knew there were some blokes across the river with tanks trying to dig in. It was a shallow, very green valley with the little river in the middle. The bridge was quite narrow and made of stone and covered in chips and holes from the fire, and I wondered why the Jerries hadn't blown it.

I was surprised that so many of us made it to that bridge and we rushed across after our carriers which went racing on up the next slope. One or two got hit, and in all the noise I heard blokes yelling; some were hit and there was a lot of smoke rolling about from burning tanks. You could smell things, bad smells, and some of that I reckon now must have been from the remains inside those flaming tanks, which were coffins and I would never have gone in one. I didn't see a single surviving tank man on those slopes, but some must have got away. There were plenty of craters there from our shelling so cover was no problem. I fell into one with two more blokes and waited for orders. After a bit a Lieutenant ran up with a bandaged arm and told us to run back to consolidate the bridge. I couldn't understand why as we seemed OK where we were. He ran off to some other blokes so we took a chance and dashed back like mad under fire to the river bank and tried to hide there among the bodies as a hell of a lot more Jerry stuff started to come down on us.

We then heard tanks and some really big bangs and the same Lieutenant ran back down to tell us to follow him. So we did, still not knowing why. And a lot more blokes ran after us with shells hitting all round, and not all made it. We were forced into cover again on the other side of the bridge and that was that. I thought, What a bloody waste, after all that effort and death. The Jerries used mortars and tanks and we stood no chance of getting back that day. But next day, after a rotten night, we went back over that bridge with tanks and this time we stayed. **99**

Gordon Smith of the Seaforth Highlanders:

66 When we went into Cheux it was one big terrible traffic jam, with MPs trying to sort it out. We had sun and rain and sun again, but there was water everywhere and it was worse by far than a city jam-up back home. We were hanging about for some time, trying to keep out of the way and waiting for orders, and there was stuff coming over. My mate Tommy said, 'Christ Gordie, if the bloody *Luftwaffe* caught us now we'd be in the shit wouldn't we, eh?' Well, there were so many of our planes about all the time that wasn't likely, but you never could tell.

At last the Sergeant-Major told us to get on down the hill in single file and then into open order and not hang about – that's what he said, not to hang about. That was his way of saying get a bloody move on or get shot. So once we got onto that slope we did just that. We split up all over the place as there was stuff coming down on us all the time. I ran as if I was in a rain shower; I had my head down and tried not to look up as I started to see all the bodies after a bit and the knocked-out tanks and I thought, 'Oh God, this is the worst part. And I called over to my mate Tommy, 'Get your bloody head down!' He was just trotting along with a sort of grin on his face as if he didn't care. Well, I ran on like mad as I thought once we get out of that valley, at least across the bridge, we'll find some cover. You see, there were all these shell craters over the other side, and plenty of knocked-out tanks to hide behind. On the slope going down there was little or no cover in the grass, just the occasional bodies and carriers and maybe a small bush – nothing really.

Well, when I next glanced round I couldn't see my mate at all, so I went down on my knees and took a proper look back, and there he was. He was lying down but looking at me and waving. And another Sergeant ran by and told me to get on so I did, but I glanced back and saw Tommy lying down and I knew he was dead. I cried as I ran on and over the bridge, and I saw the Sergeant waving the men across and he saw me but said nothing.

It was hours later before I managed to find out back in Cheux that he really was dead. I'd known him for years. **"**

Troops of the Rifle Brigade actually forded the Odon where its banks were shallower, at the more northerly end of the Epsom assault, riding on Shermans, taking the enemy by surprise and actually penetrating across the Orne and onto the westerly slope of the objective – Hill 112. Frank Bilson was a Lieutenant at the time:

" We raced across the fields from the Odon in great fashion and reached the river Orne, which was wider, and we had no idea how deep and didn't feel inclined to try it. We could not see a bridge, so one of the tank lieutenants called out that he would give it a try. There was not a shot coming at us, but plenty elsewhere. I lay on the grass of the river bank and watched the Sherman go down into the water, and it sank up to the turret and I thought, My God, the poor devils will drown! But they didn't. So they reversed their tank and we jumped on board and a few minutes later we were across and that was that. I think about six more Shermans managed it with men like that, and I learned not long afterwards that a bridge had been taken further along and more of our stuff was crossing there.

There was a broad, green slope before us, not much different from the valley tops back round the Odon, but I suppose higher – that's what made it so important. We went on up the slope and as we neared the top everyone felt elated and we wondered if we could race down the other side to Evrecy, which was the next objective. But when we crested the rise near some trees we suddenly saw Jerry tanks with infantry coming up so we halted. The lads jumped down and ran off into cover and the battle started. I then realised we were rather thin on the ground. I believe there were more of our tanks further to the north of us, those that had got over the bridge, but we became rather preoccupied and were shooting at the Jerries. Well, it didn't seem too long before a Captain ran up and jumped on one of the tanks and had a confab or something and then waved me over to him and in the racket told me to get my men back off the hill. I was flabbergasted and had no idea what was going on. It all seemed very stupid as we'd reached the main objective and were sitting pretty. So I swore like hell and called the lads to follow me as the tanks started to reverse back down the hill without waiting for us. We consolidated back near the Orne. **99**

Meanwhile, as Rommel and von Rundstedt conferred with Hitler, they may have been surprised by the frankness with which their *Führer* assessed the situation. Hitler has often been accused of living in a fantasy world insofar as his demands and ideas seemed to be so much at variance with reality on the battle fronts. It must have been obvious to him by then that after only a week or two's bombardment that the much-vaunted V1 robot bomb was having little or no effect at all on the Allies' conduct of the war. At Berchtesgaden he said: 'The overpowering aerial superiority of the enemy and his very effective naval artillery limit the possibilities of large-scale attack on our part . . . We must not allow mobile warfare to develop, since the enemy surpasses us by far in mobility.' Everything, Hitler said, depended on confining the Allies to the bridgehead, by constructing a front to block it off, then fighting a war of attrition to weaken him prior to forcing him back.

That the *Führer* could now acknowledge the supremacies mentioned, especially in the business of mobile warfare, seemed remarkable. And he was certainly speaking the truth: British battleships were using their fifteen- and sixteen-inch guns to range far beyond Caen, while the skies over the battle front hummed incessantly with aircraft of the 2nd Tactical Air Force. As for the previous German *panzer* supremacy in fast-moving warfare, lack of fuel and other factors so hampered their movements that their tank crews spent most of their hours hidden in static roles. Then, too, the grand, massive offensive by the SS and army *panzer* divisions had been frustrated. While the British 2nd Army continued to enlarge its corridor towards Hill 112 the enemy made successive attempts to blunt it and cut it in two – none succeeded beyond local level. Nevertheless, Hitler refused to allow any elasticity in defence, refused to allow a general withdrawal, and his two Field Marshals returned to France in a huff. For Rommel his end-days had almost come, as they had for his senior, though in a different way. Rommel became more convinced that the only answer to save the army from destruction was the removal of Hitler.

Yet in those crucial days, and despite all the reports of continuing Allied success back home in the media, the conduct of the battle was less than satisfactory. Montgomery had shown constraint and amazing patience with his American colleagues, whose offensive at St Lo failed, for there, despite the scarcity of *panzers* against them, the GIs were beaten back time and time again by stubborn resistance from the German Army and the newly arrived SS of *Das Reich.* The prize taken by the British at such cost over the Odon and Orne was given up, virtu-ally without a struggle. Critics, perhaps with the benefit of post-war hindsight, and invariably not having been on the spot, point to repeated lack of boldness, of timidity on the part of the British, principally of the armoured column commanders who overall seemed to lack the dash and flair of their enemy counterparts. The doyen of military commentators, Captain Basil Liddell-Hart, told of repeated checks and withdrawals by British forces when faced with small pockets of more determined Germans, that if it had not been for our great air superiority and of course superb artillerymen, who were usually scientists of perfection at the job, things would have been far, far worse. Too little initiative and determination, with exceptions. Great chances won after a hard fight were too often wasted, sometimes after comparatively light casualties.

Max Hastings refers to Montgomery's 'massive conceit' in masking the fact that his generalship was frustrated by the lesser abilities of those under him, principally the corps commanders. However, the order to abandon Hill 112 came from the commander of the 2nd Army, General Miles Dempsey, who had this comment to make later: 'It seemed obvious to me at the time that my left flank was much too exposed and ripe for a heavy blow from the enemy. That this never materialised is a fact, and, unfortunately, by the time 11th Armoured went in again it was too late. The enemy had fortified the hilltop with remarkable speed and a very terrible battle ensued.'

As Monty pointed out later, it had been impossible to retrain his new command, either British or American. The 2nd Army went into Normandy still imbued, even unconsciously, with outdated notions, ideas of battle tactics based on the 'set piece' attack, the kind of thinking that in reality gave their highly skilled, professional foe an extra advantage. The British command was, to some extent, and perhaps again more unconsciously, traumatised by the bloodbath of the Great War, the need to conserve lives. It was this that brought about such enormous use of explosive, the use of shells and bombs, rather than men, the saturation of the enemy by air power and artillery that went on and on. The infantrymen became more and more cautious, refusing to take risks after five years of war and folk including politicians back home talking of the kind of post-war Britain they wanted. Naturally enough the lads in the fighting wanted to be part of it and trod more warily, especially perhaps those ex-desert veterans like the 'Rats' of the tanks and Scots 51st Division who felt maybe they had more than done their share while many thousands of troops in Britain had been enjoying the good life for years.

For the Germans, attitudes had hardened, for following the misjudged Allied dictum of 'unconditional surrender' and other comments which played right into Dr Göbbels' hands, the soldiers of Hitler believed their homeland would be despoiled utterly by war and its break-up into zones of occupation. They fought more desperately as a result – 'The peace will be worse!' As one German ex-SS officer put it later: 'We really felt that with the terrible Bolshevik enemy breathing down our necks from the East we would see our homeland utterly devastated. I had seen what had happened in Russia and guessed how the Soviets felt about the "fascist beasts" and they really meant business. And since the Allies seemed also to have nothing but revenge in mind we saw no alternative to fighting the harder.'

The same officer also commented on Allied tactics and British generalship in particular: 'I felt when we were in the field that in a fair fight with all things equal we would always win, not because of superior bravery but through better methods which I assure you were always – ALWAYS – designed to preserve lives, or at least to win a battle with fewer casualties. We were as aware of the terrible blood-letting of the earlier war as yourselves.'

In his more fulsome *Memoirs* Montgomery states that by early July no fewer than eight *panzer* divisions had been identified on the twenty-mile front of the British–Canadian 2nd Army between Caumont and Caen. Ultra told him of the greater build-up of these divisions as the full strength of 9th and 10th SS arrived to try to seal off or cut up the Scottish corridor at the Odon. And, perhaps to the greater surprise of the Germans on the ground, the *Luftwaffe* began to make a greatly increased showing, swarms of fighters trying to intervene in the skies over the battle zone, these sorties of around 300 planes supplementing the small-scale efforts of their bombers over the bridgehead by night. None of these efforts had any appreciable effect, as Rommel complained.

The Germans' 'pegging' of their armour in a largely defensive role signified their failure and all hope of driving the Allies out of France. Added to the remains of 276th Infantry, driven back from the beaches, was the 16th *Luftwaffe* Field Division, both identified near Tilly and of little value. Whatever problems the Allies had suffered owing to the weather and other factors, these were not permanent and hardly matched those of their enemy whose 7th Army was now virtually sealed off in the boiling cauldron of Normandy by the destruction of the bridges over the rivers Loire and Seine. Knowing this as he gazed at his situation map, Monty saw that the battlefield layout now favoured his planned breakout, principally the start of the American drive south, which the General 'suggested' his subordinate General Bradley press energetically, this punch to then swing east, the start of the left hook that would threaten to trap the German Army completely. Monty emphasised the need for speed on the Americans' part, his hope that this operation, together with that planned for his own 1st Corps attack in the north, would get things moving. But the Americans had trouble in their preliminary operations to gain a suitable start line, principally because of marshy ground; this and the nature of the hard fighting on the British front would delay the actual breakout until 25 July.

Although the Americans had sufficient weight of attack, including the huge advantage of air dominance, the stubborn defence by German paras, army infantry and elements of 2nd SS made them pay a heavy price for every hundred yards gained in country ideally suited to defence. Despite all their problems with transport, the German troops did not seem in the least short of ammunition. The Americans' frustration and growing anxiety about casualties, plus slowly growing pressure from above (including the politicians at home), prompted commanders to take swift action in sacking field officers who had apparently failed. That the US Army was not very well served at first in this direction is a fact, but they learned the realities the hard way in Normandy which had proved very different to training back in America. Furthermore, once fired, commanders usually found to their dismay that there were no suitable replacements; there was no pool of experienced combat officers to draw on, apart from those fighting with the 5th Army in Italy.

The Americans' difficulty over infantry requirements, so soon after the invasion started, was echoed by the British: the Adjutant-General called on Monty to tell him baldly that there were very few fresh troops left in Britain he could call on. Although this event is recorded as having occurred around the end of Epsom (30 June), there seems to be some mystery in these events, since by around mid-July replacements supplied by the Royal Navy and RAF were beginning to arrive in the battle zone, and not all of these comprised trained infantrymen of the RAF Regiment and Marines, as will be seen. In the USA, some 30,000 aviation cadets found themselves impressed into the army. The 'freshmen' were given hurried infantry courses which took perhaps two to three weeks. The suggestion is that such measures must have already been in hand earlier. The broader question as to why after only three weeks the Allied armies in France were running short of soldiers cannot be gone into fully here, although some possible reasons are obvious as the Allies were fighting on three other fronts: Italy, Burma and the Pacific. The Allies had not had such wide-flung battle fronts to contend with in World War One. One author devoted a whole volume to this question some years ago, his contention being that as far as the British were concerned, there was never in fact any need for such shortage. The men were available in Britain, it was the planners' lack of foresight (perhaps) which resulted in surplus manpower in some directions.

Following his unsatisfactory interview with Hitler, Rommel returned to Normandy. During his absence the 7th Army had been commanded by SS General Hausser, his place at 2nd *SS Panzer* Corps HQ taken by General Will Bittrich of 9th *SS Hohenstaufen*, who would gain greater prominence at Arnhem in September.

The fight to cross the Odon and gain the Orne and beyond had so far cost the British around 100 tanks of the 11th Armoured Division, which at the start had numbered 12,050 men; it lost 33% of its personnel, some 400 tank crewmen recorded as lost. But not all the tanks were destroyed beyond use. A number were recoverable, as were the crews; probably at least half were given replacement tanks and were soon fit for action again. There was never any shortage of tanks, and morale among this branch of the army was said to be high.

The 15th Scottish Division had gone into its first battle with 8th Corps 15,005 strong; after six days of continuous action they were pulled out having lost 2,720 men as casualties, five infantrymen surviving out of every ten who entered combat. For it was of course the point units that suffered such losses, which were up to 80% in some rifle companies. The Tyneside Scottish and Durham Light Infantry, for instance, lost 400 men, the Seaforth Highlanders 300. On the enemy side, Battlegroup Weidinger had lost 636 men during its attacks from the west towards Rauray and Grainville. At the first-named location thirty-two German tanks lay destroyed on the ridge. 9th SS casualties in three days' combat were 1,145, 12th SS 1,240.

44th Royal Tanks had reached Evrecy, but violent reaction by 10th SS Frundsberg (General Heinz Harmel) drove them off. Monty (through General Dempsey) had ordered 11th Armoured to withdraw from Hill 112, which left some men of the Rifle Brigade exposed. They were pulled out at dawn on 30 June, hastened by a bombardment by two German Moaning Minnie rocket mortar brigades, assisted by the artillery of two SS divisions. In fact, the whole front of the corridor was under German fire, shells welcoming the 53rd Welsh Division as it arrived in the battle zone by night to start relieving the battered Scotsmen. The 5th Welch lost fifty men in this shelling before arriving at the Seaforth positions at le Valtru, while the Welsh Guards, newly arrived from England, lost both their CO and second-in-command, killed on arrival at the front. The 4th Welch did not escape: their new command post received a direct hit.

By then the Shropshires were veterans, along with other units that had landed on D-day of 30th Corps, which now entered the cauldron at the foot of Hill 112. In their first night they suffered an infiltrating attack by a determined SS group, some of whom used Japanese tactics, calling to their concealed opponents in the darkness – 'I can see you Tommy!' 'Where are you, Tommy?' – doubtless trying to lure unwary and nervous British troops to open fire and reveal their positions. The front exploded into a galaxy of whirring, coloured tracers, the flash of exploding grenades and bang of mortars. The British infantry of the Shropshires and Herefords called down defensive fire from their artillery packed among the muddy fields behind Cheux; twelve regiments of the RA responded, deluging the hillside with explosives. This massed fire broke up and halted the German attack, decimating the SS troops in exposed positions. At dawn a patrol of the Shropshires went out to investigate and clean up, finding twenty-five dead Germans and twenty-three machine-guns. Later, a Bren carrier patrol of the Herefords took the Esquay road, discovering a carnage of German dead and wounded with many knocked-out *panzers*. But they were well observed by the enemy who opened fire; the British CO, a Corporal, Lance-Corporal and two drivers were hit, the sole survivor managing to escape in the carrier.

Every house and farm in this attractive Norman countryside was ruined, the livestock killed; the inhabitants mostly fled. Naturally, newspapers in Britain reported jubilant French folk glad of liberation. Perhaps those in undamaged Bayeux had been, but in other well-flattened spots the Normans were understandably sullen, resentful of the destroyers of their land and property. At least the Germans had behaved correctly. One farmer asked for the loan of his intact barn by Allied soldiers was alleged to have retorted, 'Non, it is the property of the Reich!'

A real blood-letting occurred on Hill 112. Lieutenant Sam Colsen of the Shropshires recalled his first day there:

❝ It was barely daylight. The fire was coming at us from two directions and we were completely pinned down. We had dug in well enough but there was little cover and being overlooked by the enemy meant we were virtually at their mercy. When we called on our artillery it came at once, but sometimes short, which didn't help. We were really out on a limb and in no hope of relief. I had ten men with me in our position, with other sections not far away. We had Brens, Stens and the usual rifles, with a mortar platoon just to our rear, but they were as exposed as we were and found difficulty in firing at all owing to German sniping.

I had only joined the battalion as a replacement from England a week earlier, so I had everything to learn, and believe me you learn very quickly at the front – or you're dead. In my case I was and felt like a green officer, a subaltern fresh from officer school among men who were mostly very experienced by then, old campaigners who had crammed a great deal into their two weeks or so in France. In short, I had to learn the tricks from them and it was not easy to have to ask this and that from those lads who hardly felt great confidence in such a young newcomer.

When I thought we should change our position the Sergeant said, 'That would be stupid, sir, they'd only cut us to bits. You see sir, on that little hump up there is a Jerry machine-gun post. One squeeze of the trigger on that bloody Spandau and we've had it. OK?' So by that sort of comment I felt pretty stupid and wished I'd kept my mouth shut. So I lay in my hole with that same Sergeant for hours, virtually unable to move and wondering what was the point of being there at all. We could not attack, it had been tried, some of the bodies were still lying out in front of us.

I remember the first attack I was in, just hours before, at dawn. We'd got up out of our holes after eating some biscuits and drinking some cold tea. At first it seemed quiet enough; the Jerries were up the hill, several hundred yards off. The Sergeant said to me, 'Just watch me sir, do as I do, that's all sir.' So I kept crouched, clutching my pistol and Sten, with a couple of grenades in pouches. I was terrified, but my confidence grew as we advanced up that slope. The grass was short and rather yellow after all the summer sun, with a lot of shell craters that we dodged in and out of. I suppose we'd covered some fifty yards before I heard the first awful ripping sound of a German machine-gun and went down at once, my stomach retching with fear. In that second of time I heard yells as lads were hit, but the fire went on sweeping over us and some bullets clipped the ground with a sort of smacking noise. I glanced right and saw the Sergeant grinning at me and he called, 'See what I meant sir? We've no chance at all of getting up there without tank support. Come on!' And he started slithering back the way we'd come, and I saw some medics sliding forward towards the wounded and dead. And I thought, My God, so this is what it's all about! In that tiny attempt on my part we lost four men killed and six wounded, and it took the medics about an hour to get them back to the holes where they could give them proper attention before eventually a carrier got up to evacuate them under fire. **99**

Henry Billings was a Corporal with the 1st Dorsets and arrived at the base of Hill 112 during the early stages of that particular battle, though he had been in action before and knew the realities of the game:

66 When we arrived by carrier there was an artillery duel going on which was no help as we ran to some foxholes recently vacated by blokes from the Scottish division. We dived straight in and got our heads down until it got quieter. And after an hour a ration party tried to reach us but was driven back. Eventually, after another hour, believe it or not, they used a Sherman tank to deliver our grub and tea. The crew just chucked the stuff out of their hatches as the Jerries were sniping and some bigger stuff started to come over, so as soon as the tank blokes had got rid of the packages and tins they scarpered back the way they'd come. 'Windy bastards!' we called after them.

When the Lieutenant came round on his belly he said, 'Hang on chaps, we're going to give the buggers up there a bloody good stonk!' Which meant the RA were going to plaster the hilltop, and they did. It was a fantastic show. God knows how the Jerry SS stood it, but enough of them did because when our next effort went in they were waiting for us and we got clobbered. I went down with a bullet in my right side in agony and passed out. When I came to, a medic was bandaging me up and telling me I'd soon be back in the UK. So I thought, Thank God for that, and went out again. **99**

Jeffrey Cobbold had been with the Shropshires for a year or more and in action since they landed in Normandy. When they began the battle for Hill 112 he thought something bad would happen to him:

❝ We went up the hill in fairly open order in short rushes, though we soon got winded and lost chaps from the start. I called out to my mate Ron, 'I'll see you in Blighty mate, if we're lucky!' And he knew what I meant. It was mid-afternoon and very warm and the guns were banging away, lobbing shells onto the Jerry part of the hill. We used the craters to hide in but they were using mortars and there was no escaping those. To my surprise our NCOs managed to get us most of the way round the hill without losing too many men; this we did by going at a tangent, this way and that. It took some time, maybe half an hour, but at last, though still under fire, we had got near the top.

The grassy ground was brownish and burnt by shellfire and there were a lot of bits and pieces lying about, not bodies but odds and ends of equipment, and I did see some mines. We'd been warned about those but been lucky. Then, at last the Sarge said, 'All right lads, this is the last hop, get some grenades ready and we'll have a go.' There were only six of us and I thought for certain it would be the end of us. I thought some more of our company had gone round the other way, but wasn't sure. Then the Sarge nodded and grinned rather feebly and jumped up as we all did, and at once he was knocked down. He gave a sort of grunt and toppled sideways back into the hole and sat there grinning at us and waving us on and nodding. I believe he died just after that. Amazingly, we rushed on without him. The Lance-jack got it in the belly next; he fell down howling, and again I thought, This is your last moment, and I tripped over something and chucked a grenade at what looked like a Jerry post and fell head-first into another hole. I was on my own.

There was a lot of noise still going on and shouts and when I glanced up I saw a German looking down at me. He was on his knees and looked young but fierce and said 'Hands up!' So I crawled out of that hole, scared stiff, leaving my rifle, and he took my other grenade and crawled up the hill after me with stuff still flying about including our own shells. I saw heads bobbing about behind some earthworks and men talking and some machine-guns poking out of slits in heavy camouflage, and next thing I knew I was kicked into a hole where an NCO of the SS grinned at me and said in English, 'Welcome to our little home!'

I grinned at him and flopped down, almost fainting. I felt completely drained. He gave me a drink out of a small bottle. I think it must have been schnapps. I thought it was water and it took me by surprise and I choked. Then an officer jumped into the hole without a helmet on and a bandage round one hand and told me to 'Komm!' So we crawled off, with him behind me, and went over the hill at the run and doubled over with British shells falling around us and that was very bad. Then I saw some vehicles that were widely dispersed and heavily camouflaged and heard mortars banging away. I was bundled into a small truck where there was a wireless operator at his big sets and another officer with a peaked cap. They spoke together, and then the one with the cap said,

'You're from the Shropshires, right?' So I nodded, and he grinned and said, 'How are you enjoying your holiday in France?' I grinned and said nothing. He took out a packet of English biscuits and handed it to me. I took one and the three of us sat there in the truck munching away and looking out at the shells bursting. Then he asked me where I came from and I told him London. He said he had been there on a short holiday before the war and asked if Nelson was still standing in Trafalgar Square. I told him yes, of course, and so was almost everything else. So he translated this to the other bloke and they laughed and he asked me about the bombs. He said, 'You know, the––' and he made a motion with his hand and a noise supposed to be a doodlebug, so I told him, yes, they were a bit of a nuisance but not so bad.

Then two soldiers came and took me away. I went to Germany where I spent the rest of the war in a PoW camp, which was bad. **99**

Oberscharführer (Staff Sergeant) Will Botolski of 12th SS:

66 When we first moved onto the hill we found the British had withdrawn which we did not understand, though they had suffered from a very heavy bombardment. We had two depleted companies with two mortar sections and about twelve machine-guns. All the lads were very tired and usually hungry as we had been kept awake for day after day, and nights of course, by the bombardments which were very bad. The rations could not reach us and we had been living on apples found in an orchard.

When I surveyed the other side of the hill I at first saw no sign of the enemy. The grass was covered in shell holes; beyond that near the base of the hill were the remains of small trees and bushes. There had been many trees behind us but these too were shredded by shellfire. Then, on that first morning I saw signs of the enemy moving forward again. Little brown figures were hard at work digging in or bringing up equipment and I saw some carriers and trucks and a few tanks, though these last seemed to move off out of sight. We waited but nothing much happened apart from the shelling, which rarely stopped. When I was relieved I went off to find a toilet place and while I was there a very heavy bombardment started up, and as soon as I ran back to my men I found them huddled up in their holes in terror once again. But they remained cheerful after I had given them a few rousing comments, and some were required to stand to their weapons as we expected an enemy attack.

I was trying to watch very carefully and keep my nerve with all the explosions about and on our positions. Several men were hit by flying debris including splinters and carried off to safety. Then I saw the first tiny brown figures getting up to advance in rushes up the hill. I shouted a warning and all the lads manned their weapons. I told them to wait and they did. Their discipline was excellent, even though the shells kept falling around us. Then, it must have been at least fifteen minutes, I decided one of the Tommy groups had progressed near enough and ordered one of our machine-guns to open fire. Some of the Brits were cut down, the others dived into craters and we kept them there with our fire. Then I had a report from the Lieutenant that other Tommies were coming around the hill, so I ran off to watch our other posts who had already been alerted.

I was then surprised by a Captain who told me the enemy were infiltrating behind the hill. So I ran in that direction in time to meet my friend Sergeant Hilser who told me we were out of mortar ammunition. This was serious news, so I sent two men back to the dump which was not far off, but they never returned as shells caught them and they were both killed. I fell into a crater with the Sergeant and saw some of the Tommies rushing up round the hill. As soon as they came nearer we fired at them with our machine-pistols and threw grenades, killing and injuring some of them. But they kept coming and threw grenades and a splinter struck my friend who was forced to drop his weapon. I was then joined by the same Captain with some more troops and we set up such a fire on the enemy that the survivors ran back down the hill, some being hit on the way. **99**

Peter Karmann was a Private in 9th SS, one of a squad sent up to Hill 112 to assist in its defence:

66 I ran to my position when the British began attacking us with infantry. I was a rifleman and lay down in a hole with my old friend Thomas, who had joined up with me. We had been in combat in Russia for some time, and that was very bad. We had looked forward to going back to the West, but this experience too was bad, and in some ways worse because of the air attacks and terrible artillery fire that went on and on for hours and was far worse than our experience in Russia.

We opened fire on the order from a Corporal and saw Britons falling, but some set up a machine-gun and began searching us out with wide bursts of fire that knocked pieces off our hole and kept our heads down. Then someone shouted that more Tommies were coming from the side so we changed our position, and as I dropped into another hole I was hit by something in my right leg which doubled up under me. The Corporal gave my friend Tom a paper bandage and he began pulling up my trouser leg, but suddenly he was forced to pick up his weapon and begin firing again as the enemy had got very close. Then it all went very quiet for a short time before the shells started coming over once more. In that time my friend dressed my leg, which had a hole right through it above the knee, and I crawled away to see the doctor or a medic in great pain. I could not find anyone so one of the officers laid me in a jeep and drove me off to a small farmhouse, which I found was full of wounded. After about ten minutes of lying on the floor I was lifted up onto a table in the farmer's living room and operated on. It was a clean wound and in no time I was put in a truck to be taken off to a hospital in Rouen. When I next joined my unit the battle in Normandy was over and we were resting in Holland, but I was not able to fight again. 🙶

Harald Bohmann was a Lieutenant in 12th SS. He had been wounded in Russia before joining the new Hitler Youth division in Belgium where his arm soon healed and he was able to begin instructing. In Normandy the troops received a terrible baptism of fire and suffered very heavy casualties, and this affected him deeply, though as a trained soldier and officer he was forced to keep a 'stiff upper lip' and set an example.

🙶 We were quite weak in numbers though well armed, and were re-inforced by other SS units, including a mortar brigade of heavy weapons that proved so effective on all fronts. We were still in action after so many days of combat without relief and I wondered how much longer these boys would last. So many of them had been lost. As to the hill itself, it was the dominating feature in that area, though other places were higher as the enemy well knew. Unfortunately for us, though we had the defending advantage, his air force so commanded the sky that all our dispositions were visible to him, and movement of any size could only take place by night. We watched his spotter planes circling about and some were driven off or even shot down by *flak*, but more came so we knew it was hopeless to expect any of our secrets to remain that for long.

Our artillery was not too far off and very well camouflaged, but of course was easily detectable by the enemy once they went into action. Our best weapons were the mobile mortars which wreaked havoc among the enemy as they formed up and behind their lines. They could be moved about very rapidly, and because of their small size were easily hidden about hedges or bushes or camouflaged. I myself usually carried a machine-pistol, a Walther automatic pistol and grenades. I also had a flare pistol, and one night soon after this terrible battle started I used it to detect an enemy patrol that was creeping up round the hill.

It was a very dark but warm night and we had heard small sounds down the hill and stood to. After a while we realised they were getting nearer so I fired a flare, but when it burst we could see nothing. But to be sure we fired a long burst from a machine-gun across the area. Then, after a time we heard more scufflings and this time they were much closer so we opened fire and threw grenades which must have caused damage as we heard yells and the sound of men running. I fired off another flare and this time we caught them fully in the light and let off a lot of fire and saw men falling and calling out. I think some escaped, but it went very quiet then. 🙶

Edward Fischmann was a Sergeant and helped to guide some Panthers into position after dark, the crews making haste to camouflage their tanks which were driven hull-down and ready for action at dawn.

The idea was to catch any British attempt to outflank the infantry on the hilltop, and this they did.

❝ When dawn came we heard tank engines and presently realised the Tommies were working their way round the base of the hill with tanks and infantry. My captain told me to reconnoitre, so I selected six reliable men including a Sergeant I knew very well and we set off in a hurry, taking a roundabout route that offered some concealment from enemy observation. We reached the remains of a lane that had been heavily shelled and hopped cross the cratered ground until we reached an undamaged hedge, just in time to get under cover as an enemy spotter plane cruised over us.

We could hear enemy tanks approaching and soon saw some infantry advancing cautiously about 200 metres off and not yet within easy range. In any case we had no anti-tank weapons with us, so we remained in concealment to watch events. The tanks then cut off to their right into a field and began climbing the long, shallower slope that would take them onto Hill 112 itself. So I signalled my men to keep out of sight and we waited till the four Shermans had turned well away from us and then opened a devastating fire on the Tommy infantry who had no idea we were there. They were less than 100 metres from us and all but about two were knocked down. We then rushed at them and found one uninjured, who we took prisoner with us back to the hill. Meantime the tank crews had gone on with no idea what had happened to their infantry, and within five minutes all the Shermans had been knocked out by the Panthers and some of the crews taken prisoner. ❞

*   *   *   *

This comparatively insignificant-looking rise of ground known on the army maps as 'Hill 112' has been referred to by one historian as the 'cornerstone of the Normandy campaign'; certainly many who fought and suffered on the sun- and shell scorched yellowing grass there would agree. Yet it was but one hill feature to be contested through the campaign; others were Hills 61, 122, 204, 282 and 317, and all would signify in the minds of both German defenders and Allies death and destruction, and for some who survived their lives would never be the same again. The worst ordeal was to come – for the men still on their feet that is – for Mont Pincon lay ahead a few miles, by far the most dominating feature in that area of Normandy.

'No soldier who huddled down in a battened-down tank or in a hastily scraped hole on Hill 112 and came out of it alive ever forgot those sweltering summer days and fearful nights, the scream of falling shells and mortar bombs, and the sickening smell of death that overpowered all else on that mound of torn-up earth soaked in sweat and blood.' That was one writer's 'ode' to the pimple beyond the Orne, an ex-officer and holder of the Military Cross who spoke of the hill that rose so gently from the valley of the river Odon, itself little more than a stream. Major How's belief that it proved the pivot of German defence in Normandy has to be seen in context; certainly it proved that then, at the turn of the month after the Scots had thrust their corridor through at heavy cost to the Odon. But other hills became more 'cornerstones', purely local features that provided excellent defensive advantage to the Germans – always SS men who would never give ground until killed or carried off. It would be nearly three weeks before the SS troops and tanks on 112 were forced to retire following Monty's big outflanking offensives on 25 to 30 July.

There would be no memorials to the German defenders on Hill 112. Such edifices would later be erected by the victors of the 43rd Wessex and 49th West Riding divisions, mostly 'civilian' soldiers, as some historians refer to British recruits, though the same could be said of the enemy.

The failure of 2nd SS *Panzer* Corps and the other German forces to eliminate the British corridor resulted in a report being drawn up by General Baron Geyr von Schweppenburg* for submission to Hitler. In this document he acknowledged it was no longer realistic to expect the Allies to be driven out of France, instead proposing the abandonment of Caen and a general shortening of the German line to enable the *panzers* to operate in the mobile fashion they knew best in the more open terrain to the east. By this method the Germans could regain the initiative.

This report was read by von Rundstedt when he returned to his HQ in northern France following the abortive meeting with Hitler. The crisis provoked by the British thrust via Cheux had so alarmed OKW that its chief, Field Marshal Wilhelm Keitel, telephoned Runstedt in panic, allegedly saying in the course of their short conversation, 'What shall we do? What shall we do?' 'Make peace, you fools! What else can you do?' Rundstedt's response was reported by Keitel to Hitler; ever the *Führer*'s toady, the Field Marshal had been privy to and assisted Hitler's plans for aggressive war and would be hung following the Nuremberg trials in 1946. When the Schweppenburg report, duly countersigned by Rommel and Hausser, arrived at Hitler's office he flew into a rage, ranting against his defeatist generals. His personal adjutant was sent at once to deliver a small black box containing the Knights Cross of the Iron Cross with Oakleaves to von Rundstedt; with it came a letter from the *Führer* congratulating the ageing soldier on the award, the second part accepting his resignation 'on health grounds'. Rundstedt's place would be taken by Field Marshal Gunther von Kluge, who would go to the front in high optimism, discover the hopelessness of the situation,

---

* The General's tactical HQ was located by British Intelligence and bombed by the RAF, most of his staff being killed. Schweppenburg was wounded and evacuated to Paris.

become a suspect following the failed Hitler plot on 20 July and commit suicide, shortly before Rommel himself acquiesced to the *Führer*'s decision.

Rommel's chief-of-staff had warned that if the 9th, 10th, 12th SS and *Panzer* Lehr were not relieved they would be burned out within a week. The last division was in any case a mere rump of its former proud self. Hitler's adjutant travelled on to Rommel's own HQ in Normandy, his instructions to find out personally just what the situation was at the front. That the leaders in Germany had no real idea of conditions there the field commanders were convinced, among them the hard and experienced generals of the SS, such as Willi Bittrich and Sepp Dietrich. Not that it made any difference to Hitler. His orders to stand fast remained.

Von Rundstedt paid a farewell visit to Rommel, perhaps to commiserate, and in doing so reinforced the younger man's belief that their only real hope lay in removing the *Führer*, the man who had played such a part in his own advancement in the glory days. As for Rundstedt, he was typical of the old school, the stiff-necked Prussian military aristocracy despised by both Hitler and perhaps the up-and-coming SS generals who had sought new ways to win battles. Men like Rundstedt were in fact a dying breed, with their own perhaps peculiar honour code by which they set themselves apart even from others in their own army, as General Horrocks, the ex-commander of 30th Corps, discovered when he 'got to know' the Field Marshal after the war, when the German soldier was a PoW in Britain. The Britisher was General Officer Commanding Western Command and, following some conversations concerning the conduct of the campaign in France, he enquired if the prisoner had any requests to help improve conditions in their camp. Von Rundstedt's reply was, 'Yes, some of the German generals in this camp are not the sort of people with whom we are used to mixing. I would be grateful if you could have them removed to another camp.' The men concerned, although fellow Germans and fellow generals, were of the 'other sort', non-combat officers, doctors and engineers from other branches of the *Wehrmacht*. Revealing of the old Prussian concepts of snobbish militarism.

Von Rundstedt's code of 'honour' enabled him later to be reactivated by Hitler, the dictator he despised; for no matter what animosity came between them, they seemed to be at one in condemning the July plotters. To Rundstedt they were cowards who had soiled the officers' code of honour. Later, when things were even blacker, in December, he would as C-in-C issue a '*Führer*'-type exhortation to the troops before the Ardennes counter-offensive.

Montgomery's launching of Operation Epsom led to misleading headlines in the press at home, the Allied journalists in France aided in their usual propaganda style by some of the general's own super-optimistic statements. MONTGOMERY SMASHES THROUGH – Rommel's Bridgehead Ring Shattered – BIG TANK BATTLE

RAGING. He had broken through the German holding line. Rommel's crack *panzer* forces were engaged by the British spearheads in the greatest tank battle since D-day; the British were 'driving forward on a broad front; after 72 hours of the most bitter and savage fighting they had advanced seven miles; the Germans had lost 100 tanks, one officer in the field commenting – "It is a magnificent accomplishment", while another said, "The Germans west of Caen are in complete turmoil".'

The fact that no big tank battle had taken place on D-day, or that it was the British who had lost 100 tanks around the Odon, was irrelevant as the copy rolled through the censors' offices in Fleet Street and into the editor's sanctum to receive any final polishing before the night presses started to hum. Within hours the Allied nations would perhaps thrill to the latest smashing news of what could well be the decisive offensive on the western front, an attack that would send the Jerries reeling back towards Paris and beyond. If and when newspapers reached the front troops, and if they had the time to read them, then these soldiers would grin wryly, or perhaps mouth what they felt were the necessary expletives on the 'latest war news' from the people back home or over the BBC whose reporters, jolly good chaps as a whole, somehow had a habit of jumping the gun in rushing out their scripts and recordings – unless of course their editors felt compelled to rewrite such things. Towns and localities were too often 'captured' by the BBC, or 'liberated' by the press, when the reality was rather different.

Naturally, the war news was tailored for public digestion, designed to sustain morale, especially for those suffering the V1 bomb terror in southern England. It is easy decades later to be struck by the stark differences between such daily news stories and the reality given in eye-witness testimony as presented in histories such as this work. Journalists told of a 'thin crust' remaining of the German line, the enemy infantry had been cut through by British tanks and infantry who had simply waded across the Odon. In America, of course, the tabloid press used far more extravagant banner headlines; across the Atlantic sensation followed sensation. How much this kind of reporting influenced the US leaders in Washington is debatable. There is no doubt that the public on both sides of the ocean were misled by it. Bafflement and increasing cynicism would follow and start to pile up about General Montgomery.

By 2 July the 'big breakthrough' appeared to have stalled. The public was at the mercy of the media, who now told them that the British 2nd Army were busily mopping up and 'liquidating' the numerous German pockets of resistance bypassed by the great thrust, the mere remains of German units who had been committing 'jabs' into the sides of Monty's arrowhead. The enemy were suffering 'mounting' and 'extravagant' losses, and while this clean-up operation on the flanks was in progress there seemed little chance of any big-scale advance. 'Our territory' now included 'the now legendary Hill 112'. The survivors hanging on grimly there would have been interested to hear that – British and German.

One prominent Sunday paper disclosed that the troops who had just smashed Rommel's big counter-attack were first-timers; they had never before heard a shot fired in anger, 'yet they fought like veterans'. This of course referred to the 15th Scottish Division. The enemy were well acquainted with which units faced them, but the Scots could not receive any mention by name back home in Britain.

An impression of the overwhelming power of the British offensive was given by the quoting of alleged German reports. These seemed astonishingly frank, if indeed they were enemy in origin. One spoke of the 'use of air forces on an unprecedented scale by Montgomery which swept like a hurricane before his land forces', a comment hardly likely to uplift morale of Germans at the front or at home. But by this stage of the war Dr Göbbels' own propaganda machine was geared to serving up crises and reverses disguised as heroic battles by German warriors on all fronts.

If public conceptions in Britain and USA were confined to notions of 'lines' being broken through, the reality was that Caen was not the big prize, even though naturally Monty wanted it. The prize was the continued gripping of the bulk of German armour by the British–Canadian Army around the city. There were of course prizes beyond that came as bonuses: the 'turmoil' spoken of by one reporter was real enough in the German command, the aura of doom that gripped both army and SS generals as they saw their units whittled away in Monty's grinder. No matter what bravery, tenacity and nerve the Germans in the foxholes showed, it had proved impossible to unbalance the little Irish–Briton with the beaky nose, high-toned voice and eccentric headgear. His army seemed unbreakable, no matter how much local success the Germans gained, no matter how many times they caused their opponents to appear amateurish on the field of battle. Reporters, however, in writing of Britain's 'Citizen Army', tried to infer that their foe were all professionals by choosing, and thereby humbled by amateurs. In truth, of course, the bulk of the Germans fighting in the war were conscripts like them.

The impression of massed armies and tanks slugging it out did not quite gel with the scenes around the Odon, and in particular on 'Point 112', near one corner of which stood a concrete cross, the Croix des Filandriers, which somehow survived five weeks of bombardment – bombs, shells and bullets. To the Germans it stood out against the skyline. In view of the blood-letting that went on there during that summer, it seems appropriate that they christened it the Hill of Calvary. The Germans came up with other labels, then and later, such as the 'Wood of Half-trees', this referring to what was basically an orchard surrounded by a hedge. A ditch ran through the orchard which was bounded on one side by a line of tall trees. These were soon cut down in size by shells, hence the German term *Halben Baume* – half-trees. Some German tankers called it the 'box-shaped wood', and after many soldiers of the Duke of Cornwall's Light Infantry were killed there it became (for them) 'Cornwall Wood'. After the Germans had gone the army erected a temporary wooden structure with the legend painted in white, 'Cornwall Hill – July 10–11 1944'. Later, a granite memorial would be erected to the men of the 43rd Wessex Division who fell there. Beyond this, on the skyline of Hill 112, are the same trees, perhaps not wholly recovered from the battering received.

It was staying power that seemed to count as the opposing troops slogged it out through much of a July dogged occasionally by rain, comparatively small numbers of exhausted, demoralised, often hungry young men who gave importance to a slope of passing significance numbered '112'. There reporters, if any now came, would see no massed tanks and serried ranks of infantry driving on triumphantly to the Seine, Paris and beyond with flags flying. The enemy looked down their throats – or so it seemed, the positions changing as one side gained an advantage through counter-attack. The SS boys absorbed so much shelling from the massed guns behind the British positions, the Tommies wondered if they were stuck there for ever. Did Monty care? Where was the air force now? Surely the 'Tiffies' could swipe out the hidden *panzers* with their rockets, Marauders, Mitchells – flatten the cursed tormentors in mottled brown jackets. Perhaps Monty really did prefer to have the Jerries tied up there while he planned more moves elsewhere?

In any event, within a few days all talk in the press of a massive British breakthrough had vanished as the papers back home gave headline prominence to the doodlebugs – yet another source of worry to the southerners and especially Londoners in the army. Once more evacuation measures were in progress in England as the Germans launched 100 to 150 V1s each day across the Channel. So far (to 6 July) 2,754 bombs had been despatched, and these had killed by remarkable coincidence almost exactly the same number of people, practically all civilians – 2,752 in all, injuring 8,000. So it took about one doodlebug to kill one Briton, injuring more of course; the toll was said to be 'high' in London. Yet on the same day (6 July), the *London Evening News* devoted small space in the centre of its front page to announce that the main German line in Normandy had been breached.

7 Cowards and Prisoners

Not all troops performed brilliantly in battle, especially those new to the shock of it all. Men ran off, some never returned. Some units proved a let-down to their commanders who had to answer to those above for such conduct. It was not only the common soldiers who sometimes cracked; there are stories of officers and NCOs folding under the shock and strain of attack. One senior Sergeant, a veteran of other campaigns, gave up quite early in Normandy, before the fall of Caen, proving useless for further action. A Brigadier began acting so peculiarly his subordinates were obliged to take steps and have him removed. In one German attack a Captain ran off and did not stop till he reached the beaches where he sought passage to England on a landing craft. The story goes that he made it under the care of an MO, eventually being posted as an instructor and staying on in the regular army. In another case a Lieutenant panicked during an enemy attack, his behaviour affecting the men who followed him, running off towards the rear until confronted by their battalion commander with a pistol, at which point the stricken junior officer vanished, leaving his men to be driven back to their positions.*

Some of the 15th Scottish did not do well in their first battles beyond Cheux, the 10th battalion HLI in particular, who were gathered together later by their CO to receive a tongue lashing. Len Graves was a Sergeant at the time:

❝ We had a very bad time – call it bad luck, what you like. We just gave up when things got tough. We had rushed in at the Jerries and come under intense fire, many men getting knocked down. I myself was hit in the arm, there were lads screaming all around, and it was one hell of a mess. I lay there in the grass thinking, My God, this is far worse than I ever imagined it would be. Then I passed out and woke up with a medic bandaging me up. Well, I won't beat about the bush. When I got back to safety I found at least half the blokes unwounded; they had simply run back to our starting point, and frankly I didn't blame them. It was awful.

That was our first go. They went in again later and it was the same; they just weren't up to taking casualties like that, it seemed like bloody murder. Well, that evening after we'd been sorted out and I lay in a medical tent having my arm fixed, all the NCOs and officers were called

---

* One quarter of casualties were assessed battle fatigue

to attend a special meeting which took place in a barn just on the edge of Cheux. Some of the ORs also turned up I believe. I had my arm in a sling and didn't feel so bad. When we got there we had no idea what it was about, but knew we had not done well so guessed it would not be good news.

The Colonel came in with a Captain and a couple of MPs so we wondered if someone was going to be arrested. He certainly didn't need a bodyguard. He stood on an ammo crate and this is more or less what he told us:

'I am very, very disappointed with you all. You've shown me what you're made of; you're yellow, practically the whole bloody lot of you! I am ashamed of you, so there! There will have to be some bloody changes made and they won't be very nice I can tell you. I've never seen such a bloody awful performance, it really was stinking!'

We looked at each other and some of the blokes began muttering about what a fine example he was. One Sergeant near me said, 'If he thinks it's fucking well easy why the fuck doesn't he get out and do it his bloody self?' And I can tell you we all felt the same. Our opinion of that bugger went right down and I don't think we cared a shit whether he had us all arrested or what! Sorry, but that's how we felt as we thought of all our pals and the rest lying out there dead and maimed while he stood there, fat and safe and telling us we were cowards.

He said a few more things I can't remember. I think by then we were all so riled up we were hardly listening any more. He then went out and I can tell you there were a few nasty catcalls after him.

I was out of things for a bit and during that time the unit was merged with some other Jocks and did rather better, and things never got so bad again. But we lost all respect for our CO and later I believe as a result he was transferred and we had a new man who became very chatty and did a lot to pull us together again. But we never forgave that bastard. Sorry, but that's the way we felt, and still do I believe. **99**

Robert Sherrin was a Lieutenant in that unit:

66 I felt terrible as I heard our CO say such things, even if they were true. I'd never been in an attack before, and when we were ordered in again my heart sank. I'd seen so many lads go down I saw no chance whatever of success and it all seemed absolutely pointless. I thought, Christ, we've got so much artillery why not blast them to hell? It was sheer suicide to send men into such an attack against prepared positions, and frontally. I was naive to have thought all that kind of thing had gone out in the first war and they'd learned better. I was wrong, and found out that when the people at the top say ATTACK! they mean just that, no matter what the circumstances. The battalion commander has to pass on the orders and knows that if his men fail then he gets it in the neck. The trouble was that some were professional men whose careers were at stake. We were not like them, we had other jobs in civvie life and longed to get back to them and forget all about the bloody army and war. **99**

Neville Bransen was a Sergeant-Major, but not for long:

66 I was pleased I had done so well in the army. Like a fool I'd thrown up quite a good job just before the war as I saw what was coming and I was dead keen. I was made Sergeant in late 1940 after seeing no action at all and spent the rest of the war in Britain, ending up with the HLI, which seems a bit strange but they weren't all Scottish. I soon learnt in Normandy – too late – that I was not really cut out for it at all. The thought terrified me. I was not really the combat type and happier in admin, and that was it. But I had no choice but to try to set an example. God, when the shooting started I was terrified and flunked it; I just fell down in a faint and, like the rest, ran back the way I'd come. Call it cowardice if you like, I just couldn't take it. Well, just after the CO gave us that bollocking another Sergeant-Major came to me in the mess, which was a large tent in a field. He took me outside and there were two more senior NCOs. The SM said, 'You men are hereby reduced to the ranks, you're Privates from now on. Get to the Orderly Corporal and hand in your paybooks and rank badges. Now get out of my bloody sight!' **99**

Other men who decided enough was enough made the conscious decision, albeit under stress perhaps, to opt out. Jimmy was a Glaswegian in the Highland Brigade, and though his desertion took place later it was prompted by one of Montgomery's costly offensives which for some spelt the end. They would take no more.

66 We had terrible losses. I was under nineteen and saw all of my mates killed or wounded after being stuck in a heavily wooded place with the Jerries not far off. We couldn't move an inch; we were hit by shells, bullets, mortars – the lot. I lay there in a hell of a sweat, not daring to move. I called out to my mates in the din but none of them answered. Then, just for a minute or so, it went quiet and I took a quick shufti and saw them lying about dead or wounded. One of them, Tommy, was trying to call out, but he couldn't get the words out. And then the Jerries started shooting again and he was killed. I got my head down and cried and went to pieces.

There was not an officer in sight, and when it got quiet again I jumped up and ran like hell, keeping my head down, jumped over a ditch, then ran into some blokes with a Bren gun who were also trying to keep out of sight. I ran on and on into a little road where our transport was; the drivers were lying in the grass trying not to get hit. I ran down that road till an officer and a Sergeant grabbed me and I just collapsed and passed out.

I ended up in hospital, a complete nervous wreck. **99**

Freddy was in the 'Somersetters':

❝ I was hit in the left arm during an attack late in June. It wasn't serious but it did hurt and I made the most of it. I fell down in the grass with all the noise going on and my mates rushing past me. One stopped to take a look and I told him it was nothing and to go on. Then the Sergeant came along, took a look at me and told me to wait till he came back to attend to me. He gave me a bandage to try to do something myself. Well, I knew full well he'd keep me in the line, so I got up, and, crouching, ran back past our Lieutenant who shouted at me, but I ignored him and ran on past some Shermans that were moving up, and then on to our own transport. By then there was blood all down my arm, so I stopped and asked a bod to help me bandage it up. He said, 'What's it like, mate?' So I told him bloody awful, as usual. I was determined not to go back there, so after he'd bandaged me up I just walked on. I'd dropped my rifle at the start.

Then I saw some tents which I knew were our company HQ, so I avoided them and went on till I reached a bigger road and saw the transport going back from the front and all the usual stuff moving up. So I thumbed a lift and jumped in the back of a truck and went a few hundred yards before it stopped, and the next thing I knew two MPs grabbed me and hauled me off to their own truck. They saw my flashes and knew I'd run away. They said nothing as they handcuffed me and chained me to the side of their truck. I felt absolutely done in and didn't care what happened – even if they shot me. I only knew that I would never go back to the front.

Well, I was locked up for hours in that truck until an officer of our unit came and said, 'I'm ashamed of you, letting us down. You'll be charged with desertion in the face of the enemy. I wouldn't want to be in your shoes lad.'

That evening I was taken before a Provost Sergeant-Major and charged, then taken in an MP truck to a headquarters in a village near Caen and locked in a small room for several days, fed and given exercise. Then I was taken back under escort to England where I was seen by a Colonel of our reserve and charged more formally, then sentenced to three years' detention. He said: 'By God, you're lucky! They don't shoot your kind any more. Now go and do your time like a good lad. I reckon by the time you come out the war will be over.'

I was taken to the glasshouse at Shepton Mallet, but it wasn't too bad. After two years and six months they let me out and I was soon demobbed. ❞

Freddy was luckier than one unfortunate inmate at Shepton who died after being run round the square in full kit by MPs.

'Teddy' was a Seaforth Highlander, another soldier of 15th Scottish who had seen too many of his chums killed or wounded:

66 I thought I'd had enough. I reckoned I'd done my bit and we all deserved some leave in England. Instead, we were ordered back into the line, so I said, 'Fuck this! It's not fair, they're a rotten lot of bastards! Fuck Monty! I'm clearing off!'

My mates felt the same, but told me I'd get caught. I put some grub in my small pack, and when it got dark and we were off duty I simply cleared off. I knew the way and soon found a truck going back and hopped in the back without the driver even seeing me. When we reached a big dump I transferred to another truck going west, until we reached the beaches where I managed to stow away on an LST without any trouble as it was full of trucks going back for repair. That night we crossed the Channel and I could hardly believe my luck, it had been so easy. On the other side I stayed in the truck till daylight, then took a chance and walked off into the dock. No one said a dicky bird. I went off behind a shed, took off my battledress blouse, and rolled up my sleeves to make it look as if I was unloading trucks. There was a lot going on there.

After dark I hopped on a truck as it left and soon found myself in Southampton where I got on a train unseen and hopped off just before it arrived in London. I didn't see a single officer or MP to stop me. After that it was easy. I threw away my uniform and stole some clothes off a line, including some grey flannel trousers. Then I went into town where I saw a Scottish soldier and persuaded him to give me a few bob. I had some grub in a café before going to the mainline station at Euston and had no trouble getting on a train for Scotland without a ticket. When I reached Glasgow I went to my aunt's. I knew the police would be looking for me, but I changed my name and got fixed up with a ration book and all I needed. 99

'Teddy' had got away with it. He was not the only one. Other Allied deserters, perhaps in their hundreds, were on the run in London and other places. A few got mixed up in crime. It is fair to assume the problem was smaller for the Germans, but there were those among the enemy who for one reason or another decided to opt out.

Fritz Grabe had served briefly in Italy with a labour unit before going into the 1st SS in January 1944, and following training was unlucky enough to find himself under a 'rather nasty officer':

66 a Lieutenant who seemed to take a dislike to me for no good reason. Whenever there was a dirty job he always asked me to do it, and when I asked him why he said this: 'You must learn to obey, do you understand? Do not question the orders I give you. Now get on with it or I will charge you!' The job in question was running yet another errand outside the camp where he had a lady friend. He sent her letters and I felt a fool and embarrassed, but she seemed a very nice woman.

Then the invasion came and as a reserve unit we went into France and waited for orders, and as before the Lieutenant found dirty jobs for me to do. On one occasion he asked me to do his laundry, which I felt was an insult, and I had no doubt he was trying to belittle me in front of my comrades. I became heated and said, 'You can do your own damned washing!'

My comrades were amazed but understanding. The Lieutenant ordered me outside where he found a Sergeant who was told to take me to a room and lock me up. I thought, well, perhaps at least I will be safe here and not get involved in the invasion. The Lieutenant then sent for me and in front of the same Sergeant charged me with insulting and insubordinate behaviour; I was stripped of my uniform and ordered into fatigues to start sweeping up the camp and cutting the grass. I felt an absolute fool and decided right away to protest to a higher authority, or even to try to escape.

But the next day the unit was ordered to the front; the Sergeant told me to get changed and rejoin my comrades. I did so in some fear as I felt I was better off where I was. Then the officer came and told me I was to be his personal runner in the battle zone. I said nothing, and when we drove across France next day towards the battle we came under air attack and all hell broke loose. The Lieutenant ordered me to help the wounded and soon we were on the way again. We had lost about twelve men killed and wounded, and as we went on I decided that if I stayed with the unit I would be killed by some means as the Lieutenant seemed to hate me. We reached the forward area that evening and I decided to run away. I didn't feel like a criminal but I suppose I was really. Yet my action was really brought on by that swine of a Lieutenant; he never seemed to think of me as a human being. I felt he would soon start sending me on dangerous jobs and I would not survive.

I had a special comrade and told him to say nothing if I seemed to vanish. He was amazed and told me not to do it, as if I was caught I would be shot. When darkness came we were spread out over some fields. I threw away my jacket and helmet and ran off towards some farm buildings. I thought I could hide, steal some food and clothes and escape to the south, even though the MPs would be looking for me. Things did not go according to plan.

I saw some French people who were busy loading up a cart to escape the fighting and asked them for food. They seemed frightened and left me, so I went into their farmhouse and had just found something to eat and some wine when I heard a crash and three German MPs ran in and took hold of me. I was amazed and terrified and when they hurried me outside I saw the French people staring and knew they had betrayed me.

I was taken by truck to the MP HQ and charged with desertion and put in a cell. I was very worried and thought I would be shot. I had told the truth to the army Sergeant-Major, and felt sure he would call the SS to come and collect me. Well, I slept that night as best I could in the cell, and next morning to my surprise I was allowed to go and have breakfast with the MPs, who seemed quite friendly. They gave me an army jacket and cap and told me that if I behaved I could stay outside the cell while they got on with their duties. When I asked them what would happen they shrugged their shoulders and grinned. I felt sure this meant I would be returned to the SS Lieutenant and shot.

Then, to my astonishment, an army officer appeared and heard my story with sympathy. He said, 'Bloody SS! Look here, how would you like to join my unit?'

I was speechless. I could hardly believe it. Within a few minutes he had persuaded the MPs to release me and drove me off in his car to a small barracks in Amiens which was some way off. He had me fitted out with full army uniform and equipment and ordered the Sergeant-Major to put me in one of the rifle companies. Then, soon after, we went to the front and I made some good comrades and despite all the terrible battles and privations I survived. And when the Sergeant-Major gave me my army service book I was amazed to find I had a new name and number.

When August came I was taken PoW by the Americans and went to England where they never discovered I had been in the SS. Many years later I learned that the SS Lieutenant I hated so much had been killed in action. **99**

It would seem that not every *Waffen-SS* officer was imbued with the same comradely spirit. Alfred Vogelsen was a very experienced Sergeant of the 1st SS; his battles included the Balkan campaign and plenty of fighting in Russia. Withdrawn for rest and refitting in Belgium in 1943, he was used as an infantry instructor:

66 I was instructing some recruits who had completed basic training and were in need of further tuition in shooting. We were on a rifle range and I was showing them the various positions and techniques when an officer appeared in his VW jeep. He watched us for a time and then called me to him and began criticising my methods within earshot of the recruits, who seemed to find it amusing. When I tried to dismiss them the officer stopped me, so I protested that our conversation was not helpful to discipline, requesting he continue in private. He then berated me for my attitude, so I rather rudely told him to go away and leave me to get on with the job, which was to prepare these youngsters for battle. He was furious and told me to report to his office later, which I did after I had finished the training session with the recruits.

When I arrived at the officer's room he was in conversation with a Captain and kept me waiting for some time, and when he did at last speak to me he did so in front of the other officer who I could see felt very uncomfortable. I was told I had behaved badly and was not really fit to be an instructor, so I shouted at him that I probably had more experience in such matters than he had, at which point the Captain left rather hurriedly. My accuser, an *Obersturmführer* [Lieutenant] then told me to consider myself reduced to Private from that date. This order would be put in writing.

I went into battle as an ordinary Private and was decorated; the officer was killed during the first days of fighting. **99**

Officers and NCOs can make or mar any unit. And for those men who survived combat, the experience of being taken prisoner could also be the luck of the draw. Hans Holler had recovered from a leg wound received in Russia and was sent from a depot in Germany with twenty other men to the Normandy front where he joined the remains of 276th Infantry, where their new commander showed his displeasure at only receiving a mere three replacements.

66 The British were attacking and we went into action at once, passing a village in flames after air attack. It had been fortified, but the troops were killed or ran off. We were on foot, the company only supported by two armoured cars. The sky was thick with smoke and the noise from the British bombardment was great. We were shown into positions near a hedgerow and told to watch out for enemy infiltration. After a while we heard tanks and saw Shermans and Churchills coming across the fields. We didn't know what to do, but the Lieutenant told us to hold fast as the anti-tank guns would deal with the tanks – all we had to do was shoot at their infantry.

I wasn't too worried; it seemed so pleasant in that countryside after Poland and Russia. Then someone shouted and the anti-tank guns went into action and two of the British tanks went up in flames with a lot of noise. Then we saw brown figures running towards us and started shooting. But some of the tanks got very near us so the Sergeant told us to fall back nearer the village, which we did, losing only one man. The enemy infantry took over our old positions and the bullets started flying. Then the Lieutenant ordered us to counter-attack and I thought it would be the end of us. We were greatly outnumbered and some of the British tanks were on the road and shooting like mad. We moved to the right to be in a better position and the officer ordered us to advance across the field in front in short rushes, shooting from new positions. Several men fell down as they were hit. I could see we could not succeed and did not expect to survive.

Then the British started using mortars on us and both our cars went up in smoke. The noise was terrible as the British artillery started up again and the tanks rushed past us along the road. There was a lot of confusion and I lay in the grass trying to find shelter and suddenly saw British soldiers rushing at me with their rifles and Stens pointed at me. I put up my hands and they took me prisoner. I was well treated, sent back with three other Germans, given tea and a cigarette before being interrogated. A week later I was in England. **99**

As noted, the situation *vis-à-vis* the Germans on the Canadian front was rather different. Whether this really began with the incident on the beach on 6 June or following more slaughter during and after Operation 'Charnwood' in July is hard to say. It is extremely unlikely the German side ever knew of the D-day episode.

Peter Doren was in 1st SS and was captured by the Canadians south of Caen in July,

❝ and treated rather badly. I was an infantry Corporal and we were surrounded by enemy infantry and tanks for hours; all my comrades were killed or wounded, and when I ran out of ammunition I surrendered. Two Canadian soldiers took hold of me and hit me across the back and mouth with rifle butts; they then kicked me to the ground. I knew we had killed some of them, but I never expected such treatment.

'You fucking bastard!' they said, and hit me repeatedly until a Sergeant told them to stop and take me to him. He took a look at me and I was turned over to the MPs who took me away for another beating before being turned over to an officer for interrogation, and this is what he said in bad German: 'I know you're in the SS and I can see you've been given some rough treatment. You must know why.'

I told him I had no idea at all.

'Some of you bastards have murdered some of our men, so you've got to pay for it, understand?'

I told him I did not know what he was talking about and could think of no reason why his men should be murdered – outside battle.

'Well, it's fucking true, you can believe it. Now, I'm going to ask you some questions and I want answers, and they'd better be right or I'll turn you over to the police outside, OK?'

He then asked me a number of questions which I did my best to answer, though they were things I felt sure they must be perfectly well aware of. I had no wish to be beaten again, but I would not give anything away and don't believe I did. He seemed well satisfied with my answers which seemed to agree with what he knew, so he turned me over to a Corporal who took me off for some tea and a biscuit. He seemed quite sympathetic and had my wounds treated by a doctor. I was then taken away in a jeep and two days later landed in England with a lot more prisoners. ❞

Among the men of the 2nd *Panzergrenadiers* of 1st SS was Captain Siegfried Wendel, the unit debussing near Caen during a big British–Canadian attack. The troops had just been resting out of combat, but were called back to help repel the enemy offensive:

❝ We ran forward and a Captain directed us into positions astride a road and we took cover in the holes already there, under fire from all kinds of missiles. Then we heard tanks and saw Churchills entering the zone; they were taken under fire and some were knocked out. Then I saw masses of enemy infantry rushing and dodging across the fields. They looked quite funny, like little moving dots with tiny faces and smoke dancing up among them as some of our shells and mortars landed.

I told my men not to fire without my order. Many of them were new to battle and had only recently seen their first action. But they were all well disciplined and had learned fast.

The Tommies came nearer and nearer and had almost reached the road when I called for fire and we let loose a terrific cannonade which swept the fields before us and stopped the attack abruptly. Many of the Tommies were killed or wounded, the rest tried to find cover, which was difficult as they had been caught in the open. The battle went on like that for some minutes before it was our turn. A great artillery barrage hit us and we were forced down into our holes as the explosions came all around us and hit a number of our positions, which were destroyed. All cohesive defence was lost in a few minutes, and as I glanced up I realised some Tommies had reached us. I yelled to my men, 'Wake up! They are on us!'

I shot off all my ammunition in a moment or two and then threw grenades before running to another position, but found the two men there dead. As I fell into their hole a bullet hit my right leg. It was very painful, and as the enemy soldiers ran at me I tried to get away but I collapsed. I heard them shouting at me and, looking round, saw several grimy faces staring down at me. They looked angry, but then grinned and got down into our positions to continue fighting in that desperate battle. In fact, one of them fell dead a second or so later. His mates buried their faces in the grass in fear, as I did myself. Then it went quiet, and when I looked up they were grinning with relief and some more Churchills came up. I was then lifted up onto a small tank and rushed back to a command post at breakneck speed, where my wound was treated and I was interrogated.

I had nothing that was new to tell them. It was the end of my war. **"**

An unusual encounter between an SS prisoner and his captors took place in July, the witness an inter-unit liaison officer called Robert Interllin, his unusual name explained by his foreign-born parents, though he was brought up in England. Attached to 30th Corps, his job was to visit the different units to size up the situation and morale. During such tasks he was often called upon to act as interpreter as he knew both French and German.

" One afternoon I had just reached a highland battalion HQ. It was very hot and the men were standing about in their shirtsleeves before the maps discussing the latest reports. The atmosphere was tense and not very bright. I reported to the CO, who didn't say much; I could see he looked pretty worried, and since it was not my job to comment or advise I stood about awaiting developments. After a while a runner came in to report they had picked up a wounded SS Captain who was demanding to see the officer in charge. So a Lieutenant went outside and found a German in a camouflage smock under the care of a Sergeant with two MPs. He looked all in, was wounded in the leg, but quite chirpy. I'd never seen a Jerry officer, and since he was SS I thought it would be very interesting to the people at Corps if I could get something out of him. So when they brought him into the HQ I suggested I have a go at him.

They sat him down and the conversation went like this:

'Have you been at the front long? What unit are you?'

'I've been here since early June. I'm in the Hitler Youth,' he replied.

'Have you anything of interest to tell us?'

'Not really, unless you want to know about the Englishman we've captured.'

I was a bit startled, and reported this to the others. I was asked to find out what he meant.

'We have a prisoner who is of noble family,' the German continued, and this startled us even more. He then claimed the man was a prince.

'A prince?' I said, thinking how absurd it sounded as we had no such person as far as I knew in our army there.

'He says he is the Prince of Edinburgh.'

I repeated this with some laughter to the staff. The CO said, 'Get him out of here, it's all rubbish of course.'

The German seemed rather put out by our derisive attitude, so I asked him what he wanted in exchange. 'We could perhaps consider such an arrangement, if you have one of our people of higher rank? But I don't believe you have, have you?'

Well, this we confirmed, though we had a number of their men, some wounded, and all of lower rank.

'Can you describe the man?' I asked.

'He is a very proud man who will only speak to higher officers and demands to be properly treated.' He went on that the man had an English accent, but claimed to be a Scots nobleman. Yet he was only a Private. That made us all grin again, and I suggested they send him back as we would be very interested to meet this 'prince', as we'd never heard of him. The German said, 'I will be willing to act for you. If you exchange me you can get your prince back.'

When we tried to convince him the man was bogus he became quite agitated and had to be removed. **99**

8 Charnwood

General Montgomery's next blow fell on the enemy almost before he had time to recover from the crisis situation on the Odon. There was grim, some might say totally misplaced, humour in the choice of code-word for this offensive – Operation 'Charnwood', rather like the second race of the season in Normandy (at least, of that phase of the campaign).

By that time there was no longer any need to pretend that its sole purpose was simply to tie down German forces and especially armour on the British–Canadian front, even though this primary purpose remained and would continue until the campaign was won. For Monty wanted Caen, he always did; it had been a prime objective on D-day, not simply because of its importance as the Norman capital city and road junction, but because it did bar his way into the 'mobile terrain' beyond; it also happened to possess an airfield nearby, and the air marshals had pressed for the capture of such air parks from the beginning. Units of 2nd Tactical Air Force – the fighter-bombers – were using crude airstrips laid with Sommerfeld tracking by RAF construction Wing commandos in the fields behind the beach head. However, there was yet another factor: the Americans were still in trouble to the west and Montgomery pressed General Dempsey to keep on the pressure, to continue engaging much of the German armour around Caen. Since the 8th and to a lesser extent 30th British Corps had run out of steam, temporarily, it seemed obvious that the next assault should be meted out by 1st Corps in the north.

This was to be a three-division attack by 3rd Canadian (plus two armoured brigades) on the right wing, 3rd British on the left, and the fresh 59th Staffordshire Division in the centre. The British would be supported by the usual tank squadrons including 'funnies' of 79th Armoured. The number of troops involved has been quoted as 115,000. They would be supported by five regiments of artillery and naval gunfire offshore provided by at least one battleship, plus the monitor HMS *Roberts* and cruisers. These warships had been on call since D-day. In addition, extra help would be given by 43rd Wessex who would again exert pressure around Hill 112 in an attempt to prevent the Germans switching units to the more threatened area.

As a preliminary, the Canadians attacked the airfield at Carpiquet on 4 July, the area still stubbornly defended by the young panzergrenadiers of 12th SS. Fighting was fierce and went on among the hangars and aircraft parking bays, with little progress made. The Canucks would not win through here until 9 July, the day General '*Panzer*' Meyer ordered his men out of Caen and its environs, in direct defiance of Hitler's order. Meyer's CO, the youthful Fritz Witt, already wounded, had been killed by naval gunfire in June, leaving his successor to become the youngest general (at thirty-four) in the German forces.

Montgomery disclosed later that he had been considering the use of heavy bombers in a tactical role for some time. It was a new concept insofar as the large four-engined Lancasters and Halifaxes had not to date been used in the battle, apart from trying to knock out coastal batteries before D-day. Obviously, there were problems, not the least of them the 'bomb-line' – the great need to avoid allowing the massive bomb carpet to encroach on the Allied lines. Perhaps it was akin to using a monstrous sledgehammer to crack a nut, though this particular one was of a rather tough variety. For around Caen the enemy had had ample time to construct far more extensive defences of almost Great War complexity and thoroughness, deep entrenchments and bunkers that defied normal infantry and artillery weapons. There were Tigers and other armoured weapons dug in, apart from the usual 88mm guns sited to catch the advancing British tanks and other vehicles.

Montgomery felt justified in calling for, as an experiment – for that is what it amounted to – the use of Bomber Harris's massed squadrons who by now had perfected their technique of area bombing under guidance from pathfinders and a master bomber. He was, however, because of the command set-up, obliged to put his request through General Eisenhower, who forwarded it – perhaps through Air Marshal Tedder (by now one of Monty's critics). Air Marshal Harris had fought long to prevent his carefully built-up bomber force from being diverted from what he saw as its primary and vital role of knocking out German war industry; he had been very reluctant to divert even a few planes to help defeat the deadly U-boat threat in the Atlantic. Nevertheless, squadrons were briefed, Harris's proviso being that a good margin should be allowed for error, including the almost inevitable 'creep back' that occurred in bombing. The bomb line was therefore set at 6,000 yards beyond the forward British line, which must seem incredible. This decision not only ensured the German forward defences would remain untouched, it also made certain that hundreds, if not thousands, of French citizens in Caen would perish. However, the British plan allowed for the 'bomb gap' and the enemy defences within it to be taken care of by the artillery. Monty later claimed that a bad weather forecast for 8 July forced the bombers to attack the evening before; an official historian has refuted this. In any event, about 460 RAF four-engined bombers took off around 8.30 p.m. on 7 July to cross the Channel and swing east over the heads of the thousands of watching British and Canadians below.

In all such bomber raids, it was crucial for the attackers to follow up as soon as practical in order to give the shaken enemy no time to recover. Obviously, the Germans were being afforded the maximum time to do just that, for though the raid had been put forward, the ground assault remained fixed to its original timing next morning. This was a basic and serious error that would cost many lives the next day.

The concept of heavy bomber support was hardly new. Bombers had been quickly developed to attack ground forces in the earlier war, and though the Japanese had used them for years in China in the terror role against towns and cities, it was the German *Luftwaffe* which had tried out their tactical use in Spain in 1936–39 and in other campaigns since, 'errors' occurring which resulted in civilian loss of life on a considerable scale. There is no doubt that many a German general would have wished he could call up such powerful air forces to assist in his ground battles. But the types of 'heavy' bomber available to the Germans were puny compared to those wielded by Harris in 1943–45, and the enemy troops around Caen now had a first-hand chance to witness the kind of attack their towns and cities had become attuned to in the Reich proper.

Furthermore, the American General Bradley had assured his subordinate, General Lawton Collins, that heavy bomber support could be made available to him if required, but the ground troops *must* rush in at once behind the bombing. It was crucial. However, the American troops would have good cause to rue bomber support for the much-vaunted 'pinpoint accuracy' against economic targets in the Reich certainly did not come in field operations. And the USAAF were not alone on that score.

Bradley's injunction to 'rush in and you'll get it' never came about around Caen and had no chance. The Germans were served many hours' notice and prepared accordingly, and were contemptuous of the whole British operation.

But on the fateful evening of the great experiment the waiting thousands on the Allied side watched the massed bombers cross the evening sky in two great waves; they flew straight into the heavy flak hurled up against them. One bomber blew up in a great flash after being hit, another caught fire as it was disabled, the crew starting to bale out, while a third spiralled down to crash-land behind the Allied lines. Then the bombs went down, 500 and 1,000-pound high explosives, many of them of the delayed-action type; flame and fire erupted across the 4,000 × 1,500-yard area designated as the target. The soldiers watching this event cheered and cheered, waving their caps and envisaging the hapless enemy being pulverised in their holes and bunkers. A great mass of yellow, grey and black smoke erupted over the northern part of the cathedral city, where the British assumed the enemy units were hiding. In fact, there were practically no Germans in Caen itself, apart from a canteen and, so the British believed, the HQ of 12th SS.

It is said that despite all the fighting that had gone on outside the city and the bombardment, only a quarter of the French citizens had left on the advice of their prefect and the Germans. The British troops were amazed how the RAF bombers sailed on into a wall of flak that one Flight Lieutenant Pathfinder described as more intense than that over 'Happy Valley' – the Ruhr. There was a five-minute break in the raid, between the two waves. By then the city streets were filling up with debris, what one writer referred to as gigantic cubes like sugar, for many of the city's larger buildings were constructed of quarried stone blocks. As it happened, one German at least was caught in the town. Edmund Brinke was in the 21st *Panzers*:

❝ We were not stationed in the city, but outside, to the west, but there was a *Wehrmacht* officers' canteen in Caen. We were resting after being in combat. I was a Sergeant, but had never been in action till the Normandy battle began. We had not had too bad a time, though I could see the battle was going against us. We had only three armoured cars and a jeep left in our recon unit.

We had just enjoyed some well-earned refreshment in the canteen when the air raid warning went over, so we went out into the street to watch and saw hundreds of four-engined bombers in the evening sky, and this was very impressive. The *flak* was bursting among them and as they came on we wondered what their target could be. Then someone who was watching through glasses shouted they were going to bomb the city. We had of course had many air raids, but not by big bombers such as these. The man with the glasses ran off as the first bombs began exploding on the edge of the city. So we ran to our vehicles as we did not want to be caught in that kind of thing.

I had just reached my armoured car when there came several terrific explosions near us and everything seemed to come to a stop. The noise was fantastic and I had a glimpse of everything flying about me – debris and dust and red flashes. I felt heat from the blasts. It all happened in seconds. One moment I had one foot on the car to scramble up inside, the next I was lying in a pool of blood and debris against the wall of the nearest building. I felt no pain but seemed to be in a daze, a nice drowsiness, and I didn't want to get up or do anything. I also seemed to have lost my hearing. Then, after a moment, I turned on my side and saw smoke and pieces falling and more tremendous bangs which seemed to go on and on. I don't know how long this lasted, but then it was quiet but for a constant, peculiar ticking and rasping noise. And when I struggled up I saw the terrible sights of bodies among the debris, the remains of our vehicles and half a German body over one of them.

When I tried to get up I found one of my legs bleeding; otherwise I seemed to be intact, though my uniform was in tatters. Slowly, some signs of life began to appear. I saw a few people and two Germans who ran to help us. Only one of my comrades survived with me. The roof of the canteen had fallen in, so we were taken to another building and given aid. It was some time before we could be removed in an ambulance as few roads were passable. ❞

The bombers released 2,560 tons of bombs, the crews agreeing that the accuracy and concentration were excellent. 'It was a bloody good raid!' Priests and nuns were among those killed when a convent was destroyed, refugees began moving into the undamaged parts of the city, and the hunt for survivors among the mountains of rubble began. 'Evidently the complete destruction of Caen had been decided upon,' one citizen declared afterwards. 'Thousands of tons of bombs fell on one of the most historic cities in France.' Writing just after the war, a French professor stated that the bombing had been absolutely futile; there were no military objectives in Caen. All the bombardment did was choke up the streets with impassable rubble that held up the Allied advance. This was true, as the armoured and infantry units soon found out. Montgomery decided that in future such bombers must use smaller calibre bombs. 'They say there are 5,000 dead,' one French witness said, 'many hundreds are still buried in the debris . . . the piteous cries of those we could not reach will haunt us for ever.'

For the aircrews it had been a 'cakewalk', not like the terrible raid on Nuremberg in March when over ninety bombers had been lost through a combination of faulty planning and weather. The airmen had spent three to four hours on duty, first 'working for the government' on the outward trip and over the target, and once bombing was done 'working for ourselves'. There was time for a decent supper in the mess and then to the mess for drinks, perhaps even a date in town.

Despite being written off by some as a terrible mistake, the Germans did suffer: a regiment of the 16th *Luftwaffe* Field Division was said to be wiped out, and many Germans who were caught on the edge of or just outside the town were severely shaken or driven mad according to one report, with equipment lost. This kind of saturation attack would be repeated elsewhere later on in the campaign, notably at Le Havre, with more post-mortems decades afterwards and condemnation of Monty and Bomber Command.

Montgomery's old division, the 3rd, went into the assault at dawn next morning, as did the beginners on the right flank, most of the 59th's men from Staffordshire; they had everything to learn. First Lieutenant Frank Isen stepped off with one of the leading companies of the South Staffs:

❝ The terrain was fairly flat, with a few farms, and not far off, well within sight, the suburbs of Caen. We'd been tremendously bucked by the RAF bombing and imagined the Germans in chaos. We soon learned differently.

This was a big one, and much was expected of it, even though we the officers knew it was Monty's strategy to hold as many Germans off the Yanks as possible. Everyone knew this, even the men, and they didn't feel too happy about it. But we were new to the game and thought with all the tremendous support from the RAF and guns it would be pretty easy. We had hundreds of guns banging away and thought the noise was terrible and far worse than we'd expected. We were heartened by it.

I was in the lead with my company and we made quite good progress across some fields at first, but quite suddenly we started to get enfilading fire and a few men were hit. So we got down pretty quick and tried to wriggle forward, but then came under fire from those terrible big mortars and machine-guns and it was pretty horrific – I mean the lead was fairly singing over our heads and we couldn't move. I heard yells above the din and shouts for medics and a great feeling of disappointment came over me. **"**

George Wainwright was in the North Staffs, a Private going into action for the first time. He had just been finishing a last letter to his mother and added a hurried 'PS' to the effect that he expected to be pretty busy, so she should not worry if no more letters came for a while:

" We trotted along behind our Lieutenant and saw all the great smoke going up from the barrage which moved ahead of us, about 200 to 300 yards I believe, and we thought this will be easy. The RAF had knocked hell out of the Jerries and now the guns were finishing off the rest. Well, after five to ten minutes I saw chaps falling left and right and then realised we were under fire from two sides and hit the deck pretty quick. We lay there for a few minutes till I heard the Sergeant-Major yelling for us to get on and be safe – that's what he said. So we tried to wriggle on and some ran like mad; some were hit and me, I just crawled as fast as I could and then we found shell craters and flopped down into them in a hell of a sweat. **"**

John Liddings was in the South Staffs reserve company and was called along with the rest of the lads much sooner than expected and guessed things had gone unexpectedly quite wrong:

" We were holed up beside a little wood near our transport and watching the leading companies go off after the great barrage, and after about ten minutes, not much more, a Lieutenant ran up and told us to get ready. Some of us were smoking and I was swigging tea. We were all taken by surprise and scared stiff as everyone thought it would be pretty easy. That announcement meant only one thing to us: things had gone wrong. We'd been through the exercises at home in England with similar situations, with things getting all balled up, and had done exactly the same, but over there, what with all that fantastic bombing and the artillery – well, we were really shaken. And we hadn't gone far before we were under fire and everyone hit the deck and started praying and cursing, depending on what sort of a bloke you were. Then we saw medics trying to move back the wounded under fire and the sight of all that blood didn't help.

After a minute I suppose our own Lieutenant told us to follow him and we got up, crouching and terrified, as he rushed off towards the first shellholes. Well, he got there all right, but he was killed at the last moment and fell headlong into the hole. When I ran up and fell in that hole and saw him all doubled up with his eyes half open and a sort of apologetic look on his face I felt like giving up. But the Sarge jumped in, took one look, swore and said we'd be better off elsewhere as the big mortars were coming down thick and fast. There were four more of us and he forced us out of that hole some hundred yards or so into a much bigger one, where we found about a dozen other blokes all waiting for orders.

Well, the guns were still going and some bombers came over and the Sarge told us to follow him, so we did, and it wasn't too bad at first. But then we were held up again and couldn't move. **99**

Bernard Coleman was a subaltern with the 1st South Lancs of the 3rd Division:

66 We expected to take Caen after all that bombing and the barrage ahead was terrific. We led off at a good pace and it wasn't too bad. We'd been in action since D-day and done pretty well really, though naturally we'd lost a good many men and not had many replacements. At least we felt we knew the ropes, and so far I'd been lucky, with only a scratch wound across my right leg which didn't put me out of action at all. But I must say from what I knew a great proportion of the officers in all the units had been lost, which was bad as the replacements were very green and had to learn the hard way. I'd spent some time trying to teach a very young subaltern all I knew, but he was very scared and didn't seem to take it in too well and I'm sorry to say he was soon killed in the attack.

We only lost two or three men in the first half hour, but then we came right up against the first Jerry positions and had some hard fighting. I saw several Jerries behind a machine-gun, but fortunately for my group they were heavily engaged with other British trying to get at them. We threw grenades and got the lot. I saw bits and pieces flying almost before the bangs had subsided. We were on our feet and rushing them and didn't lose a single man. By noon we had captured all our objectives and felt very pleased with ourselves. We had entered the Caen suburbs but were then held up properly. We took several prisoners, however, and found they were *Luftwaffe* chaps and sent them back to the rear, and I remember someone saying, 'So that's why we've had it easy eh?' The going got very bad as there was so much mess and debris. With the Jerries well holed up it was almost impossible to make any more progress before darkness. **99**

The 6th Airborne had been in almost continuous action since the early hours of 6 June, and apart from one short break would continue in the line until the war ended following their meeting with Russian troops in north Germany near the Danish border, but that was many months away. Nobby Clark was in the 1st Paras:

❝ We hadn't had much rest since D-day and went into the attack again during Operation Charnwood. I was a Sergeant and thought we would not have it as easy as some thought. For one thing I knew the bombers had not touched the SS defences in front of us, and I also knew from experience what happened when an artillery barrage hit them. They simply got into their deep holes, if they had them, and got up to oppose us once it was over. The trouble was, they'd been able to get themselves properly organised; by that I mean they were well dug into the ground with plenty of guns too, and dug-in Tigers as well. I thought we were in for a hard time, but I kept quiet.

Well, we went in at dawn and the stuff started to fly right away and we ran like mad to get ahead of the mortar bursts – that was the way to escape those. They couldn't adjust their range fast enough; in other words, if you stayed still you'd likely get hit. We ran like hell and missed the worst of it, but of course the bloody SS machine-guns caught us as usual. But we moved like lightning and had few casualties. I jumped into a hole with a bunch of other lads. We had our red berets on as we thought it had some effect. I don't think I ever wore a helmet in all those months, except once when we were getting air bursts.

I had some glasses and tried to take a look ahead and saw ruined buildings and the city with the chimneys at Colombelles which were a sort of magnet for us. Somehow we had to get to the river and I thought, If anyone can do it we can. Well, we did, but that was hours later and by then we'd had no end of skirmishes and lost a few good chaps. My old mate Ron copped it near me and I couldn't stop as we were in a hell of a fight with some SS outside a ruined farm and had several more casualties. There were dead Germans lying about and more inside after we'd got in. We threw grenades through the lower windows and fired bursts and then crashed in and found no one alive. So we consolidated and a Lieutenant I knew quite well ran up and said, 'Fucking good show chaps! We're almost there!' Well, we got there all right, but could get no further as the Jerries were in strength over the river and the mess in that part of the town was indescribable. ❞

The plan for the three British divisions to converge on Caen and for an armoured column to dash in and seize crossings over the Orne misfired because the streets were impassable through the bombing. The city was roughly cut in two by the river and railways; it took until 10 July for the 2nd Army units to claim the northern half. It had been 59th Division's unhappy lot to enter the battle against the veterans of 12th SS; while 3rd Division and the airborne moved fairly rapidly ahead into Caen, the green troops were still fighting miles behind. Bernard Coleman:

❝ That evening we found we were completely stuck, pinned down and unable to move an inch. The Colonel sent a cheery word that every man had done well in his first battle and he knew we would do even better the next day. Well, we knew what he really meant, but next morning after yet another gun barrage we made little headway and lost more men. I think we'd lost over half the lads in my company and I couldn't see how we could get into the city with our reduced strength. In fact, I never expected to live that long as the odds seemed heavily against it.

There were small hamlets, or what had been hamlets as they were now heaps of ruins, with all kinds of possessions strewn about through the bombardment. And it was amongst all that kind of mess that the SS set up their defences and it was very hard going. We had some Churchills, but every time they went into action they'd get knocked out, so we'd be without support and at the mercy of those big mortars and even 88s and lost more men. At one point I had just three men with me. We were heads down in a little hole and almost out of ammunition. The NCOs had been lost I thought, and I just couldn't see what could be done. But we chucked the last of our grenades at the Jerries, who were very near, and then I said, 'You've done damned well lads, I'm grateful to you.' Then I thought we'd be overwhelmed by a counter-attack. But suddenly with great relief we saw a flame-throwing Churchill come up and it squirted everything in our path. We waved like mad and then rushed after it. The smell was awful, and when we saw what had been the Jerry positions there were just black lumps lying about and I felt sick. **"**

The British assault had certainly tied down the enemy, but as an experiment in Bomber Command–Army co-operation it had failed. Yet, whatever unease and criticism came the Germans had lost half of Caen, and from accounts it seems that some enemy troops did move into the ruins to try to exact an even greater price from the attackers. In his famous novel *The Young Lions*, American author Irwin Shaw describes how an American liaison officer drove into a rubble-strewn street, observing a British heavy mortar team firing from among heaps of books and other rubbish spilt from the ruins of the city university. The American was then warned of German snipers, rather roughly by a Canadian behind a machine-gun: 'Where d'ya think ya are – Brooklyn?'

At least one of the German staff found some consolation in seeing his earlier prognostications of Allied intent borne out:

" In my opinion we were right in our earlier appreciation concerning the enemy's tactics. Once having gained a foothold they have built up their forces with astonishing rapidity and been able to deluge us with artillery fire, and this has at times been impossible for us to counter. As to the air situation, it is beyond belief. The Americans are now in process of breaking out from the landing area and unless checked this will result in a very dangerous situation. In the Caen sector our forces are being bled white and the replacement situation is impossible. We simply have not the men any more to contain the pressure there. If only the *Führer* could release a division or two from the Eastern Front. **"**

So recorded General Gunther Blumentritt, Chief-of-Staff at 15th Army early in July.

The replacement situation had long badly deteriorated for the German ground forces who, after years of combat, were simply running out of men. Heinrich Luttemann was one of thousands transferred from the *Luftwaffe* in which he had served as a ground mechanic since 1936. Few if any of these men had any heart for fighting and felt out of place with a weapon; nevertheless, they went through infantry training in Germany and then France, still clad in *Luftwaffe* blue. Not until into 1944 did they receive long-pattern *Luftwaffe* camouflage jackets; their NCOs were veterans of the airborne forces. Luttemann states that in his opinion none of the rank and file felt confident in his new role, and this was proved when combat came.

After 'a lot of confusion' two companies of his division (16th) were sent to fight the British while others went off to combat the Americans. Luttemann's unit went off north of Caen, their morale sagging and apprehensive as they saw all the Allied planes overhead and the wreckage strewn along the roadside. Met by guides, they went forward into the battle zone, debussing and creeping along on foot:

❝ We heard small-arms fire so got down, trying to see what was going on. An army Corporal arrived to warn of British troops immediately in front, who we must attack at once. Our flanks were safe, at least on the right – SS troops were there – while tanks of 21st *Panzer* were on the left.

I was terrified, with all the noise. I could not see the sea but knew there was a big armada out there, with battleships shelling us. We were urged on by NCOs and soon the bullets began to fly and I heard shouts from those hit who vanished behind us. I was so frightened I just wanted to curl up and hide. But we had a loud-mouthed NCO behind us with a Schmeisser and he kept driving us on. Then I heard even louder shouting and saw brown figures rushing at us and this seemed amazing as they seemed to have appeared from nowhere. I suddenly realised my comrades, those I could see, were running away to the left, so I went after them without looking round until we were among some trees and trying to shoot back. The NCO ran in after us, but said nothing apart from telling us the enemy were Canadians.

The battle went on and on as the enemy advanced to our right and left, and after several hours we were quite out of touch with the others and our HQ. Night came. We were exhausted and lying in a ditch, cold and wet with nothing to eat or drink. The British kept shelling us and we had to stay under cover as far as we could. When it got light an army patrol came and showed us back to a broken road where there was a field kitchen, so we ate some soup and bread and drank coffee before being ordered back into action by a Captain. ❞

It wasn't long before a terrified Luttemann ran into the enemy again. He was wounded in the left leg, crawling back through the grass in pain until meeting a jeep and being removed to the rear.

Siegfried Mansenn commanded a Mk IV tank in 21st *Panzers*:

❝ We had taken up defensive positions with others of our unit before the enemy began shelling in the morning. Then we saw Shermans coming across the fields with all kinds of other vehicles behind. Although we were hull-down we were not deep enough; our turret had to be exposed, and I got down as the stuff began to fly, clattering all over our hull. I ordered our gunner not to fire until he could see clear targets, but then there were several explosions in front of our tank, and by the time he could see the Shermans were almost upon us and shooting madly. We opened fire and hit one in the left side and it stopped, smoking. But we ourselves were then hit at once. I felt a tremendous bang which shook the turret; I heard the rattle of splinters and cries of pain from my men. In one second a great gout of flame shot round the interior of the tank. I could only throw the hatch open and jump out, rolling over the grass as I was smoking. Almost at once the tank exploded in flames. I ran off as far as I could and hid under a bush before it blew up. I was in a terrible state of shock as I glanced back and realised my comrades were burning to death. It was awful.

Then I was surrounded by Tommies and taken prisoner. ❞

Helmut Grausenn had been with the 30% remains of the 319th Infantry in the Channel Islands (most of the division had been creamed off to the Russian Front):

❝ In January 1944 a party of us were sent back to Germany to help with recruit training. We were still there when the invasion came, and a few weeks later – I believe it was early July – we were suddenly told we would join another unit and be sent to the front. We were very surprised but understood there was no chance we could get back to the Channel Islands. We joined a group of replacements and fought between the 16th *Luftwaffe* Division and 1st SS.

I was a Corporal with a little experience in Italy with another unit. We were told the SS were on our right; in fact in the fighting we were almost mixed in with them. We had a lot of respect for them as soldiers, but they were very much a force on their own.

The British artillery seemed to fire at us all day and half the night. It was impossible to move by day because of the Allied planes. Then we were told to counter-attack a Canadian advance and did so. I had six men with me, and we hid in a little wood with the rest of our unit and on the signal we all rushed forward into what I thought was certain death as the enemy were in far greater numbers and we could see them a few hundred yards away with all their armour. Hell broke loose as we rushed at them, trying to fire short bursts and then drop down. Grenades were flung and machine-guns were firing at us. The grass was rather long and suitable for concealment, but I knew if we stopped and took cover it would mean certain death for us from mortars and artillery. So I ran on, hoping my men were still with me. I saw a lot of khaki figures dodging from one place to another and the bullets were flying about us. Then I dropped down to start firing short bursts and threw grenades which landed exactly on target. There was a lot of noise and screams and I knew my comrades were to the left and right of me doing as I did. But some were hit and killed and there was nothing I could do for them. Then some of the enemy tanks started to rake the grass with their machine-guns, but we had well-hidden anti-tank guns and some of the Churchills were knocked out.

Then their artillery started on us. The explosions were terrible and deafening. There were red flashes and smoke all around us. Then I saw khaki figures rushing at us and I called to my comrades to withdraw. I felt we had done a fair amount of damage. This we did under cover of the smoke from the shells. But several men were hit and we never saw them again. **"**

Georg Russeten was one of an advance party of the 363rd Infantry sent forward on reconnaissance east of Caen one afternoon in July. An experienced Sergeant wounded in Russia, he had been posted to France after recuperating.

" We went forward past another unit; a British attack was expected at any time. Observing the terrain I heard a lot of movement but could see nothing, so we went forward again, using hedges as cover beside a straight road which turned away so that we were obliged to halt as it was impossible to see what lay round the bend. Then, as we reached this point, we encountered some enemy troops in a little scout car; they saw us at the same moment. One of my men fired first with his sub-machine-gun and hit the vehicle and it ran off the road. The occupants were not hit and dived into cover at once. Our fire had put the enemy vehicle out of action and we lay flat, using what cover there was, and threw two grenades which exploded on the enemy, and I believe all were killed.

Two of my men crept forward to remove their weapons and we moved on round the bend in the road and saw a whole lot of enemy vehicles which had halted. We were seen and the bullets started flying. Several of their vehicles were shooting at us so we withdrew in a hurry, running back down the road as fast as we could. But the enemy were on our heels and shooting. Two of our men were hit and fell, and when I stopped to help them the British were upon us. Two more men were hit and we were taken prisoner. After being searched and our weapons taken we were bundled into a truck and taken away for interrogation, and that evening we reached a PoW cage and were later taken to England where I spent the rest of the war in safety. **"**

Captain Hans Gilbertus of 12th SS was also taken prisoner – but by the Canadians, and suffered similar treatment to others of his kind.

❝ I had been on reconnaissance with three lads through a cornfield when we were suddenly confronted by six or seven Tommies who surrounded us. We had no choice but to surrender. Our captors proved to be large Canadians. They snatched off our helmets and weapons and marched us back to their positions, handing us over to a Lieutenant who took us off for interrogation, one by one. When I went into the tent I was given some tea and a biscuit and a Captain asked me some questions in bad German which I refused to answer. The Lieutenant then snatched the chair from under me and I fell to the ground. I still said nothing, so the Lieutenant kicked me in the shin and took me outside. I was taken over by three large men, they may have been policemen, taken behind a tent and given a good beating. Then I was taken back into the tent where the Captain asked me the same questions, which again I refused to answer. So they took me outside again, tied me to a jeep and left me.

I was sitting on the ground, wondering what would come next. There were plenty of soldiers about; some grinned and made jokes, others seemed sympathetic. Then, as it grew dark, one of the Captains gave me some tea. When an officer called him away I realised this was my chance to escape. The man turned away so I leapt up, knocking him aside, and ran off through the bushes. There were shouts behind me, but I ran on and on, over a road and across the countryside like a madman. I heard some shots, then nothing. I collapsed into a ditch and waited a few moment, but I was not followed. I heard artillery fire and ran on eastwards, stopping several times to listen, then heard all kinds of battle noises and realised I must be close to the front line – on the wrong side. I wondered how I could get past the enemy troops.

Then came a Germany artillery barrage so I ran on once more in what I hoped was the right direction, and at last fell into a hole, and to my amazement found one of my own Sergeants. ❞

Two Germans suffered a drastic change of service when, to their amazement, they were transferred from the *Luftwaffe* into 1st *SS Leibstandarte*, the one-time 'asphalt soldiers', Hitler's praetorian guard unit who had long been expanded into divisional status to fight on the war fronts. Peter Schlieser and Edward Karl Wenter were conscripted into the air force in 1937 and had worked on bomber maintenance until late 1943, when they learned of their transfer to the infantry. They left their base at Wünstorf, travelling to the army garrison town of Münster where, after a delay of some days, they began attending lectures, along-side sailors, formerly of the *Kriegsmarine*. They learned about various infantry weapons and field tactics and did some drill. Then came an even greater shock – they would serve in the *Waffen-SS*.

Thirty of the transferees were trucked to a camp in north-west

Germany where they debussed to find SS men in grey-green, a Sergeant showing them into accommodation before marching them off for a meal. Then they were taken before an officer who told them the chance had come for them to show what they were made of. They were going to fight the enemy in Normandy with one of the seasoned SS divisions:

❝ We both felt frightened. We were hurried off to an equipment store to be fitted out with fresh uniforms and taken for a quick medical check-up, including a visit to the dentist. Then we were returned to the barracks for the night. Early next morning the Sergeant took us for a run round the camp before breakfast. Then we were formed into squads and did field training, which was hard, and went on for three to four hours. Then we were inspected by an officer, split up, and we two were despatched to the 1st SS, which amazed us.

We travelled by train to northern France and arrived in a hutted camp where a Corporal showed us to some beds. Next day we were received by a Major who examined our records before making a little speech in which he thoughtfully expressed his regret that we had been taken away from our own units, but the war was reaching a new and difficult stage and the Reich had to make the best use of its manpower etc. He then dismissed us, and that same day we joined the division on manoeuvres, which proved very exhausting and hard, with live ammunition used in a small area of the French countryside. However, although it was all very new, we grew used to the idea of being in the SS, though frightened of what lay ahead. In this we were right, as after a delay when the life we led was not bad the invasion came, and we were at last sent into action.

This was a terrible baptism of fire for us as we'd never been in action. The air attacks were very bad and we never thought we would survive. Then Edward was wounded in the first British attack; a bullet struck his arm and he was carried off in pain. I was terrified but fired my rifle and hoped for the best. I have no idea if I killed anyone, I never really looked, but simply fired when the others did. The worst part was the artillery which went on and on, and when the tanks came we simply retreated a short way to let the anti-tank guns deal with them. After three weeks of this we were filthy, starving and thirsty most of the time and lost at least half our men, and I thought it must be the end of the war. Then came a worse disaster: my family were bombed out of their home in Kiel, but because of the situation at the front I was unable to go and see them. ❞

Peter's friend Edward returned, only to be wounded again at once, more seriously in the chest, and captured by the British. After the disaster at Falaise in mid-August Peter collapsed in sickness. Following his recovery in hospital he was transferred to the SS reserve and never fought again.

Karl Lothar Voser was in one of the *nebelwerfer* rocket battalions that so plagued the Allies. Attached to 1st SS they took part in one of the many counter-attacks east of Cheux:

❝ We loaded our weapons after carefully camouflaging our hideout and received fire orders from our Sergeant-Major, and on the command opened fire. The noise of the rockets was as always terrific and we had to stand well clear. The missiles screamed on their way and we ran to reload, then fired again, and again, and in about half an hour had exhausted all our ammunition and awaited a fresh supply by truck. This never came, as not long after we were severely bombed and our weapon put out of action. In the chaos our chain of command was broken and we lost contact with our officers, so we remained in shelter for some time without orders. Our Corporal ran back to find out what was happening, but never returned. We next received a pasting from British artillery which combed the area very methodically and I received a splinter wound in the arm and ran back to get help. ❞

Hans Mischmann was attached to the 1st SS *Panzer* Corps as a messenger and often saw the top commanders. One day early in July he saw Sepp Dietrich in conference and heard the following words: 'Gentlemen, the situation is hopeless. Unless we receive some re-inforcements we shall have a catastrophe. The British have broken through here, and here, and we have a desperate situation with no means to quell the flow. I have repeatedly asked for help, but those fools do not seem to grasp the urgency of it all.' Mischmann was then seen eavesdropping by a Sergeant who sent him off on some errand.

Johannes Georg Fink was an anti-tank gunner in 1st SS:

❝ We had just arrived from our reserve positions east of Caen when we were hit by air attack and our gun destroyed. Four men were killed or wounded and we were directed to another unit who were short of men. There were three of us and we were expected by a Sergeant who showed us to three guns minus crews. The weapons were battered but still work-able, so we set to and before long were ready for action and heavily camouflaged under some bushes. We saw some Shermans coming over a hill but waited till we could read the numbers and insignia on them before opening fire. We remained unseen and knocked out three of them. The rest of the tanks came on or tried to find cover. One tank we missed almost overran us. It came straight for us with guns blazing, but one of our other guns got it with a shot in the flank. It burst into flames, slewed sideways and blew up.

Then the enemy infantry, having located our positions, opened fire and we were forced to take cover. Despite fire from our own tanks the enemy rushed at us and we were forced to run for our lives. We grabbed what weapons we had and fired and fired. One Tommy fell dead over our gun and two more were wounded. Another Tommy rushed at us with his rifle and bayonet and I tried to dodge aside, but he kicked me in the shin and I fell over. He was then shot by one of my comrades. But our position was now untenable so we ran for our lives as many more of the enemy rushed at us. When we reached a nearby wood we ran slap-bang into an artillery barrage, the splinters falling around us until we reached some more German positions and fell into a hole.

A Sergeant looked us over. We were bloody and exhausted, so he gave us a drink of schnapps and some biscuits, which were English, and we slowly recovered. But we never received any replacement guns in that battle. **99**

9 'Bring Back Some Jerry Souvenirs'

Some Allied soldiers who went to France were asked by sons or relatives, sometimes in jocular fashion, to 'bring us back a souvenir'. In any case, trophies of the war experience were routinely picked up, from bodies or prisoners. Sometimes loot of another nature was collected, though often discarded later. There was a limit to the number of oddments an infantryman could carry, especially when on the march.

Sam Whiten was with the Somersets and out of the line, enjoying a well-earned rest after much fighting and heavy casualties.

❝ The whole time I was waiting for the invasion I had one big thought in mind which was to bring back some Jerry souvenirs. I was convinced I would live through it and the battlefield must be full of gear like that, if only I could get my hands on it.

One afternoon, after I had had something to eat I asked my mate Tom if he felt like a bit of souvenir hunting. He said, 'You're joking? You fucking twerp! You'll get yourself blown up.' I knew what he meant: the Jerry SS had laid mines and it wasn't safe to go far beyond our own dugouts. But I didn't care, I thought I'd just be careful and find a few bodies. By then I'd seen enough, but they'd been too mangled and too horrible to touch – or else someone had beaten me to it.

So I strolled off with helmet on and carrying a Sten gun. The NCOs were not about and I told my mate to say nothing. There were plenty of bushes and small woods about so I headed for the nearest trees that we knew were clear of Jerry. I saw some of our blokes in foxholes, but they took no notice of me. When I reached the first trees I started to go more carefully and make sure I didn't step on a mine or tripwire. I looked this way and that and saw plenty of splinters and other oddments but nothing I wanted. Then, after I'd gone through some trees and bushes, I felt certain I could see some old Jerry foxholes and bits lying around. The ground was rather open so I went down on my hands and knees into the grass, which was quite long. In fact, I began to feel a bit scared as I'd left our own area and thought I might get shot by our own side, or the Jerries if they'd got their eyes open.

Well, I then got the shock of my life.

I blundered on hands and knees and there were three bodies, all Jerries, and they really were stinking. They must have been dead a few days and looked a horrible yellow colour. One of them had the SS-type camouflage jacket and full equipment including a rifle, but the other two wore the usual grey jackets which were dirty. Their eyes were half open and they really made me feel queer, I can tell you. I said 'Christ!' and lay flat and still for a few moments. Then I forced myself up and moved a few inches nearer the bodies in grey as they both had badges on. I really wanted to shut my eyes, but I had to struggle to get the badges off them. They included laurels, but I really wanted an Iron Cross. One of the badges had a crossed rifle with an eagle and swastika; the other one I got was smaller, round, black with a helmet with swastika.*

I felt so pleased with my finds. I shoved them in my blouse pocket and retreated backwards as fast as I could. When I got back I found the lads getting ready to move off again. **99**

Few in the army and certainly none among the public knew of the 'Phantoms', the small, officially named 'HQ Liaison Regiment' personnel. This unit was formed in 1940 to ensure the War Office staff in London were kept fully up-to-date on the front situation, which could change very rapidly. Captain Phillip Courtan had been in the unit for a year when the Normandy campaign came:

66 I had seen no action, though some of my friends had been in the Med and Italy. We reported to the War Office by radio. The sets were compact, only about 1×9 inches and quite powerful, providing the batteries were OK and the aerials properly set.

I went over with about twenty others in mid-June, split into three groups, going to 8th and 30th Corps, and we were soon testing our sets, calling the WO Q department. We called 'Q–Q–Q–Q' and waited for a reply. As soon as they sent 'A–A–A–A' we'd give them our call sign; mine was 'Hercules', the others had similar names based on Greek or Roman gods.

We first went to the fighting area during a heavy battle, which was quite a hectic business, with plenty of counter-attacks. We'd never been near action, so it was all pretty terrifying. We had maps and made notes on both the British positions and the enemy's. Although we gained a good idea of who was opposing us, you could not always be certain in a changing situation. I remember one day we saw some PoWs and took a good look at them and their docs and found they were from the *Luftwaffe*, Navy and other odds, so we guessed the Huns were scraping the bottom of the barrel. Of course, they all wore the usual equipment. As for the SS, we saw some rum customers. It was our job to interpret everything into reports and get them off by radio, but the Corps people wanted these chaps for themselves, we didn't always get first choice.

Anyway, one afternoon we'd just been into the front line and stopped for some much-needed tea to steady my nerves. I had a

* The first of these was an Infantry Assault award, the second a Wound Badge Third Class.

Sergeant with me who was a very good linguist and we saw a bunch
of PoWs, so he went over to have a chat with them. He came back
telling me he reckoned one of them was an SS officer, but trying to
appear otherwise. I said, 'What makes you think that Harry?' And he
replied, 'Because he was trying to hide his service book in his jacket.'
I must say the chap looked a lot tougher than the rest and acted rather
furtively. So I had him brought over to our vehicle to interrogate him
thoroughly, and he tried to hide his service papers by dropping them
in the grass behind him. Well, it didn't work, and when we picked
them up he just grinned and said in English, 'Well, the game's up. Can
I have some tea?'

So we gave him some in a mug with a biscuit and he proved very
chatty, though giving absolutely nothing away, though we knew full well
he was from 1st SS as they were opposite us. He spoke about his family
in Hamburg and said they'd lost everything. I told him I was sorry to
hear that, but it was the same in many of our cities. 'That's war,' he said,
and went on to ask how we were enjoying the V1s. I told him they were
being shot down in large numbers, which he didn't believe. I asked him
if he'd like to work for us, as a joke. And he said yes, as an interpreter
– 'Is the pay good?'

We had a good laugh and he went off under guard. **99**

Londoner Bill Bradley, having missed the invasion through a minor
foot operation, found himself drafted into a replacement pool and
despatched to the south, living under canvas until they were sent across
the Channel.

66 I was amazed to learn we were to join the 51st Highland Division,
and after we got across we could hear the guns at the front and next
morning went before a Scottish Warrant Officer who told us most of the
lads were 'up front' and we would go to join them that very morning. I
was frightened as I'd never been in action before, unlike a fair number
of the Jocks. So when we went off in a truck I was shit scared. The noise
gradually got louder and we saw a few unburied bodies – all Germans,
all uncovered and looking bloody horrible.

Then we met a Sergeant who divided us into two parties, and took
me with some others along a track through the trees, while a Corporal
took the rest off. We had the usual gear including rifles, and I'd brought
a few little cakes along that I'd bought at the depot in the London
NAAFI. We then had to crouch down as we came to the Highland Div
foxholes, which were very well camouflaged, and near a small wood
which I soon realised the Jerries zeroed into. Their shells burst in the
trees and sent bits flying in all directions, so it was no good thinking you
could shelter there. I dived into a hole about four by two by six feet deep
with another lad also from London, who said, 'What a fucking kettle of
fish, eh Bill?'

I didn't say much as I was too sick in the stomach and the noise was continuous, which surprised me. The guns were banging away all the time and though we couldn't see any of them there was smoke going up over the fields to our left. I felt like having a doze and a ciggie with some char. But the Sergeant came round and told us to watch our front and be ready for anything. I hardly dared look over the top of the hole, which was quite muddy at the bottom, but I did finally pluck up the courage. All I saw was a similar landscape with woods, about a mile away, fields, some bits of debris and smoke, and I believe there were some dead cows. It looked nothing like a Great War battlefield, everything looked so green. There was a lot of plane noise that went on most of the time, and every so often you saw a few dots diving over the Jerry positions and heard the *flak*. Once we saw a plane shot down, I think it was a Tiffie [Typhoon]. It went straight down into the wood in flames.

When midday came we were tired and cramped and nothing seemed to be happening until the grub came. Two blokes crawled up with a big urn of something, and then another one with some tea. They handed out cans and packs of M and V, so we started eating, and it didn't seem too bad. Then, after a while, two more bods turned up to relieve us, so we took our cans and rifles and went off for a pee about twenty yards away. We'd only just got there when all hell broke loose. Jerry shells started to come over like mad so we ran back to our hole and dived in on top of the other two, and we all huddled up in a terrific funk. The noise was terrific, with the shells whizzing over us and banging down not far beyond us. The earth clods and splinters came crashing about. This went on for about ten minutes before it went quiet again, but some of the lads said it could mean a Jerry attack.

So we gradually looked out over the top of our hole just as the Sergeant started yelling something at us. I never knew what he said, but there was a hell of a racket and I saw a lone line of Sherman tanks come into view on our left and they passed the little wood. That was the signal for the Jerry shells to start coming over again, but this time there was anti-tank fire all round the tanks and we did our best to hide ourselves as some of them were hit and blew up with a terrific roar. I felt terrible, but even sorrier for the poor beggars in those tanks. There was nothing we could do for them.

Then we heard machine-guns and the whole area was doused with tracers and big mortar bursts. I was terrified and cowered in the hole praying we'd not get killed. Then I heard the tanks rolling off at top speed across the fields and our Sergeants blew whistles and one of the other lads said, 'Fuck it! Here we go again!' We had to struggle up out of the hole and start following the tanks across the fields. I was in a terrible state but trotted on. The machine-gun fire got worse and the guns were banging away like mad. Then I realised two of the lads with me had vanished, but there were lots more all running and dodging across the grass. I had lost sight of my mate, and then tripped over something and fell headlong and saw it was a headless body of a Jock. I retched and buried my face in the grass.

The noise didn't let up and someone kicked me in the leg and told me to 'Get a fucking move on!' He grabbed my arm and I saw it was a Corporal with a Sten gun. I ran with him and saw a flame-throwing tank in action and could smell the burning. There had been some little houses near the wood ahead; these had been destroyed or were burning. The Corporal told me to follow him, so I did, and we joined up with some others and rushed towards some German holes where the ground was all chewed up, with bits of bodies lying around. It was terrible. There was an awful stench there and we ran on until we stopped near the ruined houses, the remaining tanks on the other side. I'd only just flopped down in a state and hadn't fired a shot when we were ordered to jump in a wagon, which we did, about twelve of us. We rode on a way then got out again as we reached a little lane where we found a Colonel who congratulated everyone on their fine performance.

That was my introduction to battle. **99**

Sergeant Bill Molden, the American volunteer, had survived the June battles:

66 Into July things got very bad as we'd put in a lot of attacks and lost a lot of men including all our officers. One morning we went off to the start line, over a ditch and through a hedge, up a cornfield with the Jerry fire coming at us. We just kept going and I could sense our boys going down like ninepins. The corn was on fire and the din terrific, with shells going over both ways and the zip, zip of slugs about me. I ducked down several times, I was that sure I'd be hit. We couldn't see the bloody Germans but knew they were up ahead somewhere. Then at last I did see one not far ahead and took a shot at him as he changed position. I missed him and looked round to warn the lads where they were. Then I felt a tug at my sleeve and saw it was torn by a bullet, so I jumped into a muddy crater and saw one dead Jerry who stank like hell.

Then some more of the lads joined me. I didn't know them all. We'd lost so many men the platoons were all mixed up. One boy had a Bren so I got him to set it up and blast away in the direction I gave. Then the Jerries started throwing grenades and all kinds of stuff at us, so we got out of that hole, running in two directions to try to outflank them. That was when I got another bullet, this time in the right leg. I went down yelling, but all the other lads ran on and vanished in the corn. So I was alone and trying to keep quiet, though my leg hurt like hell. It seemed ages before the tanks came up and I was able to get back and find a medic who gave me a shot and I went right out.

When I came to I was well behind the line, and two days later I was back in Blighty. My leg never healed so I was invalided out of the army. **99**

Robert Sherwin was in the reserve Dorsets and was sent over in time for 'one of Monty's big offensives'. He was unable to recall which one, though it was in July.

❝ We were in the thick of it at once. We'd never been in action but had plenty of training; the real thing was very different. For a start, there were unburied cows and bodies where we were and the smell was terrible, you couldn't get away from it. The noise was far worse as our guns and planes were at it all the time. We formed up and a Captain told us our objective was a little wood across the Odon river. He said, 'For God's sake keep your heads down. You've done it in training enough times. Let's get it over with chaps and good luck!' We knew him well; he'd never been in action either. He had a little mascot tied to the collar of his blouse.

The guns put down a hell of a barrage and off we went into the thick of it. The breeze blew the smoke back at us and the Churchills vanished into it. We heard a lot of sharp bangs and guessed the Jerries were catching the tanks and we were right. When the smoke cleared we saw most of them had been knocked out. But we ran on and on and kept ducking down until we were quite close to the little wood and couldn't see the enemy anywhere, only dead ones, and they looked awful. I wanted to stop and grab a souvenir, but each time the Corporal told me to bloody well get a move on!

Then our chaps started getting hit. I saw one bloke I knew running around with an eye knocked out. Then several more ran back yelling; some were wounded, some were just terrified. The Sergeant-Major, believe it or not, was there with his cane yelling 'Windy bastards!' trying to make them go back. One or two did, the others just lay down and pretended to be firing at the Jerries. I'd never thought about running away, but when the bullets started to fly about us and chaps were going down, some of them horribly mutilated, it took my best guts to keep going. So I did, and we found some Jerry positions well mangled up by shellfire, and bodies and bits of bodies, all SS in those camouflage suits. So we consolidated near the wood while the rest of the tanks shot the hell out of the place and we thought we'd won.

But just as I started to light a cigarette those big Jerry mortars started falling around us so we huddled down in the holes and prayed no shell had our number on it. It seemed to go on for ages before a lot of planes went in – Typhoons and Spits I think – and the racket stopped. The stretcher bearers did a fantastic job and after a bit the Sergeant-Major came and ordered us into the wood in case any Jerries were still there. There were twelve of us; all my mates bar one had copped it.

We found no Jerries alive in the wood, only one kid who was crying and he went off behind us dragging his leg. ❞

Jim Pearce drove a Sherman in the 7th Royal Tanks and went into the line in July:

66 By then the Jerries had no chance to knock us into the sea, but they were making it very hard for us. We knew from what our officers said that the enemy had concentrated most of his armour against us, so we never thought we'd have an easy time.

We went up beyond the Odon on transporters, then unloaded our tanks; ours was a Firefly with a seventeen-pounder gun which gave us great confidence as we thought if properly used we could deal with any German tank, including a Tiger. But we saw so many damaged and destroyed Shermans, Churchills, Honeys and Cromwells, we felt scared in case we were taking on more than we could deal with. But our troop CO was full of beans and a good commander. He said we'd do our best to support the lads on the ground – the Poor Bloody Infantry – and we did.

We got up early one morning and brewed some tea. We were not far behind the line among some damaged trees. We had some biscuits and bacon and felt keen to get started. Our objective was a main road, still used by the Jerries despite all our air attacks. It was a local push, not one of Monty's big efforts. When we got the order to start up it was a terrific thrill to see and hear all those big tanks in two lines. We felt invincible. By the end of that day half those lads would be knocked out or missing.

A guide showed us clear of the trees. I knew my job and liked the Sherman. It was easy to drive and I never had any problems. We were a good team. Our Sergeant was a wisecracking chap from Tyneside, a real Geordie. As soon as we reached the field we spread out into open formation and made quite good progress. Naturally, a driver's view is somewhat limited so I was rather relying on Geordie who was still up in the open with a helmet on giving me directions. But then we heard machine-gun bullets hitting us, so Geordie got down pretty quick. We could see hedgerows and weapons flashing so the Brownings on the tanks started spraying the whole area ahead.

Then came the first cracks as the Jerry 88s and other anti-tank guns got on to us. I glimpsed one of our Shermans to the left going up in flames, with bits flying all over the place. We went straight on towards the nearest hedge and suddenly another Sherman veered across our front in flames and crashed into the hedge where it stuck and burned. Two men scrambled out and I had to act fast to avoid hitting the mess. So I drove alongside the hedge as it was too thick to get through. The road swung right so Geordie yelled at me to go over a ditch. But just as we reached it there was a hell of a clanging kind of bang and we stopped dead. I could smell hot rubber and reckoned we'd lost a track. There was nothing I could do, so we all started baling out in a funk. The noise all round us was terrific, with all kinds of bangs and tanks exploding. I saw the other two survivors diving into the ditch, so I went in after them, and I heard loud yells behind me. But I couldn't stop and fell into the ditch. When I looked round I saw our gunner crawling after me with blood over his face. He collapsed before he reached us. There was no sign of the others.

I jumped out of the ditch and ran to Jimmy the gunner. He had blood all over him and was clearly past aid, so I leapt back into the ditch and we got our heads down as the Jerries were machine-gunning everywhere. Then we heard more tanks and saw that some of our Shermans had succeeded in getting onto the road, our objective. But the first one was hit and burned and that held up the rest. I said 'Come on!' to the other two, but they wouldn't move. I saw some of our infantry so ran over to them and they pointed me back the way we'd come. Just then our Geordie Sergeant caught up with me.

'What a fucking mess!' was all he said. **99**

The Churchill tank gunner David Icksen of the 3rd RTR had been disappointed by the first actions in Normandy. Instead of charging the enemy in great style they had remained in hiding, potting at targets he could not really define from a sunken lane.

66 It was all very new and not what we expected. But then came our first real action. We were lined up and roaring to go. Our squadron CO gave us a little pep talk and off we went. We couldn't hear much because of the noise from our own engine and all the other Churchills in front and behind. The guns were banging away and we had some infantry with us. It was all very exciting until we started to deploy off the lane as the way was blocked. The Jerries had it zeroed in and it was choked with destroyed vehicles including Churchills that couldn't be recovered because of enemy fire. Our CO crashed through a gap in the hedge, and as he did so his tank was hit. I heard a WHOOSH and a hell of a crash and up he went. Fortunately, the crew baled out. Then it was every man for himself as we tried to fan out in open formation along a bigger gap in the hedge cut by the engineers.

I heard one loud crash after another, but still couldn't see anything to shoot at. Our objective was a ruined farmhouse, but I couldn't see it at all and relied on our Sergeant's directions. He didn't dare stick his head out of the turret because of all the stuff flying about and was using his periscope. Then we ran into a shellhole and got stuck and I couldn't traverse the gun at all. It was terrifying as we expected to be hit any moment. But by some miracle we got out and rushed on down a slope and suddenly I could see the smoking farm buildings and our artillery shells plastering it. Then they stopped, so I started letting go with our six-pounder and saw hits all over the farm. I had no idea if we were supported or not, but the Sergeant told us to keep going.

Then I saw two more Churchills reaching the farm on the left; one went up in flames, the second vanished in the smoke, so I stopped and started using our Besa machine-gun as there were some Jerry infantry around the farm. Then the Sergeant said, 'Cut it mate!' and I saw some of our infantry running into the farm. At that moment we took a terrific hit in our left side and the tank started to fill with smoke. We needed no order to get out in a mad scramble before it caught fire. We fell over the side into the grass. Our driver's hair was singed, his face blackened. There was still a lot of stuff flying about, so we ran back and realised all our tanks had been knocked out. Apart from the two that reached the farm we'd been alone. When we reached cover we found about a dozen chaps who had survived from the squadron that had set off a few minutes before. By that night we were back in reserve and took possession of a new tank. **99**

Sergeant John Holt was also in Churchills, and took part in 'Charnwood':

66 I can't be sure. They were all much the same, those big pushes. By then we reckoned we were up against the best the Jerries had and they were proving a tough nut to crack. In fact, if it had not been for our air power I doubt if we'd have beaten them. I don't think they could have driven us into the sea, it would have been a stalemate.

We went off in great style and full of excitement. Our tank had one of the lads' girlfriend's name on it – *Penny*. We were full of beans and ready to do our bit and drove across a cratered field, past dead cattle, until we reached a crossroads that was completely full of smashed vehicles. We'd just managed to get round this mess after the other tanks when the Jerry 88s and other guns caught us. All hell broke loose as three of our tanks went up at once. But we were lucky and got off that cursed road, running alongside a hedge with two more Churchills on the other side of the road. I still hadn't seen anything, but suddenly saw a half dug-in Jerry tank through my periscope, ahead of us and through some bushes. I warned the crew and told the gunner to get on to it before they got us. I couldn't see what type it was, but had to assume the worst. If it was a Tiger we'd be lucky to escape, though even the lesser Jerry types were very dangerous.

We got in our first shot that somehow missed. Then I saw the barrel of the Jerry tank gun poking through the hedge in our direction. But our next shot got him, a real beauty somewhere on the turret. There was a hell of a flash and the turret went flying off into the air. We cheered like mad and I saw one Jerry running off with his clothes on fire, and before I could say anything our gunner gave him a burst with the machine-gun and sent him flying. We passed the blazing wreck and saw it was a Panther and felt very elated. But our excitement was short-lived. We'd hardly gone a dozen yards when we took a hit on our port track which flew off with a bang. So we got out double quick into cover, just as the Jerry machine-guns started raking our *Penny*. We were stuck there under the bushes with our heads down for almost half an hour before some infantry reached us. We started to crawl back through the machine-gun and shellfire and finally reached our starting point where, thank God, there was tea and biscuits awaiting us.

We lost most of our tanks in that action. But we had plenty more, in fact an unending stream. It was only the loss of crews that sometimes held up our attacks. **99**

The Wiltshires were in action around the Odon and Hill 112. Jim Craddock:

66 I was not optimistic as although we were fresh I'd seen too many casualties on their way to the rear and a lot of them were dead men. Still, we tried to stay cheerful, especially myself as a Sergeant, even though I'd seen no action at all. Our officers were a good bunch, but I could see by their faces they were as scared as we were. Our Captain sat in his jeep and told us he expected us to do our best, that was all he asked. We knew he wouldn't be going with us, and I suppose we resented that, but it couldn't be helped. I thought that in battle it was really up to the NCOs to do the job. Our Major was a very good chap, but unfortunately he was killed by an airburst just as we set off. He was not to know that at first, and just as well – we had enough to worry about.

Our objective was one of the little woods that seemed to be dotted all over the landscape in Normandy. We'd been watching it get a pasting from our guns and planes through binoculars, and we thought the Jerries there must have taken a beating. I was a Catholic and said my rosary, as did one or two others; I thought I'd done my best in life and had a clear conscience.

We went forward at a fair pace, a sort of jog trot; there was none of the mad rush over the grass. It was a rather peaceful scene, but for the noise. We hadn't seen a single Jerry, only one or two dead cows, and thought they must be well dug in and probably sighting on us. Well, nothing happened and we plodded on. I grinned at the nearest lads and told them to keep up. Then we heard a howl and some mortar bombs came over just behind us, and some chaps caught it. So I told the rest to run on like mad, which they did. I was over on the right, a Corporal to my left. In the next instant there was a flash and a bang and I found myself lying on the grass. I had no idea what had hit me and felt dazed and deafened. Then my hearing returned and I heard all the noise and yelling, with smoke going past. But I seemed to be in one piece, so I sat up and tried to get my bearings. I couldn't see any of the lads, only a few bundles of khaki here and there, some of them dead or wounded, others just taking cover. So I got up and called, 'Come on lads, don't stay here or you'll get hit!' or something like that. One or two got up, but the stuff was flying around so they dropped to earth again. I crouched down and saw some movement in front of me and suddenly realised I was on my own, facing a bunch of Jerries.

I was terrified and dropped flat, but as I did so a bullet nicked my back pack and I thought I'd had it. In seconds a loud voice called out, 'Come on, you're a prisoner! Put your hands up' – in English, of course. I hardly dared look up. Then I heard running and found two Jerries lying near me. They were very young and dirty and grinning and had brown jackets, and I guessed they were SS. So I let go my Sten gun and tried to put up my hands but they made me lie flat as the bullets were flying both ways. So I did so. My heart was thumping like mad, I could hardly believe what was happening to me.

Then they beckoned me to follow them. One of them crawled backwards and I followed him as best I could with the other one covering me with my own Sten gun. The first kid vanished into a hole and I slid into another one; the second Jerry slipped in beside me and asked me in German for a cigarette. I knew what he meant but shook my head. So he grinned, took out one of his and gave it to me. But I didn't smoke, so he lit it while looking out over the edge of the hole and jabbering to his mate. Then I heard boots and another Jerry fell into the hole, knocking dirt all over me. He was an NCO and said a lot I didn't understand before beckoning me to go with him. The two kids grinned at me as I climbed out of the hole and followed the NCO at the crouch with the firing still going on. We fell into another hole near a hedge, and beyond that I saw a Jerry SP gun and a jeep of some sort. There was an officer in the hole and he spoke in English: 'Welcome to the SS camp. I hope you are happy to be out of it, eh?'

I was quite relieved to be a prisoner, so I grinned and nodded. He gave me a little drink of something from a flask, it may have been schnapps. So we sat there, the officer with a helmet on and the NCO, while he asked me questions. He could see from my flash I was in the Wiltshires, but I couldn't tell him much. So he asked me what I thought of the war, so I shrugged my shoulders and said it would soon be over, we would win. He just grinned and said something to the NCO who said nothing. Then he told him to take me to the jeep, so we ran off at the crouch and jumped into the vehicle. I sat next to him and a Private got in behind. But as we started to drive off a lot more shells came down and the NCO yelled and stopped the jeep and we all dived underneath. It was terrifying to be caught in one of our own barrages. The stuff was flying all round us and splintering the jeep, which was put out of action. So the NCO cursed like hell and ran off, leaving me lying under the jeep with the other one who looked terrified and said nothing. I thought the NCO had run back to the officer, but I couldn't see much from beneath the vehicle.

Then the Private next to me seemed to get even more scared as the ground was being ploughed up around us and the noise was terrific. He shouted something and pulled my sleeve and motioned us to get out of it. I thought that mad, so I didn't move when he slipped out from under the vehicle and ran off. I thought, My God, this must be my chance to escape. There was smoke everywhere and it seemed the right moment, if only the barrage would lift. Well, the shells still came down, but landed further away. So I threw off my gear – they had removed my helmet – and rolled away over the grass. I couldn't see any Germans, but I have a good sense of direction so I ran like mad in what I thought must be the flank. I could then change direction and reach our blokes.

I didn't see anyone. The shells were still coming over and then I fell into a big crater full of muck, and I lay there for a bit, panting and hardly able to believe my luck. A few minutes later I heard the tanks, and when I took a glance out of the hole I saw Shermans coming up the rise, so I kept my head down a while and as they went past I saw some of our infantry and started waving. I was rescued, and not long after back in our lines taking hot tea. **99**

Percy Hibbs was also in the Wiltshires, but after training on machine-guns was transferred to a mortar platoon:

66 We were in the thick of it over the Orne in July and fired so many rounds the barrel overheated. My mate said, 'Fuck this chums! The fucking thing's too hot!' After a few minutes we managed to change the barrel, which was difficult as we had to keep our heads down as the Jerries were very close in the hedges everywhere. They were very good at sneaking up on us.

Well, we started firing again, but the same thing happened: the barrel overheated with a round jammed inside it. So we threw the thing out of our pit and the bomb exploded right on top of the Jerries – they were that close. **99**

Jimmy Smith was with the Glasgow Highlanders in the van of an attack when all their supporting Churchills were knocked out:

66 The crews were killed or ran back as survivors. So we were left on our own with a lot of Jerry fire coming at us, completely pinned down and unable to move. All my mates had vanished, killed or wounded. I wanted to dig in, but didn't dare move enough to get my spade off my back. Then I heard vehicles and saw some Jerry half-tracks and tanks coming over the hill. The shells were falling all round me and after a lot more noise I realised the Jerries had gone right past me in their counter-attack. So I lay quite still. All the stuff stopped flying about and then I saw a Jerry squad was coming across the field looking for British survivors. So I lay still with my arms spread out and pretended to be dead. I heard them chattering and then one coming near me; he kicked my rifle away and went on; I expected him to put a bullet in me, but nothing happened. I heard them moving about, and then our artillery started up and the shells came down so they all ran back the way they'd come. The barrage followed them so I jumped up and ran back to our lines just in time for dinner. **99**

Some Royal Scots Fusiliers were trying to clean out a ruined farm-house the enemy were using as a strongpoint. Ian Hamilton:

❝ It was full of the beggars, with several machine-guns, and we had a bad time, as although they were surrounded they wouldn't give up and kept on firing. My best mate was killed next to me. We'd been together all of our time in the army, since 1942, and I was very upset and felt like wiping out all of the Jerries, even if they did surrender. We were waiting for a tank to come up and blow the place to bits, but the silly bugger got bogged down in a hole up the road, so we were still unsupported. Then the Lieutenant said he'd try to get some help and went back and we never saw him again. I believe he was hit and killed. We got cheesed off as nothing seemed to be happening and every time we tried to move the Jerries let fly. We weren't near enough to chuck grenades into the place. So eventually, a Corporal said he'd run over to the other platoon and try to borrow a flamethrower.

He ran off and didn't get hit, and about fifteen minutes later returned carrying the thing himself. We'd never had one before and had to be very careful as they were dangerous. You had to switch the thing on a certain way before pointing it and pulling the trigger. The Corporal and one other bloke were fiddling about with the thing, well under cover as he tried to get it over his back, when all of a sudden it went off with a terrific WHOOSH and a damned great flame gushed thirty feet into the air, amazing and shocking all of us. The Corporal almost fell over with shock. But it was liquid fire and it fell on the ruins of the farmhouse and burned the Jerries who started yelling blue murder and running out with their hands up. ❞

The Glaswegian who had 'always been mad on Jock soldiers in kilts' but was put into plain khaki battledress in the Glasgow Highlanders and was 'dead keen to fight the Germans' got his wish. In France he saw so much war and death he never wanted to see another battle – 'it was sickening'. It was one searing experience that brought Jimmy McPartland to that conclusion:

❝ We were going along a little lane. France was full of them, with fields and hedgerows as tall as a small house. It was all very pretty but deadly for us as the Germans hid everywhere. Even their tanks were well concealed in little nooks and crannies in the countryside and we never knew when they would catch us out. All too often there was a machine-gun or bunch of Jerries waiting to throw grenades. It was all a deadly game of hide and seek and we had to learn the hard way. We had not trained in that sort of country in England or Scotland.

It was really hot that afternoon and I had my sleeves rolled up and my blouse slung over my back. I felt like flopping out on the grass and taking a kip. But our Sergeant was in front with a Sten and we were strolling along, very alert and spread out, when suddenly a Jerry machine-gun opens up from the hedge just in front of us. The Sergeant stood no chance and fell down over the grass. We all dived for cover, but there wasn't any. We were up against hedges each side of the road and tried to get into them, but they were thick and there was no ditch to hide in. We just had to lie as flat as we could and hope for the best. I heard screams and knew other blokes had copped it. Then, after a few seconds of this terrible surprise, I heard the Jerries moving along and thought they were going to finish us off. When I dared move my head an inch I thought I saw them over the hedge, and sure enough some grenades came sailing over onto the road. I dug my face into the grass as they went off with a hell of a crash and all sorts of stuff started falling all over me.

Then the damned machine-gun started up again, and there were more yells before it went deadly quiet again. I didn't dare move and I could hear all the summery sounds around me, flies and bees and other insects, even birds singing. I wished I was back in the UK and enjoying myself with a girl in the park in Glasgow, instead of lying there and expecting to be killed any second.

Then I heard a Sherman coming up and voices and the tank let fly with its machine-gun and raked the whole hedge before shooting its big gun. The noise was terrific and there was a lot of commotion from where I'd seen the Jerries. Then the tank came nearer and almost ran me over as it was trying to avoid the bodies in the road. I rolled aside, jumped up and fell into the arms of another Sergeant who said, 'Christ! You're a lucky one, aren't you?'

The Jerries were wiped out, but just about all my squad were killed. **"**

Fred Clark crossed the Odon with the Royal Norfolks, 'up against SS troops, with lots of casualties on both sides'. A machine-gunner, Fred found himself in a duel with an enemy gunner, and as the man behind the trigger of a Vickers he felt very exposed, unable to lie down as with the Bren.

" We could see the enemy gun location as they had set up, well camou-flaged, beside some ruined trees, so I let fly in the general direction while our Sergeant spotted with his glasses. He said I was right on target, so I stopped firing. But almost at once the Jerry MG started up again, so I pressed the tits again and gave the spot a good going over. The Vickers was a good weapon and very accurate and did just what you asked it to do. So the Sarge looked again through his glasses and said, 'That's got 'em.'

Well, to our amazement the bugger started up again, and this time the bullets were coming our way, so we all hit the deck something smartish. Then, when the fire stopped the Sarge made a more careful search but still couldn't actually see the enemy gun, though I thought I'd been sure where it was. Then one of the infantry Corporals ran up to tell us they were pinned down by a Jerry machine-gun, could we help? They could actually see the thing. My Sergeant went off with him to see what could be done. We were set up in a shallow sort of hollow in the ground with a few bushes about torn up by shellfire. The Corporal and his lads were about 100 yards to our left and in the open.

Our Sarge ran back and said he too had seen the enemy gun and reckoned they were in fact 'our' lot, but just away from where we thought they were, it was possible they had changed their position. So we moved our gun to a better spot and piled up some camouflage, bits of foliage and rocks, then let fly again. This time I could see more clearly and at first saw the flash of the enemy machine-gun, but it soon stopped as I saw my bullets cutting the whole area to pieces. The infantry lads then rushed forward and took the position, so we packed up our gun and soon set up again where the Jerry position had been – we saw their smashed MG42 and the crew lying dead. They were not a pretty sight, and I thought, That could have been us. **99**

Also in the Norfolks, John Hodges was retained in England as a reserve until being shipped across to join the battle as a replacement in July:

66 We couldn't reach the front as the road was impassable by smashed vehicles after a bit of a Jerry breakthrough. So we debussed and at once a Captain told us to watch over six or seven Jerry PoWs who were sitting by the roadside. They were the first enemy soldiers I'd seen and they didn't look too good. Their equipment was gone of course – some wore field caps, but they looked unshaven and dirty – whereas we were fully equipped and fresh. They stared at us and said something and one of our Corporals spoke to them as one knew English. We listened with great interest as he said, '*War nix gut, Hitler kaput*', and all that kind of thing.

Then we were able to get on by truck and half an hour later reached our positions as the ration wagon came with lunch. It was meat and veg [M & V] with tea and biscuits, and tasted quite good. We ate in foxholes. The chaps we relieved were also Norfolks and they looked like veterans. They didn't talk much and seemed glad to get away. I remember one young chap who looked like a schoolkid, about sixteen, though he must have been eighteen at least. He told us he was from Norwich and hoped they'd get some leave as he wanted to get married!

That evening we took our first casualties. One of the new chaps was killed by a splinter not far from me when the Jerries shelled us. It seemed a rotten place to die, stuck in a muddy hole with the shells falling about. I was scared stiff, as I know we all were. The Sergeant kept yelling, 'Watch your front! Watch your front mates!'

But the Jerries never came that night and we slept a bit till next morning when breakfast came. We felt very tired and fed up, even though we'd only just arrived at the front. We hadn't expected it to be like that, but with more movement. But right after that there was a big

Above: Canadian armour forms up for Operation Tractable.

Left: A Cromwell mounting a 95mm mortar for use against fortifications.

Below: Lance Corporal Essex tunes in to the radio link aboard his Sherman.

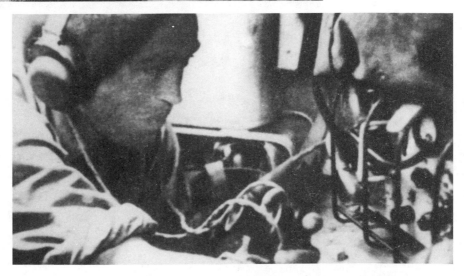

Above: Street fighting – an infantryman armed with the standard SMLE .303 rifle. Note late pattern helmet.

Right: An abandoned German 50mm anti-tank gun and dead crewman near Fontenay-le-Pesnel.

Below: Troops of 4th Dorsets pause during the advance.

Above and Right: British
wreckage on the road
from Villers and the
man responsible. The
remains of A
Squadron's 53 vehicles
shot to scrap by Michel
Wittman.

Left: Some of the dead
Britons.

Below: British infantrymen double up along
the Tilly–Caen road.

Right: Wittman's disabled Tiger in Caen, its owner escaped to be killed later on 8 August.

Below: British infantry take up new positions facing the enemy.

Bottom Right: A Tommy makes good use of a captured Schmeisser.

Bottom: Tanks withdraw as infantry advance.

Top Left: Troops of 12th SS wait to advance with Panthers.

Above: A British medic tends the wounded member of a German assault gun crew.

Bottom Left: A prisoner is searched by a Captain of the Gordons.

Below: A German Corporal lies dead in his foxhole.

Above and Right: British troops in St Manvieu.

Right: A captured French-made Hotchkiss machine-gun put to use by infantry of 3rd Division in Caen.

Below: A despondent SS prisoner is ushered to the rear.

Top Left: General Harmel of 10th *SS Frundsberg* questions captured British tank crewmen near Caen.

Centre Left: A British patrol moves warily in country ideal for defenders' ambush.

Bottom Left: A Scots Canadian supervises the burial of dead.

Below: A German soldier searches (or loots) British dead.

Above: A Scottish soldier awaits the order to advance through a cornfield at Manvieu.

Right: A turretless Sherman among the debris of the 'little wood' around Hill 112.

Below: The stream called 'River Odon' that cost so many British lives.

offensive, with a terrific bombardment which was fantastic and we all thought the Jerries had had it. But when we went into the attack, there they were again, with their weapons at the ready and we were cut down and forced to give up. It was a shambles.

I remember one of my mates I'd been in training with running past me with blood coming from his arm and side. There were tears in his eyes and he was shouting, 'Fuck this! Fuck this!'

Then the Sergeant we knew so well was killed, just as we reached our first objective which was a broken wood. He was always a cheerful chap, but just fell down without a sound. His replacement was a very different type who shouted a lot and cursed like mad. He survived the war, unlike most of the rest.

Right after that we were withdrawn as too weak to continue. I was shattered. So few of the old faces remained and we felt very low. I thought, God, none of us will see this lot out at this rate; one more go like that and we'll all have had it. We had a few replacements, but when we next advanced behind some tanks there were far fewer of us. I know this time things went better and we had few casualties. I was very surprised to find my remaining mates still in one piece and this made me more optimistic. **"**

Private Hodges' optimism was justified as far as his own safety was concerned. By the time the enemy army collapsed in August all his remaining mates had vanished, and when he returned to his old unit after a spell in a rest camp all the faces were new.

Douglas McInty of the King's Own Scottish Borderers was 'holed up' under fire from Moaning Minnies which gave them a bad time. These mortars provided the greater proportion of Allied casualties in Normandy.

" Then the Jerries started rushing us in small groups with tanks. Our anti-tank guns got some of the tanks, but their infantry kept coming and some of them got behind us, as far as our HQ company, and we could hear all the shooting, it was all very confusing. Then we heard a lot more noise, so a few of us ran back to see what was going on and found some of our chaps in hand-to-hand combat with the SS. So we joined in and all the Jerries were killed or captured. One of them was an NCO and looked very fierce, but he then collapsed in a heap and we thought he was dead. But he came round and someone gave him a drink of water. He then said this in English: 'God, what a bloody war! I've had enough, comrades!' **"**

Robert Henry was with the Gordons south-east of Caen and also had a –

" hell of a battle with SS troops. First we drove them back, then they drove us back, and there were a lot of casualties on both sides. I was hit in the left arm by a bullet, but it didn't hurt much, and with so much stuff flying about I couldn't go back for treatment. Then my mate in the hole with me was killed by a bullet in the head and I felt hopeless as I couldn't hold a weapon. When the next bunch of Jerries rushed us I just lay in the hole and hoped for the best. But they soon found me and ordered me out. When they saw I was bleeding they let me fall back in the hole while they rushed on. I watched them from the rear. If I'd had a weapon and was able to shoot I could have plugged them all. They lost a lot of men and came streaming back past me, and two of them saw me and shouted, 'We komm again soon!' So I said, 'OK mate, see you soon – in England!' 〞

John Fisher was from Cardiff, his mother English. He loved the army, but once in battle decided he must have been mad 'to volunteer for this lot!' He was in almost continuous action with the Royal Welch Fusiliers:

66 We had a lot of casualties; in my company we lost all our officers and most of our NCOs in two engagements. It was a couple of weeks before we got any replacements, but we were still considered fit for action and sent in to attack with some other mob, I think it was the Monmouths. It was really hell as the battle went on day after day and we were really worn out. We had no proper rations and kept running out of ammunition, which was a nuisance, to put it mildly, when the Jerries were right on top of us. Then we had new officers from the other mob and couldn't really get on with them or even understand them at times. They spoke differently and it was strange. Not that this mattered at all when we were in action as all you needed to know was how to shoot at Jerries, and we did plenty of that.

We saw so many corpses we got used to it I suppose, but we became plain worn out and useless, so at last they pulled us out and we collapsed into tents, too tired to eat or anything. 〞

Henry Kelly was a Sergeant with the 24th Lancers, in command of a Daimler armoured car and trying to recce a road near Caen before the big breakthrough:

66 There were three of our cars in line, with infantry and tanks behind. When we reached a crossroads I said, 'I don't like the look of this.' We couldn't see any Germans, but it was a perfect place for an ambush. So I told the driver to rev up but keep the brakes on, then ram his foot down so we could shoot across the junction at top speed.

Well, that's just what we did. But the car behind us was hit and blew up at once, and three of our pals bought it. The wreckage blocked the road; nothing could get past until a Sherman came up and pushed it aside. But the tank was hit so we had a hell of a jam with us stuck out beyond. I knew very well that the Jerries were probably closing in on us at that very moment. So I told our driver to reverse a few yards, then go like hell at the small hedge on our right and try to rejoin our lot across the fields. He did this, but our rear wheels got stuck in the undergrowth and nothing he did could shift the thing. So we were in real trouble and baled out – just as the Jerries opened fire and our car went up in flames. We just managed to crawl and run back to safety. "

Ron Colsen was a Bren gunner with the North Staffs:

" We were in position east of Caen in July, on a small hill overlooking an orchard where the Jerries were forming up for an attack. We could see them quite clearly doubling among the trees, and some vehicles. We were well dug in and waited. We'd had dinner and tea and felt quite comfortable as it was hot in the sun, but we didn't expect the peace to last long. Our Sergeant used his glasses to give us a running commentary on what was going on. 'The bastards are forming up,' he told us. 'Now they're having a conference. Trying to get their guts together I reckon.' Things like that.

Then it went quiet and we felt it was about to start. We sighted our weapons and waited, and waited and nothing happened. Then, after a few more minutes, a single half-track appeared out of the orchard and rushed off down a bank, disappearing in a cloud of dust. So we wondered what the hell was going on. Well, we soon got our answer. There were a lot of planes in the sky and a few seconds later a load of bombs came down and landed smack on the orchard, completely destroying it. Great clouds of smoke went up and we thought, Christ, nothing could live through that lot!

Well, believe it or not, ten minutes later about thirty Jerries came rushing out of that place, yelling like mad, straight up the hill at us. They were some 500 yards away; we could hardly believe it. At the same time they started to shell us quite heavily, so we had to get our heads down for a bit. But our Sergeant kept yelling at us, so we had to keep popping up to shoot at the Jerries, though even then they never gave up and kept coming right at us until the last of them were knocked down, only about ten yards from our holes. "

The capacity of the enemy to absorb the most horrific punishment from air and artillery bombardment surprised the Allies over and over again.

Rennie MacDougal was a gunner in an armoured car of the Fife and Forfar Yeomanry:

" I liked my job in the cars. We had the best of the war I think, but on one day everything went wrong.

We were going along at a fair pace north of Caen in our Staghound car. The little lane seemed peaceful, with no sign of any Jerries, though we guessed they had to be near. We were at the point of our column and felt very vulnerable. But all continued peaceful for the first mile, before we reached a slight bend in the road at about thirty miles an hour. Then there was a hell of a bang and the car went straight into the ditch on the left and caught fire. There was a terrible yelling from our driver, who I called Jack, and we knew we were in big trouble. Our Sergeant yelled at us to help Jack and get out of it. So with my pal Geordie we tried to drag Jack out of his seat; his legs were buckled up and he was whimpering with agony. The whole front and underside of the car was alight and we knew if we didn't get out of it pretty quick we'd be fried, or more likely blown up when the tanks caught it.

We managed after some difficulty to get the lower side door open while the Sergeant jumped out of the turret hatch, only to be hit by fire and fall dead on the road. We jumped into the ditch, trying to drag our mate with us. But the bullets were spraying all along the hedge and we had to fall flat for a while. The rest of the column had stopped, but they started up again, trying to avoid running over our poor dead Sergeant. It was all like a terrible nightmare. The next car went up like a bomb, the lads inside screaming terribly in the flames. Then damn it if the next one didn't get it too, but thank God the crew got out in time. The column tried to reverse and we progressed back along the ditch. Then the Jerries set up a gun and started shooting along the lane and we could hear the yells from our lads being hit. We lay flat in the ditch praying to God we'd be OK.

Then some of our tanks got into action and the Jerries were killed. The tank CO rode up and shoved all the wrecks aside and then they raced on past, the whole column following in dashing style, and at last the medics rushed up to help us. But our chum Jack was dead. **99**

Stephen Kershaw was another 'yeoman', a Sherman tank commander with the County of London regiment:

66 We were advancing near Caen and going great guns along a lane when the tank ahead was hit and went up in bits like a rocket. We were very shaken as we knew them, but it was too late to do anything, so we tried to get round the bits and pieces, just the lower hull really, with smoking wreckage all over the place. We'd just got past when we were hit ourselves. I'll never forget that sound as the 88 hit us just below the turret. It was a sort of crack on a tin, but very loud and at once I found myself lifted up with the turret still round me in a mad kind of hot blast that carried me right out of the tank hull. I must have lost consciousness, but only for a few seconds, as I next found myself half in and half out of the turret, over the hedge and in a field. For a moment I felt fine, but then a great feeling of disappointment came over me and I realised my legs were twisted and trapped and I felt awful pain which grew worse, and I passed out.

I remember a great deal of noise of the battle and I seemed to be in a semi-conscious state, and not caring any more. This seemed to go on and on, until at last I half came to and heard voices and vehicles and someone said, 'Half a mo' chum, we'll soon have you out of it.' They gave me a shot of morphia and I went right out again, and glad to. When

I came round I was on the operating table and the MO said, 'You'll be all right old chap, we've just taken a few bits out of your legs. You can have a good sleep now.'

Well, I did, but I never walked again. **"**

John Timpson was 'scared stiff' when he went to the front as a replacement for the Berkshires in July. Posted into the 3rd Battalion he found himself 'in the thick of it at once':

" I was only nineteen and of course had never been in action before. The noise was devilish, I'd never heard such a din, it went on for hours and hours. We ran forward to take over some positions the Jerries had lost while our point infantry chased them. I found a big hole with all sorts of bits and pieces, and another chap I didn't know jumped in beside me. I think he must have been a veteran. He started scooping up all the bits as souvenirs, grinned at me and said he regularly sent stuff home, though he wasn't sure if it all got through. I was too scared to think about such things.

Then, after a hell of a lot of noise, we saw the wounded coming back, the first I'd seen, and I was really shocked. One chap was in a very bad way with his arm hanging off and his mate supporting him. Others were limping or holding their heads and covered in blood and I felt faint just to look at them. The bloke with me saw my face and offered me a cigarette, but I didn't smoke. He said, 'You soon will mate. I never smoked till I came here. You gotta take something or your nerves will go.'

I felt very bad and wished I'd gone into some safe service, as a driver, or RAF ground crew, anything but that stupid business. I thought about trying to get away from it, but I knew they dealt severely with cowards – or thought so. So I put my head down and tried not to look at the wounded at all. But then the Jerry shells started to come over and I felt even more terrified. All sorts of splinters were falling over us, some were just lumps of earth or bits of trees, but something hit me and I jumped with fear. The bloke with me just took it calmly, smoking away, grinning and saying nothing much except, 'Christ! I could do with some tea, where have those buggers got to?'

The tea came when it got quieter and darker, and I'd never been so glad of a cuppa. It made me feel a lot better, except that I'd ruined my trousers, and this didn't endear me to the other chap who said, 'You'd better go over there mate and do the best you can.' I felt so ashamed and awkward and terrified. I thought of the Jerries catching me doing my toilet business. It was something I'd never thought about before – trying to use the toilet in the middle of a battle. Fortunately, I had some paper and clean clothing, but it was a very difficult time and I felt so embarrassed and needed a proper clean-up. My new mate said to me, 'Don't worry mate, we all get the runs now and again. You'll get used to it.' **"**

James Heaton was another armoured car crewman, a driver with the Northants Yeomanry:

❝ We were out of the line enjoying a rest when our CO called for volunteers for a special job – an easy one. So like chumps we said we'd go, without knowing what it was about. He told us one of the General Staff officers wanted to have a look for himself up front, that sort of thing. This sounded just the job and we wondered who it could be, even Monty or Ike? We spruced ourselves up a bit and reported to the CO's tent and found the GSO waiting. We shook hands but couldn't recognise him, so felt a bit disappointed. A few minutes later we set off, the officer sitting inside and seemingly very thrilled, except that he kept wanting to look out. We told him he could for a moment a bit later on, but it could be dangerous. He said he understood perfectly, so the Sergeant let him stand in the open turret as we cruised past the artillery positions and then the foremost infantry foxholes. There were several tracks and lanes, but it seemed safer to cruise slowly along beside a wood and hope for the best. The CO had warned us to 'take jolly good care of our guest', but we felt it rather dangerous and foolish for a GSO to be sent across the front line.

But nothing much happened. We saw some of our infantry who warned us the Jerries were near, and this seemed to excite the officer who had a pistol at his waist, and I thought, I bet he's itching to have a go with that, silly bugger!

I was right! He ordered our Sergeant to stop the car so he could clamber out and go ahead on foot. The Sergeant said he wouldn't advise it, but the officer insisted and said one of us could escort him, 'If it'll make you feel better!' So our gunner went with him, carrying a Sten gun, and I watched them crawl away alongside a tall hedge, and I grinned as I wondered what we'd tell the CO if we lost the fool. The pair dropped down and I laughed as the Sergeant said, 'I hope the silly twerp gets nicked, but if he loses Nobby I'll kick him in the balls!'

A little while later we were not too surprised to hear shots, and then they came rushing back to get into the car. The officer was red-faced, grinning and very excited. I drove the car back in reverse and soon reached our lines again. Back in our camp we dropped off the officer, and in our own tent Nobby told us what happened.

'The silly sod insisted on going forward by himself, then called me to tell him where the Jerries were. I hadn't a fucking clue, but I reckoned they were about all right. So I told him, "Do you see that big tree there sir?" He said yes, and I told him "They're there!" So he pokes his pistol through the bushes and lets fly. I was trying not to laugh and sure the Jerries would open up on us any second. He was pleased as punch; he'd been in action against the enemy. I reckoned he felt he deserved a medal, the silly arse!' **❞**

As shown, not only natives were put into county regiments. Bill Norris was a real Cornishman, however, in the Duke of Cornwall's Light Infantry:

❝ I was from Truro, and we did have a lot of Cornishmen of course, but others from all over the place, even a couple of Jocks. But I remember this bloke from London; he had the accent, very broad too, and I suppose we all thought of him as a Cockney. I know when we went into action he used to curse and swear about everything, usually the little irritations, you know, the poor food or no rations turning up or cold tea, all sorts of silly little things. One day we had a Jerry prisoner come in who was wounded and bleeding. The little Cockney ran forward, whipped out his own bandage – we always carried some – and started binding up this Jerry. Then a most amazing thing happened: the German spat in his face and pushed him away. This is what the Cockney said: 'You stinking fucking bloody Nazi sod! You ungrateful bastard. I've a good mind to kill you, you bugger!' He gave the Jerry a hefty kick and ran off in disgust. ❞

The Highland Light Infantry were in action against the SS, 'the bloody SS who were giving us a bad time, counter-attacking and, frankly, we'd had enough'. This was Jimmy Partridge's feeling in late June as his unit was awarded a short break of two days out of the line. 'We did some grumbling, but the officer said, "Don't worry lads, it'll all be over soon and we'll be in Berlin eating off Hitler's table!" That's exactly what he said, and one of the lads said, "You must be fucking joking sir!" The officer didn't answer, and as soon as we returned to the front we went into an attack and the officer was killed. We buried him there, on the spot, and the same bloke who'd been cheeky wrote a little note on an old envelope for the grave, which said, "This chappie wanted to eat off the *Führer*'s table."'

The Durham Light Infantry of 50th Division had been in action in France in May–June 1940, then fought their way across North Africa with the 8th Army. By late 1943 they were being readied for the invasion. Reg Noakes from Durham joined them for the big party, and in Normandy one damp day in late June rode up to battle on a tank, deploying on foot across muddy fields as the rain started to fall again.

❝ I had some chocolate and was eating this and thinking of the old days back home as a kid. I let my mind wander off a bit too much. Next thing there was a flash and a hell of a bang and I was thrown across the grass and found myself looking up at the sky and wondering what the hell had happened. Then I felt a terrific pain and couldn't move my right leg. Some of the lads ran to me and started bandaging my foot and yelling for the medics. Two came with Red Cross armbands, lifting me back to the road where they laid me on a carrier and I passed out. When I woke up I was in the operating theatre with a male orderly telling me

I had lost a lot of blood but would live. Later, I found I had lost my foot through the mine I stepped on. **99**

Author Bernard Fergusson wrote a history of the Black Watch which he called *The Black Watch and the King's Enemies*, and it was to help deal with those enemies that Corporal Fergus McGinty travelled across the Channel in June 1944. Surviving into the following month, he and his mates found their way barred by a German strongpoint: 'We had some Churchills in support, one of them a flamethrower. The Germans were holed up in an earth bunker, nothing else, and wouldn't surrender. We put a lot of fire into them with no result and then the flamethrower went in and we got the result we wanted, but not one we would have preferred. The stench was terrible, and after the first squirt we heard the awful screams that went on and on, so I ordered one man to go forward as far as he dared to throw in a bundle of grenades to put the poor devils out of their misery.'

Not exactly the most popular of men in the army, the Military Police nevertheless did an essential job in various ways, sometimes getting involved in the sharp end. John Trollope was an MP Sergeant and one day in July was sent forward to assist in traffic control:

66 Soon after we arrived the Jerries put in a big counter-attack and we found ourselves in the middle of it. We were scared as we had never been in action and were forced to take cover with our pistols drawn. One of us had a Sten. The noise was terrific and a lot of our transport was set on fire. I really thought we were going to be killed or captured.

Then came a short lull, and a Lieutenant ran up and asked us to help him with two prisoners who were being difficult. So I went with him, with one other man, through a thick hedge where we found a Sergeant covering two SS men of the worst kind. They were obviously being very truculent. The battle was still in progress in the fields around us, and we were really scared and in no mood for trouble with prisoners. So we ordered them to come with us, but they refused to move. We grabbed them roughly and dragged them back through the hedge, but one of them broke free and ran off back to the hedge and started to scramble through it. I heard a shot and saw the Jerry fall head-first into the hedge. He'd been shot by the Sergeant. The other German was shaken and went off with us quietly. **99**

Bill Centro was of part-Italian parentage and a soldier in the Royal West Kents, better known as the 'Buffs', but to his surprise was transferred as a replacement in July to the Duke of Cornwall's and went over to Normandy with a couple of dozen other new hands. They were split up, and with two other men Bill was shown to the DCLI foxholes where a Lieutenant turned them over to a Sergeant, who in turn put them in charge of a Corporal:

❝ It was very frightening as we'd never been in action and the guns were banging away all round us. Two of us were shown into an empty foxhole where we tried to make ourselves comfortable. Of course, we'd been in foxholes in training, but this was different; there were shells landing nearby and we had to duck down as the bits and pieces flew over us. After a while two men brought tea and biscuits. One of them said, 'Make the most of it, it's all you'll get till morning and breakfast – if you're lucky!'

Later, the Corporal came round to check on us, warning us a Jerry attack was expected, so we were scared stiff and kept looking out of the hole, but we couldn't see anything but fields and broken trees. But it all began soon after darkness came, so we tried to hide in the bottom of the hole, even after the Corporal started shouting something we couldn't understand and all the shooting started. We were too scared even to put our heads up and the noise got a hell of a lot worse, with all sorts of shouts, yells and bangs of grenades going off. But we still stayed in hiding. Then it went quieter, with only the artillery blazing away not far off. Suddenly the Corporal appeared near our hole and said, 'You fucking windy bastards! Don't you know the Jerries have attacked us? We've only just driven them back. You silly bastards – you're not much use, are you? Come on!' And he made us move to another hole next to his. Next day we went into the attack and my new mate was killed. ❞

Although not normally in direct danger, only occasionally from enemy counter-battery fire, the field gunners were worked hard. James Fogarty was a Captain with an RA twenty-five-pounder unit:

❝ We were ordered to prepare for a heavy stonk on the German forward positions and stocked up as much ammo as possible. At 0400 hrs we began our barrage and this went on for two hours, by which time the lads were worn out. We had relief teams ready and they took over, but as they did so the Germans began some counter-battery fire, just a few shells to begin with, but they were fairly accurate and I didn't like the look of things as we had so much ammo lying about near the guns; if that lot went up the weapons would be destroyed. So for safety's sake I ordered our three batteries moved. This was not too popular with the lads, but they soon buckled down when some more Jerry shells came over, almost bang on target. We moved in about ten minutes to another site about 500 yards away to the left and in no time were banging away again.

Then we had a call from our Colonel to cease fire for five minutes, then concentrate on the Jerry rear, which we did. In this time our infantry were attacking. On this day we fired off 10,000 rounds from our three batteries alone and wore out our barrels, which had to be changed. ❞

Other personnel, too, though not in the combat units, faced danger. John Fielding was a truck driver in a Royal Army Service Corps field squadron:

❝ We were working flat out to keep the men at the front supplied. I took up all sorts of supplies – ammo, food, blankets, and personal items such as toothpaste, anything. One afternoon we had a rush job as the guns had fired off so much ammo they were running short. We had a convoy of twenty trucks all bound for the same battery, but halfway there the first one was hit by a lucky shot from a German gun battery and went up like a rocket. The road was completely blocked so we were stuck there waiting for the MPs to organise a bulldozer to move the wreckage. The two men in the truck had been pals of mine in England.

We'd all felt like turning round and getting out of there, but we were stuck and couldn't move in any direction. A few minutes later several more bursts came, but these were further away and not near the road. But it blew part of the hedgerow away, and at once one of the Sergeant MPs rushed up to try to direct us through the gap. It was a hell of a muddle, as the hole was right next to the middle of the convoy, but at last we were slowly moving through it into the field as a diversion. But when we had driven our trucks to the end of the field we found we couldn't get back onto the road. So the MPs started rushing about trying to find a tank to make a path for us. Before they could succeed a flurry of German shells arrived and these smashed a long line of the hedge and in a few minutes we were able to get out of it. ❞

Perhaps almost as least enviable as the job of the infantry was that of the medical staffs at the Casualty Clearing Stations, or field hospitals. Alan Turnhouse was a nursing orderly assistant:

❝ In July the casualties were coming in so fast we could no longer cope. So we sent off for some assistance, but before they could arrive two MPs brought in a German PoW who they said was a medic and keen to help. So we asked him to do some odd jobs and he worked really hard, and during a very brief break for some tea he told me something about himself.

He'd studied at Bonn University, hoping to become a doctor, but had been called into the army in 1942 before he could qualify. Naturally, he ended up as a medic in the German Army and had been on the Eastern Front where he said things got so desperate they had to use paper bandages, which by 1944 were common in their army. He thought we were lavishly equipped and said he would like to stay on to help with the wounded, as for one thing he was learning a good deal. His name was Hans, but then the MPs came to take him away. Our Captain MO intervened and told them he had proved so valuable he wanted him to stay.

So he did, for quite a long time, and was fitted out with a British battle-dress with a PoW patch on it as the MPs insisted. He left us after Falaise, profuse in his thanks, and was removed to England. **99**

Edward Lancing was a Sergeant with the Monmouths and the sole survivor of one of the abortive attacks on Hill 112:

66 I remember telling myself we'd never get out of it alive, I was that pessimistic. But somehow we did – for the moment. There were open fields to cross, some with corn, and the shells and bullets set it on fire. When I reached the little ridge with my platoon I found only six left with me. We tried to consolidate, but the Jerries mortared us and it was impossible to dig in. We had to slide back on our bellies over the hilltop with bombs coming at us. When I finally reached a little shellhole I looked round and found I was completely alone.

That was the end of our attacking that day. **99**

John Tim Railton was a Sergeant-Major with the 23rd Hussars:

66 The first battle is always a testing time; some men lose their nerve or run off, or go to pieces. We'd left England in fine fettle and distinguished ourselves by not losing our nerve. But one chap I had with us was a tank gunner who'd been a good soldier with no black marks whatever. He always performed very well and I had no complaints against him. But in that first action he went to pieces at once.

I had left my tank to try to help a wounded Corporal off the road when one of the Sergeants in charge of another vehicle yelled for help. We were in action and the noise was great and I had no idea what the problem was, though I could see his vehicle was stopped and he was blocking the road. When I ran to him he said, 'Give me a hand will you? Billy's gone nuts!' I asked him what he meant. 'He's gone off his rocker in here!'

The Sergeant got down into his turret and I guessed he meant the chap had gone haywire with panic and wanted to get out. Then I saw the hatches fly open and the driver leapt out and looked round as if waiting for something to happen. The next moment this kid called Billy, who was the gunner, appeared and he jumped out too. The Sergeant waved at me and shouted but owing to all the noise I couldn't hear what he said. Then Billy ran past me and I tried to grab him but he slipped away, with the driver standing by doing nothing. I ran after the boy but he disappeared behind the tank in front, and at that moment another tank up front got hit and burst into flames. So I got back into my own vehicle and tried to see Billy and got a glimpse of him running across a field like the clappers for a moment before he was bowled over by German fire. **99**

Ron McAndrew of the Seaforth Highlanders was involved 'in one of Monty's big attacks', and had a bad time:

66 We had to advance over open fields with the Jerries throwing everything at us. Then I found I was alone with only one of my mates. There was no one else in sight and we had no idea if they were all dead or wounded. So we decided to stay where we were and see what happened.

By that time it had quietened down, and though we were in a little dip and could see ahead quite a way, everything behind us was concealed. Then we heard voices shouting and saw a lot of Jerries running and crouching over the field in front of us. So we waited till the nearest one got close and then opened fire. I'll never forget the looks on their dirty faces. They were only about twelve yards away and we got the lot of them. The rest were further off; they fell to the ground and started chucking grenades at us. But they weren't sure where we were and missed by a mile. We kept quiet, really wanting to beat a retreat, but didn't want to show ourselves.

Then, when nothing happened, the Jerries started getting bolder and crept towards us, trying to see how many we were. We did exactly the same thing: at the very last moment we jumped up and let fly at them and got the lot – about five of them. I don't think one survived. Then we ran back to our own positions and found we'd been completely alone.

Just as we reached our positions my mate was hit by a bullet and collapsed. 99

10 Goodwood

Post-war publications on the battles in Normandy were, to coin a term of more recent usage, anodyne, straightforward chronicles outlining military operations, such as the *Short History of 21st Army Group* (HMSO) and others, including the by then Field Marshal Montgomery of Alamein's own two accounts. This was perhaps to be expected, for in the years following the collapse of Nazi Germany any ruffles that had occurred in the Allied camp were either concealed or glossed over. Monty's own memoirs of 1947 on the campaign were in the set tradition of military history from a commander's point of view. His strategy and ideas and management were set down in uncomplicated fashion – without hint, that is, of his more personal problems, and specifically of his near dismissal in July 1944.

A somewhat more penetrating history with far greater detail, as one might expect from a first-rate journalist, appeared a few years later when, for the first time, controversy arose over Monty's handling of the battle, and hints of difficulties with his colleagues were disclosed. Not of course to the extent of scathing criticism of General Eisenhower who, as one more recent historian has mentioned, rode around in a limousine accompanied by a sycophantic staff and mistress. Whether or not Ike's driver was his mistress is still up for contention, whatever the late Kay Summersby's denials. As to a 'sycophantic' retinue, most commanders' staffs appeared that way, though in Monty's case by all accounts his helpers were very carefully chosen for their ability and diligence. But Chester Wilmot's account, *The Struggle for Europe* (Collins, 1953), did bring fresh sidelights and highlights by its use of German archive material and Allied sources.

It would be decades before new generations of historians, perhaps following the trend set by David Irvine, set out to dig down further into the personalities involved at the top in the conduct of the battles in 1944. In this respect it can be seen that this younger set of writers, admiral and diligent in their researches, stood apart from their predecessors insofar as they were not around at the time and were therefore bereft of the ethos of those times. This does make a difference, especially in an era when digging the dirt is part and parcel of the publishing game, when every slant and nuance of a subject's personality is delved into. When such facets are added to the inevitable hindsight some highly readable accounts can and do emerge, even if, as indicated, the later set of historians are without the ingredient of actual experience of the times to set against their scholarship. Perhaps in a sense this is a good thing.

But many publishers in these times are not content with a mere 'well rounded' biography; colourful anecdotes there must be, especially if they smack of the sensational or salacious. Nothing like that has appeared about Montgomery, and is not likely to, despite hints from one leading writer. Monty, despite his calling for the sending into battle and often certain death of men by the thousand, was human, and his quirks are by now well known. We are only really concerned here with his conduct of the Normandy campaign.

In his superb work, Chester Wilmot, it can be noticed, refers often to General Dempsey passing out the orders, and in such a way that one concludes the plans laid were his own. It has been said that in the case of Operation 'Goodwood' his chief Monty issued only a general directive, that the actual scheme in detail was Dempsey's, but that in the execution of it the two corps commanders went awry and lost their jobs as a result. Max Hastings has remarked that every operation until then had been meticulously planned, but adds that no sane general would have conducted a battle as Goodwood was conducted. This is not a precise quotation, but that is the gist of it. And of all the successive 'Monty offensives' mounted after D-day it is Goodwood that has come in for most scathing comment. But, once again, it is necessary to look at the relationship between Monty and his boss Eisenhower and the state of 2nd Army in early July 1944 before examining the battle itself.

Later, Monty would claim, with some justification, that the reinforcing of the German front, the imminent transfer of *panzers* to the American sector and their replacement with three infantry divisions was justification enough for yet another great blow by his 2nd Army. General Bradley stated that he never saw Goodwood as other than a 'holding operation', in other words a continuation of the set strategy to pin most of the German armoured strength on the British–Canadian front. Yet, later on, Bradley stated that all hope of Monty continuing as Allied ground forces chief vanished after the failure of Goodwood, which seems something of a contradiction. It implies that the intention of Monty was a decisive breakthrough into the plain beyond Caen and an end to positional warfare. The truth seems to be that Montgomery and his commanders did, on the one hand, see their continuing role in the first context, one all lamented, but without doubt also expected much from the offensive in terms of a big breakthrough.

As to General Montgomery continuing in his role as C-in-C land forces, it had already been agreed that once the Normandy business was concluded he would step down and the Americans would run their own show, though to Monty the notion of running a battle beyond that by a 'committee of generals' was anathema, and of course he had no great admiration for his boss as a combat general. Somehow, Americans like Patton had arrived in Europe smothered in ribbons, and their allies may well have been a little dubious as to how they came to gain these.

Monty's other great and increasing problem was deeper and not solvable. On 14 July he wrote to General Sir Alan Brooke, perhaps the only person he really confided in on military matters, commenting that while his army was very strong, it was passing its peak, for many of the best-trained soldiers had been lost, the replacements were not so well trained, and of course being inexperienced were often also lost before they had 'earned their keep'. He may well have felt that with the serious losses suffered his army would soon no longer have the leverage to carry out grand assaults. Montgomery then signalled Eisenhower about his next attack, and in using a few ill-chosen phrases led his boss to believe that the big one was about to win through and create the conditions for the British commander's planned American pincer to the south and east. Monty said he would 'set the front aflame'; there was to be a big showdown (he told Brooke). Three '*panzer*' divisions would smash through the German front to Falaise and beyond.

There was of course the political angle that went far beyond relations between Monty and Ike; as American strength grew so did their political clout and the British government must have been well aware that in calling Roosevelt's country into Europe on such a scale they were handing over the prime weight of power, which would and did mean that the Americans gained leadership in the post-war scene. As Nazi propaganda had assured, Britain would end up bankrupted to the Americans and lose its Empire in the bargain, the Soviet–US bloc presiding over international affairs.

As General Eisenhower gazed at the situation map at SHAEF, doubtless with his aides around him, including Monty's critics Lieutenant-General Morgan and Air Chief Marshal Tedder, he saw very little change in the battle lines. With no experience of directing operations, certainly not in a modern war against foes such as the Germans, Ike, though not unaware of the need to destroy the enemy army, was primarily a soldier whose lofty position as team manager desired above all to see the red, white and blue colours enveloping all of France. Back home the great American press was showing signs of impatience; the US War Department too reflected some disquiet at the slow pace of Allied gains, apparently completely remote from the realities and Monty's plan. Eisenhower wrote to Montgomery expressing his own jitters, that the Germans seemed to be sealing off the bridgehead and calling for an all-out offensive. He too had become painfully aware of one fact, that no more American infantry reinforcements could be expected until September. With losses running as they were this was serious news. The only additional strength he could count on was in armour, when General Patton was released from the fiction of FUSAG (First US Army Group) in England and could take command of the newly activated 3rd Army on the southern sector of the American zone.

Meanwhile, General Bradley had told his chief, General Montgomery, in conference that owing to ammunition shortages and the need to gain a better jump-off point his Operation 'Cobra' must be postponed some days. This Monty accepted.

It was in part these pressures which hastened Goodwood. The plan hatched by Montgomery and his army commander General Miles Dempsey called for an assault by three armoured divisions, covered by the usual massive artillery barrage and with a huge air bombardment. It was to be a grand 'demonstration' of armour, one the Germans could not ignore. It would convince Rommel that there, around Caen, was the main point of effort and that this coming offensive was the breakthrough attempt the Allies hoped would link up with a second landing around Calais. For the British deception plan still worked to perfection; 15th Army still gazed out to sea across the Straits, expecting a fresh invasion fleet bringing the 1st US Army into action. In a sense, this British success rebounded on them, as we shall see; Monty's latest pressure blow resulted in a German reaction beyond the knowledge of his intelligence staff and without doubt brought not merely far heavier losses but all the succeeding disappointment and crisis of confidence in his leadership and the capabilities of the British–Canadian Army.

None of this really affected the British commander's overall strategy, but it is necessary to go into exactly what Montgomery had in mind when he launched Goodwood, if only to try to understand how he came to be so criticised. It is risking tedium to reassert the same contentions; one need only examine the evidence to confirm the same strategy and the errors of those opposed to him at SHAEF and in Whitehall.

In signalling Ike about the new assault Montgomery used phrases like 'setting the whole front aflame' which somehow so enthused Ike that he replied effusively in clear expectation of a big breakthrough. This belief was concrete and confirmed later when he came to make his report to the US Chiefs of Staff in which he spoke of a thrust to the Seine and Paris. Obviously, Monty failed to make his real intention clear, and not only to his chief: when officers of his staff travelled to London to try to arrange the necessary scale of air support they took with them more detailed plans for Goodwood which undoubtedly also provoked greater expectations in some quarters. This air plan included a request for more help from Bomber Command (beyond the routine *blitz* from 2nd Tactical Air Force), and at first Air Chief Marshal Harris demurred, being well informed as to the results of the recent bombing of Caen. He was persuaded to change his mind when the use of smaller frag-mentation bombs was suggested. Notably, heavy bombers of both the RAF and US Army Air Force were to be called in to assist in both Goodwood and Cobra.

There is no indication that Eisenhower ever saw the detailed Operation Instructions issued by General Dempsey for the offensive, which was to begin 18 July, with a feint attack to go in during the night of 15th–16th from the Odon salient by 43rd Wessex Division – i.e. against Hill 112. It seems that General Montgomery himself did not see these orders until 15 July; he then sent a memorandum to the 8th Corps commander, Lieutenant-General O'Connor, who would be the executive of the plan, and at no point is any mention made of forcing any great breakthrough to the Seine and Paris. It emphasises the prime need to 'write down' German armour so that it is of no further use in the battle, to gain a good bridgehead over the river Orne, and to 'generally destroy German equipment and personnel'. Paragraph two of this document is concerned only with emphasising the need to maintain balance on the eastern flank, a bastion on which the whole campaign rested. If it became unstable then operations on the western flank would cease.

Montgomery also redefined the task of the three British armoured divisions which were to dominate the area Bourgebus–Vimont–Bretteville, but armoured cars could reconnoitre south-east towards Falaise 'and spread despondency and alarm' and discover 'the form'. Meanwhile, 2nd Canadian Corps, now responsible for Caen, would finally clean out the suburbs of any remaining enemy and gain a very firm bridgehead to cover the build-up area for Goodwood. Only then would 8th Corps 'crack about as the situation demands'. In other words, O'Connor should feel free to exploit as he might.

Before the operation commenced, however, 2nd Army intelligence began receiving reports of enemy reinforcements moving into its sector, which meant Montgomery's plan continued to work. However, this strengthening went well beyond expectations and directly affected the coming British offensive. Not only that, errors in staff planning resulted in fiasco, as we shall see. For a start, a minefield laid by 51st Highland Division was overlooked and no time remained to clear a path through it. Then the air force let it be known they would not have sufficient aircraft to take care of the German guns located by the Bourgebus ridge; they would have to be attended to later, and the artillery would find these enemy weapons at extreme range.

Crucial to the contentions made is the fact that as late as 17 July General Dempsey further curtailed 8th Corps objectives, instructing O'Connor to 'establish Armd. Divs. in the areas Vimont, Garcelles–Secqueville, Hubert Folie–Verrieres'. This further, clear instruction showing Goodwood's objectives did not reach SHAEF; one must therefore lay the blame for resulting contention and bad relations at the door of Monty and his staff. Ike and his HQ continued to expect a massive two-pronged breakout (including Cobra).

Major How, in *Hill 112*, expresses the opinion that the previous 'first race' (Epsom) had achieved far more than was recognised at the time (and later), that the British breakthrough beyond the Odon so seared the enemy commanders (Rommel, Hausser etc.) that they considered the battle lost. Apart from which, of course, it had completely foiled the Germans' own plans. But Rommel, soon to be removed from action, did ensure that the threatened sector beyond Caen was heavily built up.

British intelligence, despite some master coups, failed to realise the extent of enemy reinforcement opposite them. The *Luftwaffe*'s 16th Field Division was located to the north-east and directly in the path of the bomber assault; the 21st *Panzers*, or remnants, were also known to be still in the sector, with remaining elements of 1st and 12th SS. Unrealised was the number of guns opposing – 1,632 of them, including around eighty of the deadly 88 and 105mm *flak*/anti-tank guns and 272 multi-barrelled mortars (Moaning Minnies). The Germans had organised no fewer than five defence lines, including six battalions of 1st SS and two battle groups of 12th SS, the latter equipped with eighty tanks all told. About thirty-six Tigers of the independent heavy tank battalions – probably the entire strength of these monsters – were also gathered to oppose Goodwood.

SS General Sepp Dietrich had picked up the old Red Indian and Australian aborigine trick of putting an ear to the ground to detect enemy movements. It had worked in Russia, but in Normandy there was hardly any need; the sound of 700 British tanks rattling and rumbling towards the front via Bayeux could be heard for miles. Furthermore, the *Luftwaffe*, daring the skies by night, took photoflash pictures of this nose-to-tail traffic. So Rommel and his staff were well informed that another great 'Monty blow' was about to fall and must have marvelled at the wealth of matériel continually at their enemies' disposal, an enemy cut off from their main base by an unpredictable Channel which, with the weather as it had been, showed a persistent pro-German bias.

General Montgomery's apparently unflappable front of supreme optimism concealed anxieties, and these would increase once it dawned on him the extent of the rift opening up like a disastrous chasm between Ike and himself. In mid-July this was not yet evident. There is no doubt that the British commander also, privately, nurtured hopes for the coming offensive. How could he not do so? If a great breakthrough did come, then most of his problems would vanish. But what of his subordinate, Miles Dempsey, a man virtually unknown to the public before the Normandy battle and not named in the press until after it was underway? Said to be a shy type, he had not reached such a position of command without ability, being chosen over the heads of far more experienced commanders such as Ritchie, Rennie and O'Connor, to name but a few. Lieutenant-General Dempsey's own hopes were recorded in his diary before the offensive began: 'I have every confidence in the army to do what the C-in-C wishes of it, which is to hit the enemy in such a way that they are once again compelled to dance to our tune.' If the General had any expectations beyond that he did not record them. His reactions to what followed will be given.

The Germans were not fools. They were not deceived by the feint attack across the Odon, a bloody battle by the county battalions of 43rd Wessex, of which more later. Rommel's HQ signalled to Field Marshal

Kluge that the 'local' attacks across the Odon between Maltot and Vendes could be the prelude to the large-scale attack expected during the evening of the 17th 'for making a breakthrough across the Orne'. All the German units around Caen were put on high alert. The 12th SS battle group was ordered to move up by night to Liseux, their original starting point on 6 June.

Rommel had been in the habit of touring the front daily, and he made no exception on 17 July. He visited the 276th and 277th Infantry, who had repulsed a heavy British attack the night before, then called on SS General Bittrich of 2nd *SS Panzer* Corps, also conferring there with Sepp Dietrich who warned him to drive in a small VW jeep rather than his larger Mercedes staff car, this prudent advice owing to the constant attentions of the enemy air forces over the battle fronts. Rommel scorned this advice, setting off from the SS HQ at about four p.m., apparently anxious to get back to his own HQ before nightfall as news had come in of another enemy breakthrough.

'All along the roads we could see transport in flames; from time to time enemy bombers forced us to take to second-class roads,' recalled his adjutant, Captain Lang, later. After two hours their car was still encountering burning German transport, some recently strafed, with enemy planes in the vicinity. At Livarot the Field Marshal's car turned off into another side road, intending to rejoin the main highway near Vimoutiers. But over the first town they saw a cluster of enemy 'dive bombers', and their plane spotter, Sergeant Holke, shouted to the driver, Daniel, that two planes were coming along the road towards them. The driver put his foot down, trying to reach another little side road they hoped would provide some shelter.

The two planes were Spitfires of No. 602 (City of Glasgow) Squadron, the lead aircraft piloted by the CO, Squadron Leader J. J. Chris Le Roux from South Africa. It had been an unusual day insofar as they had met the *Luftwaffe*, Le Roux destroying two of the enemy aircraft. They were now on their second sortie of the day, and it was the CO's 20mm cannon shells that ripped into the left side of Rommel's car, the driver Daniel's left shoulder and arm being shattered. The Field Marshal was hit in the face by flying glass and received a blow on the left temple and cheekbone, causing a triple skull fracture which rendered him unconscious. Rommel's other aide, Major Neuhaus, received a shell through his pistol holster that broke his pelvis. The car went out of control, struck a tree stump and turned over into a ditch. Captain Lang and Sergeant Holke dived into shelter beside the road; Rommel had been thrown out when the car overturned and was left lying in the road some twenty yards behind.

It took some forty-five minutes to find transport which ferried Rommel to a French religious hospital; later, he was transferred to a *Luftwaffe* hospital at Bernay, about twenty-five miles away, still unconscious and not expected to live. A few days later he was moved again

to Vesinet, near St Germain, but by grim paradox, the first habitation
Rommel was carried to by the uninjured aides was the little nearby
village of Ste Foy de Montgommery. The British General's old adversary of the desert war was laid low and would never enter combat
again.

Though operations by 12th and 30th Corps would continue, the
major role in Goodwood went to 8th Corps which would pass its three
armoured divisions (11th, 7th and Guards) through the 1st Corps
bridgehead.

Between 0545 and 0630 hrs on 18 July the greatest tactical air *blitz*
ever went in against the German forces arrayed east and south of Caen,
some 1,100 heavy bombers of the RAF, 600 of the 8th US Air Force,
plus 400 medium bombers of the US 9th Air Force bombed every
known enemy position, the latter using fragmentation bombs with
instantaneous fuses and completing their work by 0745 when the
ground assault was to begin. The 3rd British infantry division of 1st
Corps struck east and south-east; 11th Armoured Division advanced
south behind a rolling artillery barrage, the tanks soon vanishing in
smoke and dust as fresh waves of bombers swept in to attack the fortified villages in the path and on the flanks of the advance. The British
armoured phalanx consisted of regiments in three columns, spread
across a 1,000-yard front, probably providing the most impressive
spectacle of the campaign, and having crossed the Caen–Vimont
railway lines the 29th Armoured Brigade advanced to the second which
ran from eastern Caen through Tilly la Campagne. Opposition had
been negligible, the effect of the frag bombing had been terrific, and the
Germans struggled from their shelters in dazed conditions, or remained
under cover, to be rounded up by the British infantry.

The village of Cagny had been pulverised by the bombing, but when
the leading British tanks climbed the nearby railway embankment
around 9.30 a.m. they came under fire from 88s and Tigers that had
somehow escaped the bombing. One tank regiment remained in the
vicinity as flank guard to engage the enemy while the other two pressed
on towards Bourgebus. They had now gone beyond the British barrage,
and came under fresh fire from undamaged portions of the little village
strongpoints in their path. By an extraordinary fluke, the parts of these
hamlets untouched by bombing all faced the British advance. From
these positions the Germans resisted with every weapon, including anti-
tank guns, and the leading elements of 29th Armoured were stymied.
They had gained six miles, and were now taken on by long-ranging fire
from 88s and Tigers; their infantry component had become embroiled
in mopping up on the flanks. This aspect and others would come under
fire from critics (including higher officers) later, especially the decision
to use a huge tank wedge when, according to one expert, squadrons
supported by infantry would have done the job better.

Meanwhile, Guards Armoured had pushed on behind the 11th, to be hit in the flank from Cagny and Emieville as they swung for Vimont. Their advance was then barred more directly by German tanks and guns hidden in the orchards of Frenouville. The offensive ground to a halt. Bourgebus ridge was reinforced by Panthers of 1st SS, these panzers using perfect defensive country consisting of sunken lanes and ruined villages in the bocage, amply supported by infantry and anti-tank guns, including 88s. The enemy on Bourgebus defeated attempts to advance, and very unfortunately for the attackers their RAF ground-to-air liaison officer was lost in the morning's fighting, so the Typhoons could not be called in to deliver their rocket salvoes accurately. Nevertheless, O'Connor ordered his two armoured division commanders, Roberts and Erskine (7th), to continue the assault regardless of casualties. The tanks were mere mass-produced machines, now churned out in great numbers by the huge factories in Britain and America which had in peacetime produced cars and civilian trucks. Major-General Erskine was reluctant, critical of this mass use of his armour, seeing no point in sending his tank crews into a trap – which is what it had become, a killing ground that became something of a grave-yard for the British tanks. Erskine pleaded that his units were still strung out back to the Orne, and there was insufficient room to manoeuvre between 11th and Guards Armoured. Not until six o'clock did his tanks enter the battle zone; by then it was too late. 29th Armoured had been fighting desperately to ward off a counter-attack from Bourgebus by fifty to sixty German tanks.

The Guards took Cagny, but in further trying to force a way through the enemy anti-tank gun screen they lost sixty tanks. By evening 11th Armoured had lost 126 tanks, of which forty were complete wrecks, the rest either recoverable or out of action through defects. With its remaining less-than-half strength it consolidated north of the Caen–Vimont railway. Despite the huge aerial *blitz* of that morning, some localities ahead of the British assault had remained intact: Touffreville, for example, target of the 3rd British infantry, held out until late afternoon when it was finally bypassed by troops riding on tanks who cleared out two further villages of an enemy said to be too be-fuddled by the bombing to offer resistance. The same force attacked from two sides, the southern probe being repulsed.

The 21st *Panzers* on Bourgebus were worn out and relieved by 1st SS during the night of 18th–19th. On the second day of the offensive it became clear that a great and prolonged slogging match had developed in which the hoped-for continued heavy bomber support would not be forthcoming as the squadrons were (supposedly) preparing to help the American break-out in the west. Despite this, most of the fortified villages were cleared during heavy fighting by the British and Canadians and it soon became evident to Montgomery that his main purpose was being achieved, for the Germans had indeed been yet again forced to dance to his tune, reinforcing their front against him with elements of not only 9th and 10th SS from the 43rd Wessex sector, but 2nd *Panzers* also, apart from more units of 1st SS.

On the afternoon of the 20th a thunderstorm broke over the battle-field. Torrential rain turned the countryside into a sea of mud, effectively cancelling out further operations. It was the end of Good-wood. 'The storm which burst over Caen on July 20th was a minor squall compared with the tempest that raged at SHAEF and at Leigh-Mallory's H.Q. over what was regarded as Montgomery's "failure",' wrote Chester Wilmot. Eisenhower's aide, Captain Butcher, commented that the air marshals were completely disgusted that once again the army (Montgomery, in fact) had failed and they were left without their precious airfield sites south-east of Caen. The SHAEF staff's belief that the latest Monty blow was a real breakthrough was fostered by one of the General's own special announcements stating that British and Canadian forces had 'broken through'. As Wilmot comments (as a defender of Monty's strategy), the announcement was premature and indiscreet, for by then – even on the 18th – the attack had stalled. Naturally, the great air bombardment had in itself made the front pages in Fleet Street and in America, and this followed by Monty's statement was enough to set greater expectations in train.

The day following the launch of Goodwood the front page of the *Daily Mail* typified the press reaction to the latest Monty offensive, and the public soaked up the great news:

CAEN: THE BIG BREAK-THROUGH
Mightiest Air Blow of All Time Launches the Great Offensive
ARMOUR NOW SWARMING INTO OPEN COUNTRY

The 'great Battle of France' had begun, the column announced, supported by the mightiest air force ever engaged in a land battle. General Montgomery had hurled the British Second Army against the line of the Orne. In a few hours 'this splendid fighting machine' had burst across the Orne, through the Germans and into the plain beyond. The greatest air operation in history, directed by the Allied air commander-in-chief, Air Chief Marshal Sir Trafford Leigh-Mallory, had resulted in 7,000 tons of bombs being dropped on the enemy, for the loss of only nine aircraft. There was (of course) no sign of the *Luftwaffe*.

The basic story was heavily repeated in greater detail by reporters who called the air *blitz* 'Terrifying to watch', a 'Shuddering, Blazing Nightmare', while one of the *Mail*'s veteran star reporters, Ward Price, in his column on page one stated 'The Enemy Knew Nothing' of our preparations, which was of course nonsense. Ward Price was the journalist who wrote a card-covered book in the 1930s entitled *I Know These Dictators*; he had been one of several duped by Hitler and Mussolini, rather like Lloyd George and others even more notable.

The great publicity afforded Monty's latest race certainty was, fortunately perhaps, swamped within hours by an even greater news story, the attempt to kill Hitler by some of his own generals, principally the combat veteran Count Stauffenberg, whose satchel bomb was ill-placed beneath the conference table in Hitler's East Front HQ and failed to remove the *Führer*. As the combatants slithered about in Normandy mud the Allied press gave the dictator's escape greater prominence. The great 'breakthrough' into the plains beyond Caen was shunted aside, the public's notice diverted – not that the people could know of the waves now breaking about their favourite general. At staff level the top British airman renewed his attacks on Monty by assuring Ike that the British Chiefs of Staff would support 'any recommendation' he cared to make with regard to Monty's future. That was the measure of Air Chief Marshal Arthur Tedder's dis-enchantment with the General he had worked with well earlier. It seems extraordinary, to put it mildly, that a British officer of that status should have virtually recommended Montgomery's dismissal to the American chief. At least, though it has been suggested Tedder and his friends did not want a change of command, it is hard to see any other course in their minds, even though they must have known full well that sacking Monty would have been disastrous in the extreme for public morale and at that stage of the war. In any case, there was no one to replace him – certainly not Eisenhower – though some did suggest this. It was as well Ike refused.

Fuelled by this sniping which fitted in with his own feelings, Eisenhower mentioned his fears to Winston Churchill who was visiting the bridgehead. On 20 July, the day Goodwood finally closed, the American chief conferred with his field commanders Generals Bradley and Montgomery. At this meeting Ike was 'deeply disturbed' to hear that the bad weather had further postponed Cobra, but why he should have been so is not easy to fathom. Without 'air' and with mud hampering the troops on the ground there could be no question of an American assault. Ike was reportedly then 'amazed' to hear from the British land chief that he was 'well satisfied' at the outcome of Goodwood. From the viewpoint of his own misconceptions this is understandable. The American's constant, naive preoccupation with all-out, all-of-the-time, all-along-the-line attacking was anathema to Montgomery, who unlike his boss had really studied the art of modern war, if 'art' it can be termed; perhaps 'scientific application' is the better phrase. For, as any real field commander knew, the way to success was to apply concentrated pressure on one point of the enemy's front to achieve breakthrough. Even Ike's fellow generals knew this – and practised it. Ike's way would have got the armies nowhere, or at best slow progress in the extreme.

It was doubly fortunate that Montgomery had General Sir Alan Brooke on his side, a man called by one of his biographers as 'a master strategist'. It was Brooke who continued to ward off the ill-judged attacks on Montgomery, defending him and his strategy, especially to Churchill, whose ear he was frequently privy to. Churchill was no admirer of Montgomery, affronted by the General's abstemious ways perhaps, more inclined if anything to see matters in the simpler, more impatient manner of Eisenhower, wont to interfere in matters beyond his grasp and office, even though he was head of the War Cabinet. Yet the Prime Minister was able to grasp the essentials of the basic Normandy strategy once Monty had explained it to him, as he did. So the usual batch of press photographs depicting the PM beaming from behind his cigar and at one with his generals again reassured the public at home that all was indeed well in France.

Yet behind the scenes at SHAEF, Goodwood was mistakenly written off as a failure because it had achieved neither the expected big break-through or even its tactical objectives, which presumably meant the airfield spaces. The actuality of Monty's successful operation was ignored, for while less of the enemy's armour had been written off than hoped, 2nd Army had succeeded in pulling in even more *panzers* onto their front, thus making it (in theory) even easier for the Americans to break out in the west.

The alarm bells clanged loud and long once more in the corridors of the German headquarters. Field Marshal von Kluge (one of Hitler's favourites) had taken personal command of the battle in Normandy. So threatened was *Panzer* Group West (7th Army now in charge of the American sector) that they diverted the fresh 116th *Panzers* to the British front, while 2nd *Panzers* (*Wien*), about to be taken out and placed south of St Lo (facing the Americans), was brought back to the Caen front. This meant that just before Bradley launched Cobra no fewer than seven German *panzer* divisions plus four heavy battalions of Tigers faced the British and Canadians, while opposing 3rd US Army were just two *panzer* divisions and no heavy tank battalions.

Furthermore, the Germans' faith in a seemingly impregnable defence system five belts deep had in fact been pierced by a tank army thundering on behind a bomb carpet and rain of artillery shells. The German C-in-C's optimism on taking office had, within hours, been shaken so much by Goodwood that he felt compelled to compose a defeatist letter to his *Führer* in which he described his army as helpless in the face of the enemy's overwhelming air power. There was no way a strategy could be formulated to combat its 'annihilating effect', 'unless we give up the field of battle'. Kluge described how whole armoured formations had been caught up in bomb carpets of the greatest intensity, so that they could afterwards only be extricated from the torn-up terrain with great difficulty. The effects on the infantry, whether good or bad troops, was terrible; they too were more or less annihilated, the psychological effects of such aerial terror worthy of special consideration. Kluge confessed he had gone to the front with the 'fixed determination' of carrying out Hitler's order to stand fast, but his experience had now shown him that such a policy could only mean the end of the army.

No matter how graphically his generals described conditions at the front (and Hitler had no intention of seeing for himself), the *Führer* read such reports as more defeatism from them, and in the wake of his near-death felt a paranoiac suspicion of all of them – but especially those who seemed to him to have lost their nerve.

The actual cost to Montgomery's army (apart from the considerable tank losses, and counting only the first two and most intense days' fighting) of Goodwood was perhaps low, comparatively speaking, and especially so when compared to the insane bloodbaths of the earlier war: on 18 July the number of killed, wounded and missing totalled 521 (11th Armoured 336, Guards 137, 7th Armoured 48); on the 19th the total was 499 (399, 33 and 67 respectively), or only 1,020 all told. The 1st Corps lost more – 1,192 – from the one-and-a-half infantry divisions attacking. This compares with 3,817 for the previous three-day assault on Caen when no comparable tactical bombing took place.

These low casualties among personnel did not stop Monty's critics, who soon learned of the heavy tank losses, some then and since asserting that Monty halted all his offensives as soon as the casualty rate grew. But there would very shortly be a fresh target for these critics, plus quite a few at the sharp end. Cobra began at half-cock on 24 July when the air armada turned back owing to bad weather. Next day the heavies of the USAAF went in, but the medium bombers changed their route, and contrary to the agreed plan came in from the west, i.e. following the lines. As a result the two leading American battalions waiting to assault were hit by bombs and put out of action. Casualties, including one CO, all needed to be replaced.

Whatever beliefs and misunderstandings resulting in controversy later, the British troops at the front of Goodwood went through the usual ordeal. Captain Edward Jones attended a major O Group briefing shortly before the assault began. His job was that of liaison between 8th Corps HQ and 11th Armoured:

66 I well remember that day, just hours before the op began. We were gathered in a big tent and had just received a short pep talk from Lieutenant-General O'Connor, who emphasised it was a very important, major operation from which great things could be expected, and I quote him exactly. From that we gathered Monty thought this the big effort that would carry us right away from Caen and to the Seine. I know I left that meeting with a feeling of great optimism that was not borne out by events. But, later on, I came to see that it really was part of the overall plan, because soon after it finished in all that mud I saw a situation map and noticed how many more Jerry units had been pulled in on us. 99

Sergeant Tom Braithwaite commanded a Sherman in 11th Armoured:

66 We'd had many briefings of course since landing in Normandy, but the one before Goodwood stands out in my mind because our officers told us it was the biggest thing yet, as we would see. Well, from that we jumped to conclusions I suppose, and we all hoped of course that the period of rather stagnated fighting was over and we could get going at last. I know I was very optimistic, and when we saw all that terrific air power it went to our heads. Then we had our columns lined up ready to go behind a fantastic gun barrage and I felt nothing could stop us. We really did look a marvellous sight, hundreds of tanks all stretched out behind, and we felt we must surely burst right through the Jerries and win a big victory. Well, I felt later it was a big let-down, but later still I could see we had won a victory as the fighting had been very hard and yet we had advanced some miles, despite everything the Jerries could throw at us. 99

Staff Sergeant Rick Reynolds of the Guards Armoured also gained the impression of something bigger than usual:

66 We attended a briefing some hours before jump-off time in which a Colonel told us it would be the biggest offensive ever undertaken by a British army, and by that we thought he must mean bigger even than the things they did in the First War. I thought he must be referring to all that air power, as I knew quite a bit about the earlier thing when they'd used thousands of guns. I think in Goodwood they used under 800. Anyway, we were all keyed up, even though some like myself would not be going into action. Whenever we had a big attack going in it did affect everyone before, during and after. I know I went out and took a look over the tanks and some of the lads I knew and everything was very impressive. Later on, after it had ground to a halt and I saw the casualty lists, I noticed only two blokes I knew had copped it, and in view of the scale of the thing it seemed amazing. I remember too one of our staff officers telling us that Monty had in fact got what he wanted, and we knew what he meant. On one occasion I happened to overhear a conversation between a Captain on our staff and a chap from one of the armoured squadrons and he remarked how Ike didn't seem to know his arse from his elbow – that's exactly what he said, but I didn't poke my nose in to enquire further. 99

John Brown was a Sergeant in charge of a Sherman in 7th Armoured:

66 I was at Alamein, which was a hell of a battle; Goodwood was too, but in a different way of course. We went in last and it wasn't too bad, fairly easy in fact, but once we got involved we were soon stopped by 88s and Tigers and all kinds of hold-ups because of congestion on the routes etc. I personally was not so optimistic with my experience of

the Germans, but it was hard not to be tremendously impressed by all the air force did for us. I wondered later how they felt when it all came to a stop. By that stage of the war I suppose I'd got used to such events, and when we were stopped it didn't surprise or worry me. I knew we'd win in the end. **99**

The Germans, fully expectant, had their own ideas before Goodwood, during and after it closed down in the rain.

Stabsfeldwebel Hermann Krischne was responsible for maintaining up-to-date intelligence reports at 21st *Panzer* HQ:

66 We had many reports of enemy movement, the building of bridges and that kind of thing, and it became obvious to us that Montgomery was about to launch another offensive. We had been greatly weakened by the many battles since 6 June, but put everything we had into the line. When the big air raids came they were the most fantastic experience. I myself found shelter in a deep bunker, but even this was severely shaken by the blast of heavy bombs, and when the smaller planes came it was even more terrifying in some ways as we were subjected to a rain of fragmentation missiles that seemed to go on and on. We shot down one or two of the enemy, but without fighter protection we were rather helpless and cursed the *Luftwaffe* and especially Göring every day for their uselessness.

When the offensive started everyone had to stand to and the fighting came our way. I myself was forced to man a machine-gun even though I had very little experience of actual combat. I fired off a belt or two but the enemy went off in another direction, to my great relief.

After the battle was over we counted our losses and the enemy's and found that almost all our casualties had been caused by the bombing. Even so, when I came to assess the situation map later I found the enemy had gained a good deal of ground and of course we had finally lost Caen. It was, however, seen as a defensive victory from our side. **99**

Lieutenant Richard Dischen was on the staff of 1st SS and often saw Sepp Dietrich, who did his utmost to bring every available unit into combat during Goodwood:

66 Dietrich saw it as the most serious British effort so far to break through beyond Caen. I heard him say that only a miracle could hold us together if they did get through. But we had had ample time to regroup and build up defences and many remained intact after the fantastic air raids, so overall things did not go too badly, even though it was obvious the British had greatly extended their salient into our territory and we had no chance to erase it. I myself made many visits to the front units and even though they had suffered greatly from various privations their morale remained amazingly good. **99**

The commander of 1st SS *Panzer* Corps, Sepp Dietrich, made this after-action report to General Hausser:

66 The enemy have put everything into this latest offensive, and it has failed in its objective to gain ground beyond the bocage. We have maintained our overall cohesion in the face of unprecedented air attack and mass tank formations. Yet I must say the position has inevitably deteriorated, as we have lost a good deal of ground, and this can only be to the enemy's advantage. I see their next effort as being the most crucial for both them and us. They have suffered tremendous losses in armour, but I suspect this is not of great concern to them, as they seem to be most profligate in this direction. Naturally, I lament the total and disgraceful absence of our *Luftwaffe* yet again from the battlefield. 99

General Hausser himself had been saddened by the wounding of Rommel, and even more shaken by the attack on Hitler, having received the news with mixed feelings. On the one hand he had come to look on the dictator as a madman with an obvious suicidal desire to ruin Germany; on the other hand, he could see little or nothing to be gained by assassination. In short, he was on the horns of the same dilemma that faced every German general. He had always tried to steer clear of the political angle, especially the crazy notions of the man unfortunately wielding a certain power over him and his comrades – Heinrich Himmler. He preferred by inclination as a career soldier to remain in the military sphere, and in Normandy he had found his greatest challenge.

'My view, gentlemen, is this: sooner or later – probably sooner – the Allies will break out of their bridgehead, and when that happens we will not have the mobility to stop them, because of our drastic fuel situation and the usual orders from above. Our only hope is to try to extract a very heavy price from our enemy and trust in God that our fate will not be too severe.'

This is the gist of comments made to subordinates and comrades by General Hausser after Goodwood.

On the same day the press announced the 'big breakthrough' at Caen came news that gave a clue to the manpower situation in Normandy, even though no direct hint was given:

AIR CREW RECRUITS FOR ARMY
– Some Even Going to Civilian Jobs
Thousands of young men who set their hearts on becoming R.A.F. pilots after the Battle of Britain and who, after years of training and study, were finally accepted for air crew duties are now, by War Cabinet decision, being drafted into the Army or even civilian roles.

The papers went on to allege that 'manpower needs can now be measured', that in addition to the similar redrafting of naval personnel made known the day before (18 July), air crew took so long to train that they would not be ready in time to take part in combat before the war ended. One correspondent put it this way, and one can well imagine how such absurd comment was received in air crew messes and billets throughout the UK: 'By transferring to the Army, recruits will have a much better chance of getting into action.' The poor lads concerned were, of course, as dismayed and outraged as the *Luftwaffe* recruits and trained air crew to find themselves wielding rifles under army discipline on a barrack square and in the field. The same correspondent went on, fatuously, 'Although bitterly disappointed at losing air crew status, many will nevertheless welcome a clear-cut decision on the surplus.'

The writer was right on one count, far more than the public could realise. The RAF had indeed far more fighter pilots than they needed; this the correspondent blamed on the rapid retreat of the *Luftwaffe*, which had affected both American and British pilot training programmes. The fact was that Fighter Command had been maintained for years far beyond the strength needed; when the Desert Air Force was constantly short of combat pilots in 1941–43 there were hundreds literally idling in Britain in dozens of squadrons, supposedly guarding the nation against a scale of *Luftwaffe* incursion which the Air Ministry knew could never come. For since May 1941 the bomber arm of the *Luftwaffe* had been reduced to a bare minimum in the West. The Germans found difficulty in scraping together 300 bombers or so to launch Operation 'Steinbock', the 'Baby Blitz' early in 1944, and since this was a declining series of night raids not one of Fighter Command's many day fighter units became involved. It was different for the US Army Air Force, which had taken on the role of smashing the *Luftwaffe* fighter force defending the Reich. The American fighter groups were very strong and of greater range than the British. Even so, a cutback in training at home was in order, and this included the several bases churning out British air crewmen across USA and in Canada.

Hundreds of fully trained airmen had been waiting months for a posting to combat stations even though Bomber Command continued to lose considerably in its raids on Germany and had suffered many thousands of casualties attacking nearer continental targets. Surplus fighter pilots there were, certainly, but to be thrust into khaki at such a stage after long and expensive training was, to put it mildly, demoralising. Then, too, the papers spoke of transfers to civilian roles in work of 'vital national importance', which must have been pure propaganda. After the war trained and even combat veteran air crew (usually non-pilots) found themselves working on routine clerking jobs, for example at RAF Records Office Gloucester, alongside civil servants and regular office personnel of the service, obviously an odd anachronism, awaiting return to civilian life. It was astonishing to read the small print in these reports of reshuffles, of air crew allegedly carrying out 'all manner of jobs to fill in time. Trained pilots on full-time fatigue duties can be found at many RAF stations.' If this refers to the cleaning out of ablutions then it is not believable. Not even the RAF authorities could have been that stupid.

Instructors also became victims in this comb-out. The Air Ministry announcement concluded: 'The Royal Air Force is most reluctant to lose the services of the airmen volunteers affected, many of whom will have had service in the A.T.C., but the highest strategical demands of the war must naturally transcend all other considerations, and it is in this spirit that these young men are being asked to accept this new situation.' The report also mentioned that 'a large part' of the RAF Regiment was 'also being surrendered'.

The surplus storesman John Stewart was ordered to report with two other similar tradesmen to his Orderly Room at RAF Burtonwood, then a huge and still growing base consisting of great hangars filled with every kind of service requirement – though not aircraft. By 1944 a growing number of American personnel were being drafted into the location, which would in fact become known as a US base, though for a time, from 1945 onwards, it served in part as No. 101 Personnel Dispersal Unit, a service euphemism for 'demob centre'. One of the cavernous hangars was converted into partitioned 'departments', tiny cubby-hole offices, like some bureaucratic honeycomb, but one the exiting servicemen willingly entered, bemused as they went through the rather complicated, but not over-long, process of being removed from the active duty rosters of the RAF. Each man, having gone through the red tape process, would then find himself in a much larger department; in fact, it was rather like a mini-Woolworths, with rough counters split into different displays containing all the various items of civilian apparel a grateful government deemed him due.

But all this was still in the planning stage of some chairborne genius in Kingsway in July 1944, for even though the servicemen's friend, the *Daily Mirror* and other papers had begun talking about 'demob group' numbers etc. No one was yet to be sent home from the services – unless in a casket or wheelchair. John Stewart was certainly apprehensive, like his two colleagues, as they beheld the fearsome caricature of the Station Warrant Officer regarding them in the Burtonwood Orderly Room that day in July 1944, probably wondering what misdemeanour they could possibly be guilty of. What relief they gained was at once shattered by the SWO's announcement, almost like one of impending doom: 'He told us that owing to a "certain situation" we, along with a lot more surplus bods, were being transferred into the army. This hit us like a bombshell, though at that moment we never imagined we would be put into the damned infantry!'

Stewart and his chums had to return to their Nissen hut billet to pack their gear at once and travel to Kidderminster by train, where they were met by an RAF Regiment NCO who told them they would now go into training with them:

❝ I popped up and asked him what for, and he said 'Riflemen.' In other words, as infantry. We were so amazed we just looked at him blankly and then began to swear. It was the usual sort of Nissen camp; we were shown into a hut and left to ourselves. Then, after a while, a bunch of blokes came in all kitted out in battle gear and after chucking off their stuff onto their cots they got talking to us and said they'd been 'shanghaied', as they put it. We ate in the cookhouse and next morning had to draw battle gear including rifles and line up with the platoon for parade, and then go off for a run round the countryside. We weren't used to that and at last collapsed, as did some of the others. At that time we wore khaki denims, but still had our Raff uniforms, battledress and sidecaps.

Somehow we crawled back to camp and had a meal and the same day were kitted out with army battledress with no flashes and some of those horrible floppy berets, which we hated. Then we started battle training with pig sticker bayonets and Sten guns on the range, crawling about over the grass, chucking grenades. The instructors knew their stuff, but we were obviously cheesed off I can tell you, and scared about what would happen as soon as they decided we were ready for action. There were RAF Regiment soldiers there in other companies and those beggars were dead keen and couldn't wait to get over there and into action. They too were re-kitted in army battledress and looked a darn sight better than we did as they'd always been bulled into their own regiment training.

I did about a month, or less, before we were paraded and told we were going to France 'to help Monty', and the CO said he knew we'd do well and not let the side down – by which he meant the Raff. We felt really scared and next day went off in dribs and drabs by train and truck, eventually ending up I think in Weymouth. It was late July or early August. I remember writing to my mum and telling her not to worry if she didn't hear from me for a while. She was alone in Northampton as dad had died from cancer before the war and there were no other children.

When we got to France it seemed pretty quiet at first, though we saw masses of stuff, men, tanks and all sorts of gear everywhere. As soon as we were paraded before an army Colonel we had a meal then went off to the front in trucks. I was practically pissing myself, I was that scared. It was getting dark and it took some while before we finally debussed and were given orders to move up in single file behind a Sergeant. I had no idea where or what unit we were going to. In fact, like my mates who were still with me, we actually thought we were still going to be with the RAF Regiment lot. We should have known we were by then in the army proper. A Corporal showed up and numbered off a dozen of us and led us away through the trees and we began to see all the mess of war debris – old equipment and foxholes etc. Then he told us to open up in file as we were in range of the Jerries, so I really felt sick. We crouched down and saw blokes huddled down in foxholes with rifles and other weapons at the ready. It was a kind of stand-to time I learned, in case the Jerries put in a dusk attack.

Then I heard the thud-thud of guns and a lot of other racket some way off and before I knew it we were dumped in a hole and left to it. The Corporal vanished and a voice called over, 'Just come from Blighty, mate?' We looked out and he shouted, 'Keep your fucking head down!' And we reckoned he must be a Geordie.

We were right. He said it was the 50th Northumbrian Division and they'd had a bad time, but things were quiet at the moment. Then other voices started calling, and not all Geordies by any means:

'Have you got any fags mate?'

'Have you brought any booze?'

'Got any skirt, chum?'

Things like that. It was very funny and quite strange. But we were tired and hungry and dying for some tea. When these other chaps heard we were Raff types they were amazed and said, 'Monty must be getting hard up!' It made us think the 2nd Army must have suffered a lot of casualties if they had to take blokes like us.

As soon as it got a bit darker supper came round, three blokes with urns of grub and tea, which was very welcome. We ate and drank and the Corporal came and dropped into our hole and started to tell us what to do if the Jerries came. 'Do you see that hill over there and that wood? Well, that's where they are. They've got a few tanks but don't worry about them as we've got plenty of anti-tank guns on the flanks to take care of them. If they come, do nothing until you hear my whistle, then pop up and let the bastards have it – OK? Now, two of you can get some kip when you like, but one bod must remain awake – OK?'

So that was our introduction to the battle of Normandy. Next morning the Jerries did attack and gave us a terrifying time with shells and machine-guns and we just cowered in our holes with no room to move and unable to go to the loo or anything until it all went quieter and the Corporal shouted, 'The buggers have had it!' He meant the Jerry attack had been stopped by our artillery before it really got started. When we dared look out of our holes we saw fires burning over in the wood and planes finishing them off and two tanks burning. We were very relieved and hadn't fired a shot. **99**

Corporal Alfred Jones was a trained infantryman of the RAF Regiment, quite suddenly briefed in this fashion:

66 'Lads, at last we've a chance to show what we're made of. We've been ordered to France in an infantry role to support the army. I don't know the details, but we'll be going soon.'

By that time some non-Regiment lads had arrived and some of us were putting them through their paces. They'd had no training at all and were only tradesmen. This was amazing to us and we guessed the army people must have taken a lot of casualties.

Not long after that we were briefed again and left for Weymouth in convoys. When we arrived in France we were issued with all-army gear, but still had our Regiment flashes, but to our great disgust a Colonel told us they would have to go. There was an argument and our officers protested strongly, but it was no use. For some reason they would not allow us into action as Raff Regiment blokes. We were forced to change into army blouses etc. and those awful floppy berets. I can tell you our hearts sank and morale dropped so much we had to have a special pep talk from our CO who told us to keep our chins up at all times; no matter what the army people said, we were still there to uphold the RAF traditions.

Next day we went forward in convoy. I can only speak of our own lot, about two companies I think with the usual rifles and Stens and a few Brens. After a half-hour ride we debussed and lined up to be inspected by a Colonel who said how glad they were to see us. We were then numbered off into squads and soon found ourselves in the front line east of Caen and under fire. It was our first time in action, and from then on every day until the breakout we were in combat, apart from a few half-day rests. We had a rough time as ordinary line infantry and I reckon took 50% casualties. By that time we'd made a few advances and been bloodied, as they say. It was what we volunteered for, though none of us had expected to get it that way. **99**

Whoever ordered the RAF Regiment lads to relinquish their unit status made a bad error of judgement; the decision was not Monty's. After Falaise they were withdrawn and returned to England – 'We considered ourselves lucky to find many of the old faces still about, but many weren't.'

Among the many and varied uniform insignia seen about Britain's town and city streets during the war were the somewhat rare beige coloured berets of the Reconnaissance Regiment. Peter Vassell joined the unit when it was formed in 1943, retaining his rank of Sergeant:

66 We were different insofar as we wore brown berets and had our shoulder flash, otherwise we were employed in much the same way as the recce units with divisions, but with one difference. Apart from being a scouting regiment we were given special roles which included probing independently to find out the layout of enemy positions, reporting back to whichever corps we were attached to. In my case our company was attached to 8th Corps during the breakthrough period south of Caen.

We used various armoured and scout cars, some American, and went off to reconnoitre an area south-east of Cheux where we thought there could be a weak link between the SS forces opposing us. We went forward cautiously late one afternoon and ran into a small German patrol which tried to ambush us but failed and they were all killed. From their documents we discovered they were from 9th SS, which we had been warned had just come into the battle. This was important information and was radioed back in code to Corps.

We then pushed on with care as it began to get darker. We thought we had in fact entered the enemy area and then heard vehicles which were off the little lane and we expected to run into them at any moment. We had no intention of getting caught, so six men went forward on foot with Stens and pistols and some grenades while our vehicles were turned round as quietly as possible for a quick getaway. The lane was thickly lined with hedges, but there were no trees. We could not believe the Germans had no guards out, so one of our Sergeants produced a German helmet, put it on and strolled nonchalantly along the road and then made a sign that it was safe to proceed. But when we reached him he motioned us into a little gully, pointing to a long line of vehicles further along the road. There were tanks and other vehicles in the fields strung out in open order and camouflaged.

It was getting quite dark and we felt we'd seen enough. But our Lieutenant decided we needed a prisoner. I myself was too scared to try anything stupid, I had a wife and kid back in London, but our Sergeant with the helmet, who I knew very well as a bit of a daredevil, volunteered to see what he could do.

I was all keyed up and never thought he'd get away with it and was looking back to see if we could reach our vehicles before the Jerries caught us. Well, bold as brass he went off into the gloom as he thought he knew a bit of German and could get by while the rest of us got under cover. He vanished and I thought I saw him go over a hedge. I was almost wetting my trousers with nerves when, after about five minutes, he reappeared, and to our amazement he had a Jerry with him. It was only a kid and he looked terrified. Needless to say we bundled him back hastily into one of our cars and got out of there. And by the time we got back to base we'd found out plenty as the kid told us everything we wanted to know. He was from 9th SS and said he was with its reconnaissance battalion who hoped to go forward at first light.

We had a lot more adventures, but did not always get away with it. 〞

Bill Gates was a Private in the Marines, and had volunteered just before the outbreak of war, as an eighteen-year-old rather disillusioned by unemployment in Plymouth, and of course with a youthful zest for adventure. By the summer of 1944 he was an experienced naval soldier who had seen no action:

❝ We were paraded outside the barracks in Plymouth where we'd been stationed for some weeks after a spell aboard one or two battleships at sea. Frankly, I was bored stiff with it all and wondered if I could transfer to the RM Commandos. So it came to me at any rate as a great and fantastic surprise to be told we would now be going to France to fight the Germans. Of course, it was all very amazing, and we had then no idea what was awaiting us on the other side.

As soon as we got over there we were met by a Marine Colonel and another high army type who looked us over and congratulated us, and I thought, Aye, aye! Now what? And sure enough came the big bombshell: we were to go into the line as *army* infantry. You could have heard a pin drop for a moment, then there was a great yell of anger. It really happened, and like nothing I'd ever come across as we were well disciplined. I suppose the officers had behaved in a friendly fashion hoping to soften the blow. Well, I could see by their faces they were very surprised. The Marine Colonel called us back to attention and said it was very important for the war effort that certain sacrifices had to be made. And without further ado he marched us off and army NCOs showed us into a store where in great confusion and some anger we got out of our Marine gear and into the army stuff. And were we chuffed! I've never heard bods swear and cuss so much, it was that bad, and the army bods beat a quick retreat. I think they thought we might take it out on them. Of course that couldn't happen.

We were taken off in very bad mood to a tent cookhouse where, believe it or not, some blokes threatened to go on strike-mutiny. The NCOs were very sympathetic and tried to keep order. Then a Captain came and appealed for calm. He stood up on a table and tried to speak, but men were blowing raspberries and making other rude noises. When at last he got a word in he told us that he would speak to those in charge and see what he could do. So he then jumped down in a hell of a lot of noise and vanished out of the tent.

Well, we ate the grub, which wasn't too bad, and after that when we got outside we were called together by our own officers and the CO said this. It was a Colonel who'd come over with us: 'Lads, I'm very sorry you've had such bad news, but I'm afraid there isn't anything I can do about it. I'm as much under orders as you are. So we'll just have to lump it and do the best we can. But I do assure you I'll do my utmost to see you aren't swallowed up in the army. That's all.'

Well, there was a lot more grumbling as we went off in trucks to another depot where we were issued with the usual weapons. I was not all that unhappy myself as like a fool all I could think of was getting into action. But a lot of the blokes and especially the old hands refused to wear the stupid berets and no matter how much they were told to get 'properly dressed' they just wouldn't put the things on. Of course, once we got to the front we put on helmets and that was different.

We were sorted out and taken off in file and ended up among bushes and trees and the usual foxholes and saw the brown jobs, as we called them. No sooner had we arrived and started to get the feel of things than a fight broke out. I heard one of the army jobs call out jokingly, 'Christ, look who's here – it's the flippin' Marines!' Well, the next thing one of our blokes landed him one on the kisser and there was a hell of a ruckus until a Sergeant rushed up and restored order. He said, 'Don't you silly twerps know the bloody Jerries are just over there? How do you think they feel when they hear us fighting among ourselves? They're laughing their bleedin' heads off of course. Now settle down or you'll be on a fizzer!'

We couldn't sleep as we weren't used to huddling up in holes and I thought, God, what a bloody mess. It wasn't what I expected. And next morning came our first action when the Jerries shelled us and we had to move back because of all the stuff coming down from the trees. Then we went forward and into an attack. I'll never forget that first one. All the excitement had worn off and I felt scared with all the noise and the fact we might be killed any second. And I was very surprised I couldn't see any Germans, only trees and fields and smoke and a small wood over to our right as we rushed forward. Then I heard yells and half looked back and saw blokes falling and I thought, Christ Almighty! It'll be me next. But I rushed on behind one of our Sergeants, a great big bloke who seemed afraid of nothing, and I felt so long as I stayed behind him I'd be OK. Well, we fell into a shellhole and he laughed and, believe it or not, said, 'This is the lark ain't it, me lucky lads!' We had about six of us with a Bren gunner who started firing, but at first I was too scared even to look out of that hole.

Then we all had a go, just taking quick pot-shots and ducking down again, and in one quick second I saw camouflaged Jerry helmets moving behind some bushes but I've no idea if I hit anything. Then the Sarge said, 'It's time to get moving lads!' and jumped up, and straight away he got hit in the chest and fell back at our feet. We gaped down at him; his eyes were wide open, like his mouth, and there was blood oozing out of his blouse and I felt sick. But a Corporal with us jumped down and tried to put a bandage inside his jacket, but it was no use. Our Sarge with the big laugh was stone dead. We were really cut up and I don't think the Corporal felt like ordering us on. The Jerries were pinning us down anyway and it would have been suicide to show ourselves. Fortunately for us some Shermans came along and gave the Jerries such a pasting that we jumped up and went in after them and found six or seven Jerries lying about dead. They all looked very young and I suppose I felt sorry for them.

An army Lieutenant ran up, looked us over, asked if we were Marines, so we said yes, and he laughed and said, 'All aboard for the Skylark!' and led us off again. Well, he didn't last the day out. By nightfall he was dead. He wasn't a bad bloke but a bit young and I think new like us. We took over 50% casualties in that first attack and not until a week later were we given a day off from combat and went back a mile for a bath and change of underwear and a decent kip and some better grub. I survived that battle, but many of my Marine chums never saw England again. 99

Andrew Barham was another Marine who found action at last, but not under naval auspices. A Corporal, he was never short of the courage to step forward:

❝ When we were told on parade that the army needed us in France I stepped out to ask if we would be allowed to retain our own officers. The reply I received did not sound promising, and our worst fears were realised. In the very sudden move across the Channel and immediately afterwards I somehow got separated from my closest pals, who ended up in another company. That was blow number one. Number two came when we had to hand in our Marine gear and there really was a near riot. After all, we had volunteered, every one of us, to serve in the Marines and were very proud of our traditions. To put us into army uniform was about the worst thing they could have done as we lost all our cohesive unit spirit and things went from bad to worse as we had no chance to get into the feel of things but were thrown in at the deep end. For that reason I believe we suffered far more casualties than we need have done, and I'm afraid I've never forgiven the army for that. ❞

During the seven weeks following 6 June, the Germans brought up twenty extra divisions to reinforce the eight already in western Normandy, while the Allies landed thirty-six. But few, if any, of the enemy divisions arrived intact or at full strength (apart from the SS units of course); they were thrown into the battle in piecemeal fashion as parts of regiments, battalions or even companies. This was in large measure due to the air interdiction programme carried out by the Allied air forces. Over the weeks following their arrival they were whittled down to a strength of two or three battalions each. From D-day until 23 July 7th Army and *Panzer* Group West lost 116,863 men killed, wounded and missing; replacements numbered only 10,078, this figure not including the 1,000 *Luftwaffe* field soldiers sent to General Meindl's 2nd *Fallschirm* Corps, of whom he reported 800 were withdrawn in short order as unsuitable for combat.

German tank losses amounted to 250 in six weeks, which may not seem extraordinary in view of the intensity of the battle, but only seventeen replacements arrived at the front, this at a time when German tank production was at its highest ever. In the three months May to July the factories turned over 2,313 *panzers* to the army, but losses amounted to 1,730 overall, and as shown, it proved almost impossible to move the vehicles from the depots to the Western Front.

That was only one of the Germans' difficulties. Their communications system was near breakdown owing not only to Allied bombing but French sabotage, both by violent and more subtle means. The cables had in many cases been laid by the French engineers who made sure connections were incorrectly set, which resulted in maddening delays and breakdowns for their enemy.

Even late in July, the German staff, and General Speidel in particular, insisted in believing a second Allied landing in northern France was imminent; British deception measures continued to work splendidly so that 15th Army in north-east France counted forty-two fresh Allied divisions waiting to cross the Channel around Calais. As a result, of the eighteen German divisions held in readiness, only three were released for the Normandy front.

Despite all their misfortunes caused by the bad weather and renewed German attempts to interfere, the Allied build-up across the Channel had been an amazing success, so that before July ended a huge number of men and impedimenta had been delivered to the bridgehead:

	Men	Vehicles (all types)	Stores (tons)
American	903,061	176,620	858,436
British	663,295	156,025	744,540
Totals	1,566,356	332,645	1,602,976

One of the most remarkable facts about the stores build-up was the great American success in improvising landing facilities following the destruction of their own Mulberry harbour in the June storm. The Americans had proved that it was possible by energetic, determined measures to land stores in large quantities direct onto the beaches. Also, lest an impression has been given of the greatest effort being made to destroy the enemy on the British–Canadian front, General Montgomery remarked that the Americans had 'eaten the guts out of the German defence' – on the US front, that is. Their twelve-day battle for St Lo after the launch of Cobra cost them 10,000 casualties, this sacrifice a measure of the hard fighting, and the enemy suffered greatly too. General Hausser reported to 7th Army that his total reserve consisted of only three infantry battalions and pleaded for help on the western sector. He was told to expect *Panzer* Lehr, or what remained of it, once it had been relieved by a fresh infantry division on its way from Belgium. As for the so effective nebelwerfer (heavy mortar) battalions, the three brigades could not be spared from the eastern (Caen) sector. Eight German infantry divisions were sent to Normandy following the fall of Cherbourg, six went to oppose 2nd Army.

*   *   *   *

❝ They advanced across the meadows, unchallenged for the first few yards and filled suddenly, as they always were at such moments, with the wild, unreasoning hope that this time it was going to be easy; until the first shell quavered down on them and they were out there, soft, human flesh clad only in khaki serge, with the angry splinters of steel whining among them . . . **99**

This opening to a British infantry attack from Alexander Baron's *From the City, from the Plough* (Jonathan Cape, 1948) could have been any one of several, similar little hills that dotted the Normandy countryside. In fact, it referred to Mont Pincon, described by that author on good authority as the key in that sector to the whole battlefield, 1,200 feet above sea level and a dominating road junction controlled by the Germans who had fortified its forward and topmost slopes in their usual expert manner with machine-gun, mortar and rifle nests, with the standard crop of 88 and anti-tank guns dug in at suitable points, interspersed with tanks and the odd Moaning Minnie battery, everything cunningly camouflaged to blend in with the summery landscape and lull the weary British infantrymen into daydreaming that it might be a walkover.

No veteran of the 43rd Wessex would believe that – those that remained in the decimated battalions of south-west county regiments allotted this nut to crack. They had suffered their early baptism of fire around the Odon, then the Orne and Hill 112, leaving these killing zones behind them, littered with the ugly debris of war and the corpses of many a once fresh-faced boy from England – or Hitler's Reich. On their right, some miles off, the Yanks had at last begun their Big Push. If things went as Monty hoped the boys from Brooklyn and Minnesota and many another state of the Union would swivel left and chase the Jerries and Krauts back eastwards across France to the Seine and beyond. If things went well the Jerries would see themselves being trapped and would flee from the last of the bocage east of Caen, and at last the 2nd Army's tanks could swan off across the plain in pursuit. If things went well.

The situation in Normandy at the start of Cobra, which itself depended heavily on British support, was this. *Panzer* Group West on the British–Canadian front, had continued as shown to be given priority. On that sector General Dempsey's fourteen divisions were holding down the same number of German divisions, the latter having an estimated 600 tanks, at least, according to Intelligence, and that after their heavy losses. Of the German divisions, five had been at the front less than two weeks. In the west, General Bradley fielded fifteen divisions in the 1st US Army, but now a further four were in reserve to become General Patton's new 3rd Army, which it was hoped would be the 'pursuit corps' to exploit the coming breakthrough. The Americans were opposed by a somewhat motley collection of German units, battalions and battle groups totalling about nine divisions with 110 tanks; only one of these 'divisions' had been in action less than a month, the 5th Parachute, which according to Hausser was 'completely untrained'.

Whatever the American approach to battle or their opinions of the

British and German way, the 1st Army commander, General Bradley, had followed Eisenhower's dictum of attacking on a broad front. Weeks of this had provided little result; only after a far more concentrated punch at St Lo did the breakthrough come, but the comparatively weak enemy formations opposing them had by then been worn out. Even 2nd *SS Panzers* were down to fifty-seven tanks by 23 July, while *Panzer* Lehr had been reduced to about fifty tanks and assault guns.

Yet, once the Americans began to slice through the German front, Field Marshal von Kluge did his best to start transferring *panzers* to stop them. Meanwhile, a Canadian assault on the Bourgebus ridge had been bloodily repulsed. Montgomery now ordered General Dempsey to make a change of plan to frustrate the enemy's attempts to halt the American drive: 8th Corps would switch its armour from the Orne to Caumont and attack on 30 July, also using 30th Corps to seize Hills 361 and 309, which was the western half of Mont Pincon (Operation 'Bluecoat'). By this move Montgomery hoped to cover the American left flank and prevent 7th Army using the area as a 'natural pivot'. 8th Corps comprised 15th Scottish, 6th Guards Tank Brigade, 11th and Guards Armoured Divisions; 30th Corps; the 43rd, 50th Infantry, 8th Armoured Brigade and 7th Armoured Division.

Although there was a dearth of German armour in the area south of Caumont, the enemy had been in possession all through the campaign and, in addition to the heavy defences around Mont Pincon, had laid extensive minefields in the rather rugged countryside. Once more the weather intervened. Heavy rain saturated the ground and low clouds hung in the sky on the morning of 30 July, forcing 200 bombers to cancel bombing. But 1,000 heavies and mediums did strike at the enemy, yet despite this new and terrifying *blitz*, as soon as the 43rd Wessex went into the advance they were halted by a dense minefield and a deep-sided stream the tanks could not cross. While 11th Armoured tanks were also held up by mines not detonated by the bombing, 50th Infantry and Guards brigade tanks stormed the first German defences, and following a further air *blitz* in the afternoon the tanks and infantry reached the top of Hill 309 by dusk. They had advanced five miles. The Scotsmen dug in, but the 43rd were in trouble.

Bill Simpson had, like thousands of other British and Canadian troops, found that 'Those big offensives were all the same: terrific prep-aration, and then a little bit of an advance with knocked-out tanks and heavy infantry casualties. It happened over and over again, and it's not easy to remember which [offensive] was which.' That was inevitable. As the weeks went by the surviving soldiers found themselves in a blur of attack and counter-attack through hot sunshine or rain, with green fields and woods and cottages rubbished by constant fighting. At the front Monty's grand overall strategy did not seem at all apparent, even though officers knew its purpose; yet even those with the pips on their shoulders became carried away at times into believing their latest sacrifices signalled 'the big breakthrough'. But a great number of young officers had gone from the battle since D-day, either marked down by snipers as easily identifiable, or else removed in the many attacks at the head of their men. It seemed incomprehensible to the tired troops that their enemy could take so much terrific punishment from the air and artillery and still come up fighting. Bill Simpson was of the portion of the 'Ox and Bucks' Light Infantry not converted to glider troops in 1942:

❝ It was after Goodwood. The Jerries hit us with artillery, SP guns, tanks and infantry, trying to split us in two. Our guns took care of most of them as usual; all their tanks and guns were destroyed or retreated. But we'd taken such a pasting that all we wanted to do was fall down and have a good kip. But the Lieutenant said we had to go out on patrol and make sure no Jerries had been left behind. So off we went, about twelve of us with a Sergeant who I knew very well. His name was also Bill.

We crawled out across a field and found a few dead Jerries and one or two wounded, so sent them back under guard. Then we found a Jerry machine-gun intact with lots of ammo, and not far away this young chap without his helmet, who was trying to hide. So we got hold of him and he kept looking round and seemed shit scared, so our Sergeant reckoned there must be more Jerries about. Well, he'd hardly said that and told us to search around when there was a burst of fire and both the Sergeant and the Jerry were knocked down. The Sergeant had a bullet in the back and kicked up a hell of a row; the Jerry was killed, hit in the chest. By then we were all flat on our bellies, trying to see where the fire had come from. But the Corporal said, 'It's no use, let's scarper!' So we crawled back to our own lines, taking the Sergeant and the Jerry machine-gun with us. ❞

Captain Gerhard Berger was with the 9th SS and fought on both Hill 112 and Mont Pincon:

❝ It was my task to assess the situation on both these commanding heights and to call up reinforcements as required. But this was easier said than done; the whole area was under constant artillery fire and the planes came over regularly. I had a jeep shot out from under me twice and was reduced to running about until I could get more transport. Then, as for the reinforcements, these themselves became so heavily engaged that there were none to call on. The British tried everything to dislodge us from these hills, which were certainly of great importance to both sides, but they never succeeded in defeating us and we withdrew our remnants in good order when threatened with outflanking during their last big offensive. ❞

Raoul Heinz Wagner owed his French first name to a mother who hailed from Alsace-Lorraine. She married her German husband before the First World War. Raoul was seventeen and in 9th SS and spent the whole period helping to defend its slopes against successive British attacks by various county battalions:

❝ We too suffered badly. The casualties were very heavy, and our food came erratically and was usually cold. We had tea or coffee and, of course, the latter was not real and all drinks were usually held up and arrived half cold or stone cold. We grew filthy as facilities were almost non-existent and it proved impossible to leave. We were not relieved once in a four-week period and in that time lost many of our NCOs and officers who lived in the same miserable conditions. I often saw no hope of leaving that cursed hill alive. It was red with the blood of both sides, but I have to say mostly British as they were the very brave attackers and lost far more men than we did. ❞

Peter Winkler was in a small squad of 12th SS who found themselves trapped near the base of Mont Pincon by the British advance:

❝ We lay in the grass and among bushes under artillery fire, quite unable to move. We had been on our way to reinforce the 9th SS; we were all that could be spared and we felt we could be kept by the 9th to help them throughout the battle, which became very fierce. One of my comrades was struck by a splinter and died in my arms. This was a terrible shock as we had trained together in Belgium and been in the battle together since 6 June. I laid him down on the grass and I cried, but the Corporal saw me and told me to stop, but he himself was then slightly wounded and told us all to run off to better cover. He crawled after us but was then killed by a bullet before reaching us. Then a senior Private directed us to set up our machine-gun and we drove back the advancing British.

When it got dark we heard a lot of movement and thought we would be surrounded. We could see nothing so one of the men shot off the only flare we had, but when it burst and we stared down the hill we could see nothing at all. So some of us fell asleep from exhaustion while the others tried to keep watch. We had no idea what was going on and were without orders. Then, as it got light, the first bombers arrived and we suffered the worst air raid yet. We had dug holes but they were quite unprotected from the fragmentation bombs that burst above and about us, and two more lads were killed. We were very exposed, so the senior Private told us we must go further round the hill, and as soon as the last bombers left we did that and on the way met a patrol of the 9th SS who sent us in the right direction. We found an artillery position where we were able to get some coffee and a little to eat. Then an officer sent us off with a Sergeant and we were back in the battle again. ❞

Ted Bartram was a Lance-Corporal with the Somersets:

❝ We were already weakened by our previous encounters with the SS on Hill 112, and frankly thought it far better to let the air people and artillery deal with them. But we were called together yet again and told to do our best. And I looked at the few lads left in the platoons and thought what a stupid waste. But we had to get on with it. It was useless to try to walk or even crawl up that damned hill; we'd tried everything, and always ended up having to slither back on our bellies to escape. So this time, as the artillery started up again, we made a mad dash and fell head-first into the brown grass and tried to wriggle forwards on our bellies, and made quite good progress at first. But after about a hundred yards or so the Jerries started mortaring us and the casualties began and in a few minutes we were completely stuck and unable to go forwards or backwards. The air was alive with machine-gun bullets while the bombs were falling all round and behind. At last it got quiet and I knew very well the first man to show himself would be shot. I heard moans from some of our blokes hit, then someone shouted and ran back down the hill and that started it. The survivors tried to follow him, and I saw no alternative but to do likewise. When we reached cover again – those that did in all that fire – I counted twelve blokes left. It had been another massacre. **"**

When the Duke of Cornwall's lads had a go Reg Beckwith went in with them. A long-serving Private, he had a wife living with his aunt in Cornwall and had almost given up hope of ever seeing them again:

" When we went forward again it wasn't so bad as we'd had a bit of a rest and some good grub and a pep talk in which the Colonel told us the Jerries were definitely going to break at any time. But then we saw the Somersets and we could see by their appearance they'd had a bad time. I remember some of our lads calling out to them as we passed and I don't think one bothered to answer, they were that bushed, and who could blame them.

We knew the damned hill and hardly needed any briefing, and late one afternoon after the usual artillery stonk we started off, and I followed our Corporal in a sort of sideways advance along the side of the hill. Then we started to hear the rattling Jerry machine-guns and hit the deck. We fell into a shellhole and were stuck. Two blokes tried to get up and run on and were hit at once. One fell dead at my feet, the other one's arm was shattered and he sat there swearing and carrying on until the Corporal told him to 'bugger off back down again' which he did. Whether he made it safely or not I've no idea. When the planes came in again we managed to gain about a hundred yards, doing the old zig-zag trot again before we had to dive in a hole. By then there were four of us and no one else in sight.

We were stuck there until dark when two blokes came up with a Bren and a Lieutenant who said he had some more men coming up and we could infiltrate under cover of darkness. Well, we were not in the least optimistic as we knew the Jerries would be alert. So, after getting our guts together, we climbed quietly out of the hole, with the Lieutenant in the lead and the Bren gunner ready to cover us. We made little noise in the darkness and to my surprise reached a small rise with not a Jerry in sight, and the officer told us he reckoned we had outflanked them up the hill. He told us to dig in and be ready to fall back into the holes if the Jerries popped up. We had made a very significant advance.

After a bit, with us digging as quietly as we could, the Jerries suddenly started to machine-gun the whole area and the tracers were flying everywhere. We were lying in our half-holes and I heard a sort of grunt and moan and guessed someone had been hit. But it was no use trying to move for a bit. Then the machine-guns stopped and we had a look round and found the Lieutenant with a wound in his chest. He said, 'Sorry chaps, I think I've had it.' Then he coughed and wheezed and was dead. At that moment a Sergeant appeared from nowhere, sized up the situation and told us to hold on while he went for more help. He made one bloke help him off with the dead officer and we hung on there for an hour before the same Sergeant reappeared with two mortar men and bits of their weapon. The other bloke came with the barrel and they dug a pit, making a hell of a lot of noise, despite all we told them. Sure enough, it was too much for the Jerries who opened fire again and one of the mortar blokes copped it at once; the others dropped down, and one of them said, 'Bugger this, we can't fire now. Anyway, we've no bombs.' Well, we had a few choice words to say to them as they cleared off back to fetch some ammunition. But we never saw them again. Their pal was dead.

At daylight we were relieved and somehow managed to get back down the hill intact for some grub and tea. **99**

John Castle was a subaltern with the Hampshires, and although well aware their latest assault was part of Operation 'Bluecoat', saw it as no different to all the previous attacks they had made. In fact, it had become a routine, and one he personally felt would probably end with his company's extinction.

Sergeant Henry Chaisten was an ex-Grenadier in Guards Armoured and described his first taste of action in Normandy in mid-July just south of Caen during Goodwood:

66 It was our very first time in action. We were all keyed up and excited, and when the commander gave us the signal our drivers put the Shermans in gear and we roared off. The guns had been hammering the Jerries but so far we had not seen anything at all of the enemy. All that was about to change. We went off in great style in clouds of dust and hadn't gone far when the lead tank carrying our Captain went up in a sheet of flame. It was so sudden I was taken completely by surprise and barely heard the explosion against the general din of all our tank engines and the gunfire. It took a few minutes to get past the wreck and we were very shaken as there could be no survivors.

I got down in my turret and used my periscope but couldn't see anything remotely resembling a Jerry position, but they were about, as we found out a second time as a tank behind us went up with a much louder bang and we knew we were really in action at last. Then I saw some grey-brown figures running, but before I could give a command my chap at the Browning let them have a burst and got one of them. Then I saw targets, dug-in Jerry tanks and guns which had been very well camouflaged but were visible from the sides as we went past. My gunner swung his turret as we went by and started to let fly. As he got off two shots a shell glanced off the front of our hull. Then we were past and firing like mad and I cheered as I saw a Jerry Panther go up in a queer blue flash with bits flying everywhere.

Then we went round a bend in the road and found a number of Jerries running in all directions and gave them a real pasting. When I had a second to look behind I saw only three tanks following, but I thought the rest were hidden round the bend. I found out differently later. We were then held up by mines and a/t fire and went into a ditch, but were able to continue firing. 〝

John Veasey mentioned that even after converting to armour, the Guards always maintained their strict discipline:

❝ We were always being reminded we were not in the army! But the Guards! And the officers and NCOs never let us forget that. I can see now that it did help to hold us together when things got bad, as they did at times.

When we went into that Goodwood attack we were tremendously excited at a chance to show what we could do. I was a driver and had long mastered the job and thought if only I could survive long enough I would do a good job. I was of course very apprehensive as even though we had not been in action we knew very well the reputation of the German tank boys, and especially their 88s.

When that first tank went up in flames I was well back down the column and I thought, I'm damned glad we weren't in the lead! You expect losses, but first time in they do hit and shake you more than somewhat. And we had known our Captain a long time. So on we rushed and then a second tank went up and we had to take avoiding action and still hadn't fired a shot. But then I began to see Jerry infantry and tanks and stuff and my heart leapt as all the guns started banging away. The smoke obstructed my vision and it was hard to keep on the road. In any case, it was madness to keep on like that and after a few minutes we deployed over some fields and were then held up, and a long slanging match began against the Jerries which went on for hours. I don't know how many miles we had gone, but it all ended in disappointment, as for a tank soldier to be stuck in static fighting like that was a dead loss. 〝

Edward Carmichael was a Corporal and ex-Irish Guard, though from London, and had a nastier shock than usual in his first action:

❝ It was after we'd been stopped and were stuck out on a limb; too many tanks had been knocked out behind us and we were rather exposed. But our commander, an RSM, told us we were surrounded; the Jerry infantry had got behind us. This was near a ruined village which was full of them. We got scared then. A splinter had actually come right through the driver's visor and missed him, but it bounced about inside and wounded the gunner. I had been loading and aiming and also had a hand with the radio to change net, as they used to call it. So for a while I was loading and firing as the gunner lay on the floor of the tank moaning after the splinter hit him in the side. I didn't like the look of things, we were too vulnerable.

In a short time I realised we were about to run out of ammunition and told the RSM, and he said, 'Christ, prepare for all-round defence!' I had ammo left for the Browning, but then of all things it was struck by a burst of fire and ruined. So we took up our Stens, which we carried, and prepared to bale out fast before we were brewed up.

In a moment the RSM told us to scarper out of it, so we got out quick and under fire and the gunner was hit and killed. We were shaken and fell over in the grass, and before we could even raise our weapons the Jerry SS blokes were on us and it was all over. They put their guns at us really close and shouted and we dropped our Stens. I'll never forget the look on the RSM's face at being captured – he was really sick! In fact he let off a mouthful at the Jerries and they laughed. They hurried us off under fire from all sides until we reached one of the ruined houses, and they left us alone for a bit under guard, there was so much going on. The RSM said we could try to escape, but then an NCO came in and took him off somewhere and my mate the driver went off to sleep, as if he hadn't a care in the world!

After a while one of the Jerries gave us some foul-smelling coffee – I suppose it was supposed to be. I couldn't drink mine but my mate Nobby scoffed his and went back to sleep. So I got up and stretched my legs, with the one Jerry watching me closely. There were two broken windows and it got rather quiet, apart from the guns banging away and shells going over. Then, after a few minutes, the Jerry, who was quite young, started talking to me, in a quite friendly fashion, but I hadn't a clue what he was talking about so I just nodded and grinned. Then he pointed to my shoulder flash and said 'Eerland?' and I reckoned he meant 'Irish', so I said yes, Irish Guards, but told him I was from London, and he couldn't understand that. Then more firing started up and he went to watch the window and I gave Nobby a kick as I thought we might have a chance to escape. But he was out to the wide, as they say, and I gave up. In any case, I thought I might stand a better chance alone if the RSM didn't come back. I didn't fancy spending a few months in a Jerry PoW camp.

Then another Jerry came in so I got down on the ruined carpet in that room, which had once been a bedroom but the furniture was gone. They chatted and looked at me as I pretended to lie down next to Nobby and try to get some sleep. Then the Jerries went out of the room and I nudged Nobby awake and told him we could try to escape. He said, 'Not me mate, we'll get shot!' And he closed his eyes again, and though I tried to persuade him he was having none, so that was that.

After a minute or so I heard the Jerry come back and look in on us, and he probably thought we were asleep as I kept my eyes closed. But when I heard him go out and our guns started up again I got up, went to the door and couldn't see him. So I went to the window and climbed out without trouble and dropped down, then I ran like mad towards some bushes and dived straight in them. I got caught up in brambles or something but tried to get myself concealed and be still. The noise went on and I thought I heard yells, so guessed the Jerries had found I had gone. But the shelling got worse and no one seemed to come looking for me. So after a while, as it grew cold, I crept out of the bushes and started to crawl back the way we'd come. I saw our tank and went to it, climbed inside in the dark and found one or two bits and pieces including my scarf, got out again and hid under the tank for a bit before crawling off again.

I went about one hundred yards like that before getting up at the crouch until I saw some more ruins and one or two dim lights and hoped I'd reached our chaps. But then I heard Jerries so got down quick. I hung about like that in the grass until it was much darker, then I went on but changed direction slightly and managed to miss the Jerries, who were in occupation of another ruined village. I felt whacked out and hungry and thirsty as I'd had nothing since breakfast. I then reached some trees and lay up for a bit. Then I could see the flashes from our gun lines and the shells were going right overhead, so I ran this time and after a mile of seeing nothing I heard vehicles and got down. A few minutes crawling over the grass in a field and I definitely heard British voices, so I went a few more yards and called out, 'Oi!' and someone yelled, 'Who the hell are you mate?' And I called 'Irish Guards – escaped prisoner. OK if I come on?' And someone yelled, 'Come on mate, you're OK now chum.'

A few yards on and I stumbled into a foxhole. A few minutes later I was eating grub and drinking tea. **"**

*　　*　　*　　*

General Montgomery's strategy in Normandy can be likened to the famous RAF 617 'Dambusters' Squadron attack on the Moehne Dam in May 1943. Successive hammer blows by the Barnes Wallis mines were needed to break down the great edifice. When it burst the effects seemed catastrophic, though in fact it was mostly impressive; the enemy soon recovered. The same could not be said of the German armies' defeat in France.

There had never been any quick way to smash through them; Montgomery had shown this. No amount of concentrated *blitzkrieg* seemed to work. But the Germans' line bent here and there while overall the weakening effect of the successive offensives was about to pay the Allies handsome dividends. The sweeping, rapid drive by Patton's 3rd Army was made possible by the intense crumbling operations carried out over nearly two months before the American ever set foot in France. Commendably and expertly carried out, Patton's victory with his new pursuit corps served his ego and brought that army great kudos, so that after the war many Americans who had served under him in the heady days of late summer 1944 were proud to proclaim they had fought in Patton's 3rd Army. How many of them appreciated the great sacrifices made not only by their fellow Americans but especially by the British and Canadians to enable their triumph?

Late in July, as indicated, Monty saw the Germans as ripe for collapse through the final blows from both armies that would generate the rout and pursuit. A certain situation now arose that might have placed him in an awkward position *vis-à-vis* his own plan and American allies.

The enemy, uncharacteristically, allowed a gap to open between 7th Army and *Panzer* Group West, re-designated Fifth *Panzer* Army by this time. It was hardly typical German practice, simply a measure of the overstrain on SS General Hausser and his severely stretched command. It had the overtones of fiction. British infantry, advancing during the night of 31 July, discovered a woodland trail, with not a German soldier in sight. Going forward in single file they found themselves on the outskirts of St Martin des Besaces, and by dawn four armoured cars of 11th Armoured had bypassed the village and driven on through the Forêt L'Evegne as far as the river Seuleuvre, five miles on. The impossible had happened, for the reconnaissance cars now found a bridge intact west of Beny Bocage and radioed HQ to send a column of tanks to secure it. Six light tanks (probably Honeys) arrived, but too late. The Germans finally woke up and plugged the gap. As a result the British drive stymied and a set-piece battle developed to clear the enemy from St Martin.

This thrust had caught the Germans completely by surprise, for although Hausser had lost Avranches to the Americans, he had been about to or was in the process of securing his right flank when Montgomery sent in 8th Corps to dislodge it; the German commander lost his pivot and found the important communications centre of Vire under direct threat. Units of the depleted 21st *Panzer* were hurried forward as a race developed to bolster the sector, but too late. They were defeated, and on the morning of 1 August British scout cars were approaching Vire. Now a second great chance to plunge in behind

Hausser's front facing the Americans presented itself. Tanks of the main 11th Armoured force were rumbling along less than five miles behind the armoured recon units. There was practically nothing to stop them, and it must be said that it would have taken a Patton to snatch a dazzling coup from the wide-open situation now put to the British.

The German divisions supposedly covering the area were ten to fifteen miles to the west and north-west of Vire; they had been constantly tied down and harried from here to there by successive crises. 9th SS began to move, but would need at least a day to reach the threatened town, owing of course to the Allied aircraft overhead waiting to pounce on anything moving in daylight. Meanwhile, a gap seven miles across had opened between them and 21st *Panzers*. The opportunity was there. Vire was practically deserted, as the cars of 11th Armoured discovered.

What, one must ask, were the feelings of those scout car crews when they heard the next orders? For instead of the British tanks of 8th Corps crashing into the town and securing it they were ordered to divert south eastwards towards Flers. This is the kind of historical detail omitted by Monty in his memoirs, as are the subsequent odd corners that throw light on events in these crucial operations before the German collapse. For Vire was on the boundary between the British and American armies, and in fact the town was one of General Bradley's objectives. Yet surely, with such an opportunity this kind of protocol could have been overlooked and the town snatched and handed over (with suitable British politeness) to the Yanks when they arrived?

In the event, and despite Monty's assertion in his memoirs that the Germans 'had not evacuated Vire', the enemy were now permitted to rush in reinforcements and harden their right flank, and in the fighting that followed 11th Armoured was halted on the Vire–Vassy road, the Guards Armoured at Estry, and only by skilfully handled small German battle groups which snapped at the flanks and heels of the British columns. But 9th SS was severely hit as expected by fighter-bombers and Typhoons of 2nd Tac and lost heavily. Yet the 'administrative clean-up' shown by Lieutenant-General Dempsey on that day and the lack of dashing aggressiveness meant a grand chance wasted.

However, by 3 August the Germans facing 8th Corps were in real trouble and almost incapable of offering effective resistance. But 30th Corps (50th Division and 7th Armoured) made little or no progress in trying to capture Aunay and Villers Bocage, still in German hands after weeks of confrontation. As a result a different kind of storm erupted about the heads of the respective corps commanders as the CO of 2nd Army issued ultimatums to his deputies in the field – 'Get on or get out!'

General Erskine decided his 7th Armoured (the Desert Rats) had a dangerously exposed flank, this due to Bucknall's tardy progress; 7th Armoured was halted, for it had never been part of British staff thinking or practice to take risks over exposed flanks. One is reminded of the state of terror Hitler himself experienced in May 1940 when he saw Rommel leading his own 7th *Panzers* in France. The unit had raced on far into the enemy's vitals. The *Führer*'s anxiety seemed odd in view of the far more colossal gambles he had been taking politically and militarily for years. In that event, his fear seemed justified when (again) 50th Division and armoured units of the BEF hit into Rommel's right flank south of Arras, bringing crisis and some grossly exaggerated signals from Rommel himself telling of an attack by 'hundreds' of enemy tanks. But now Rommel was out of it, the mantle of crisis lay on Hausser and others.

The British command, however, now showed it could be as ruthless and intolerant of failure as the Americans. Dempsey dismissed Bucknall, Erskine was also sacked (replaced by Major-General G. C. Verney), and so was the Royal Artillery commander. It was perhaps the final straw for General Miles Dempsey, who had already shown his dismay by recording his private thoughts in his diary: 'I am bitterly disappointed with the conduct of Goodwood which has resulted in such serious losses. Mistakes have been made which I feel ought to have been avoided.' To which he now added: 'I have had to replace my two corps commanders, with Monty's approval. Whatever hopes we had for the offensive, very little has been achieved, even though we realise it has cost the Germans heavily and put exactly the right kind of pressure on them, also to help our American allies go forward. Our very fine army is being bled and this cannot continue.' To these frank comments must be added those of Lieutenant-General Bucknall, who continued to record his experiences:

❝ We have done our utmost to fulfil the C-in-C's directives which we are perfectly aware are designed to tie down as many German divisions as possible. This has resulted in considerable losses, and I fear if the present rate of attrition continues we will not be able to sustain such offensives, at least not on this scale. Goodwood has cost us dear in armour and morale; the men see very little gain for the losses sustained. Some units have been decimated and need to be completely reinforced and rested before attempting further combat. In my case I have had very little sleep owing to the intensive nature of the battle, with frequent and determined German counter-attacks which, though held, have been of concern at times.

The fact is, this is all a very great strain on all of us at the front as we have it must be admitted been forced to unlearn and relearn as we go along, which is the way of hard experience. I myself have not been up to the job in my own opinion, and this has been confirmed by my dismissal by the Army CO. I fear whoever takes over will himself be obliged to go through the same process of indoctrination, particularly if he is a desert veteran. ❞

Feelings through 7th Armoured were said to be aroused by the loss of their commander, but as is fairly well known, that division had not settled into the bocage type of warfare after its long battles in the open deserts of North Africa. But then, their enemy had also been placed in a similar position; as shown, many of the veterans in 21st *Panzer* and other divisions were stifled by the nature of the Normandy countryside, especially those with long Russian front experience. However, the Germans soon saw the great defensive potential of the terrain and used it to their advantage. The Desert Rats would, however, soon come into their own again once the plain well beyond Caen was reached.

Lieutenant-General Brian Horrocks was himself a desert veteran, having served under Monty from 1942. He was watching a rehearsal for the Salerno landing at Bizerta in June 1943 when a low-flying German fighter strafed the beaches, a bullet hitting him in the stomach. Several operations followed, and by the end of July 1944 he was almost well again; in fact, on that day he attended a Cambridge hospital for a final injection. However, a medical board had refused to classify him A1, though he felt completely fit again and ready for action. He had watched the battle develop in Normandy with growing impatience to get back into the war, but he had heard nothing from his former boss Monty. Then, the day following his visit to Cambridge, he received a telephone call from the War Office to tell him General Montgomery was sending a plane to collect him the next day (2 August), the same day 30th and 8th Corps lost its commanders in Normandy.

'This was splendid news,' Horrocks was to write later in his memoirs[*], especially as it meant he would again command his desert veterans of 30th Corps. After taking off from Northolt in Monty's aircraft, he persuaded the pilot to overfly his cottage at Winchester so that he could wave to his wife and daughter in the garden of Yew Tree Cottage. Horrocks made this very English departure before facing up to the heavy responsibility of taking over a leaderless British corps who would by the time he arrived be well aware they had fallen below par.

As soon as the new broom landed on a dusty Normandy airstrip he found doubts welling up inside him. He had been 'out of it' for fourteen months and was as fresh to the Normandy countryside as the others of African experience. In fact, of course, all of the men who had landed in France were new to that terrain, but only a small proportion overall were 'desert men'; most of the new corps CO's friends were still with the 8th Army in Italy. Yet, as he was driven through the lanes crowded with traffic, he was hailed by a tankman who called, 'Glad to see you back, sir!' That young officer, who knew the General's face from the desert, proved a tonic for Horrocks, and more was to come, for he now began to recognise more and more men he had last seen in Africa. At Monty's 'tac' HQ, Horrocks found not only his old boss (and new one), but General Eisenhower. The American, on spotting the arrival, went

[*] *A Full Life*, Collins, 1960.

forward to shake his hand, assuring him there was nobody he could be more pleased to meet.

Horrocks had good reason to feel a trifle uneasy as Monty scrutinised him carefully inside his map caravan; the penetrating blue eyes could discern perhaps the sickness still occasionally plaguing him. But Horrocks passed the test and Monty ran over the current situation on the 100-mile battle front. Horrocks (or 'Jorrocks' as he was known to his chums, including Eisenhower) well knew that criticism of Monty was growing in Britain, at least in some circles – 'This was all very different from the adulation of the 8th Army days.' Yet he knew very well the Monty strategy, recalling the briefing given back in April at St Paul's School in London. That simple strategy had worked; it had enabled the Americans to capture the Cherbourg peninsula and now start their breakout; the whole front was starting to pivot eastwards from the Caen sector, from the holding hinge of the British–Canadian front.

From Monty's HQ Horrocks went to meet his more immediate commander, Lieutenant-General Dempsey, a 'quiet, self-retiring personality' that hid a rather tough character. They knew each other and had both served at staff college before the war. Dempsey gave out his orders, writing left-handedly, not mentioning the fact of his air crash so very recently when his observation Auster had turned turtle on landing. Then Horrocks went off to see the 30th Corps units. 'It soon became clear that the gloss had been taken off that magnificently trained army . . . seven weeks' hard fighting . . . had taken its toll.' Casualties had so drained the front units they were weakened and exhausted. It was a general's job to watch a division's 'psychology'; some went into battle and won success, never to look back, while others suffered defeat at the start and somehow never recovered.

Horrocks spent several days visiting the infantry units at the front, giving little lectures to officers and NCOs, using a situation map fixed to the back of a truck to put his view across. This was something he excelled at, so much so that thirty years later he would score an unlikely hit on television doing much the same thing before the public as he recounted some of his battles in the war.

One amusing sidelight came when the General discovered he was the 'owner' of a mobile farm, a collection of chickens and cows maintained by his chief admin officer, Brigadier George Webb, the farm animals used principally to provide eggs and fresh milk for the Corps hospital. The farm moved with the unit, but their chief mentor George Webb was killed later in the campaign.

At first, there was no levity to be found in the battle itself as Horrocks discovered the trail of losses suffered by 43rd Wessex in their battles for Hill 112 and Mont Pincon. But in writing later that their casualties were 'distressingly high', he surely erred in quoting the 5th Battalion as 'reduced to 500 men'; a battalion still that strong after so many attacks would have been considered virtually untouched by the norms of that battle. When he returned in sombre mood to his HQ he was unexpectedly hailed by his Chief-of-Staff, Brigadier Peter Pyman, who ran to him yelling, 'We've got it!' The General had no idea what he was referring to, and could hardly believe his ears when Pyman repeated and enlarged on his outburst. They had captured Mont Pincon.

It seemed that some tank troops had shown boldness and initiative, something not always too evident in that arm. A Captain had led his six or seven tanks in a night advance along a narrow track up and around the hill, the slope difficult enough to send one tank toppling over into a gravel pit. The rest pushed on through mist until they realised they were on the summit – and without infantry support. The Captain reported his success and called for reinforcements; the 4th Wilts responded, though they had only just come out of forty-eight hours of continuous combat and were exhausted. Spurred on by their Colonel who led them off in transport, they debussed and went up Mont Pincon in single file, securing the hill which their General knew even before leaving England was the dominating feature in the whole of that region. It had featured in the sand-table exercises. Its capture came as a great relief to all, and morale soared.

Yet, in view of the German claim that they had not been defeated but merely withdrew to avoid being outflanked, the British victory seems rather hollow. How many hundreds died or were wounded in trying to wrest the feature from the enemy is not known. It was the same on Hill 112, the cursed pimple that had cost both sides so dear. During the night of 3/4 August patrols of 53rd Welsh Division found the enemy had gone. All around the slopes that had suffered so much punishment from shells and rockets and bullets the worn-out, dirty, stubble-chinned Tommies rose up to stretch their aching limbs, hardly daring to believe that once again they could move without being shot at. When they advanced cautiously up and over the hill they found it littered with bodies and debris, burned out, blackened hulks, semi-graves and Britons who had reached goals only to be killed and remain unburied for days.

Some days later, soldiers drove up in a truck carrying a large signboard which they erected on Hill 112, it read:

CORNWALL HILL
July 10th–11th 1944

The makeshift tribute was replaced later with a granite monument to the fallen of 43rd Wessex Division who died trying to take the hill, perhaps a respect marker for Mont Pincon also.

For Lieutenant-General Horrocks the good days had come swiftly; he would not have to slog it out for weeks in Normandy. With his commander he sat atop the Mount, directing the fire of 300 guns wherever he wished, having perfect observation across the enemy's remaining territory.

11 Totalise to Victory

Justification for Montgomery's strategy was about to come, though some would remain sour for ever as to his part in the victory that resulted in the end of the German occupation army in France and Belgium.

There were contentions in other directions – proud SS soldiers who would not admit they were defeated on the hills facing the British. The exhausted Wiltshires who toiled up Mont Pincon laden with ammunition and other gear fell asleep over their spades on digging in atop the summit, well aware the enemy had not decamped but were themselves holing up all round them. Yet the wedge the Germans had inserted there had gone, and that same night (6 August) 2nd Army forced a crossing over the Orne at Thury-Harcourt, and the enemy's door began to creak open. The great battles that had so worn down both sides since D-day ensured that Patton and his 3rd Army could motor in comparative safety across the southern front. Not that the Americans lacked opposition; the counter-attack at Mortain proved that. Neither were Patton's commanders all quite as driving and dynamic as their general; one of them (Major-General Grow) halted his 6th Armoured Division for twenty-four hours while units went back to clean up 'a pocket' in their rear. Some Americans could be as timid as their allies.

Having allowed the enemy to punch up Vire, when Bradley's troops arrived at the town they were met by staunch opposition. But the town fell, while the enemy command tried desperately with half measures to effect a big counter-thrust at the Americans. Montgomery had directed that his allies should sweep round towards the Seine, exploiting any weak point in the enemy front to the full; Bradley ordered Patton to go all out eastwards. Field Marshal von Kluge's response to this dire situation was to report to Hitler's HQ that the only sensible course was to withdraw to the Seine. The *Führer*'s decision, as always, was not only to hold fast but to counter-strike with every available division. On 4 August he decreed that eight of the nine *panzer* divisions must attack the Americans from Vire-Mortain to the coast at Avranches. Amazingly, Hitler also ordered the *Luftwaffe* to throw in its last reserves: 1,000 fighters must be thrown in to support the blow that would hold the Americans and perhaps permit an orderly withdrawal on the British front. Hitler ordered that the attack must not begin until 'every gun, tank and plane' was in place; this was impossible in the prevailing situation, with the position growing more critical by the hour. When Patton's men reached Le Mans the fresh 9th *Panzers* from southern

France were diverted to try and stop them. And owing to the continuing severe British pressure only 1st SS could be spared to move against the Americans; this unit – or what remained of it – would join 116th *Panzer*, 2nd *Panzer* and 2nd *SS Das Reich* in an assault at Mortain. The panzer-grenadier division 17th SS were and had been in combat against the Americans but were hampered by two factors: a complete lack of tanks, and attacks by French partisans. Their defensive front ran from Le Mans to Mortain; the division was not directly involved in the counter-thrust.

Due to start just after midnight on 6 August, the German commanders faced insurmountable difficulties, and not only from the enemy. General von Funck, commanding 47th *Panzer* Corps (the newly formed 'spearhead'), reported to General Hausser that not only had 1st SS failed to arrive, but 2nd *Panzer* had not received the promised tanks and assault guns, that the commander of 116th *Panzers* had 'made a mess of things again and should be relieved'. This meant (he stated) that it would be several hours before the attack could begin. That was at ten p.m., which meant a possible delay until first light, which would be fatal in view of the enemy air activity. Indeed, the German build-up had been well reported so the American command had ample time to prepare. Nevertheless, Hausser insisted the attack must go in as scheduled. As a result 2nd *Panzer* managed to attack with what it had and advanced seven miles towards Avranches where they were stopped, the Americans remaining in possession of the high ground outside the town. On the right, though aided by early morning fog, the Germans made no progress, and at dawn the enemy assemblies were at once found by marauding Thunderbolts and Typhoons who began their deadly work of destruction.

All that following day the suffering Germans on the ground complained bitterly of the complete lack of *Luftwaffe* cover: 'The activities of the fighter-bombers are almost unbearable. Air attacks of such intensity have never before been experienced.' The 1st SS was stopped, while 116th *Panzers* had not even started. By the evening 7th Army reported the offensive had made no more progress, this almost entirely due to the air attacks which had got worse so that no German unit advanced 'one step'. Typhoons caught one German column of 200 trucks and sixty armoured vehicles on the open road and decimated it with their rockets and 20mm cannon. Yet Hitler insisted they try again, this time reinforced by two SS divisions from the British front. It was too late. Bradley's troops snatched the initiative handed them by the American and RAF airmen and the Germans were thrown onto the defensive, with 84th Corps complaining that 'weak men were deserting and the good men could no longer hold such a wide front'. The news got worse for the enemy command: the Canadian army had struck hard towards Falaise. In the south there was little to stop Patton's raging columns as they raced on past Le Mans and Angers on the Loire, just a few security battalions and one regular infantry battalion, with 9th *Panzers* directed back to Mortain by Hausser.

Hitler demanded 'blind obedience' from his commanders; von Kluge complied, possibly anxious lest he be implicated in the Bomb Plot conspiracy, for the list of arrested military and civilian suspects was growing and heads would soon roll, though a vengeful *Führer* had other ways to execute the guilty or weak who could not prove their loyalty. In the field the generals attempted to follow von Kluge's orders, and the fate of 7th Army was sealed.

Meanwhile, on the British front the adventures of Lieutenant Reg Hall of the SAS had continued following his daring peep behind the enemy lines just after the first landings on 6 June:

66 We had somehow managed to survive all those weeks behind the enemy front. At times it had been quite hair-raising as we were often forced to seek cover at minimum notice, with Germans quite close by. And when one of our men wandered off to do his business one afternoon and never returned we thought he'd been nabbed and the game was up. In fact, he had met an old Frenchwoman who had invited him into her house for some refreshment and he rather lost count of time. If she had been somewhat younger we could have understood. As it was I felt he deserved a bit of a rollicking for giving us such a scare. We then moved off as we felt our security had been compromised.

Early in August we received fresh orders by radio to reconnoitre south-east towards Falaise to find the form, so we set off on foot, with a good stock of apples and, I must say, a few more supplies audaciously dropped by an RAF fighter which had no trouble finding our marker north of Mont Pincon. We tramped on, stopping every so often near a major road to observe enemy movement and radio a report or two. Then, towards dusk, we stumbled on an enemy HQ.

We had crossed a field by going round the edge of it. It was a bit gloomy and as we reached the other side we heard vehicles and voices so we dropped down and I went forward with my Sergeant. We looked through a hedge and into a woodland clearing and saw several vehicles well camouflaged and some with aerials extended and guessed what we had found. We then moved right round the camp and saw not one guard, so were able to move in to a better position to try and read some insignia and identify them. But it was then too dark. So we returned to the rest of our lads and went back a way to set up camp in the bushes and have some tea and grub. Then I went off again with another chap who was very good at German until we were back in the vicinity of the German HQ. Then we went forward on our bellies until we were actually underneath one of their trucks with an aerial and my man did his best to listen in. It was not easy, as some Germans kept coming and going, but after half an hour he gave me the thumbs up and we made a very careful withdrawal.

When we got back to our little camp my chap reported that they were of the 9th SS and had a tactical headquarters and were about to move. In fact, before it got light next morning and after I'd had some kip, we heard them packing up and leaving. We went off to watch them go and then radioed a report to our people.

That was in fact our last adventure, as immediately after that the big drive to Falaise began and we were withdrawn. All we had to do was lie low until some Canadians arrived and we greeted them – with appropriate comments, I may say. **99**

On 6 August, partly as a result of Hitler's orders, the German Army in Normandy began its irrevocable collapse. Events in the almost quite separate battles proceeded in an inevitable sequence; in the north the German front at Caen trembled as the troops and commanders found the Americans rolling up their comrades in the south.

Field Marshal von Kluge had moved almost all his forces west of the Seine where, unless a miracle occurred, they were sitting nicely, ready to be scooped up or destroyed by the Allies. To enhance this opportunity, General Montgomery set in train his final operation, choosing no racetrack as inspiration for a code, but the word 'Totalise'; if a new verb, it would be seen very shortly to signify the total destruction of 7th Army. The task was given to the newly constituted 1st Canadian Army, so designated no doubt for political reasons. Every 'Canuck' was a volunteer for overseas duty, but the force also included 1st British Corps.

The plan put forward by the Canadian General G. C. Simonds was innovative. Simonds was an efficient, ruthless scientist in war, much like Montgomery in these respects, and not afraid to try new ideas. Bearing in mind the errors in recent operations, Simonds decided to pass up a heavy preliminary artillery bombardment; the guns would commence firing at zero hour in the night assault. But there would be air strikes carried out both sides of the proposed corridor by Bomber Command heavies, with American heavy and medium bombers attacking ahead of the assault columns in daylight. A wedge would be punched through the German frontal defences by four tight-packed armoured columns, a four-tank front comprising the usual flail tanks, combat tanks and infantry behind in armoured carriers. These were converted Canadian 'Priest' 105mm SP guns with the weapons removed. The great problem with all these offensives had been the depth of the German defences around Caen. The enemy had had ample time to prepare several lines of strongpoints backed by tanks and artillery of all kinds, and too many had survived previous attacks. This time the infantry would bus three miles into enemy territory before dismounting to attack on foot.

Extraordinary measures were arranged to overcome the problem of darkness. Bofors guns would fire tracer each side of the route, green marker shells would be put down ahead, and special radio beams would be laid for lead vehicle navigators to track; all the following drivers needed to do was stick closely to the tail light of the vehicle in front. There would also be another night combat innovation, the use of searchlights beamed onto the cloud base to reflect light over the landscape, assuming there were clouds enough to make it effective. The moon was due to rise around midnight.

The four-column armoured phalanx would drive along the Caen–Falaise highway, while on each side other forces would quell the German defenders and hold off attempts to strike at the flanks – two British brigades on the eastern side, two Canadian on the west. In a pre-op pep talk the Canadian Army C-in-C General Crerar told his senior officers that the potentially decisive period of the whole war was at hand. 'I have no doubt that we shall make 8 August 1944 an even blacker day for the German Army than that same date twenty-six years ago.' Crerar was referring to the utterance made by General Ludendorff after the great British offensive of the same date in 1918.

During the evening of 7 August, 2nd Canadian and 51st Highland Divisions assembled south of Caen, formatting into their four columns. At eleven p.m. the Bomber Command pathfinders arrived and began their usual precision job of marking the target areas each side of the proposed attack corridor, and following the thirty-minute aerial bombardment the British–Canadian attack force began to roll behind a creeping barrage.

Almost at once all the careful preparations and precautions seemed to be nullified. Added to the dust and smoke from the bombardments came a German smokescreen, blinding the lead navigators. Chaos increased as some vehicles deviated from the set course; others ran into deep bomb craters, some into the enemy, being hit and lighting up the fog like blazing beacons. Following drivers found it difficult to see the dim tail lights ahead and the 1,000-vehicle phalanx began to waver. 'The chaos was indescribable,' one officer commented later. The enemy too were driven to some confusion, hearing rather than seeing a tremendous din before and around them. Firing broke out, 88mm guns and other German weapons untouched by the bombing and artillery shooting almost blind. Drivers blundered away from the route and in trying to regain cohesion were fired on by their own troops. On paper it had seemed a feasible, original plan; now it began to look stillborn.

Yet among all the confusion some officers began to restore order, leaping from their vehicles, using flashlights to guide erring drivers back on course. And, amazingly, in due course the infantry debussed only 200 yards off their designated point. By dawn the Highlanders were three miles inside enemy territory and well established. Their Canadian comrades had met tougher opposition, but were achieving their objectives. But when full daylight came a thick mist held up operations and the Germans began to recover.

Captain Michael Sanderson took part in that wild drive, an experience he has never forgotten. Every detail is imprinted into his mind. In some ways it was a nightmare, yet tinged with mad humour here and there. In fact he managed to laugh about it later, when in daylight he looked back over the hours of confusion and death.

❝ We were all keyed up as we climbed into those carriers. There was an almost holiday spirit about the whole thing, despite all the hard and bloody fighting we'd been through, and I suppose expected. The Germans were as lively as ever we thought; they will not take it lying down. Something's bound to go wrong, it always did. Yet, with so much optimism about, that we really had worn the Jerries down, we went off into the darkness in great hopes.

The fireworks provided by the air force had been terrific, very heartening, and we only saw one plane shot down. When that was over the artillery started up, just as we began to move. But almost at once a great wall of dust and smoke hit us and it was choking. I got out my hankie and tried to cover my face, but I was forced to look over the side to see what I could. It was like a London pea souper, but into that was a stench of explosives after the bombing and other smells which I only realised later was from a German smokescreen. The lads were joking and cursing and soon we saw that there were vehicles going off track; one actually hit us and we had something to say about that. It went on and on but we still managed to get forward and then came under fire. But in all that fog it was possible to make out both our own vehicles and occasionally enemy soldiers who were trying to surrender. We had to stop several times to take their weapons and direct them to the rear. It was quite a long and confusing night and very unlike any other battle I'd been in, as we had very little fighting to do.

We jumped out at one spot to deal with a Jerry machine-gun nest and lost two chaps doing it. Then we got back in our carrier and went on. When dawn came an officer ran up and directed us into a little orchard where we debussed exhausted, even though we'd been more or less sitting down much of the night. The mist was thick and we could see almost as little as we had during the drive. It was some hours before we began to get fire and went off into the usual sort of attack, and I was wounded in the knee and evacuated. The battle for Normandy was over by the time I was reasonably fit for action again. ❞

Bernard Fielding from Edinburgh was a Corporal in 51st Highland:

❝ When we went off some of the lads were whistling and singing '*Mairzy Doats*'; we were in very good spirits. I'd been in Normandy about a month. I went over as a replacement and had been in some pretty rotten fighting and seen too many good lads get hit and removed, most of them dead. I thought, If this bugger doesn't work I'll feel like kicking Monty's backside! We thought he was a very good general you see, but with so many men getting hit and us not getting anywhere much, morale did sink at times. But we were under Canadian command and they seemed full of optimism. I remember one Canuck Captain coming round to inspect us and he shouted, 'Up the Jocks! We'll give 'em hell boys, whaddya say lads?' And we cheered him and went off again in good heart.

Well, it was a bit chaotic, but to our amazement when things looked like a complete balls-up we found we were almost in the right place and had a bit of a kip in our blankets before breakfast, and then things began to liven up. The sun eventually came out, the Jerries woke up and off we went again. I had a good pal called Henry and I'm sorry to say we got separated that day. I don't quite know how it happened, but later I found he'd been killed. It turned out a big success though. **99**

The German 346th Infantry Division was formed in the autumn of 1942 and sent to France next year. A two-regiment, 'static' division, it did duty in the St Malo area of Brittany until spring 1944, when it was transferred to Le Havre, north of the Seine, its commander Lieutenant-General Erich Diester. Thrown into the fighting against the British around Caen, by mid-June it had only thirty-five to sixty men left in its companies, with six anti-tank guns. These remnants faced the 3rd British Infantry at the time of Totalise.

Friedrich Hoppener was a Captain with the division and recalled how they watched the great air raid that night at the opening of the latest British offensive. Things had gone fairly quiet on his front, though they guessed it would not be long before the enemy began attacking again:

66 We had taken one or two prisoners during the last attack and knew we faced the same 3rd British Infantry, and that once the attack got underway to the south they would start to put pressure on us again. We had so little left with which to stop them, I fully expected my people to be overrun, and that is what happened.

I was asleep in my dugout before dawn when the alarm sounded and I ran out to use my glasses to try to assess the scale of the enemy attack. There was the usual firestorm of artillery and then I saw tanks and infantry advancing. We manned our weapons and I distinctly recall one Private saying his rosary on his knees, which amused and saddened me. Within half an hour he was dead. We fired off all our ammunition and knocked out some tanks, but there were too many of them and they bypassed us so that in no time we found ourselves out of ammunition and surrounded. We had to surrender. I gave my pistol to a British Sergeant who told me I would not be needing it any more. I must say, considering the difficulties we were very well treated and a few days later went to England where I found a new education beginning, because not long afterwards in the PoW camp near Derby we began to have political discussions organised by the British in which we were allowed to express any opinions. It was all very illuminating and helped me no end after the war. **99**

While the weakened 346th Infantry had defended the sector north of the main south-east railway out of Caen, the 272nd, veteran by now of the battles since D-day, was stationed south of that route and directly in the path of 51st Highland. Sigmund Regel was a Corporal and in his post on duty when he heard the first night bombers come over:

❝ I soon saw the 'Christmas Tree' markers come down and then various pretty colours on the ground, some quite near us and I sounded the alarm. When the bombs started to fall all round we were all in shelter, but the detonations were terrific and some men were killed, others including myself badly shaken. And when at last the planes had gone the artillery started and we knew we were in the way of a big new offensive. We tried to man our weapons but the shellfire was intense for a few minutes before it moved behind us. Then we found we could see little in the great fog and our Captain said we were putting down a smoke screen to make it even harder for the enemy to see what he was doing. There were searchlights in the sky, but they could not prevent the smoke and fog from confusing everything.

Then we heard a great deal of noise from vehicles including tanks and our officers told us to wait until we could see some targets. This was very hard, but at least the gunfire had moved on. Then at last we were amazed when a great host of enemy tanks and other vehicles suddenly appeared before us and they began firing as we did ourselves. But the battle was over almost as soon as it began because they were so close they simply overran us and many of our men were taken prisoner including myself. I was herded up by some infantrymen, stripped of my equipment, given a kick in the rear and pointed behind them. I was in a state of shock, it had all happened so quickly. I found myself with other comrades marching past an endless column of the enemy until at last we were taken by policemen to a truck and driven off. I think about an hour later we were given some tea and biscuits and the NCOs and officers taken off to be interrogated, they didn't bother with us. ❞

The German 85th Infantry had only been formed in February 1944 from disbanded and remnant units and encamped in the rear area of 15th Army until the beginning of August when all at once it was hurried forward to the Caen sector where it soon came under attack by the 1st Polish Armoured Division, which comprised three armoured regiments, one 'Highland' battalion and two infantry battalions, plus one motor battalion. A British Colonel had a chance to visit the Poles on a number of occasions in the liaison role: 'I always found them to be very friendly. Their one big ambition, of course, was to get at the Germans. The business before the Falaise battle was their first big action and they did have a lot to learn, as had we all. I think they did as well as most.'

Heinrich Laser was a Sergeant with the German 85th Infantry when the Poles went in to attack them on 9 August:

66 We had no idea then that they were Poles; if we had then we might have acted a little differently, for I have to say there was very bad feeling through the war against them for their supposed atrocities in 1939. Of course we had been duped by our Nazi masters, but we only found this out later. When we saw the enemy tanks and infantry attacking us we had no reason to assume they were other than British or Canadian. We opened fire and a fierce battle developed. Then, after a while some of the enemy got as far as our positions and hand-to-hand fighting took place. I remember all the noise and confusion and shouts and shooting going on, and one of the men yelled, 'Polen!' and we all had a great surprise and I believe the fighting became even fiercer. There was real hatred on both sides and not one prisoner was taken by us. It was a very hard fight and I'm sorry to say a bitter one, beyond our norms to that time. When it was over we had retreated in some disorder as the enemy were in far greater strength. Their tanks simply ran over us, and I mean that literally; some wounded Germans would have survived.

I can now understand their feelings and respect them, but at the time their kind of fighting did not help us to try and treat them as usual foes. I mean their dirty fighting. I will not say more. 99

Obviously, there would be no tea and biscuits and polite conversation behind the Allied line for German PoWs on the Polish front – if they had taken any.

For the Canadians west of the Caen–Falaise highway and railway, the German 89th Infantry guarded territory with 12th SS on their right. Known as the 'Horseshoe' division owing to its unit symbol, it had been built in 1944 from reinforced regiments of the Replacement Army and trained in Norway before being moved to Normandy in late June, where its process of decimation began. Collapsing on 8 August, the remnants were taken out of action.

Don McLeod of the Argylls recalled the drive south before Falaise:

66 We were moving along in carriers against the Jerries who were running away in panic as their whole army fell apart. But then we heard shooting ahead and had to get out and deploy for attack. Some men came running back and said they'd been ambushed. The road was wide open, with no cover, so the Sergeant told us, 'Go easy now, lads.' So we went forward on our bellies, stopping to listen, but heard nothing in our sector. Then some of us went round the flanks where the grass was quite long, and after a few minutes we heard someone yell, 'I've got the bastard', and we were amazed when he stood up holding some German SS kid by the scruff of the neck. He was the only one left of an ambush party. He'd had a machine-gun and had knocked down a lot of our

platoon. He got quite a beating before he was allowed to go back as a PoW. "

The Germans' situation was now desperate, that of their commander von Kluge especially so as Hitler's suspicion of him grew and no firm orders came from the *Führer*'s HQ. It was as if the German command in Normandy was paralysed, like a rabbit waiting for a snake to strike it down. Kluge was himself in this condition, unwilling to issue any order that contravened his *Führer*'s wishes. While Montgomery urged General Bradley to use a long hook eastwards, the Americans were still too engaged around Mortain to fully comply. Even so, the enemy watched in dismay as Patton's four divisions drove on, virtually unchecked. There would be some contention after the war as to exactly whose plan it was to forge on in the south, all the leading generals, including Patton, claiming the credit. It was certainly in overall terms in compliance with Monty's original scheme. As for von Kluge, he used the added (and safer) weight of SS General Hausser's and Eberbach's opinion that the attack towards Avranches was unsustainable, but that '*Panzer Group Eberbach*' should disengage at Mortain and drive off the enemy forging northwards. Eberbach was an alleged 'staunch Nazi' so von Kluge felt such weight would perhaps persuade Hitler, which is what happened; for once the *Führer* agreed. Not that his decisions now carried any substance that could affect events, which were moving rapidly to a climax and the end of 7th Army in Normandy as the Allied jaws began to close on the many thousands of enemy soldiers facing entrapment around Falaise. The 1st Canadian Army drove south, the British 2nd Army forged on from the north-west and west, while the Americans enveloped Alencon and then fought north to Argentan.

There was only one force of men who might yet try to hold open the jaws and enable some of the doomed army to escape – the SS troops. The proud, then undefeated SS divisions that had entered the battle in June and July were now themselves reduced to remnant status. Lieutenant Eduard Kempner was still commanding a much reduced company of 12th SS:

" We were indeed in a terrible situation. We had lost all our heavy weapons and had only one machine-gun with little ammunition. I had about twenty young riflemen with which to try and form a blocking position against the British–Canadian advance. We ran forward under artillery fire and got into what little cover there was among the bushes and were soon in action against the Tommies who were advancing on a broad front. We managed to stop them for a short time but lost half our men and were forced to fall back to a new position. And so it went on, hour after hour, until we ran out of ammunition. I then had six men left and had to hunt around desperately to find some food, water and above all ammunition. We were completely cut off from command and in fact never saw them again. That evening, while we tried to get a little rest, we were surprised by the enemy troops and captured. We were not badly treated, but in a very bad way from our privations. **99**

Gunther Hase was also in 12th SS and lost his comrades during a big attack when they were split up: 'I lay in deep grass, trembling and terrified as the enemy soldiers raked the whole area with machine-gun fire and sent in tanks which crossed the ground this way and that trying to force out any stragglers. In the end I saw it was useless and gave up. They pushed me about and took all my possessions and my watch and gave me a kick which sent me sprawling, and off I went behind the Tommy lines under guard and met a few of my comrades, which was a great relief.'

As the Germans were forced back so they were obliged to retreat in increasing haste as all ranks became aware of the trap closing on them. The generals, including those of the SS – Bittrich, Hausser and Dietrich – were forced to save their necks in the hope of fighting another day, certainly of trying to stop the Allies on the German border. Kurt Meyer, however, virtually charged himself with the almost impossible task of forcing open the jaws of the Allied armies closing in so that as many troops as possible could squeeze out of the increasingly narrow bottleneck around Falaise:

66 I had a jeep, one radio truck and some dozen men to try to organise defences in all directions. There were men streaming past us by the thousand, all ranks and every type of vehicle, the whole lot under constant threat from air attack, and every so often this happened. Many hundreds were slaughtered as they tried to escape along congested roads on which the dead, dying and many horses were causing nightmare scenes of obstruction.

I was forced to go on foot with my men. We were trekking west when all else was moving the other way. These fugitives gave us little notice and none stopped to enquire about the situation, and even less what could be done. I could see that although the situation appeared hopeless, with a few small groups I might be able to hold back the oncoming Allies long enough for many of this bedraggled and beaten army to escape. That is what happened, as by a miracle I found some three hundred of my own men, though not all 12th SS, and organised a few battle groups. I then showed them into the best available positions from which to conduct defence and by that same evening we were in combat again with the British and Canadians. The fighting was severe and we were forced out of our holes time and time again over several days during which we virtually lost all sense of time and date.

In the end I was down to about one dozen men; the rest were killed, captured or vanished, and I saw we could do no more. We were surrounded by the enemy and I told every man to look after himself and try to break out eastwards if possible. I also told them they were free to surrender if they wished.

I myself elected to remain in hiding and see what opportunity to escape came after dark. I felt reasonably confident I could reach German-held territory again. However, things did not go as hoped. I was hiding in some bushes in the hope of getting some sleep when I heard British soldiers combing the terrain and got down into my cover as far as I could. But it was no use, as they started firing into the under-growth, so I was forced to reveal myself. Several Tommies ran up and searched me and I was marched before a young officer who looked over my papers before taking me off to a radio truck where I saw a higher officer who had me interrogated by another man who spoke reasonable German. I was given some tea and biscuits and almost collapsed, I was that exhausted. And so began my long period as a PoW. Later on in England I was charged with war crimes of which I had no first-hand knowledge, but that is another story. **

Lieutenant Vernon Hapsley of the Herefords had been employed carrying despatches to corps headquarters but diverted his driver to Falaise. By then the enemy forces had been massacred, taken PoW or escaped. Ten thousand Germans lay dead in the fields and roads of the area, with very many horses and destroyed vehicles. The slaughter had mainly been the work of the air force and artillery:

** There were MPs directing the traffic and it was impossible to get through because of the carnage. So we left our jeep by the side of the road and went off on foot down a sloping, sunken road which was literally thick with bodies and wreckage. The stench was awful and there were flies everywhere. I had never seen anything like it and saw my driver was shaken too. We went on and he picked up a few bits and pieces, helmets, medals and badges, that sort of thing. I saw a German officer in a car whose head had been blown off; it was lying on the seat beside him. He held a pistol, so I steeled my nerves and took it. The face on his head was quite rosy and had a silly look on it and was not really bloody. I looked into his briefcase which contained papers which I decided to take back to our CO. There was also a wallet with family photos and I kept that too, but lost it later. He had a lot of medals and badges and my driver stripped these off. There were a lot more sight-seers about. It was a fantastic scene and one I would never wish to see again. **

Hans-Ulrich Jägerman was a Captain on the operational staff of 1st SS:

** We were in some panic as the enemy pincers closed in on us and all control of the battle was lost, but we believed that what units there were would continue to fight to allow as many troops of Army Group B to escape as possible. We burnt all superfluous documents, grabbed what weapons we could and thought we might have to fight our way out. I saw Sepp Dietrich drive off in a command car with escort; the rest of us took what transport was available and did our best to follow. Then we met a group of leaderless infantry and a Colonel told us to get re-organised and act as rearguard. I had no choice but to do as ordered. I had about twenty men so formed them up and returned to where we had started to try to set up an ambush against whichever Allied troops reached us first. The men went into whatever cover available, an old barn or destroyed farm buildings, while some dug holes. I climbed up into a roof space to observe and soon saw an enemy column racing towards us.

We waited until they were stopped by wreckage on the nearby road and then opened fire. Panic resulted and many of the enemy fell, and some of their vehicles caught fire. But they soon recovered and began trying to surround us, guessing we were no more than a rearguard and unsupported. So we rearranged our positions for all-round defence, but the enemy made good use of cover, using trees and hedgerows, and we were soon under fire from all sides. It was a very difficult situation and as the officer in command I had to decide what to do next. My decision was to try to break out in small parties, one covering the other, and go eastwards.

This proved very difficult as the enemy fire was continuous and they had the means to hand to destroy all the buildings we were using. Despite this, half the men rushed out along the road with a Corporal leading them, firing as they went. We threw grenades against some of the enemy who tried to rush us. Then we tried to follow the first group into the road; two men were hit and killed at once, but we could not stop. We ran like mad along the edge of the road, straight into some of the enemy who were killed or wounded. In this process we lost three more men. Then we came under the covering fire of the first group and reached comparative safety. But not for long, as the enemy came on with tanks and many infantrymen and we were obliged to run for our lives, and by then we had no more bullets to fight with and our only thought was to escape.

When we reached the next village we were exhausted and under observation by an enemy spotter plane, and we had no hope of resuming the fight – or so we thought. Then one of our men ran to me and reported he had found an army truck convoy full of supplies. We ran off and found twelve trucks parked all over the road without any sign of occupants. There were supplies of all kinds, even weapons, which seemed strange. We filled our pockets with food and ammu-nition and felt completely rejuvenated. We then tried to board the vehicles, but discovered to our dismay they were all out of fuel, which was why they had been abandoned, yet not destroyed as they should have been. So we left them, undecided as to what to do. The Corporal had vanished, probably one of the wounded, so I promoted a likely substitute and told him to get as much of the supplies unloaded as possible and hide them in the bushes, and then we would destroy the vehicles.

This we did, then took up fresh positions in time to meet some enemy troops thrusting up the road. This time they had tanks in the lead and we could do nothing about those. So we let these pass, but once the infantry came along in smaller vehicles we opened fire and did tremendous damage. Then I ordered my men to disengage and follow me along a path. We escaped, and after a long march found some of our own transport that evening and were able to retreat in good order to the Seine. There we found absolute chaos, with many troops trying to cross the river by all manner of makeshift craft. I took a party of men some way alongside the water and found two old rowing boats, managed to lash them together, loaded up some wounded, clambered in and against all odds managed to reach the far bank. The scenes on both sides were awful. There were masses of dead horses and corpses and equipment lost through the constant Allied air attacks. But we managed to fight again. **99**

Corporal Swencla Gonblance was a Germanised Pole whose family had become naturalised following the Versailles Treaty. He had grown up in Germany. By the summer of 1944 he was a retreating survivor of 716th Infantry, a few of his unit mixed up with many other remnants in the roads and fields around Falaise.

66 We were under almost constant air attack. I had taken to the fields with a comrade who was also a Corporal, but even then we had some narrow escapes from tanks and bullets as the planes attacked over and over again. There were hundreds of dead bodies choking the roads, wrecked and burning transport, and we wondered how we could escape such a hell. Every time we thought we had found a safe route we found others there already. It was all a wild scramble, with horses going mad under the air assaults, and the stench was bad. I saw many sights among that mess too awful to describe.

We went into a large field of corn that was on fire in places. All we carried was a few personal possessions and our rifles, but nothing to eat or drink. Then we met a Captain who was foolishly trying to stop everyone and organise a defence. He held a pistol, but no one took any notice of him; we were too far gone for that. Then at last we reached a stream, but it was red with blood from men and horses and several vehicles had fallen into it and poured out their petrol. Some were on fire. We fell down from exhaustion, intending to wait until dark and escape. But the Allied artillery was shooting up the whole area and we heard tanks and other vehicles. It was impossible to sleep. When dawn came we were too tired to go on. Then we saw enemy tanks and infantry and threw away our rifles in great relief and began walking towards the enemy.

Soon we were drinking tea and eating biscuits. That was the best meal I ever tasted. "

*   *   *   *

Field Marshal von Kluge wrote a farewell letter to his *Führer* advising him to end the war, that by the time it was received he would have taken his own life. Hitler's reaction, as recorded during an interview with two other generals, was to insist he would go on fighting until a decent peace became possible or – quoting Frederick the Great – 'one of our damned enemies gives up in despair'.

Hitler's opinions of his enemies had been perhaps confounded most by the performance of the 'shocking crowd' – the Americans, the men who had only 'come over to make money, or for adventure, or to see something new, to be in something exciting for once. Not one of them has a political opinion or a great ideal. They are rowdies who quickly turn and run and could not stand up in a crisis.' These sentiments had been readily absorbed by the *Führer* when presented to him in a report by his man von Neurath who had allegedly interrogated 'hundreds' of American prisoners in Tunisia (following their first blooding in November 1942). With all their faults, the 'damned Yankees' had proved Hitler and his professional militarists wrong. As for the 'English', they had under Churchill succeeded in forming the coalition which was bringing defeat to the 'Thousand-year Reich'.

The Battle of Normandy officially ended on 19 August. Then General Montgomery – soon to be elevated to Field Marshal – could start reckoning up his score card. It ran like this: twenty German Army, corps and divisional commanders killed or captured, two wounded, two dismissed (one suicide); about forty German divisions eliminated or mauled, losses over 200,000; over 3,000 guns captured; tanks destroyed over 1,000; British and Canadian casualties 68,000; American casualties 102,000. The war was not over, but it was the end of the beginning.

Bill Kershaw of the Cameronians was driving on past Falaise and the great number of bodies and wreckage when two Germans were found sitting in an undamaged truck. When pulled out they seemed petrified, trembling and almost paralysed following air attack. 'They'd been in the thick of it and couldn't stop trembling; they'd lost their nerve. I'd never seen human beings in such a pitiful state. We told them to start walking westwards. That was only the start of it all.'

When General Sepp Dietrich reached the Seine he found chaotic conditions, for the bridges had been destroyed by air attack and thousands of German soldiers were trying by every desperate means to cross the river under assault from the air. The *blitzkrieg* tactics formulated by the OKW staffs in the late 1930s had been perfected by the Allies. Bill Kershaw: 'As we neared the Seine the bodies and wreckage were even thicker on the ground, and along the river bank where the Jerries must have been in complete panic to get across. It really was the worst smoking mess we'd seen, though I believe Falaise was even worse. There were all sorts of souvenirs to be had, but we were all so sick of it we left most of it behind.'

Almost 100,000 Germans had been compressed into an area some ten by twenty miles, with Allied troops driving in on them from all sides but the east, the narrowing gap that was finally closed on 21 August. Before then about 50,000 escaped to fight again. Certain censures flew about thereafter, with an 'untidy' situation prevailing as the respective Canadian, Polish and American units tried to maintain some semblance of cohesion in their boundaries. It was in these closing days of the Normandy campaign that Patton suggested to his boss Bradley that he be allowed to push on north and drive Monty into another Dunkirk. Indeed, General Montgomery has been blamed by some Americans for permitting a sizeable number of Germans to escape, even though he was not on the spot to exhort the Poles and Canadians to greater efforts.

Later, Lieutenant-General Horrocks cited 500,000 German casualties in the ten-week campaign, with 211,000 taken prisoner, while much later Max Hastings quoted German losses at 450,000 men, including 240,000 killed or wounded. Weapons losses comprised 1,500 to 2,000 tanks, 3,500 guns and 20,000 vehicles. The number of horses, which the Germans used profusely, were uncounted.

In fact, the disaster was worse than that at Stalingrad in the winter of 1942–43, and if Hitler's generals had forced their will on him Germany might have capitulated, though the 'unconditional surrender' policy announced by the Allies seemed to have precluded any terms but that. The Nazis had interpreted Allied and especially American statements even more literally, and naturally, to mean the Allies would dismember Germany and inflict a life on the population not worth living. But, above all, the fear of retribution falling on them from the 'Bolshevik hordes, the mongols from the East' made the troops fight on the harder, no matter how many had surrendered in the West. The exhortation of Montgomery to his men before D-day to 'kill Germans', crude as it was, had nothing on the vituperations of Ilya Ehrenburg of the Soviet Union – 'Kill! Kill! Kill!'

The most accurate slant on the scale of the German losses in the West is seen in the returns of surviving personnel and matériel submitted by Army Group B after the campaign. The very strong SS divisions, Hitler's élite 'fire brigade' units, had suffered especially badly, for these formations had entered combat up to 18,000 strong:

2nd *Panzer Division (Wien)* – one Infantry Battalion, no tanks, guns

21st *Panzer* Division – four weak Infantry Battalions, ten tanks

116th *Panzer* Division – one Infantry Battalion, twelve tanks, two gun batteries

1st SS Division – a few weak infantry detachments, no tanks or guns

2nd SS Division - 450 men, fifteen tanks, six guns

9th SS Division – 460 men, twenty to twenty-five tanks, twenty guns

10th SS Division – four weak Infantry Battalions, no tanks or guns
12th SS Division – 300 men, ten tanks, no guns

Figures for the other German units are not known, but 17th SS who fought the Americans left Normandy some 8,500 strong, having lost some 7,000 men and most of their artillery.

Finally, and several decades after these events, what of the fighting qualities of our soldiers as displayed against their comparatively new enemy, the Germans, in Normandy? Such questions could never, of course, be asked in wartime, or indeed for long afterwards. In a letter to General Brooke, Monty wrote: 'The trouble with our British lads is that they are not killers by nature.' Geoffrey Chater, who ended the war a Colonel and who we last heard of recovering from 'Moaning Minnie' attacks at Cheux: 'From my experience I must say there was in general no lack of courage among our fighting troops. But as the war neared its end they tended to become more cautious. They saw no point in sacrificing themselves when they knew with absolute certainty the war was being won. And in any case we had such overwhelming air and gunpower they believed it sometimes better to let the Jerries be beaten that way. It certainly saved many lives.' Montgomery himself told a historian: 'I never had the slightest reason to doubt the abilities of our men in general, it was just that they did at times lack the overall fanaticism of the better German troops, and there were certainly shortcomings in their training. In that respect I do in part blame myself.'

General (later Field Marshal) Templar, like Monty, also gravitated in time to head the General Staff, and made comments detrimental to the state of 'Tommy's' fighting spirit, comparing them less favourably with the lads of the earlier war. If his opinion was justified, then one must look to factors in society, rather than in their training, even though the latter was of great importance. People in general were more sophisticated, with greater knowing and certainly bigger expectations in the 1940s. The gung-ho, almost blind patriotism of the Victorian era had gone. The disreputable Boers of the South African war were replaced by the wicked Huns under Kaiser Bill in 1914, and by 1939 those horrible, warmongering Germans had become Nazis (every one of them) under the bloodthirsty monster Adolf Hitler. But five years of wartime propaganda, not to mention years of pre-conditioning before, no matter how factual in part, had failed in the main to instil hatred or the killer instinct in most Britons. Overall, whatever Monty said he thought of our enemy, when it came down to cases he was seen as a 'proper chap', in the sense that he was a 'bloody good soldier', and nothing excited more respect in the Tommy than a worthy opponent.

The British had suffered, a proportion of them, from the *Luftwaffe*'s attentions, which hardly promoted goodwill towards the Germans across the Channel. Many had not suffered at all, apart from the inconveniences of rationing and the blackout, while a number enjoyed the war, and for a variety of reasons. It is impossible to generate hatred among a population which has not suffered under the brutal heel of an occupier. For most of the soldiers in Britain destined for combat on the continent the only knowledge of the German enemy had come via the media; few had actually seen a German. No matter how much their Sergeant instructors bawled at them as they rushed at straw-filled sandbags with bayonets fixed, when it came to the crunch they invariably treated their enemy with fairness, especially if he was hurt. It was not practice (though it happened) to ill-treat even the SS men captured, the chaps with the lightning flash insignia they had been hearing about for years and years as real swinish Nazis of the worst type who were Hitler's darlings.

And it really didn't matter if these same Germans found their Tommy opponents lesser soldiers in attack; it was rare for them to be dislodged. The shortcomings among Britain's army of 1944 were more than made up for in other directions. The same could not be said for the *Wehrmacht*, hitherto the greatest, most professional fighting force the world had seen.

If it is possible to view the Normandy campaign (from this point in time) as being a 'fair fight', then that is only marred perhaps by the atrocity angle that broke into public knowledge via Anthony Eden's announcement in the House of Commons in mid-August. If some British troops received and had time to peruse the front pages of newspapers in Normandy then the report would have confirmed the belief in SS devilry, or otherwise confounded those who had recently discovered these enemy soldiers to be much like themselves. In any case, the other side of the coin was not generally known, and remains so to this day.

12 The Match Won

'The battle in Normandy was crucial to the outcome of the war. That may seem an obvious point to make, but it is worth remembering that but for the Allies' great sacrifices in that campaign the Red Army would never have beaten their enemy.

'When the battle began we were relatively weak on the ground, in other words the beach-head force had barely reached the minimum strength to hold off German counter-attacks. Fortunately, when these came we had just built up enough strength to beat them off, but it would not have been so easy without the tremendous support given by the RAF.

'Opposite us were some of the finest troops of the German Army and SS; we knew they were there before we sailed, but in some cases we were unsure of exact strengths and other details. The problem was that though some German divisions had been diluted by an intake of foreign "volunteers", including Russian Mongols, we ourselves had a great preponderance of untried troops who though of sufficient courage lacked the experience necessary to do a really effective job in France. That kind of experience can be very costly when you are up against the Germans.

'The Americans were in an even worse position because practically all their forces had no experience whatever; those that had were fighting in Italy. I had certain misgivings about some of their optimism and these proved justified here and there. I refer of course to the lack of armour and special vehicles on Omaha beach, though in other areas they were well served.

'When the really ding-dong fighting began we were in a very good position to see off the enemy whose attacks were often ill-timed and ill-co-ordinated and certainly lacking in essential features such as artillery and air support. However, we could never write off the Germans militarily, until they were dead or surrendered. When I heard of fresh SS divisions on the way from Poland I knew we had to spoil their plans and took steps to put in my own attack to disrupt their preparations. In this I was ably assisted as always by the air force who made life hell for the enemy before he even reached the battle zone. In some cases the Germans lost all their transport and even armour before entering battle, which had a very bad effect on morale.

'I saw a few Jerry prisoners and they looked utterly dejected and of no further use. Interrogations proved what they thought of the war and Hitler and the hopelessness of it all. Yet, whatever such men said it had

little effect on the course of the battle. The remaining Germans kept at
it as long as they were able, by which I mean until they were killed,
captured or ordered to withdraw.

'As to the successive offensives carried out in July–August, they did
have a very serious cumulative effect on the enemy who was gradually
ground down until at last the dam broke and he was forced to concede
the field after suffering enormous losses. In that period, which was very
difficult for me, I had to contend with various problems and HQ staff
who seemed to have little or no idea of not only the strategy I was
pursuing but the meaning of a battle at all! The whole concept was to
destroy the enemy army on the battlefield, so that our own forces were
completely free to swan off eastwards with little or no opposition –
which is exactly what happened. I had allies with me who were perfectly
well acquainted with the true situation on the ground and I did my best
to advise all concerned as to my policy. Unfortunately, I put in a few
gaffes which gave the wrong impression. I tried my hand at publicity,
which the Yanks did all the time; I was not very good at it and should
have kept my mouth shut! The trouble was, I had a completely in-
flexible optimism about the outcome of the war and that particular
battle. I just knew we could not lose; the difficulty lay in convincing
others.

'A battlefield can be a very strange and lonely place for a commander,
insofar as although he has his staff the vital decisions are his alone and
these affect the lives of thousands. The responsibility is very great, but
I had no complaints. I was a career soldier and had at last got what I
wanted – command of a large army in battle.

'As far as the composition of our British army is concerned, I would
have much preferred an indigenous "pursuit corps" who could take up
the reins so to speak once a breakthrough had been made. This was not
possible to form in the time left to me from my appointment in
December 1943 until the invasion. It was impossible to implement such
a radically new concept in an army in the time available. Such a corps
would have been based on the highly mobile concept of tanks and
infantry in armoured carriers, with all the necessary supporting arms,
but all under the control of one commander. It would have been the
ideal group to carry through the offensive from the moment we reached
the Falaise gap. As it was we had a rather muddled situation, with
Canadians and Poles and British coming up against the Americans, and
it did prove a headache to get the boundaries and axis of advance in
place. But the great fault was the lack of real drive on the part of the
commanders on the spot which bedevilled me no end throughout my
battle front experience from Egypt to the Baltic. I have to admit we were
not nearly as good in the pursuit as some of our allies, the Americans –
and, if you like, the Germans. However, the Guards armoured did a
terrific job in their dash to Brussels and I believe surprised even the
Americans.

'As far as the British soldier is concerned, I have always believed him to be the best, or at least an equal to the Germans. The trouble was that our men did not always get the right type of training or directions for battle; they understandably grew tired of bull and that kind of thing, especially drill which was intended to keep them busy and in a fair state of discipline. But too little attention was paid to field training in the modern manner, especially in co-operation with armour. This was the great fault in North Africa and the problem was still not resolved by 1944. To get that "Army of Liberation", as it came to be called, anything like prepared for such a great undertaking was a heck of a big job. There was so much to do and I'm afraid not enough of the right kind of people to help do it.

'In the last resort we won the battle, despite all the difficulties mentioned, and that is the main thing. I can only say I was heartily grateful to all who served under me and put up with all my quirks!'

Field Marshal Bernard L. Montgomery

Epilogue

One grey, blustery morning in 1944 I set off for work on my bicycle as usual, meeting an older, little man also on a machine (one that was far too big for his short legs). As we battled along he remarked on the weather adding, 'It's started then'. He meant of course the Allied invasion of France, just announced on the eight o'clock news.

All these years later, I wonder how many lives were lost across the Channel in the fifteen minutes or so it took us to reach our firm in the Midlands on that morning of 6 June. As a youngster and despite some experience of the *Blitz*, the uglier realities of war did not strike home.

Much later, a long-term interest in the military and those dangerous years of World War were expressed through various ventures, both as a hobby and professionally. A spell earning a living as a dealer in militaria brought various correspondences from wartime generals into my hands, such items had become part of the collecting scene. Then, various writing and publishing projects entailed radio and press appeals for testimony from war veterans. This material plus much gathered through the valued help of a friend in Germany would have to wait until a later date to be published.

Ample literature on the deadly contest in Normandy in June–August 1944 has also come about from which I have been able to draw not only facts, but my own conclusions and opinions which are expressed in this work. Some of these books are listed in the Bibliography.

Edmund L. Blandford

Appendix Tank Production

Report by the Select Committee on National Expenditure and replies from the Government (1942 and 1944).

26 August 1942:

❝ The decision to go into large scale production of 6-pdr guns ought to have been balanced by a plan so timed as to produce tanks to carry the guns when they were ready. In fact, time was wasted in working out the tank plan, especially in the stage of design ... The story of tanks and six-pounder guns seems to show lack of decisive direction, division of responsibilities as between tanks and guns, and failure to consult manufacturers until a late stage in the work on the design have led to failure to make full use of manufacturing resources in getting timely production of effective weapons. Other examples of similar failure have come to notice in the case of self-propelled artillery. There has been a division of responsibility based apparently on a distinction between a tank carrying a gun (which has been treated as a 'tank'), and a gun mounted on a tank chassis (which has been treated as self-propelled artillery).❞

11 March 1944:

❝ The general conclusion of the first report was that there had been faults in organisation which had led to avoidable waste of time, money and material resources ... Changes have been made in the organisation which substantially satisfy the Committee's recommendations (eg that the responsibility of the War Office and Ministry of Supply be more closely clamped together). The Committee was influenced to make its second report by the consideration that unfavourable comment was prevalent about tank production. In the review of the position, it is impossible to avoid the general impression that, measured in terms of production of tanks fit for current battle requirements, the British manufacturing effort of 1943 has fallen far short of realising expectations or being fully effective, and has involved what appears to be a wasteful use of national resources ... The main fact remains that apart from the Valentine tank in Russia and the limited use of the Churchill in Tunisia, no British tanks in 1943 have been considered worthy of a place in the main battles; British tanks issued to British troops have gained a bad reputation both for mechanical reliability and fighting arrangements; that British factory workers have seen very large quantities of completed tanks broken up, or parts (finished and half-finished), piling up to be taken away as scrap; and that these things have combined to create a psychological atmosphere about British tanks among all concerned with handling them which must have unfortunate effects and which in our view deserves the urgent attention of the War Cabinet. The past record, in fact, puts the onus of proof very heavily on those who now claim that all is well with the organisation for tank production . . . The 'new organisation' has not fully made good and the expectations recorded in the earlier Report have not been fulfilled. **"**

In its reply of 2 August the War Cabinet included comments from General Montgomery:

" In the fighting in Normandy we have defeated the Germans in battle; and we have had no difficulty in dealing with German armour once we had grasped the problem. In this connection British armour has played a notable part. We have nothing to fear from the Panther and Tiger tanks; they are unreliable mechanically and the Panther is very vulnerable from the flanks. Our 17-pdr gun will go right through them. Provided our tactics are good we can defeat them without difficulty. **"**

General Lees:

" The Churchills stood up to a lot of punishment from heavy anti-tank guns. Several tanks were hard hit without the crews being injured. They got across some amazingly rough ground (in Italy). **"**

The Cabinet reply continues:

" Further methods of strengthening such links (between the troops in the battle lines and the design and production organisation) are continually being studied. Officers with recent operational experience are kept in close touch with all stages of development . . . It is agreed that it would be a national disaster if the country were to fail during the war to build up a first-class organisation for producing British tanks. With the growth of experience in industry and in Government establishments, this objective is being progressively achieved and the Committee need have no fear that every effort is not being exerted towards that end. **"**

Bibliography

From the City, From the Plough, Alexander Baron, Jonathan Cape (1948)
Memoirs, Field Marshal Viscount Montgomery, Collins (1947)
Normandy to the Baltic, Field Marshal Viscount Montgomery, Hutchinson (1947)
Dawn of D-Day, David Howarth, Collins (1959)
The Struggle for Europe, Chester Wilmot, Collins (1952)
Caen–Anvilof Victory, Alexander McKee, Souvenir Press (1964)
The Turn of the Tide, Arthur Bryant, Collins (1957)
Hitler: a Study in Tyranny, Alan Bullock, Odhams Press (1953)
The War, Flowers-Reeves, Cassell (1960)
So Few Got Through, Martin Lindsay, Collins (1946)
The Longest Day, Cornelius Ryan, Gollanz (1960)
My Three Years with Eisenhower, Harry Butcher, Simon & Schuster (1946)
North-West Europe, John North, HMSO (1953)
A Short History of 21st Army Group, HMSO (1953)
Overlord, Max Hastings, Guild (1983)
A Soldier's Story, Omar Bradley, Eyre & Spottiswoode (?)
Montgomery: Master of the Battlefield, Nigel Hamilton, Hamish Hamilton (?)
Flamethrower, Andrew Wilson, Wm. Kimber (?)
Hitler's Legions, Samuel W. Mitcham, Leo Cooper (1983)
A Full Life, Lt-Gen Sir Brian Horrocks, Collins (1960)
Invasion, John St John Cooper, Beaverbrook Newspapers (1954)
The Normandy Campaign, Hunt-Mason, Leo Cooper (1976)
Panzers in Normandy, Eric Lefevre, After the Battle (1983)
D-Day, Tiger Books (1994)
Hitler's Second Army, Edmund Blandford, Airlife (1995)
Hill 112, Major J. J. How MC, Wm. Kimber (1984)
Phantom, Philip Warner, Wm. Kimber (1982)
German Paratroops, Volkmar Kuhn, Ian Allen (1974)
Storming Eagles, James Lucas, Arms & Armour (1988)
Invasion, Haupt-Feist, Feist (1968)
Hitler's Teutonic Knights, Bruce Quarrie, Patrick Stephens (1986)

Index